Angel Sanctuary

story and art by Kaori Yuki
vol. 18

Angel Sanctuary

Vol. 18
Shôjo Edition

STORY AND ART BY KAORI YUKI

English Adaptation/Arashi Productions
Translation/Arashi Productions
Touch-up Art & Lettering/Bill Schuch
Design/Izumi Evers
Editor/Jonathan Tarbox

Managing Editor/Megan Bates
Editorial Director/Elizabeth Kawasaki
Editor in Chief/Alvin Lu
Sr. Director of Acquisitions/Rika Inouye
Sr. VP of Marketing/Liza Coppola
Exec. VP of Sales & Marketing/John Easum
Publisher/Hyoe Narita

Printed in the U.S.A.

Published by VIZ Media, LLC
P.O. Box 77010
San Francisco, CA 94107

Shôjo Edition
10 9 8 7 6 5 4 3 2 1
First printing, February 2007

www.viz.com
store.viz.com

PARENTAL ADVISORY
ANGEL SANCTUARY is rated T+ for Older Teen and is recommended for ages 16 and up. This volume contains violence and mature situations.

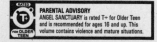

Angel Sanctuary

story and art by **Kaori Yuki**   vol. 18

The Story Thus Far

High school boy Setsuna Mudo's life is hellish. He's always
been a troublemaker, and his worst sin was falling incestuously
in love with his beautiful sister Sara. But his troubles are
preordained—Setsuna is the reincarnation of the Lady Alexiel, an
angel who rebelled against Heaven and led the demons of Hell
in a revolt. Sara, in turn, is a manifestation of the angel Jibril.

Rosiel, the new leader of Heaven, proposes a meeting of all
parties to work out a peace accord. None of the rebel angels
trust him, but all plan to attend.

Rosiel has imprisoned the angel of destruction Sandalphon, who
has possessed Metatron's body. Sandalphon can only use
Metatron's body for a limited time, and must create a new body
of his own for his soul to inhabit. He plans to impregnate Sara
so that he can possess her child.

Raphael, who rescued Sara after her trial, has fallen completely
in love with her. Her refuses to free her, knowing that she will
go straight to Setsuna. He leaves her locked in his mansion
when he leaves to attend the peace meeting. While he is out,
Sandalphon escapes from containment and finds Sara left alone.
He confuses her with nightmares and convinces her that he is
Setsuna. Setsuna and his crew arrive to rescue Sara, but they
are too late—Sandalphon has infected her mind with his
nightmares. They also find that Lucifer is there, having arranged
the entire situation to suit his devilish plans.

Now Setsuna, Kato and the other rebels face Lucifer in battle
once again. Setsuna manifests his power as the reincarnation of
Alexiel, and as his astral power surges forth, his wings and eye
miraculously heal. The battle with Lucifer begins in earnest.

Contents

天使禁猟区 (てんしきんりょうく)

Angel Sanctuary

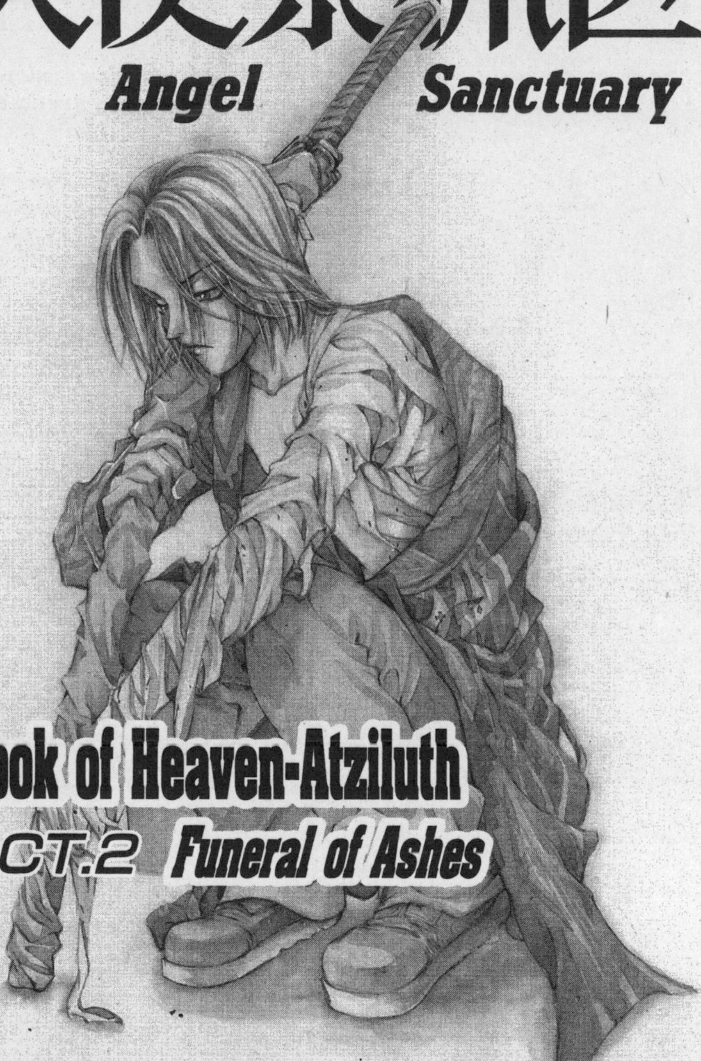

Book of Heaven-Atziluth

ACT.2 Funeral of Ashes

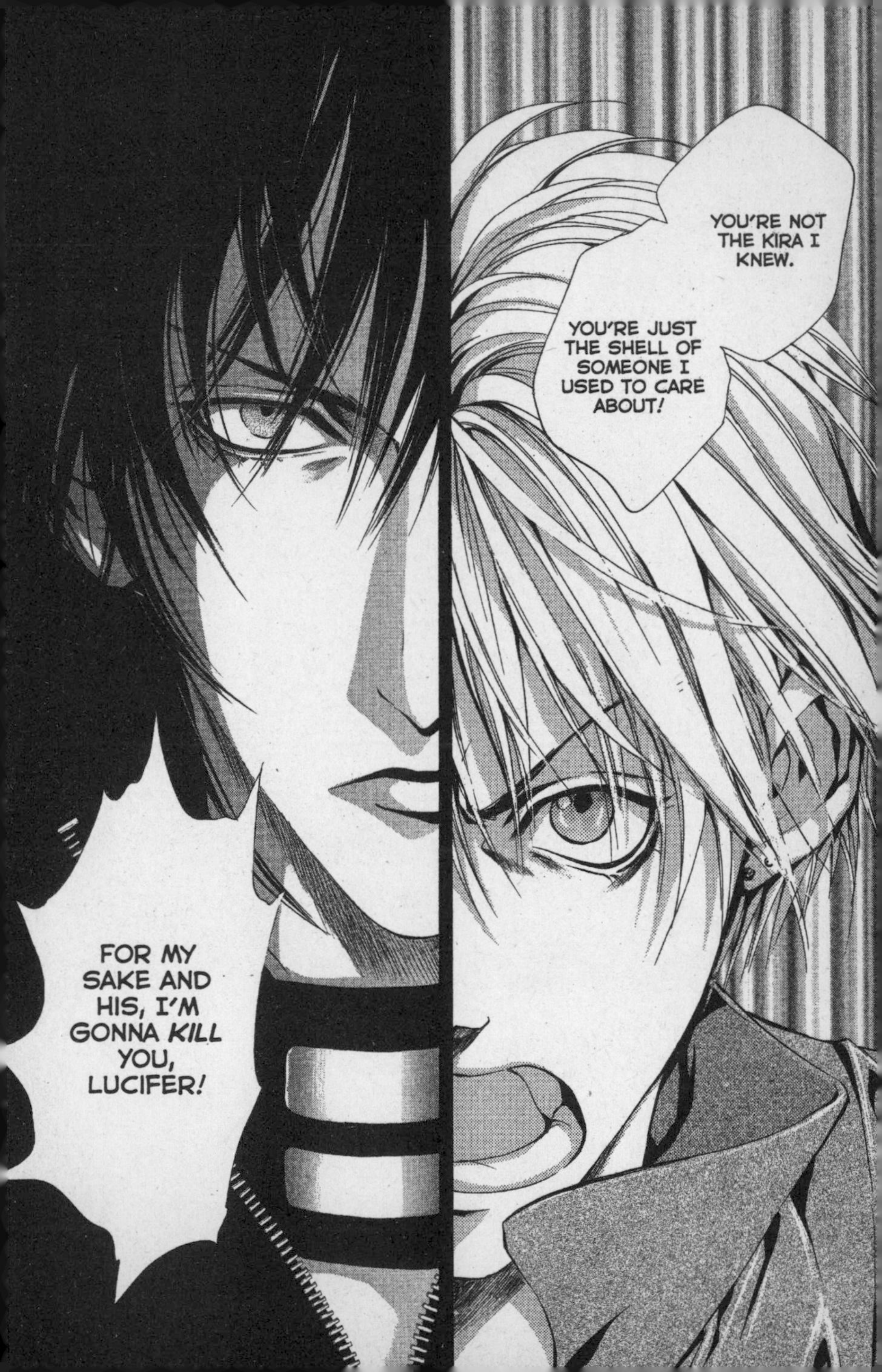
YOU'RE NOT THE KIRA I KNEW.
YOU'RE JUST THE SHELL OF SOMEONE I USED TO CARE ABOUT!
FOR MY SAKE AND HIS, I'M GONNA *KILL* YOU, LUCIFER!

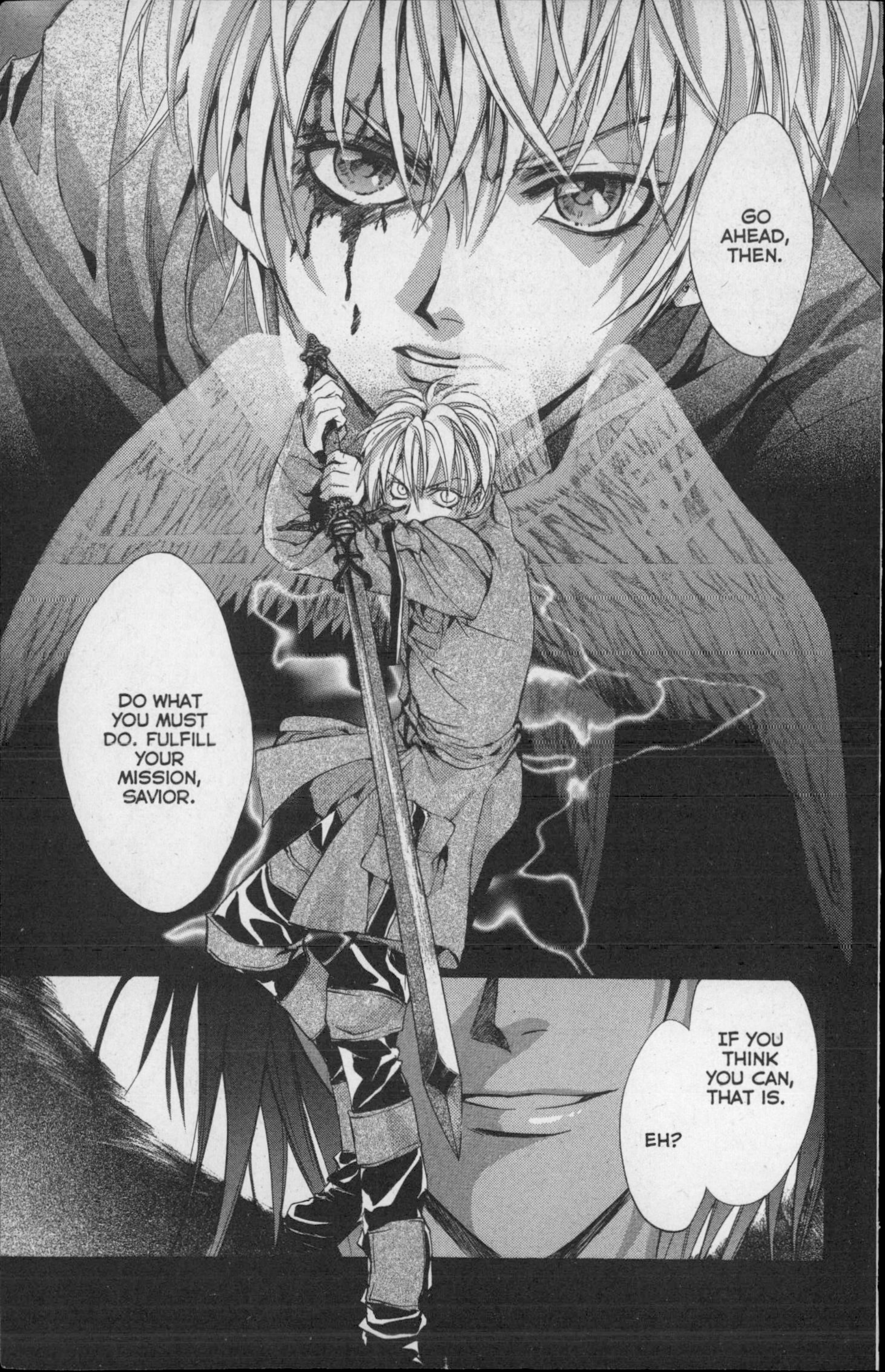
GO AHEAD, THEN.
DO WHAT YOU MUST DO. FULFILL YOUR MISSION, SAVIOR.
IF YOU THINK YOU CAN, THAT IS.
EH?

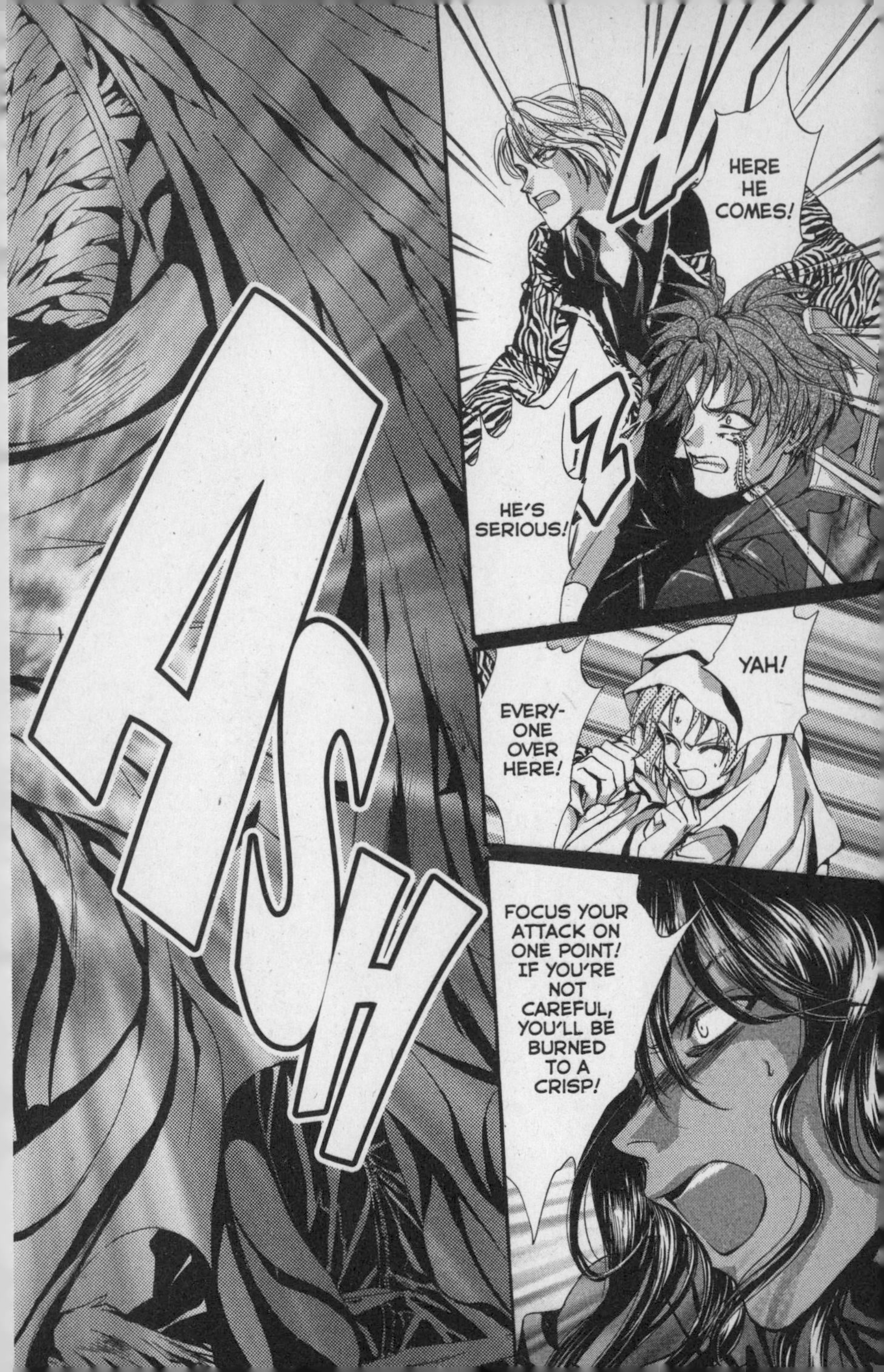
HERE HE COMES!
HE'S SERIOUS!
YAH!
EVERY-ONE OVER HERE!
FOCUS YOUR ATTACK ON ONE POINT! IF YOU'RE NOT CAREFUL, YOU'LL BE BURNED TO A CRISP!

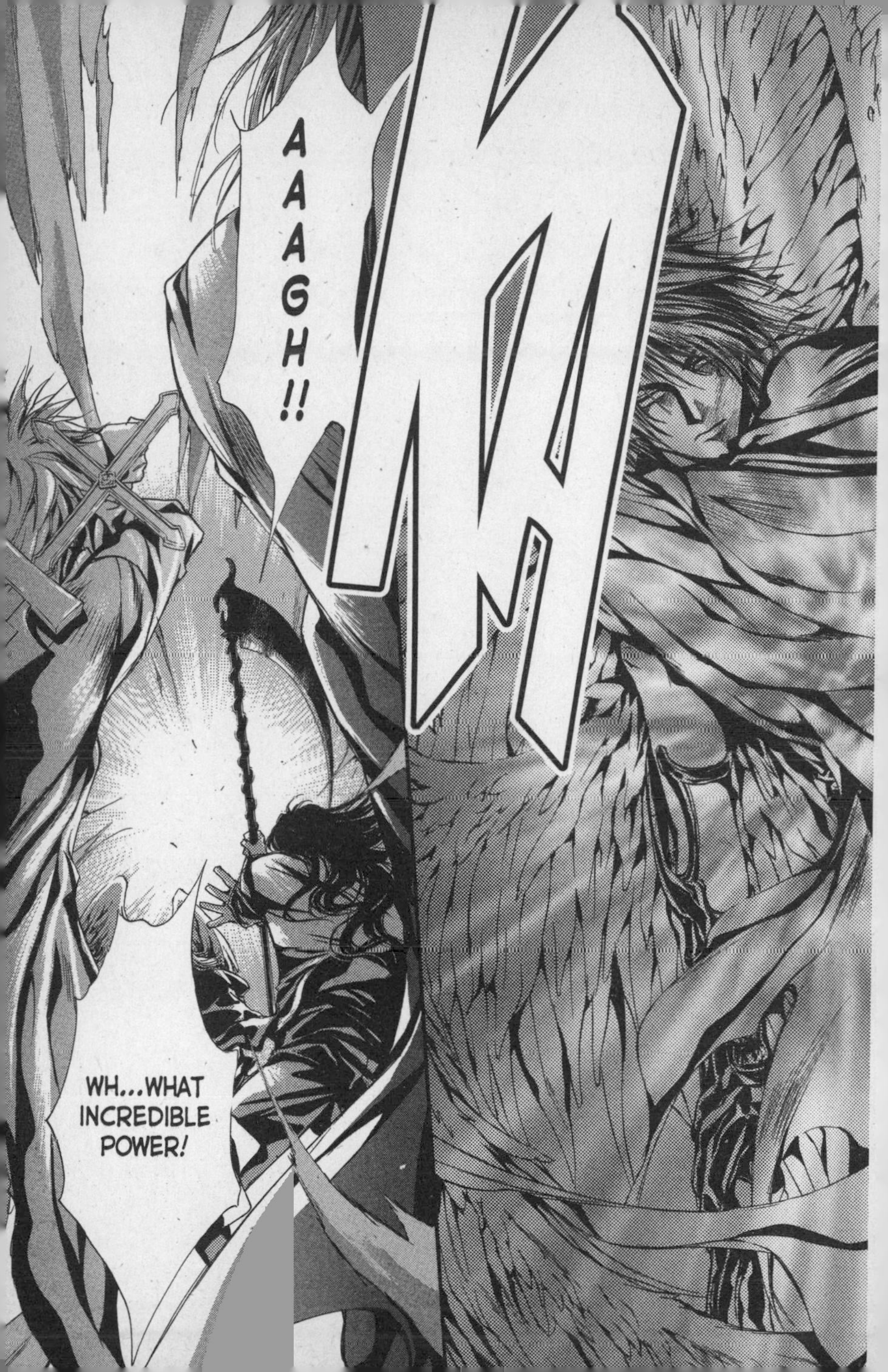
AAAGH!!
WH...WHAT INCREDIBLE POWER!

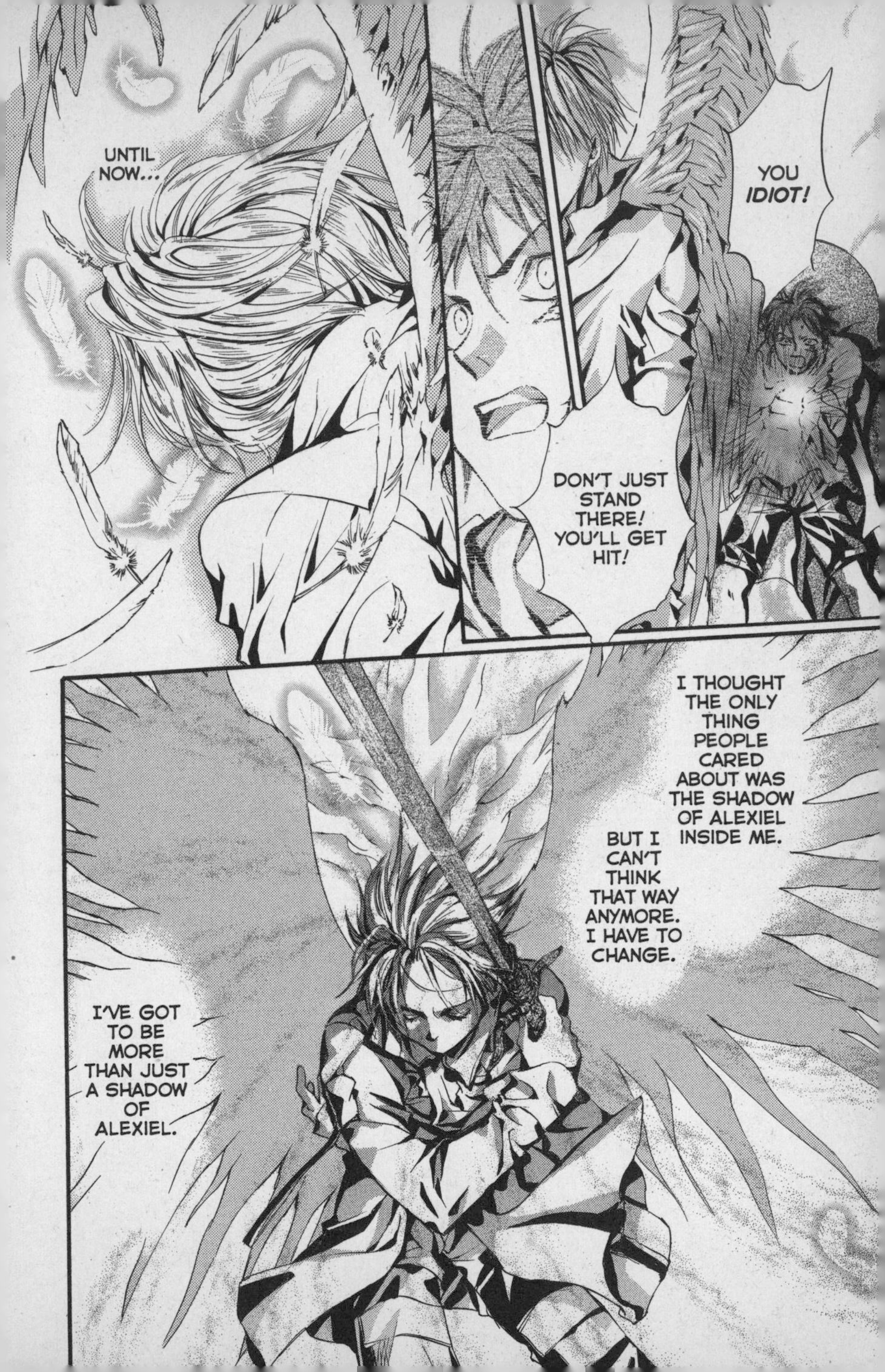
YOU *IDIOT!*
DON'T JUST STAND THERE! YOU'LL GET HIT!
UNTIL NOW...
I THOUGHT THE ONLY THING PEOPLE CARED ABOUT WAS THE SHADOW OF ALEXIEL INSIDE ME.
BUT I CAN'T THINK THAT WAY ANYMORE. I HAVE TO CHANGE.
I'VE GOT TO BE MORE THAN JUST A SHADOW OF ALEXIEL.

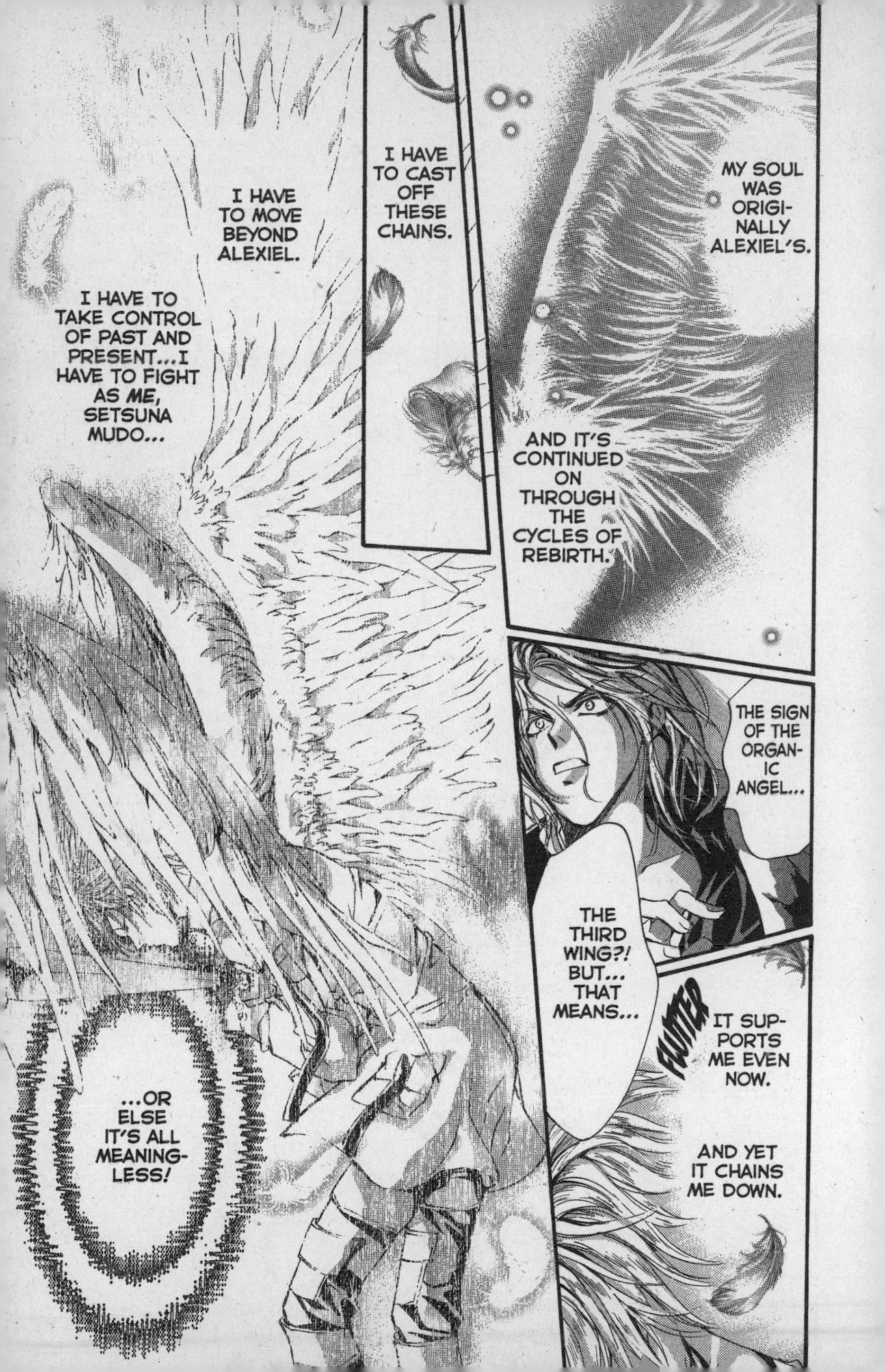
MY SOUL WAS ORIGINALLY ALEXIEL'S.
AND IT'S CONTINUED ON THROUGH THE CYCLES OF REBIRTH.
THE SIGN OF THE ORGANIC ANGEL...
THE THIRD WING?! BUT... THAT MEANS...
FLUTTER
IT SUPPORTS ME EVEN NOW.
AND YET IT CHAINS ME DOWN.
I HAVE TO CAST OFF THESE CHAINS.
I HAVE TO MOVE BEYOND ALEXIEL.
I HAVE TO TAKE CONTROL OF PAST AND PRESENT...I HAVE TO FIGHT AS *ME*, SETSUNA MUDO...
...OR ELSE IT'S ALL MEANINGLESS!

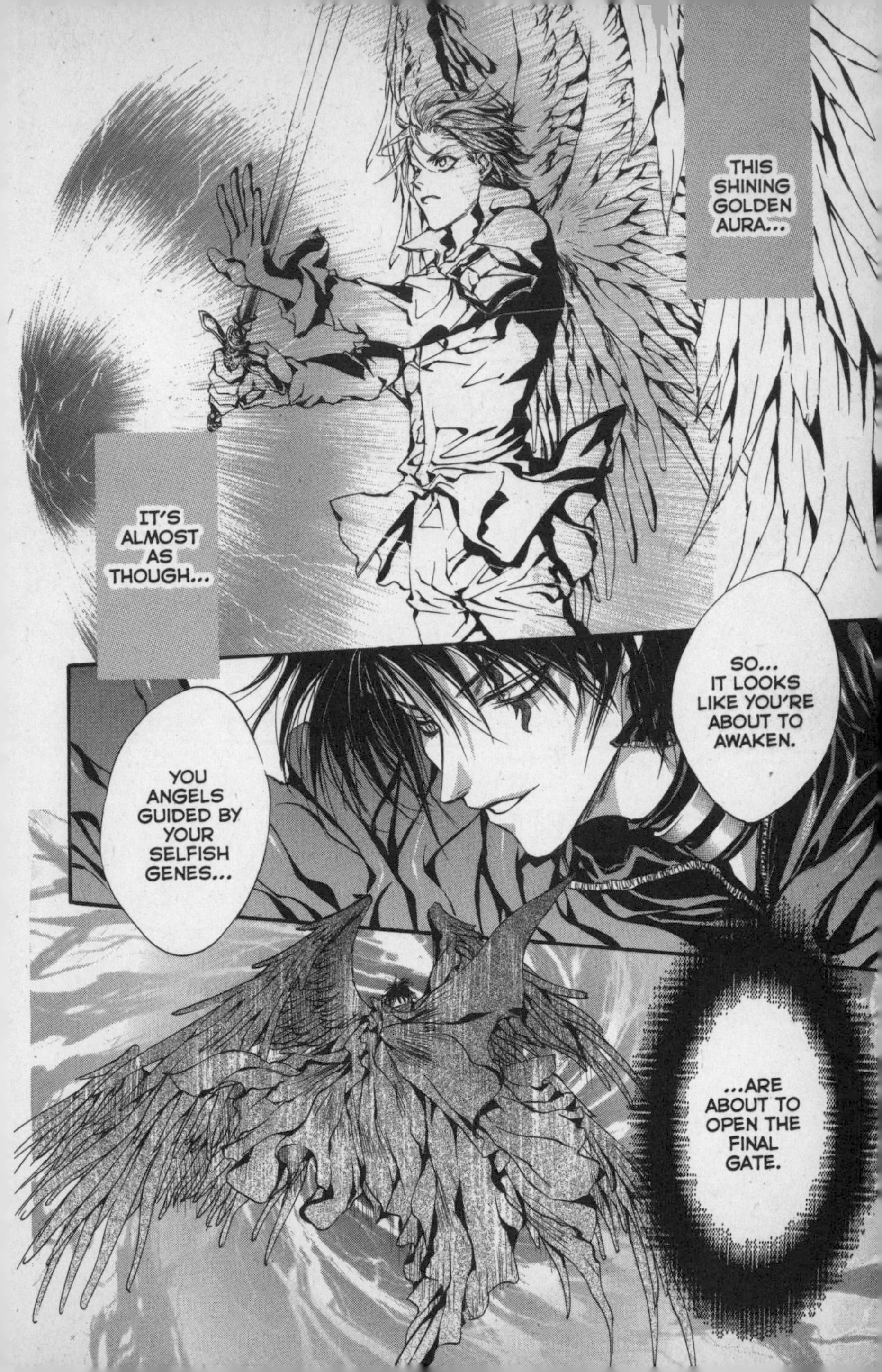
THIS SHINING GOLDEN AURA...
IT'S ALMOST AS THOUGH...
SO... IT LOOKS LIKE YOU'RE ABOUT TO AWAKEN.
YOU ANGELS GUIDED BY YOUR SELFISH GENES...
...ARE ABOUT TO OPEN THE FINAL GATE.

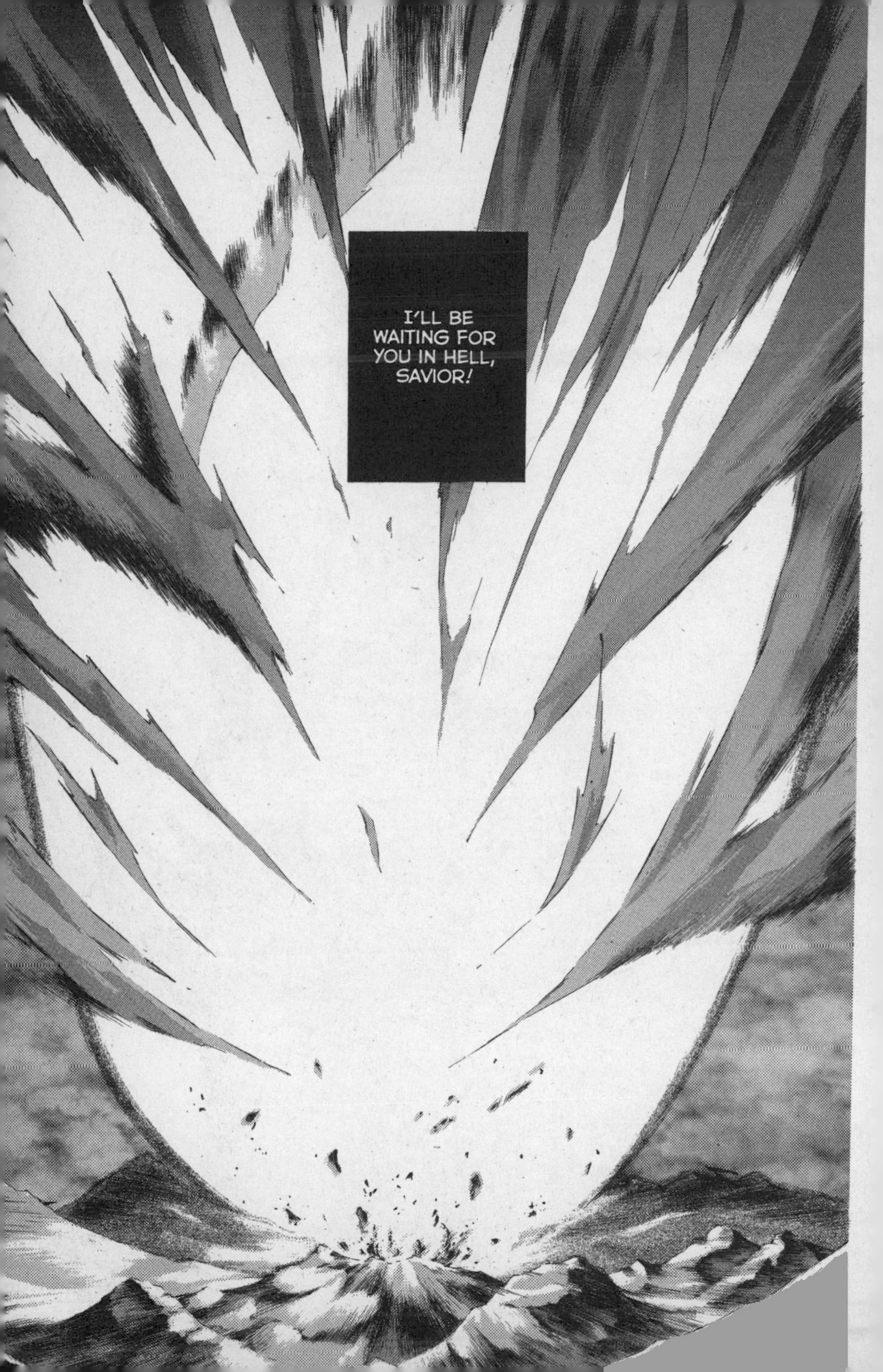
I'LL BE WAITING FOR YOU IN HELL, SAVIOR!

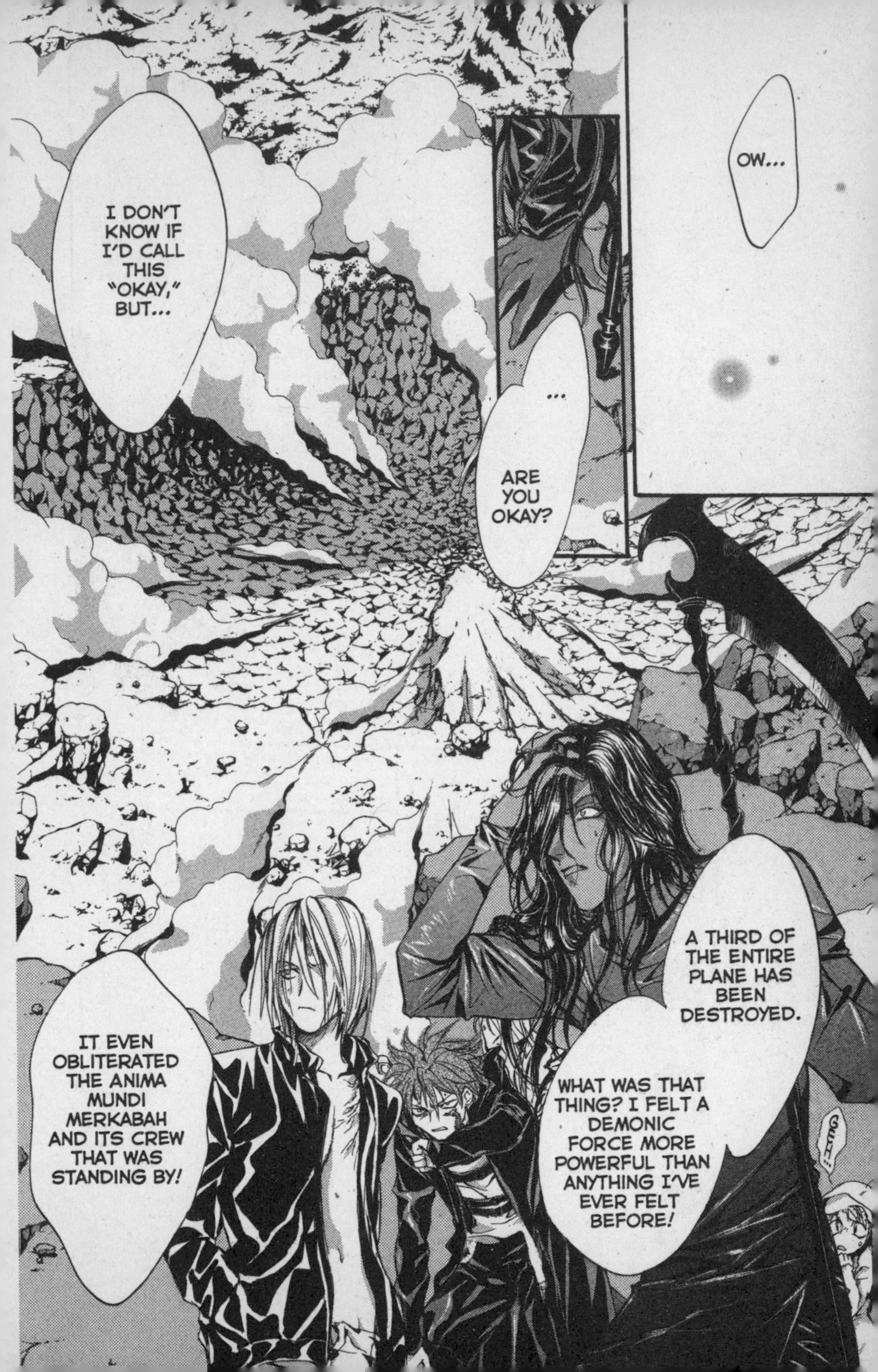
OW...
...
ARE YOU OKAY?
I DON'T KNOW IF I'D CALL THIS "OKAY," BUT...
A THIRD OF THE ENTIRE PLANE HAS BEEN DESTROYED.
GEEH...
WHAT WAS THAT THING? I FELT A DEMONIC FORCE MORE POWERFUL THAN ANYTHING I'VE EVER FELT BEFORE!
IT EVEN OBLITERATED THE ANIMA MUNDI MERKABAH AND ITS CREW THAT WAS STANDING BY!

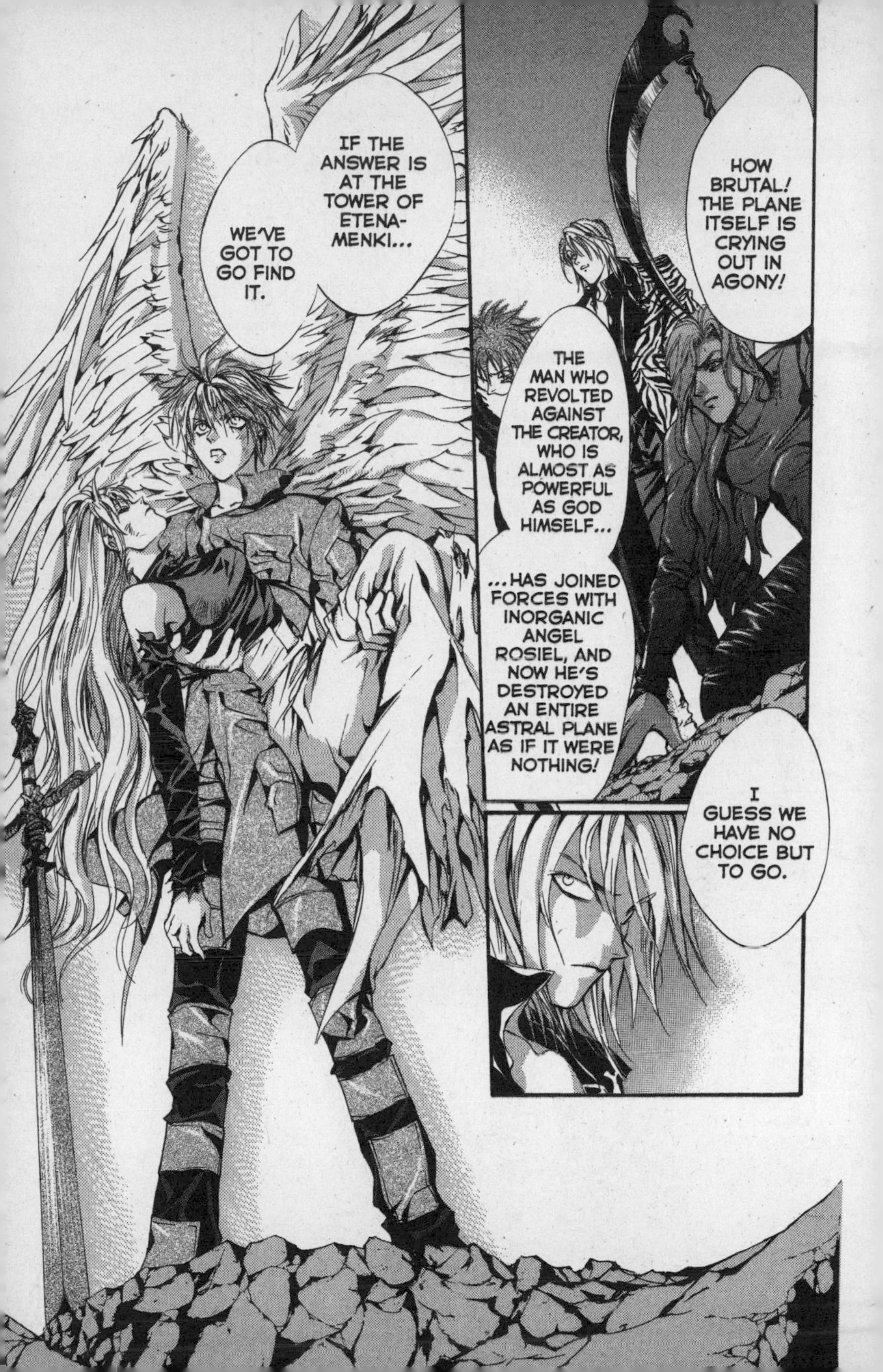
HOW BRUTAL! THE PLANE ITSELF IS CRYING OUT IN AGONY!
THE MAN WHO REVOLTED AGAINST THE CREATOR, WHO IS ALMOST AS POWERFUL AS GOD HIMSELF...
...HAS JOINED FORCES WITH INORGANIC ANGEL ROSIEL, AND NOW HE'S DESTROYED AN ENTIRE ASTRAL PLANE AS IF IT WERE NOTHING!
I GUESS WE HAVE NO CHOICE BUT TO GO.
IF THE ANSWER IS AT THE TOWER OF ETENA-MENKI...
WE'VE GOT TO GO FIND IT.

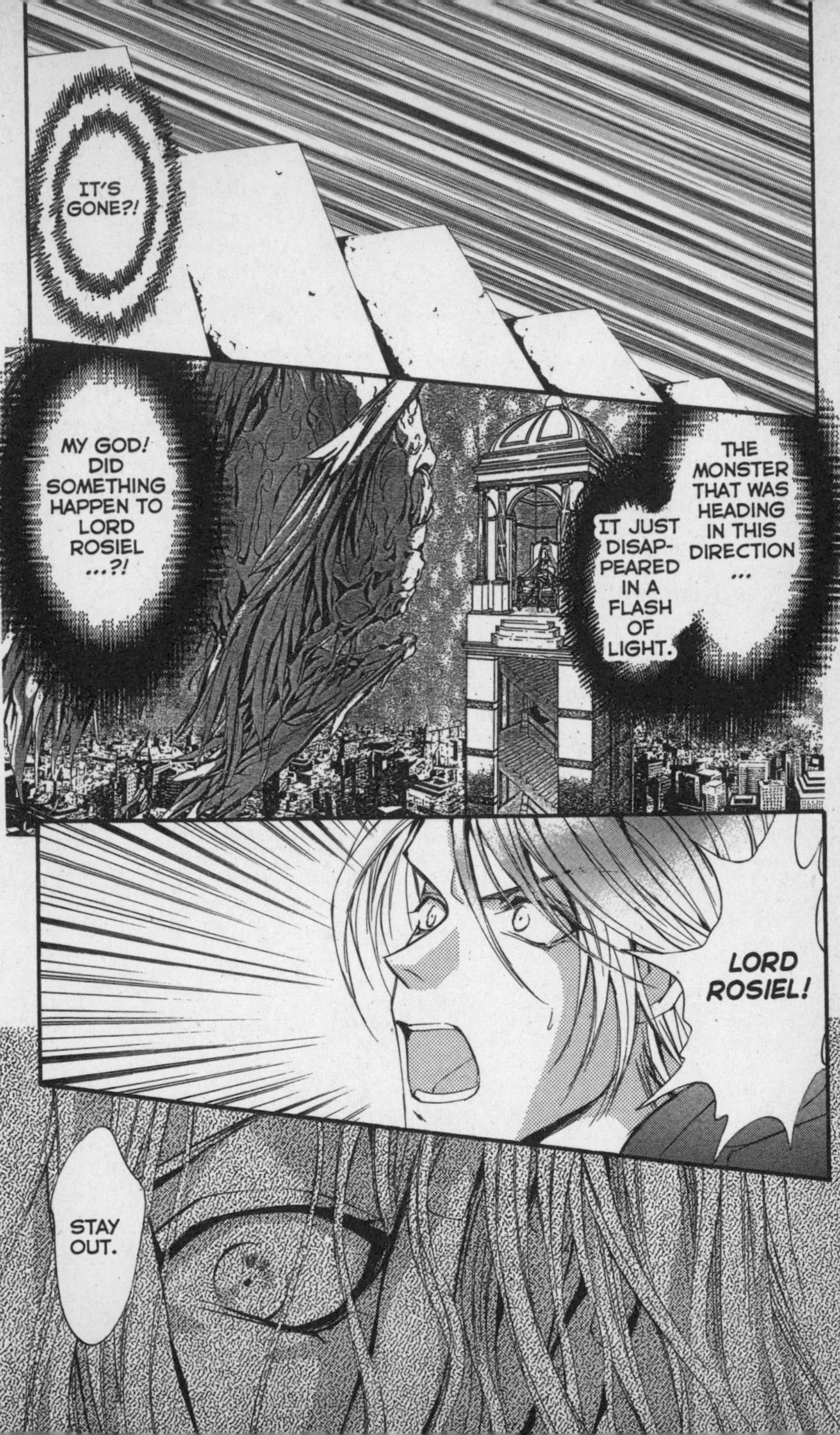
IT'S GONE?!
THE MONSTER THAT WAS HEADING IN THIS DIRECTION...
IT JUST DISAP-PEARED IN A FLASH OF LIGHT.
MY GOD! DID SOMETHING HAPPEN TO LORD ROSIEL...?!
LORD ROSIEL!
STAY OUT.

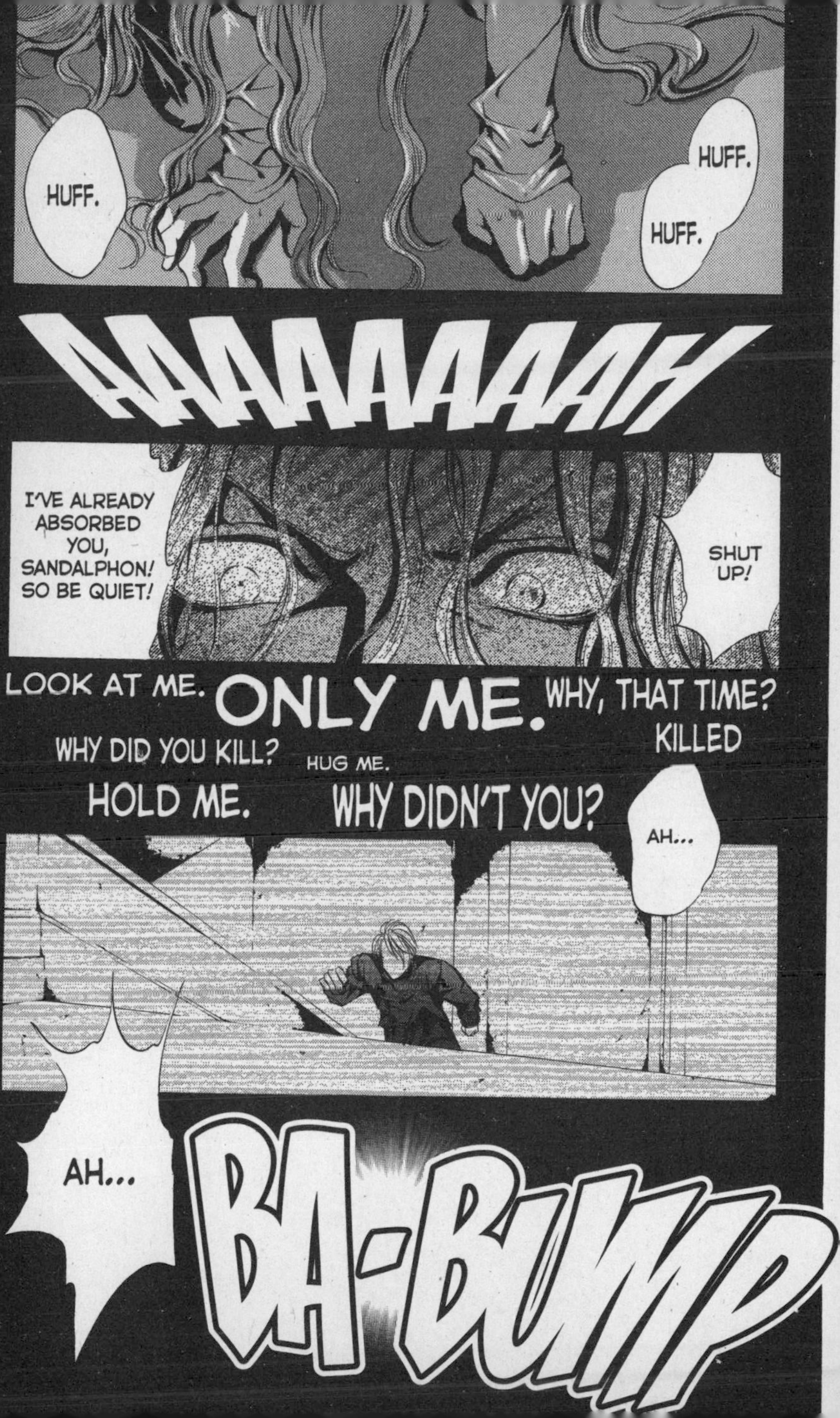
HUFF.
HUFF.
HUFF.
AAAAAAAAH
SHUT UP!
I'VE ALREADY ABSORBED YOU, SANDALPHON! SO BE QUIET!
WHY, THAT TIME?
KILLED
ONLY ME.
LOOK AT ME.
HUG ME.
WHY DID YOU KILL?
WHY DIDN'T YOU?
HOLD ME.
AH...
BA-BUMP
AH...

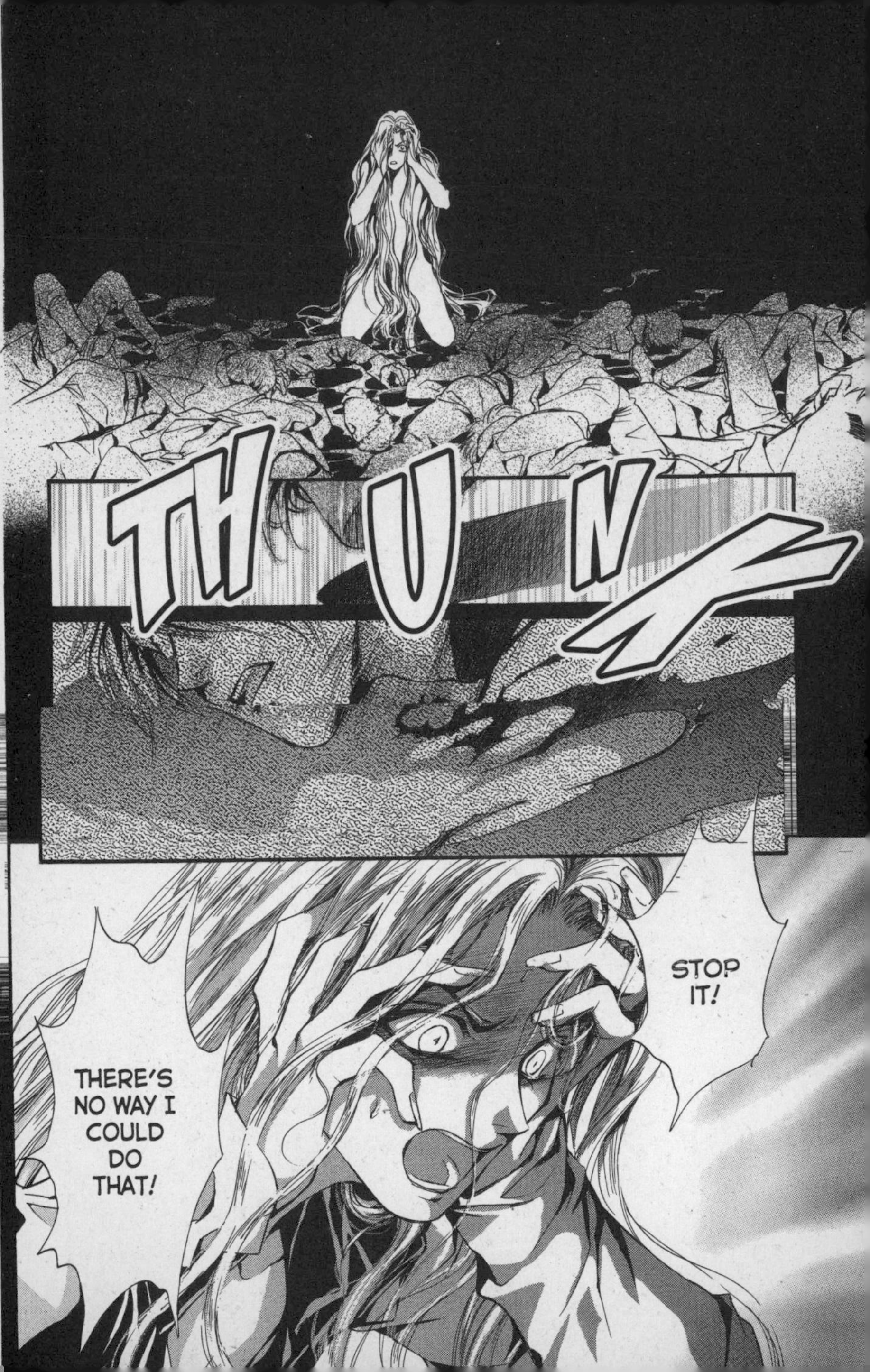
THUNK
STOP IT!
THERE'S NO WAY I COULD DO THAT!

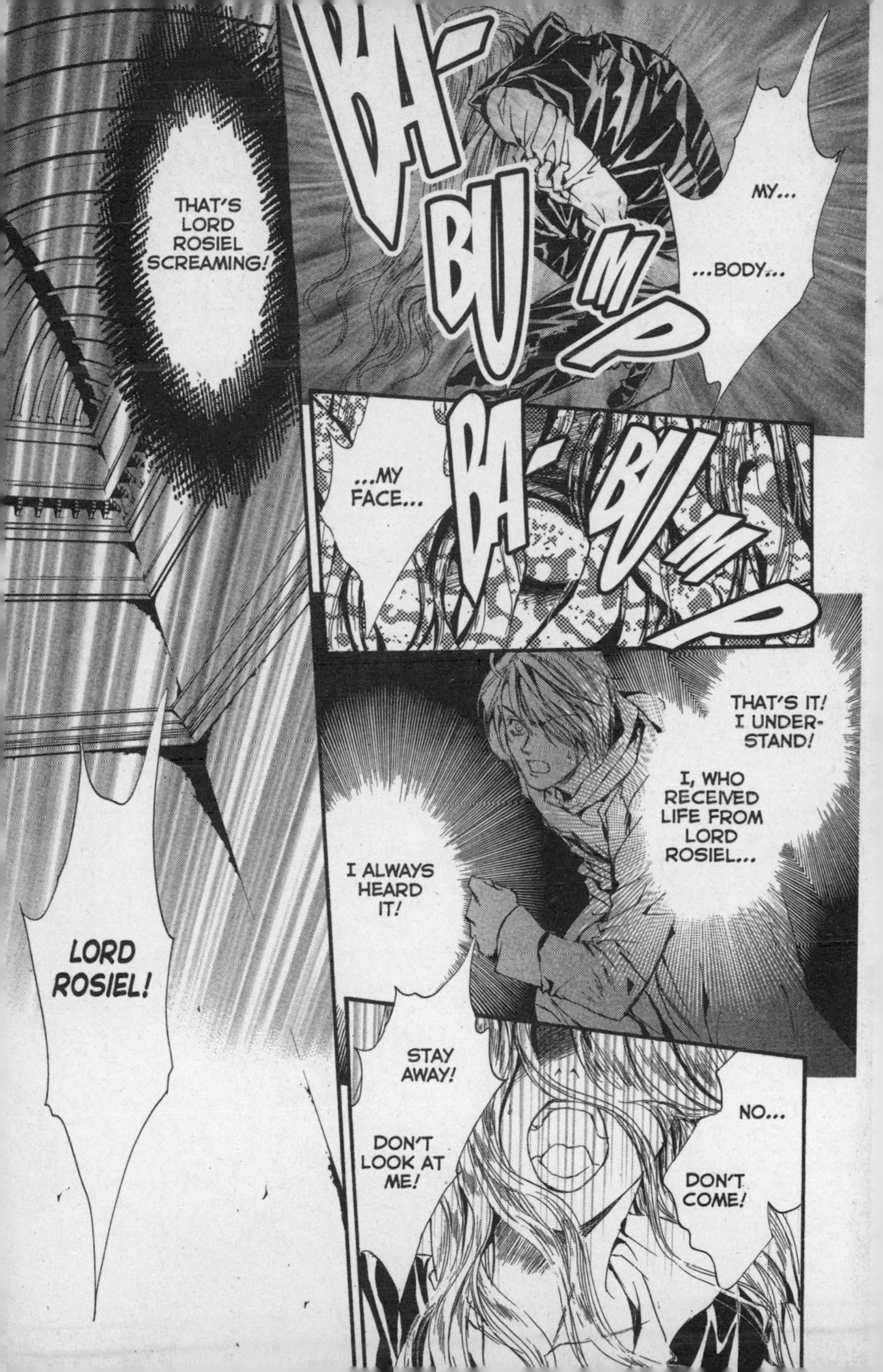
BA-BUMP
MY...
...BODY...
BA-BUMP
...MY FACE...
THAT'S IT! I UNDERSTAND!
I, WHO RECEIVED LIFE FROM LORD ROSIEL...
I ALWAYS HEARD IT!
NO...
DON'T COME!
STAY AWAY!
DON'T LOOK AT ME!
THAT'S LORD ROSIEL SCREAMING!
LORD ROSIEL!

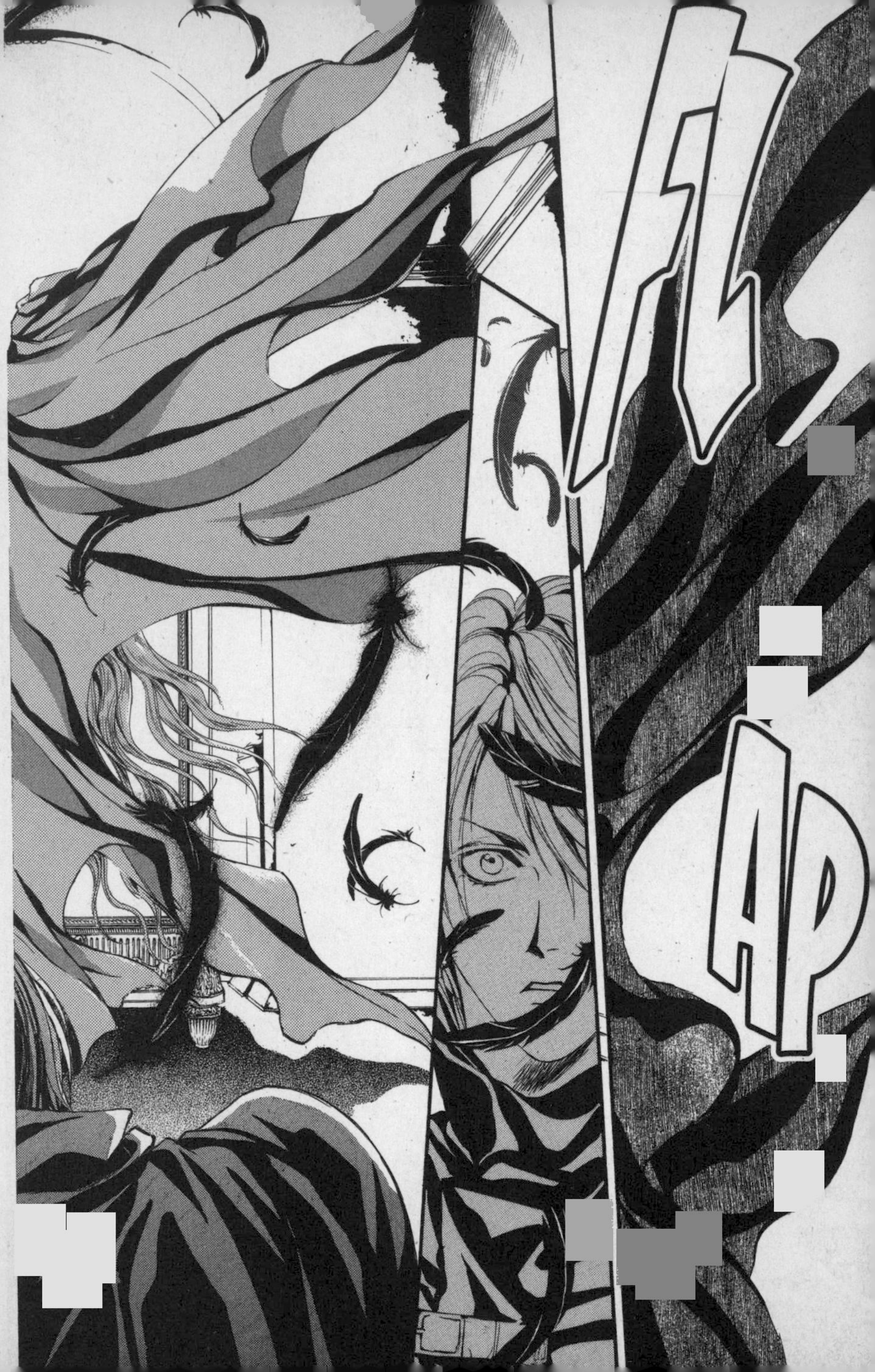
FLAP

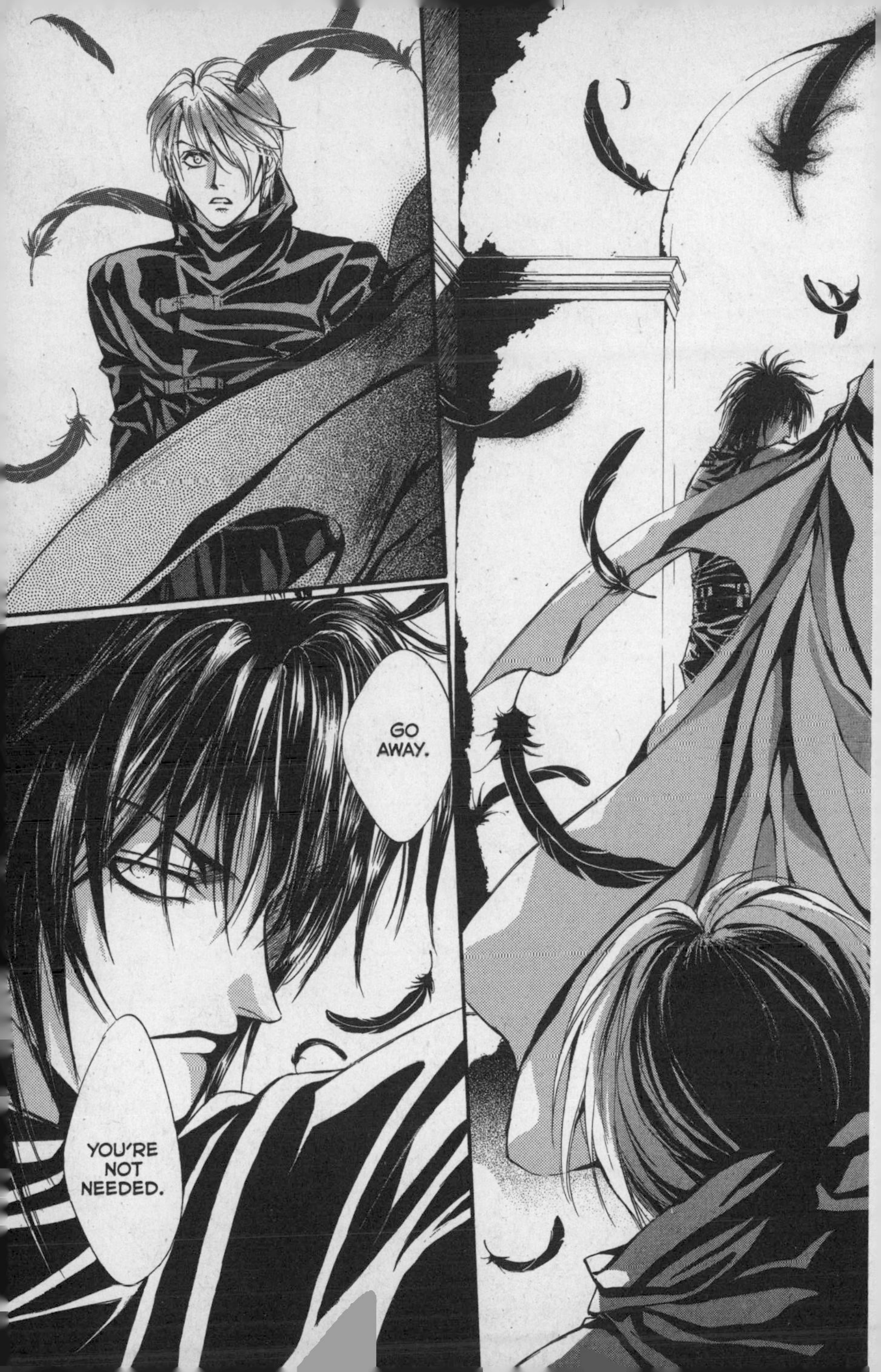
GO AWAY.
YOU'RE NOT NEEDED.

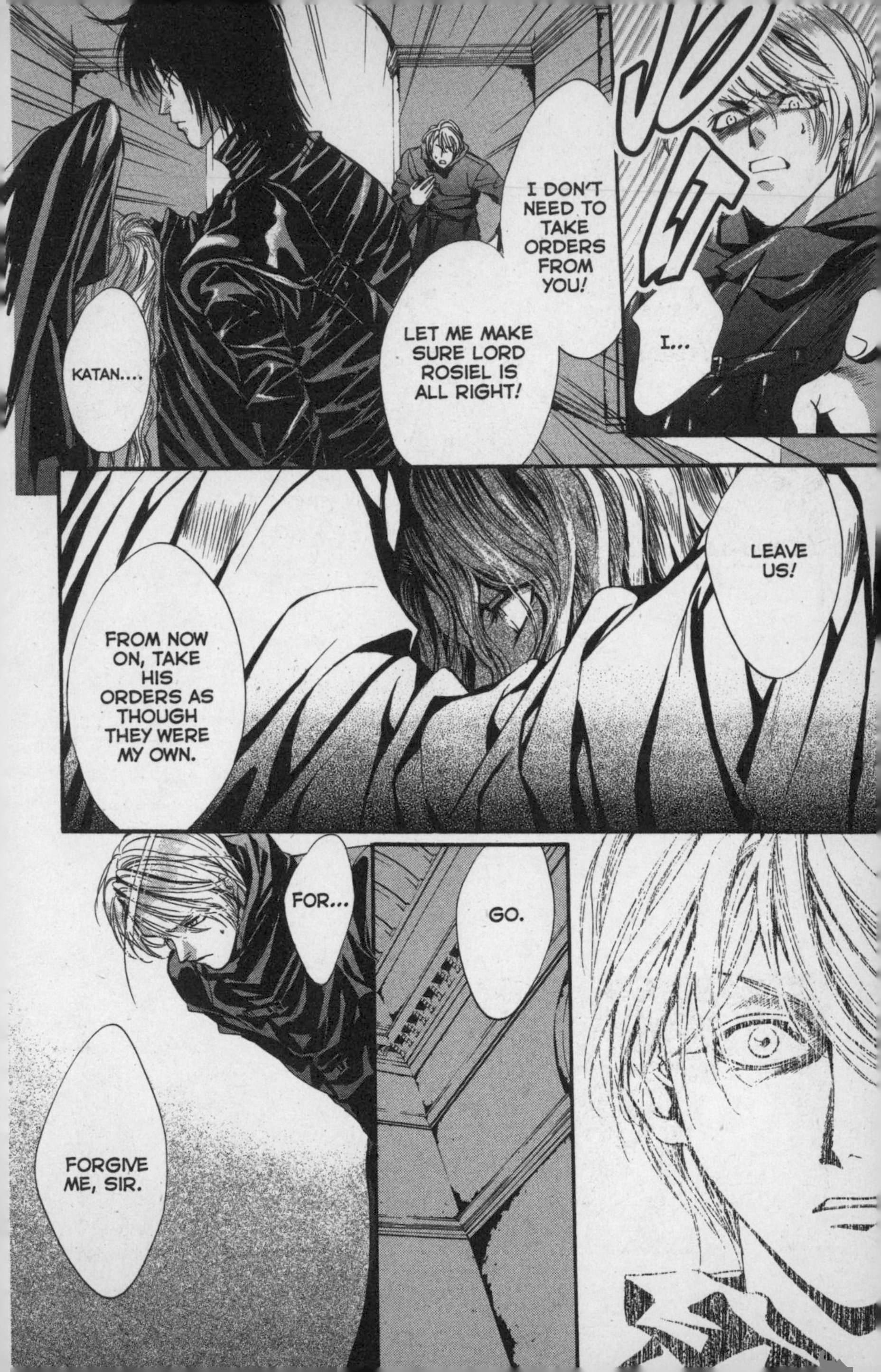
I...
I DON'T NEED TO TAKE ORDERS FROM YOU!
LET ME MAKE SURE LORD ROSIEL IS ALL RIGHT!
KATAN....
LEAVE US!
FROM NOW ON, TAKE HIS ORDERS AS THOUGH THEY WERE MY OWN.
GO.
FOR...
FORGIVE ME, SIR.

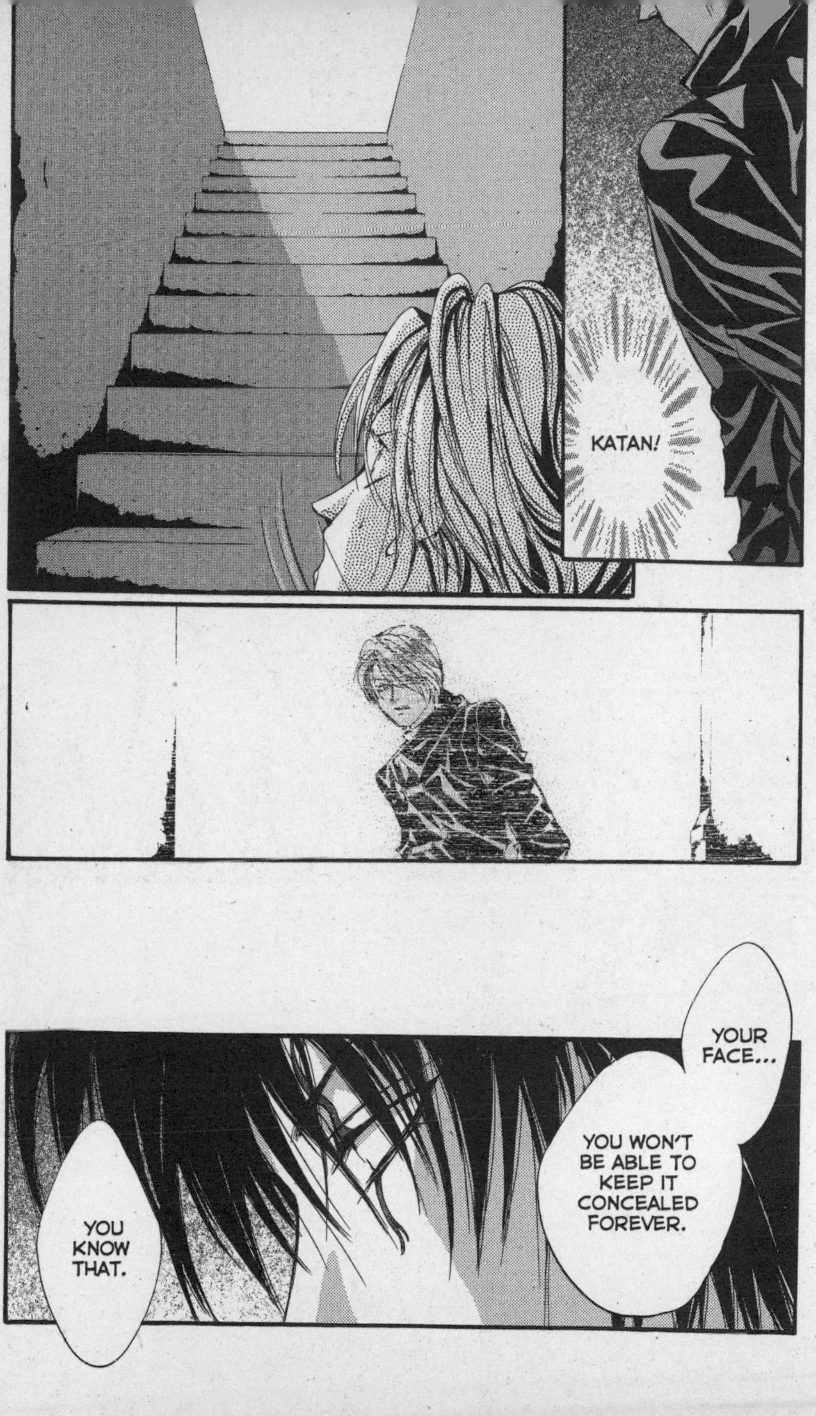
KATAN!
YOUR FACE...
YOU WON'T BE ABLE TO KEEP IT CONCEALED FOREVER.
YOU KNOW THAT.

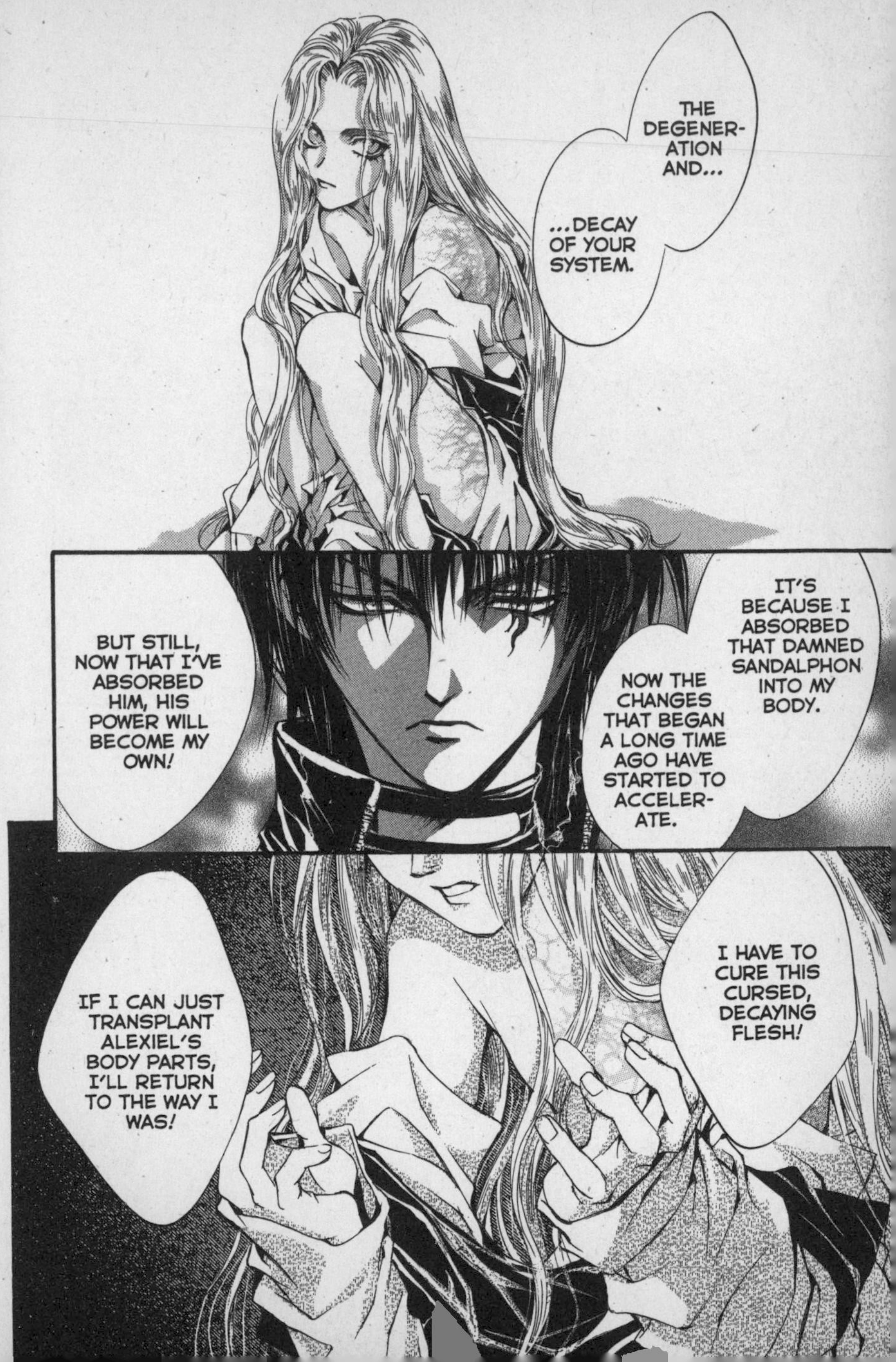
THE DEGENER-ATION AND...
...DECAY OF YOUR SYSTEM.
IT'S BECAUSE I ABSORBED THAT DAMNED SANDALPHON INTO MY BODY.
NOW THE CHANGES THAT BEGAN A LONG TIME AGO HAVE STARTED TO ACCELER-ATE.
BUT STILL, NOW THAT I'VE ABSORBED HIM, HIS POWER WILL BECOME MY OWN!
I HAVE TO CURE THIS CURSED, DECAYING FLESH!
IF I CAN JUST TRANSPLANT ALEXIEL'S BODY PARTS, I'LL RETURN TO THE WAY I WAS!

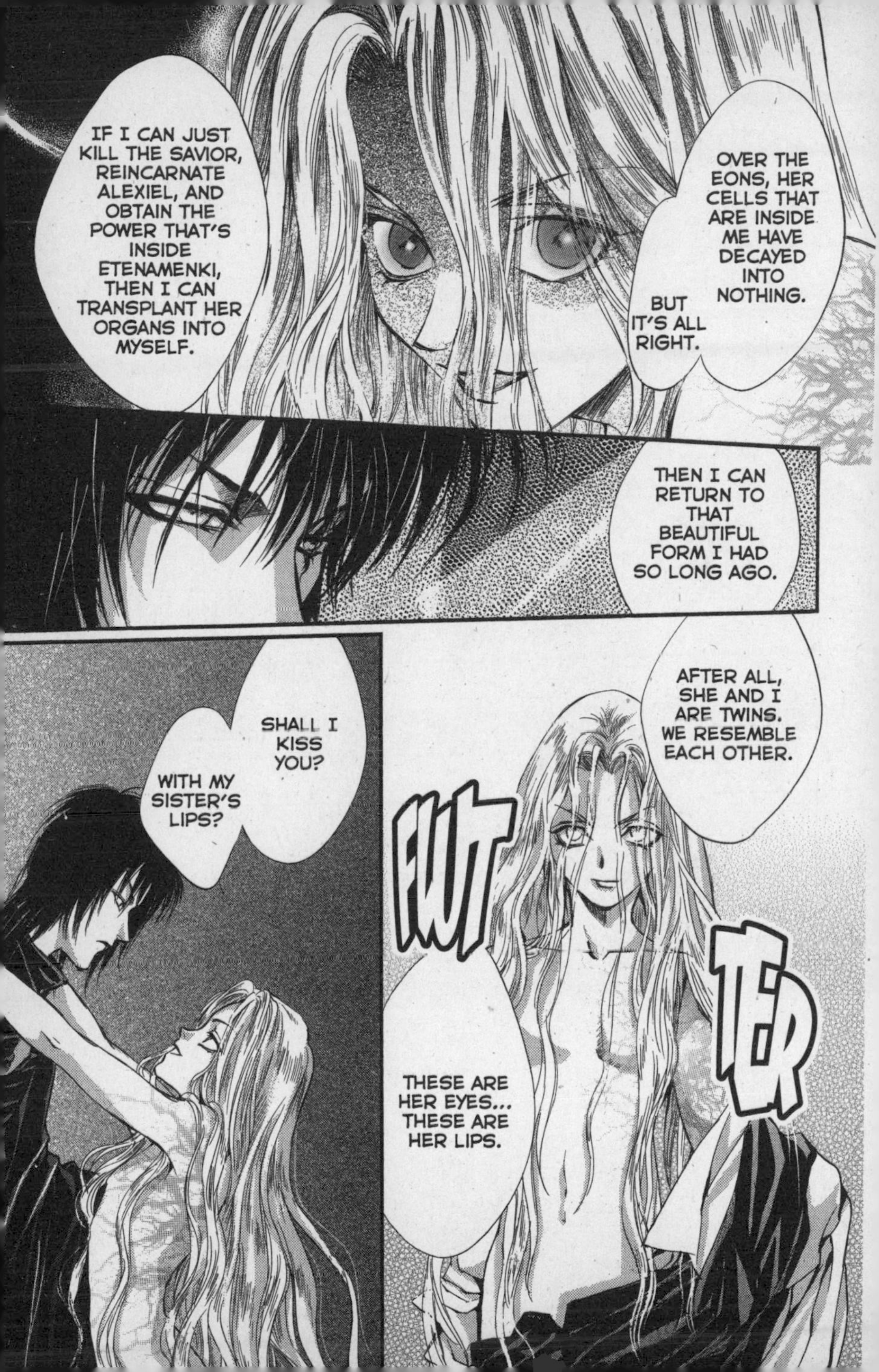
OVER THE EONS, HER CELLS THAT ARE INSIDE ME HAVE DECAYED INTO NOTHING.
BUT IT'S ALL RIGHT.
IF I CAN JUST KILL THE SAVIOR, REINCARNATE ALEXIEL, AND OBTAIN THE POWER THAT'S INSIDE ETENAMENKI, THEN I CAN TRANSPLANT HER ORGANS INTO MYSELF.
THEN I CAN RETURN TO THAT BEAUTIFUL FORM I HAD SO LONG AGO.
AFTER ALL, SHE AND I ARE TWINS. WE RESEMBLE EACH OTHER.
FLUT
TER
THESE ARE HER EYES... THESE ARE HER LIPS.
SHALL I KISS YOU?
WITH MY SISTER'S LIPS?

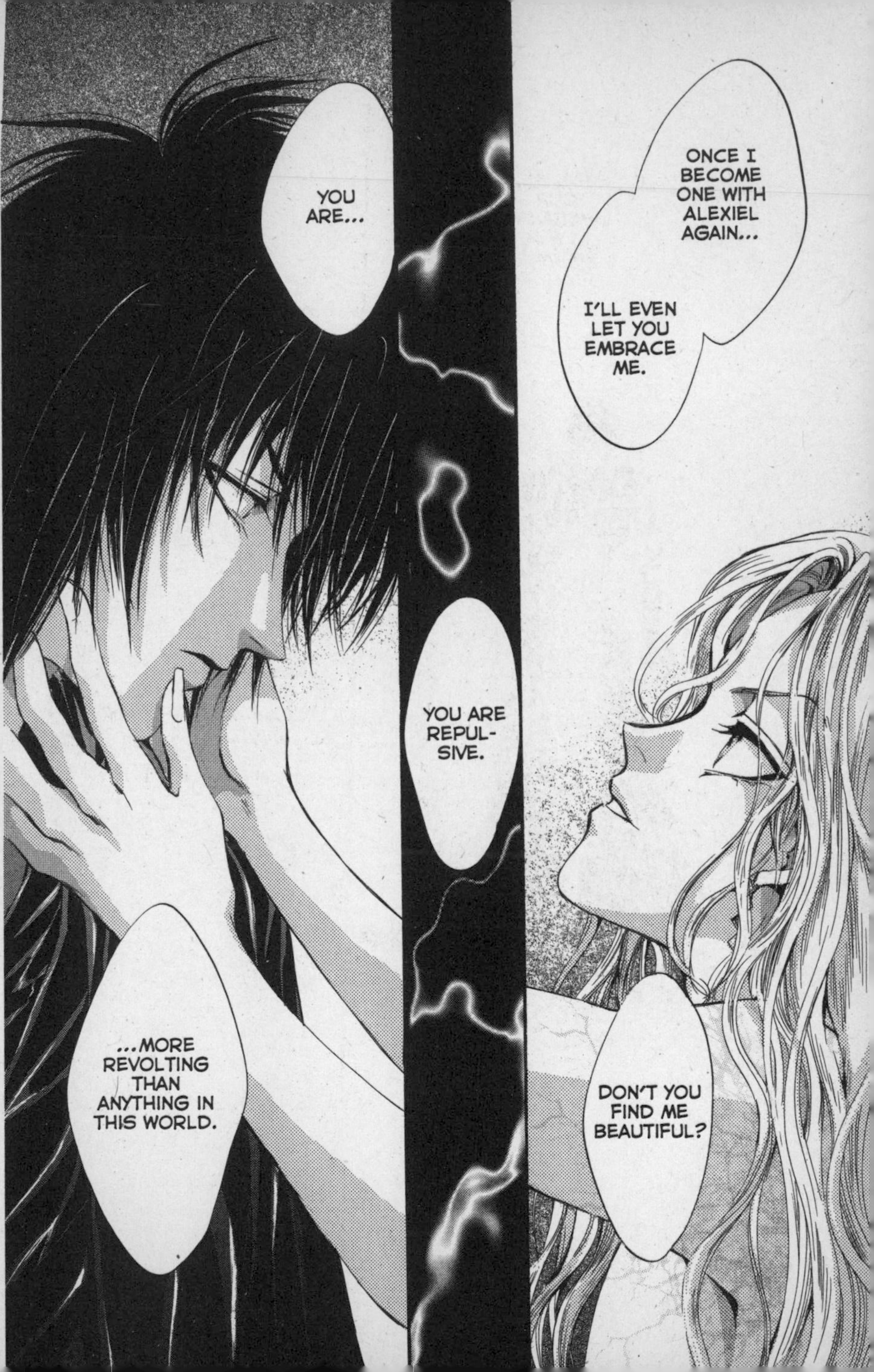
ONCE I BECOME ONE WITH ALEXIEL AGAIN...
I'LL EVEN LET YOU EMBRACE ME.
DON'T YOU FIND ME BEAUTIFUL?
YOU ARE...
YOU ARE REPUL-SIVE.
...MORE REVOLTING THAN ANYTHING IN THIS WORLD.

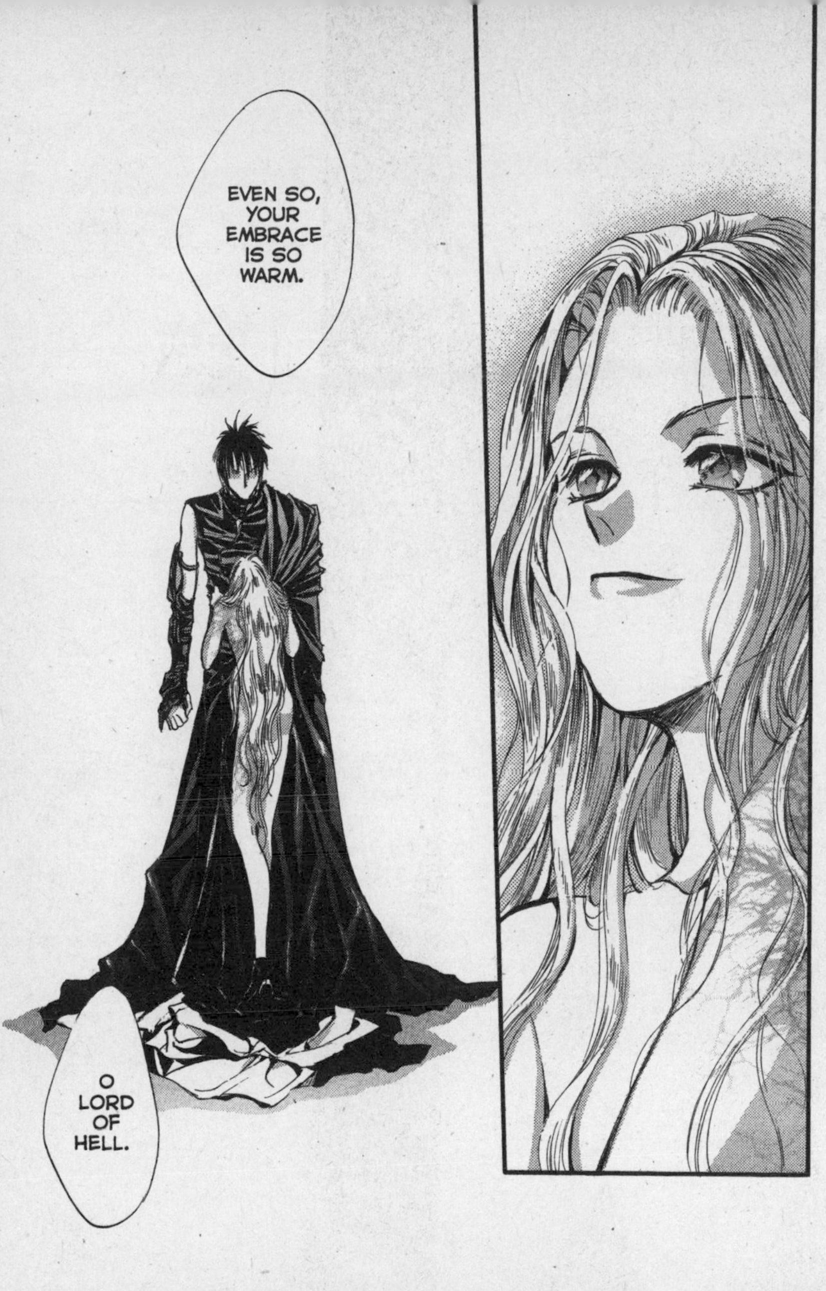
EVEN SO, YOUR EMBRACE IS SO WARM.
O LORD OF HELL.

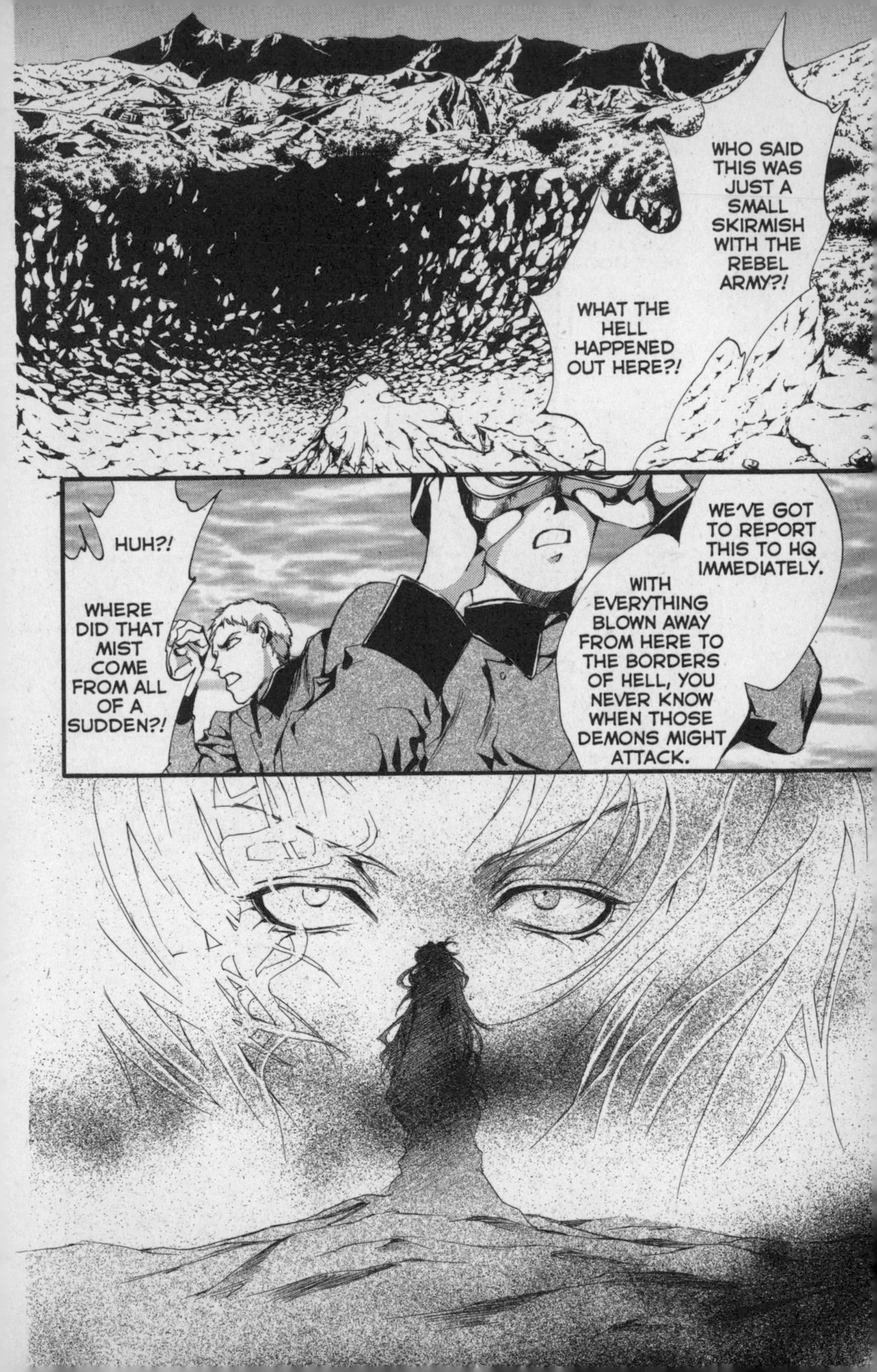
WHO SAID THIS WAS JUST A SMALL SKIRMISH WITH THE REBEL ARMY?!
WHAT THE HELL HAPPENED OUT HERE?!
WE'VE GOT TO REPORT THIS TO HQ IMMEDIATELY.
WITH EVERYTHING BLOWN AWAY FROM HERE TO THE BORDERS OF HELL, YOU NEVER KNOW WHEN THOSE DEMONS MIGHT ATTACK.
HUH?!
WHERE DID THAT MIST COME FROM ALL OF A SUDDEN?!

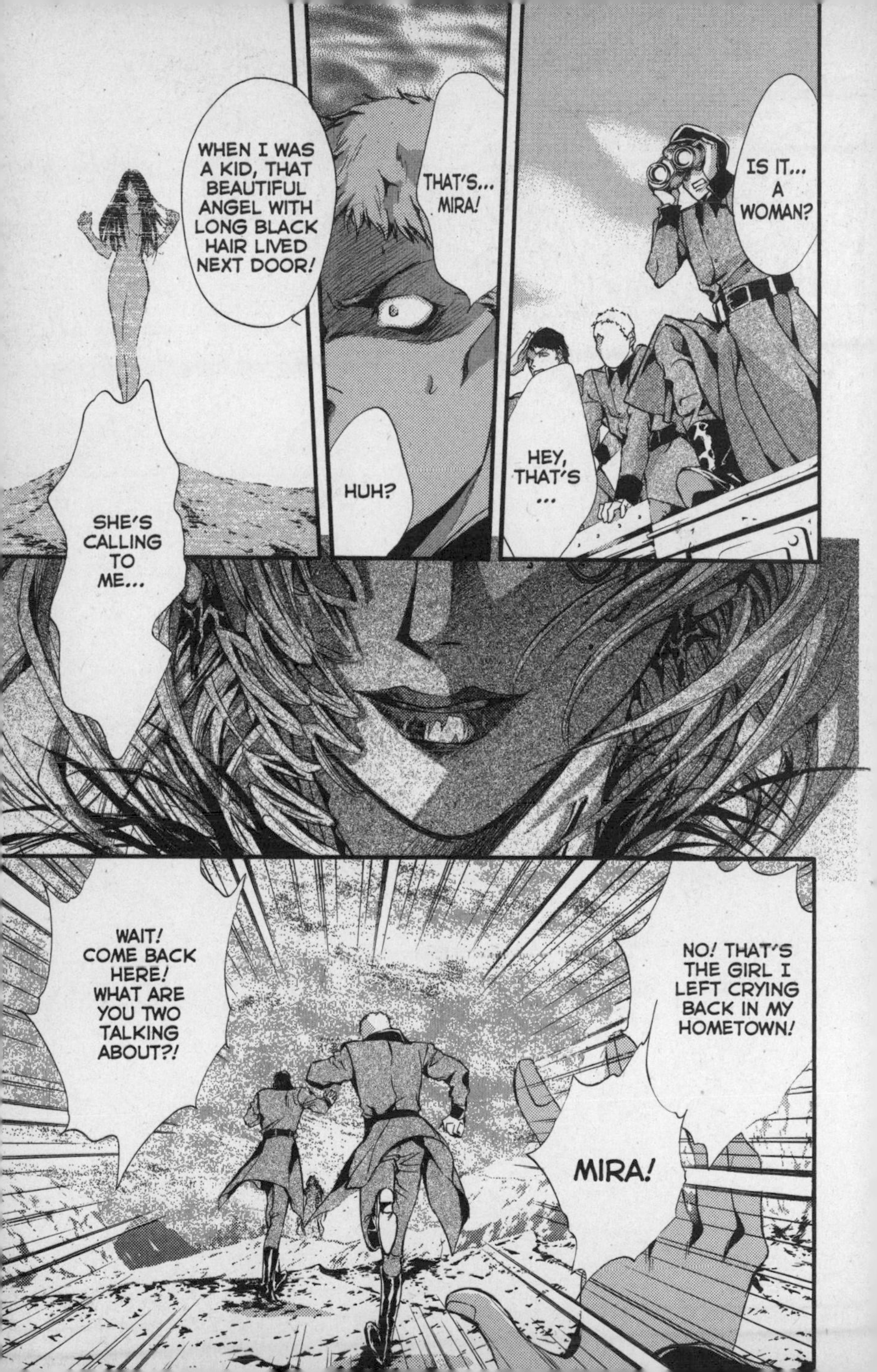
IS IT... A WOMAN?
HEY, THAT'S...
THAT'S... MIRA!
HUH?
WHEN I WAS A KID, THAT BEAUTIFUL ANGEL WITH LONG BLACK HAIR LIVED NEXT DOOR!
SHE'S CALLING TO ME...
NO! THAT'S THE GIRL I LEFT CRYING BACK IN MY HOMETOWN!
MIRA!
WAIT! COME BACK HERE! WHAT ARE YOU TWO TALKING ABOUT?!

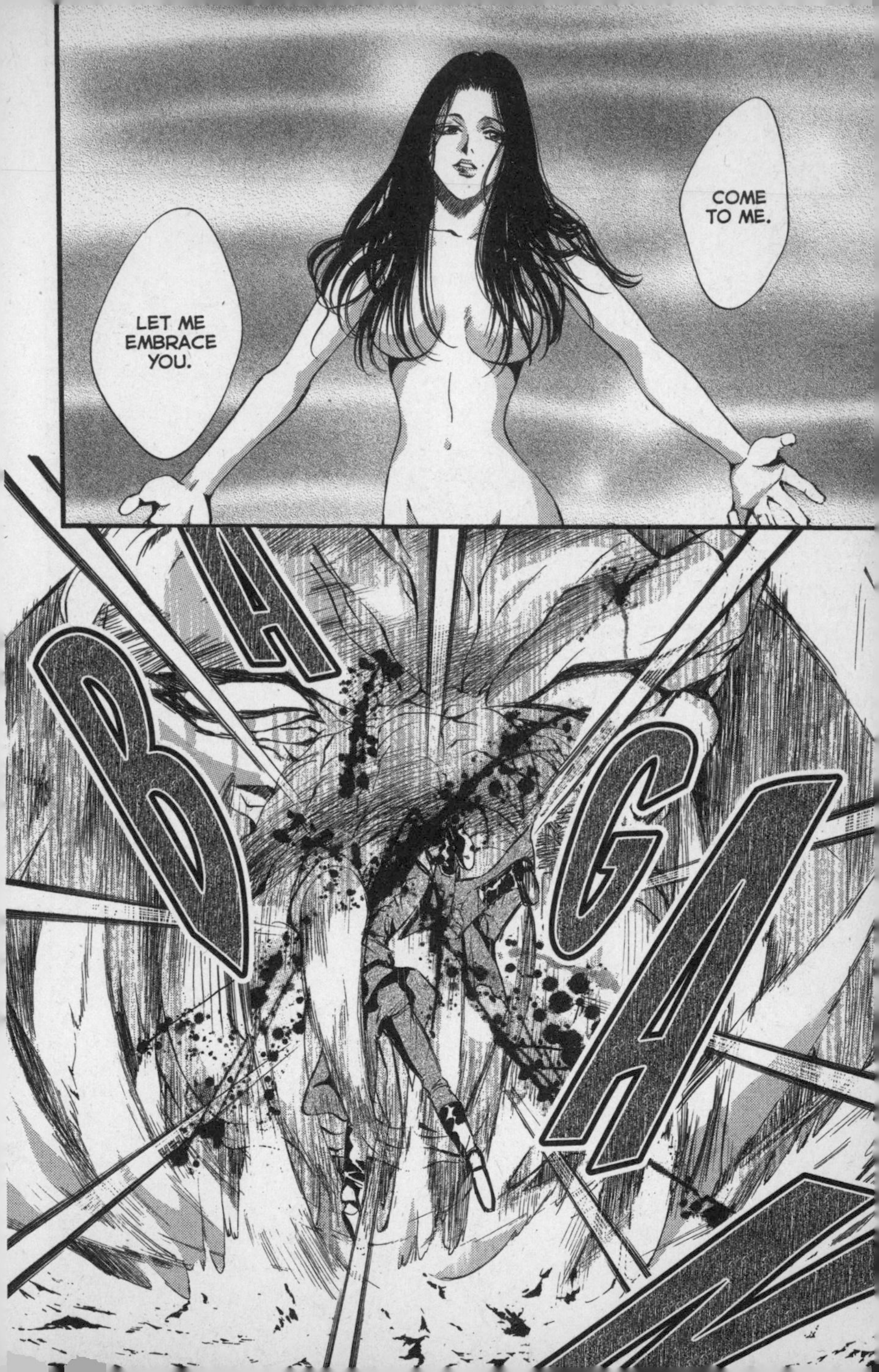
COME TO ME.
LET ME EMBRACE YOU.

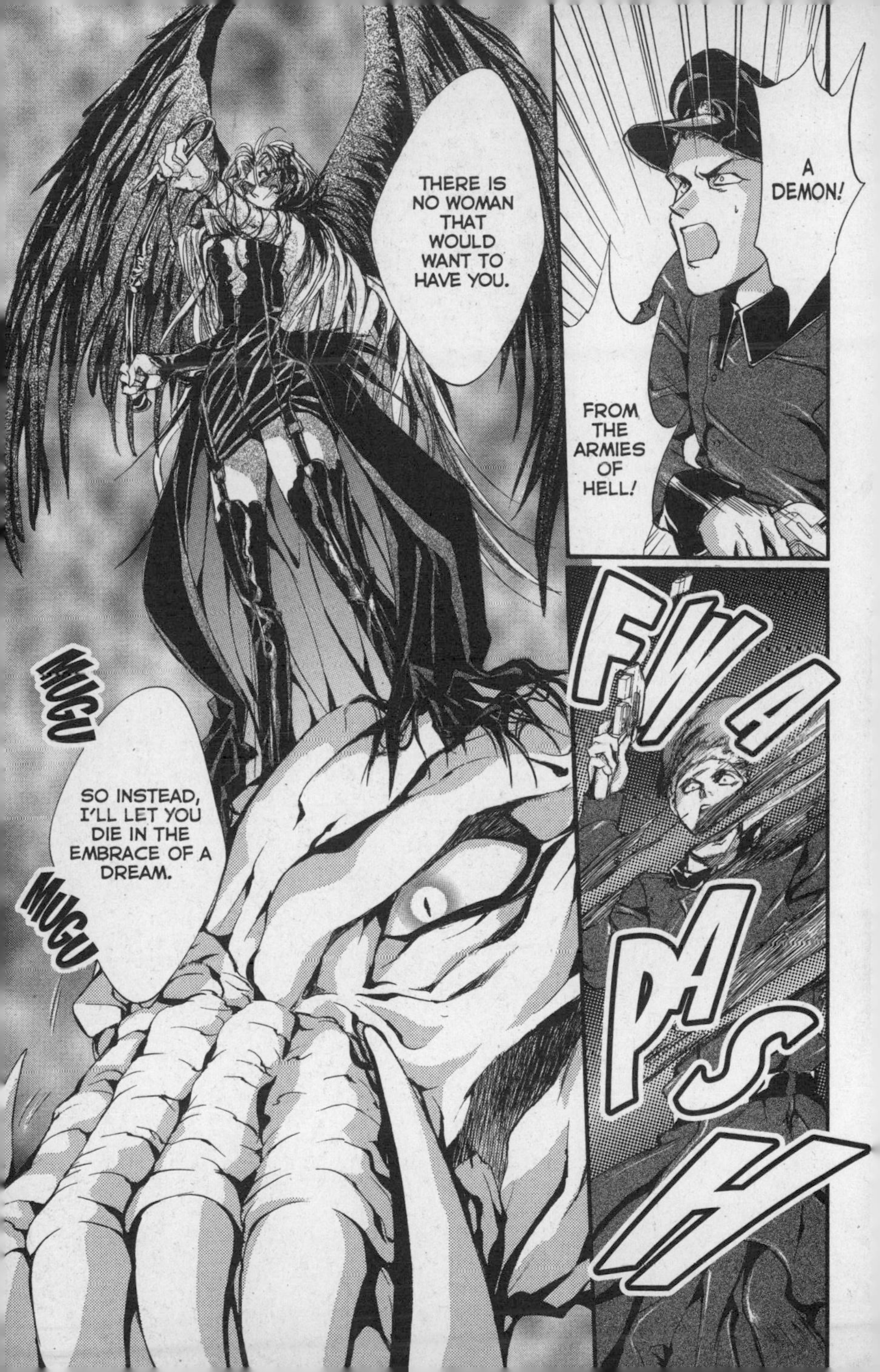
A DEMON!
FROM THE ARMIES OF HELL!
FWA
PASH
THERE IS NO WOMAN THAT WOULD WANT TO HAVE YOU.
MUGU
SO INSTEAD, I'LL LET YOU DIE IN THE EMBRACE OF A DREAM.
MUGU

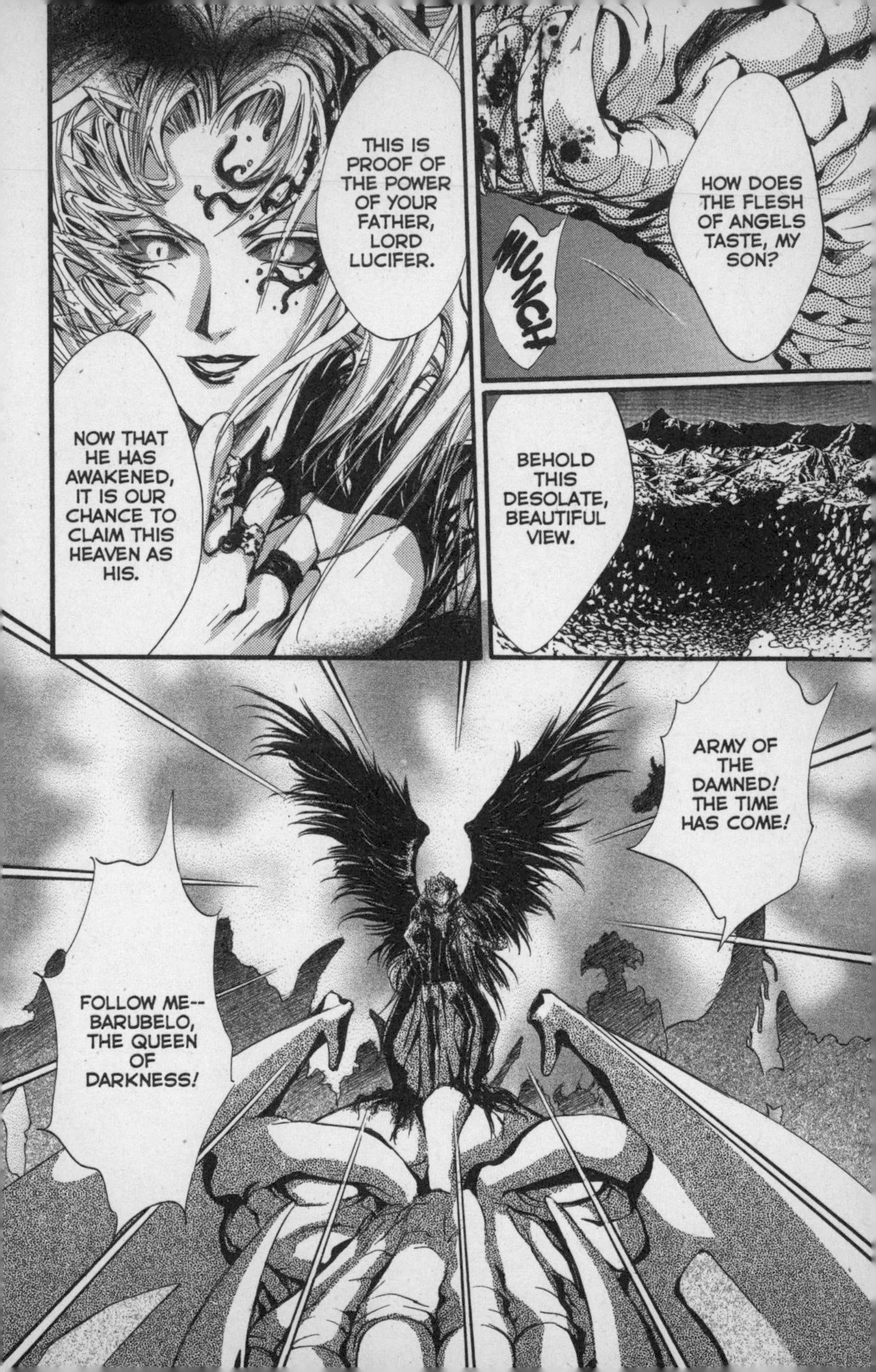
HOW DOES THE FLESH OF ANGELS TASTE, MY SON?
MUNCH
BEHOLD THIS DESOLATE, BEAUTIFUL VIEW.
THIS IS PROOF OF THE POWER OF YOUR FATHER, LORD LUCIFER.
NOW THAT HE HAS AWAKENED, IT IS OUR CHANCE TO CLAIM THIS HEAVEN AS HIS.
ARMY OF THE DAMNED! THE TIME HAS COME!
FOLLOW ME--BARUBELO, THE QUEEN OF DARKNESS!

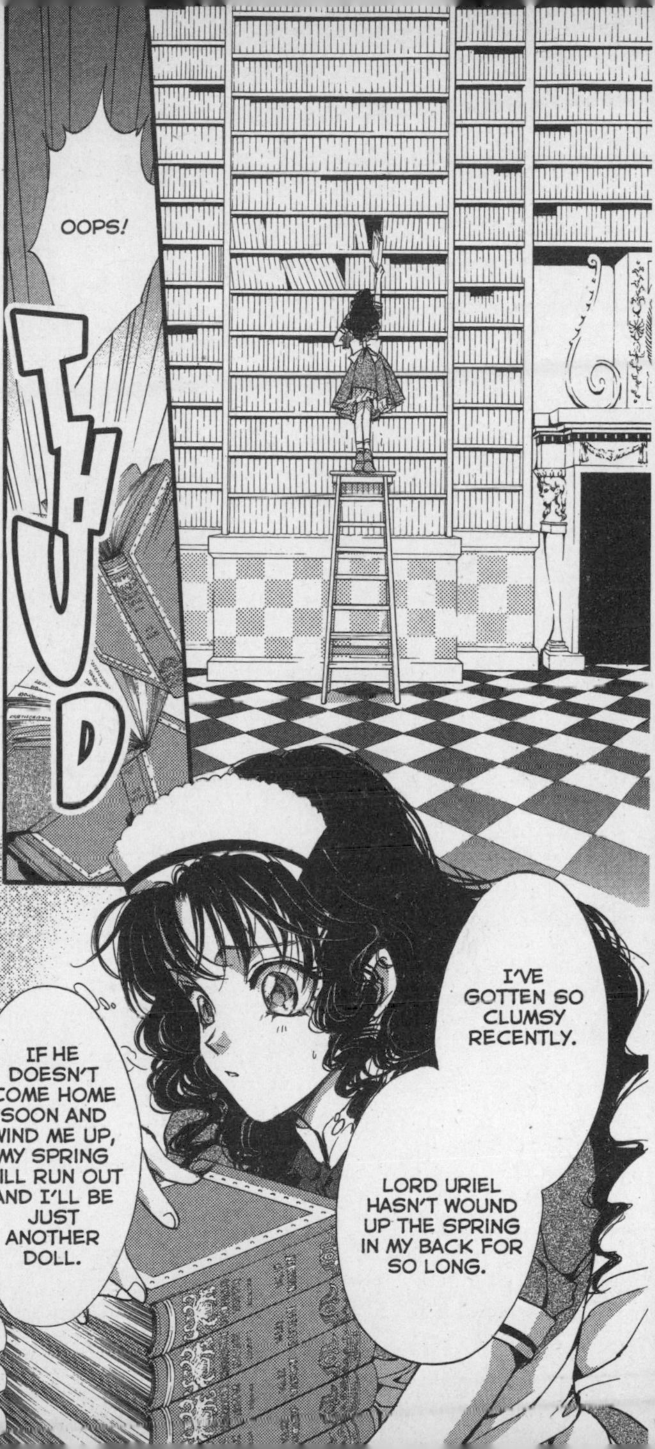
OOPS!
THUD
I'VE GOTTEN SO CLUMSY RECENTLY.
LORD URIEL HASN'T WOUND UP THE SPRING IN MY BACK FOR SO LONG.
IF HE DOESN'T COME HOME SOON AND WIND ME UP, MY SPRING WILL RUN OUT AND I'LL BE JUST ANOTHER DOLL.

Volume 18! I'm hoping I'll be able to meet you all very soon! Honestly, it's been hell correcting these comics--it's driving me nuts! I think I've even caught a cold! It's the second one I've had this year (actually, it started at the end of last year and lasted through New Year's). I don't know why, but even when I get sick I don't run a fever. I haven't come down with a high fever since I was a student. Now my throat hurts (cough) but I'm too busy to take medicine, or even eat for that matter. My eyes hurt and my head aches. Have I totally destroyed my body? Ugh. Maybe I've wrecked my ability to monitor my health! Agh!

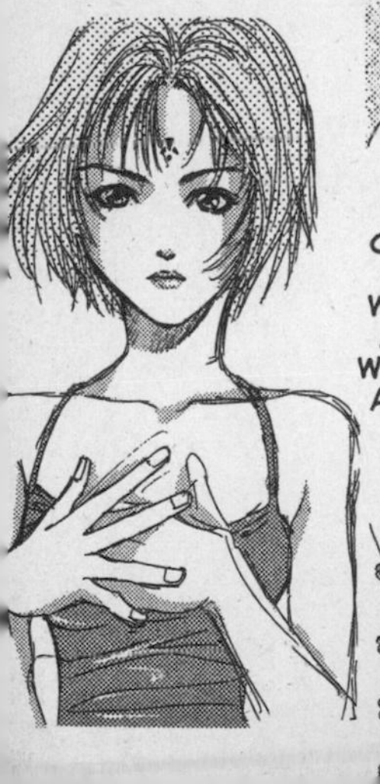

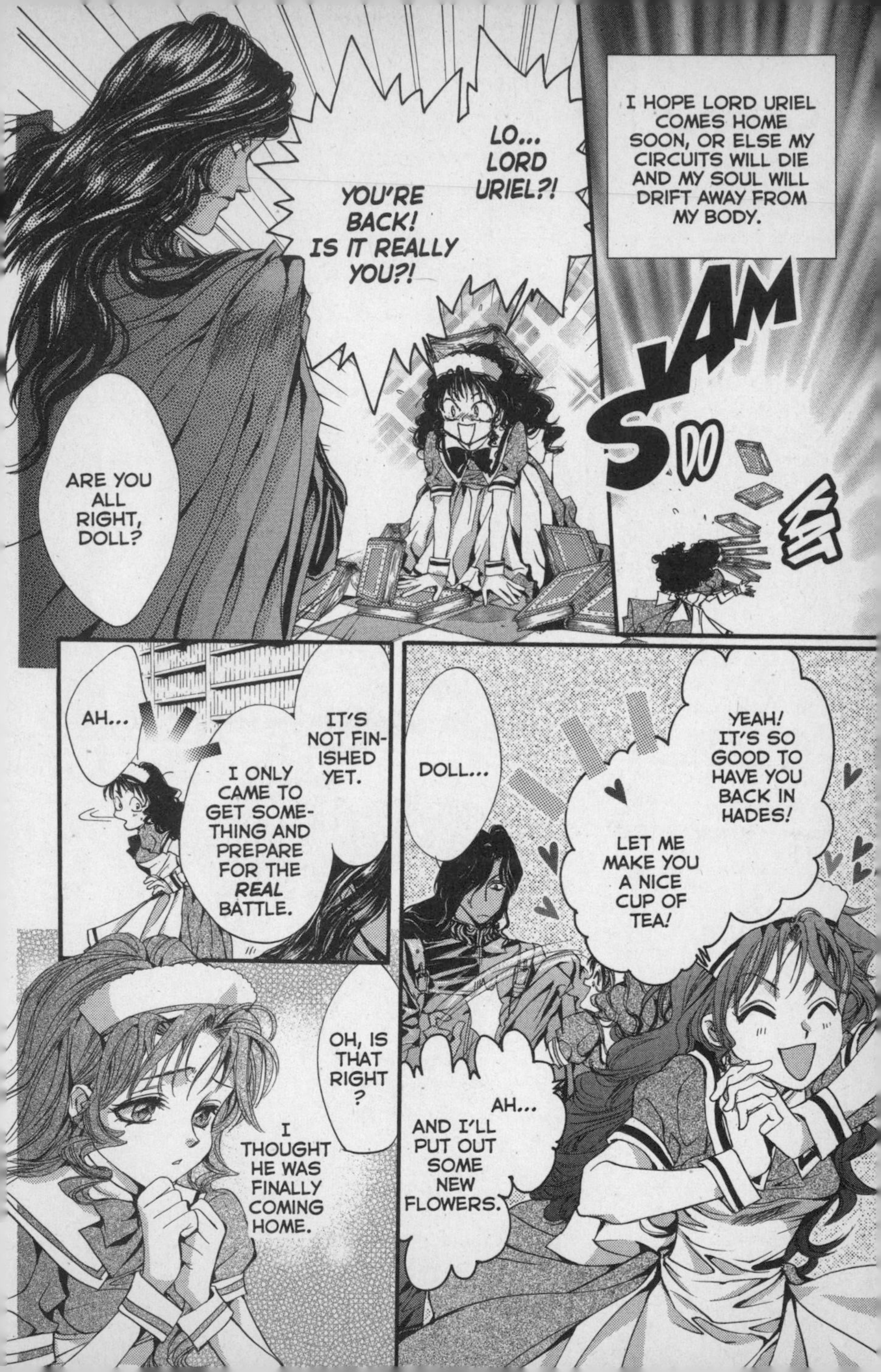
I HOPE LORD URIEL COMES HOME SOON, OR ELSE MY CIRCUITS WILL DIE AND MY SOUL WILL DRIFT AWAY FROM MY BODY.
SLAM
DO
LO... LORD URIEL?!
YOU'RE BACK! IS IT REALLY YOU?!
ARE YOU ALL RIGHT, DOLL?
YEAH! IT'S SO GOOD TO HAVE YOU BACK IN HADES!
LET ME MAKE YOU A NICE CUP OF TEA!
DOLL...
AH... AND I'LL PUT OUT SOME NEW FLOWERS.
IT'S NOT FIN-ISHED YET.
I ONLY CAME TO GET SOME-THING AND PREPARE FOR THE *REAL* BATTLE.
AH...
OH, IS THAT RIGHT?
I THOUGHT HE WAS FINALLY COMING HOME.

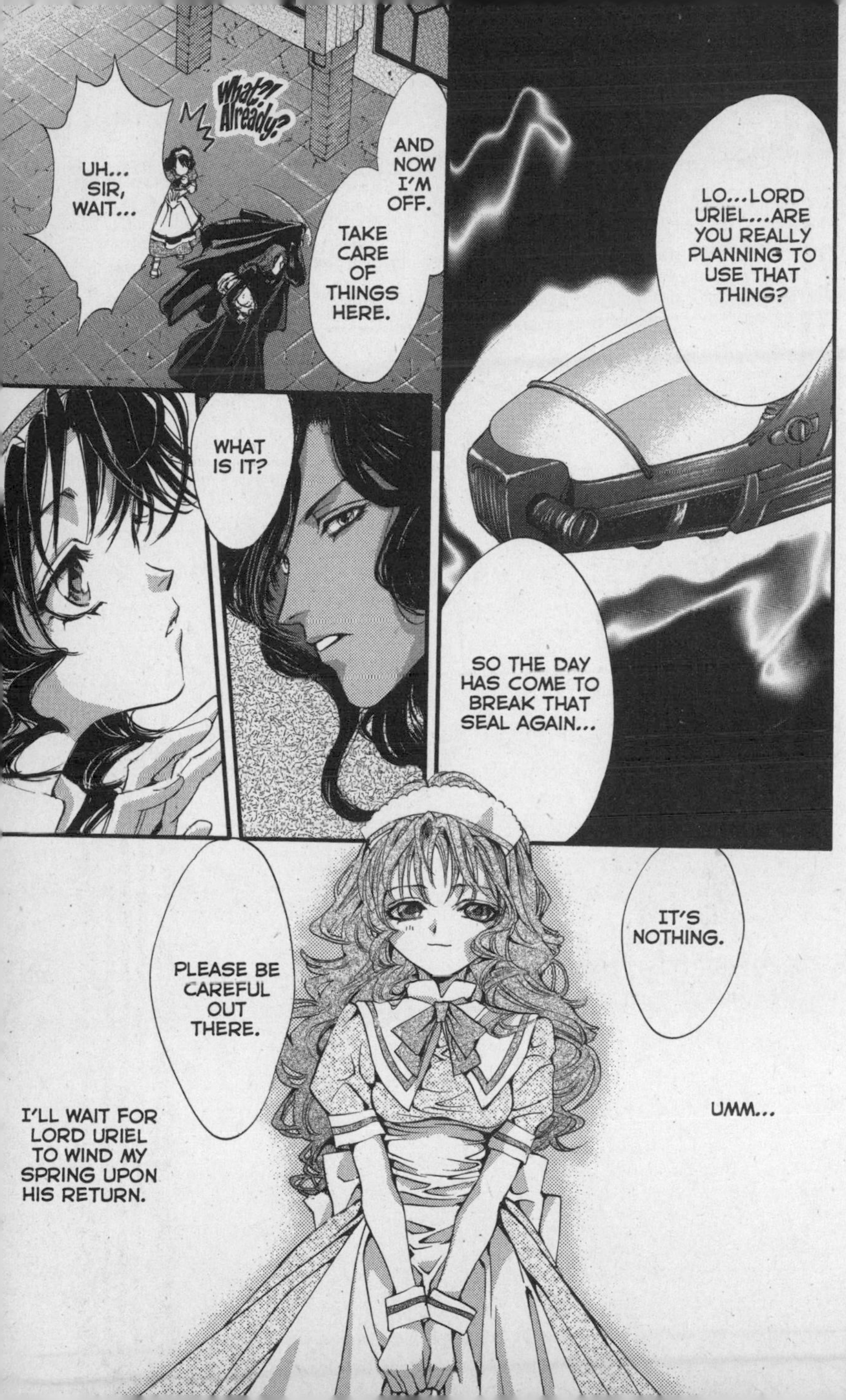
LO...LORD URIEL...ARE YOU REALLY PLANNING TO USE THAT THING?
SO THE DAY HAS COME TO BREAK THAT SEAL AGAIN...
AND NOW I'M OFF.
TAKE CARE OF THINGS HERE.
What?! Already?
UH... SIR, WAIT...
WHAT IS IT?
IT'S NOTHING.
UMM...
PLEASE BE CAREFUL OUT THERE.
I'LL WAIT FOR LORD URIEL TO WIND MY SPRING UPON HIS RETURN.

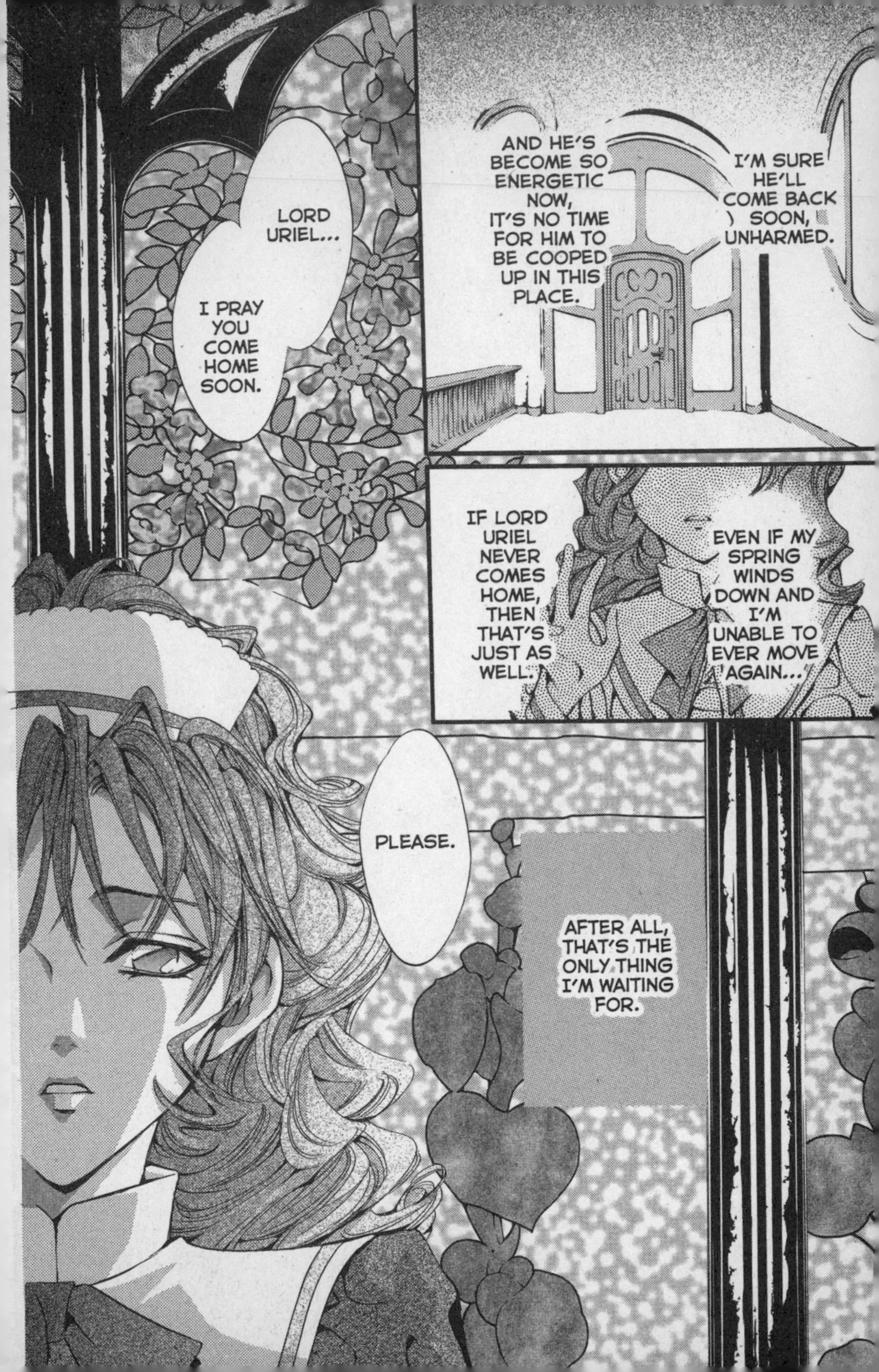
I'M SURE HE'LL COME BACK SOON, UNHARMED.
AND HE'S BECOME SO ENERGETIC NOW, IT'S NO TIME FOR HIM TO BE COOPED UP IN THIS PLACE.
EVEN IF MY SPRING WINDS DOWN AND I'M UNABLE TO EVER MOVE AGAIN...
IF LORD URIEL NEVER COMES HOME, THEN THAT'S JUST AS WELL.
LORD URIEL...
I PRAY YOU COME HOME SOON.
PLEASE.
AFTER ALL, THAT'S THE ONLY THING I'M WAITING FOR.

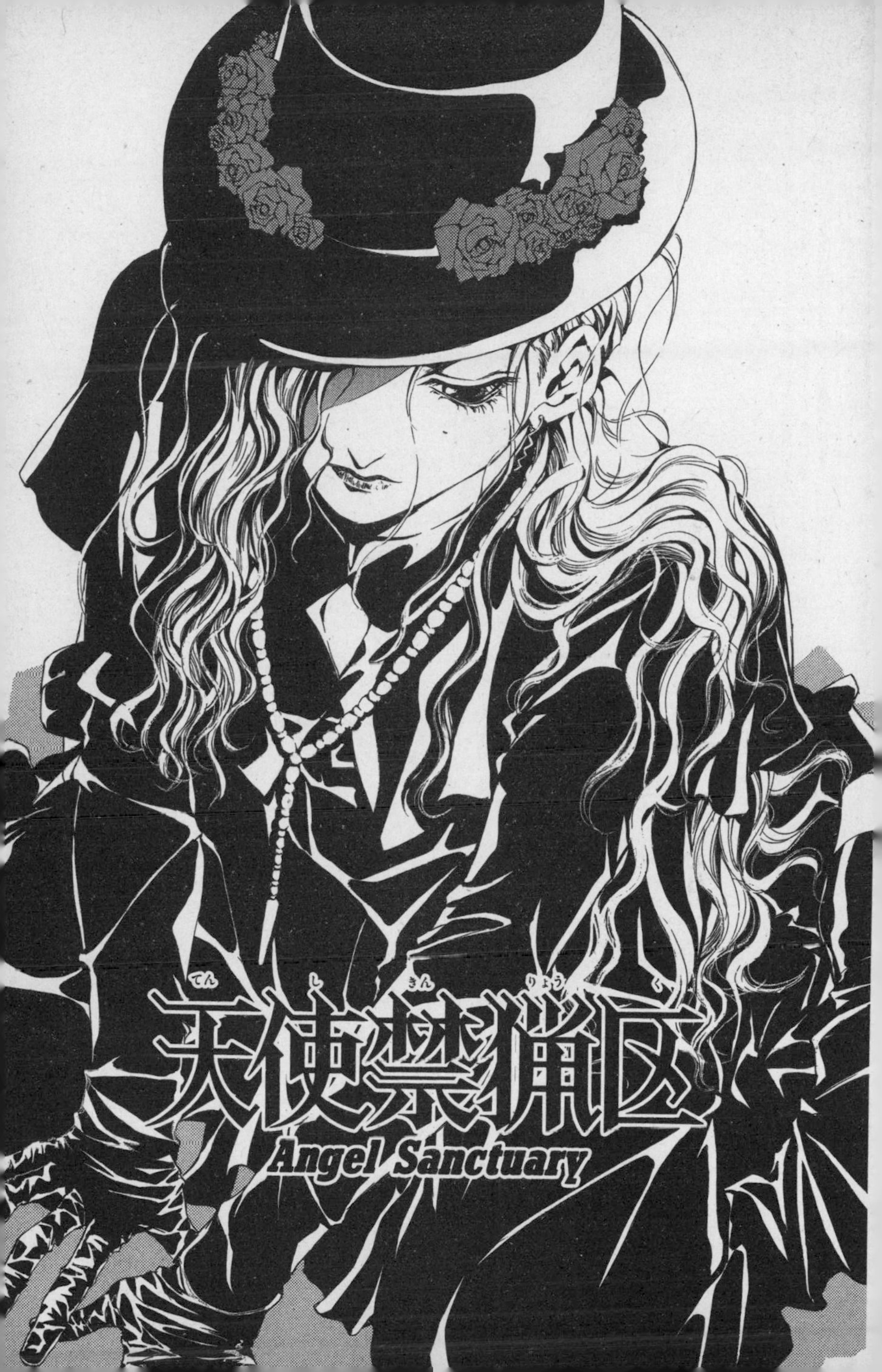
天使禁猟区
てんしきんりょうく
Angel Sanctuary

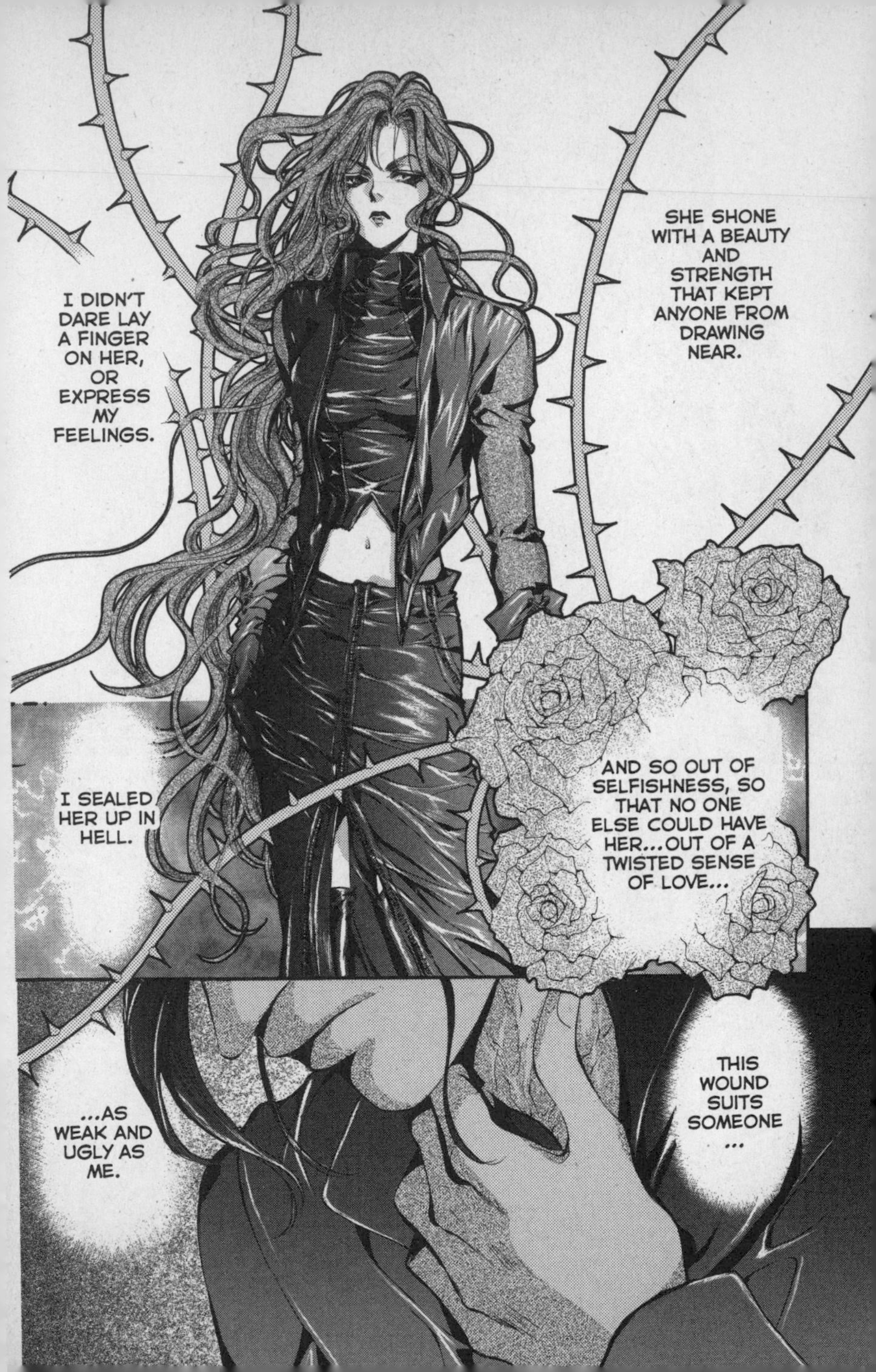
SHE SHONE WITH A BEAUTY AND STRENGTH THAT KEPT ANYONE FROM DRAWING NEAR.
I DIDN'T DARE LAY A FINGER ON HER, OR EXPRESS MY FEELINGS.
AND SO OUT OF SELFISHNESS, SO THAT NO ONE ELSE COULD HAVE HER...OUT OF A TWISTED SENSE OF LOVE...
I SEALED HER UP IN HELL.
THIS WOUND SUITS SOMEONE ...
...AS WEAK AND UGLY AS ME.

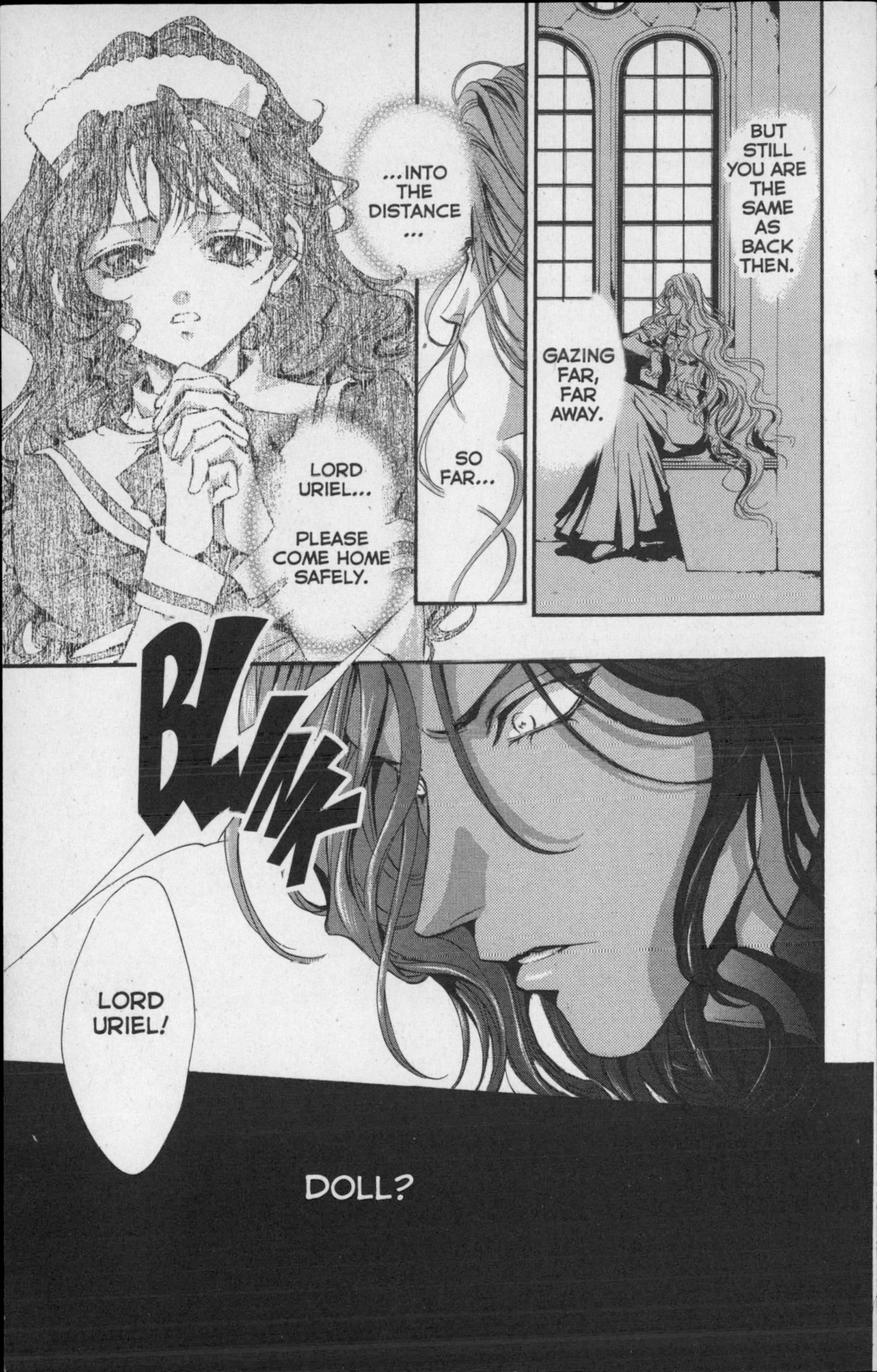
BUT STILL YOU ARE THE SAME AS BACK THEN.
GAZING FAR, FAR AWAY.
...INTO THE DISTANCE...
SO FAR...
LORD URIEL...
PLEASE COME HOME SAFELY.
BLINK
LORD URIEL!
DOLL?

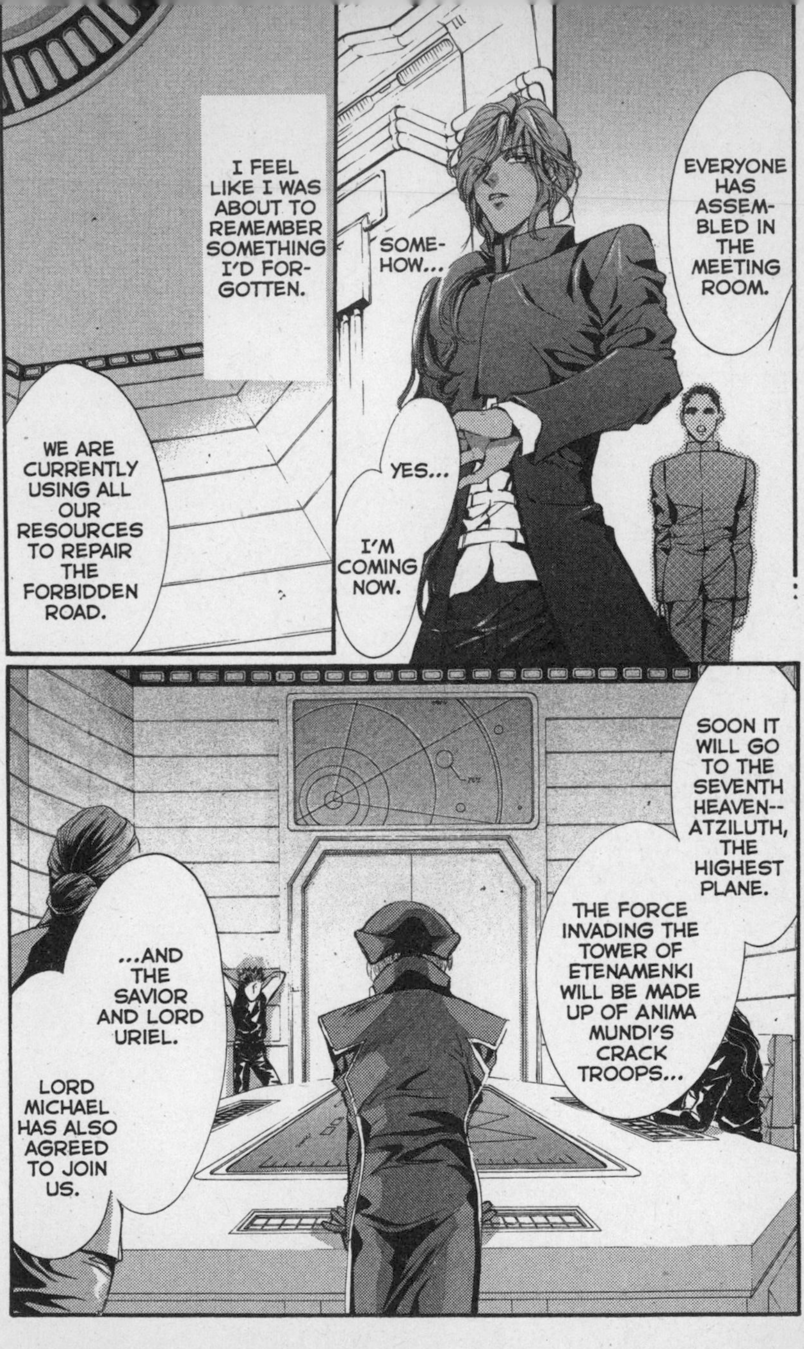
EVERYONE HAS ASSEM-BLED IN THE MEETING ROOM.
SOME-HOW...
YES...
I'M COMING NOW.
I FEEL LIKE I WAS ABOUT TO REMEMBER SOMETHING I'D FOR-GOTTEN.
WE ARE CURRENTLY USING ALL OUR RESOURCES TO REPAIR THE FORBIDDEN ROAD.
SOON IT WILL GO TO THE SEVENTH HEAVEN-- ATZILUTH, THE HIGHEST PLANE.
THE FORCE INVADING THE TOWER OF ETENAMENKI WILL BE MADE UP OF ANIMA MUNDI'S CRACK TROOPS...
...AND THE SAVIOR AND LORD URIEL.
LORD MICHAEL HAS ALSO AGREED TO JOIN US.

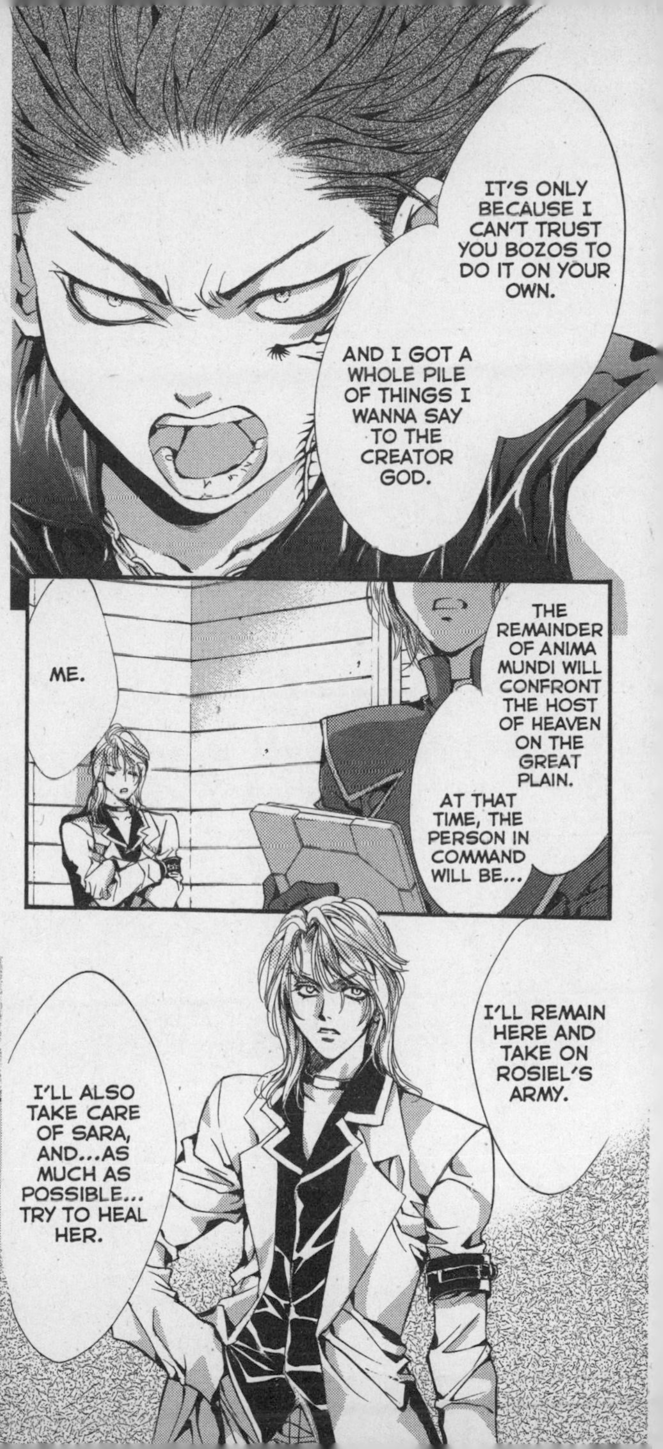
IT'S ONLY BECAUSE I CAN'T TRUST YOU BOZOS TO DO IT ON YOUR OWN.
AND I GOT A WHOLE PILE OF THINGS I WANNA SAY TO THE CREATOR GOD.
THE REMAINDER OF ANIMA MUNDI WILL CONFRONT THE HOST OF HEAVEN ON THE GREAT PLAIN.
AT THAT TIME, THE PERSON IN COMMAND WILL BE...
ME.
I'LL REMAIN HERE AND TAKE ON ROSIEL'S ARMY.
I'LL ALSO TAKE CARE OF SARA, AND...AS MUCH AS POSSIBLE... TRY TO HEAL HER.

Aah...do you guys even remember Doll? There are a lot of pictures of people cos-playing as Doll (I received some from fans, and from web-sites) and they look so cute in those maid outfits. I like them, too! And hey, I found some interesting Angel Sanct web sites. There're lots of 'em. Even some about Kira, and about Asmodeus. Some have horoscopes. I wrote on a chat, but used a fake name so nobody recognized me. Heh heh heh. I want to make a website, too.
But I can't find anybody to build it for me. By myself, I can't do anything but surf, read mail and chat. My PostPet name is HamHam the Hamster, but so far no friends have signed up.

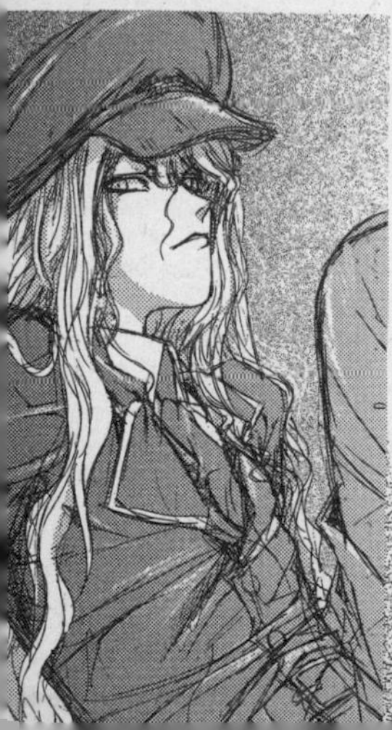

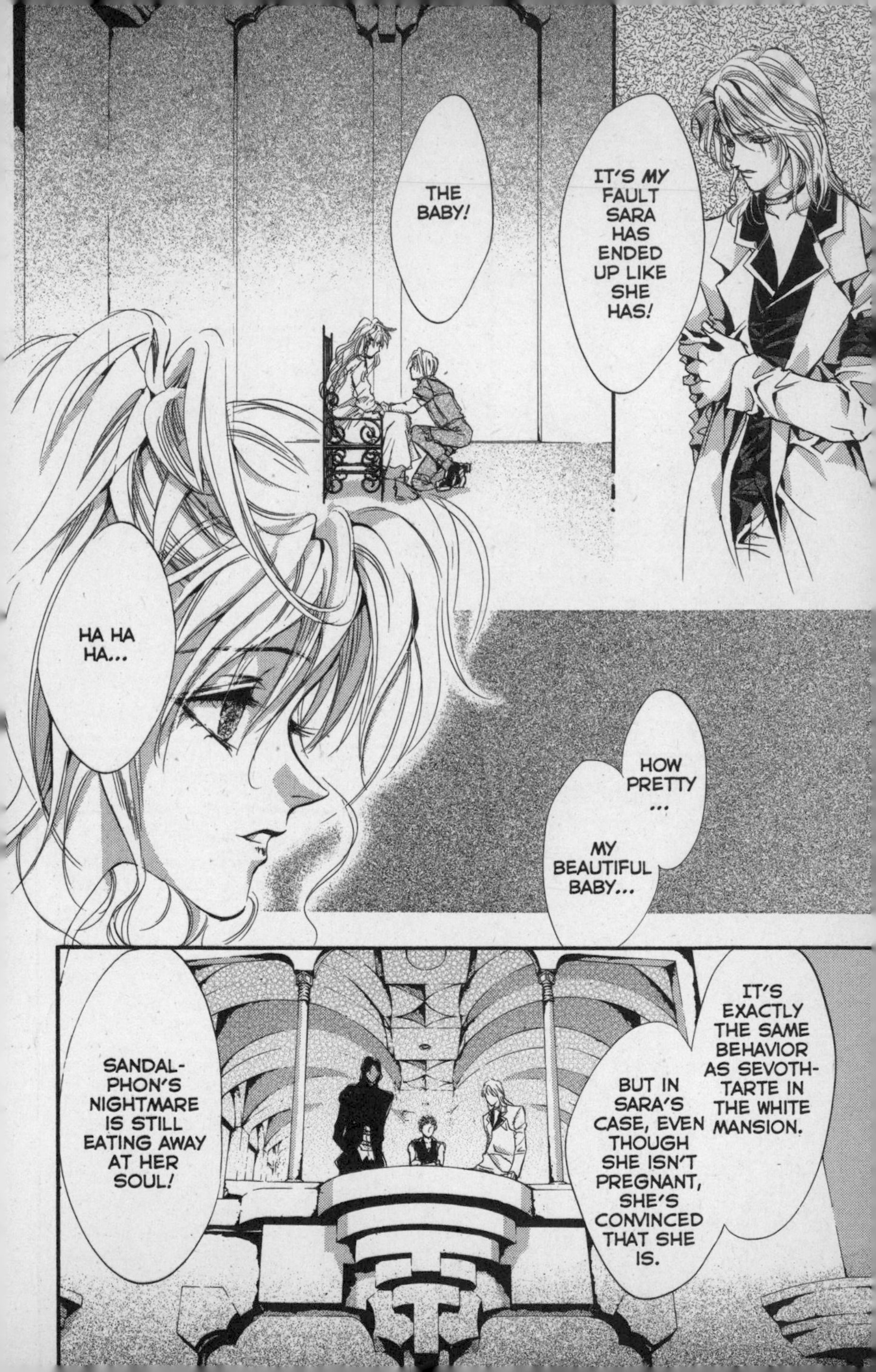
IT'S MY FAULT SARA HAS ENDED UP LIKE SHE HAS!
THE BABY!
HOW PRETTY ... MY BEAUTIFUL BABY...
HA HA HA...
IT'S EXACTLY THE SAME BEHAVIOR AS SEVOTH-TARTE IN THE WHITE MANSION.
BUT IN SARA'S CASE, EVEN THOUGH SHE ISN'T PREGNANT, SHE'S CONVINCED THAT SHE IS.
SANDAL-PHON'S NIGHTMARE IS STILL EATING AWAY AT HER SOUL!

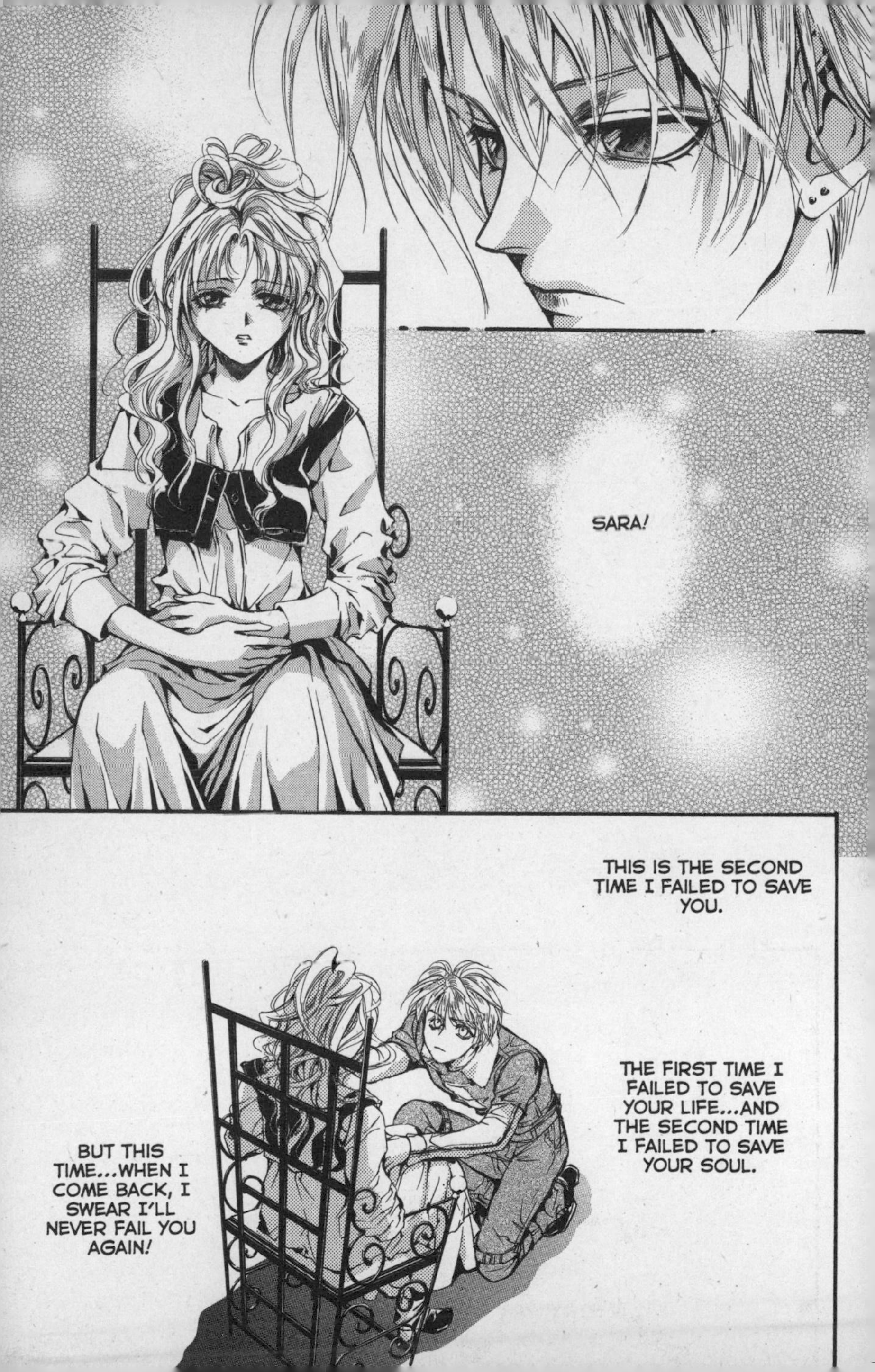
SARA!
THIS IS THE SECOND TIME I FAILED TO SAVE YOU.
THE FIRST TIME I FAILED TO SAVE YOUR LIFE...AND THE SECOND TIME I FAILED TO SAVE YOUR SOUL.
BUT THIS TIME...WHEN I COME BACK, I SWEAR I'LL NEVER FAIL YOU AGAIN!

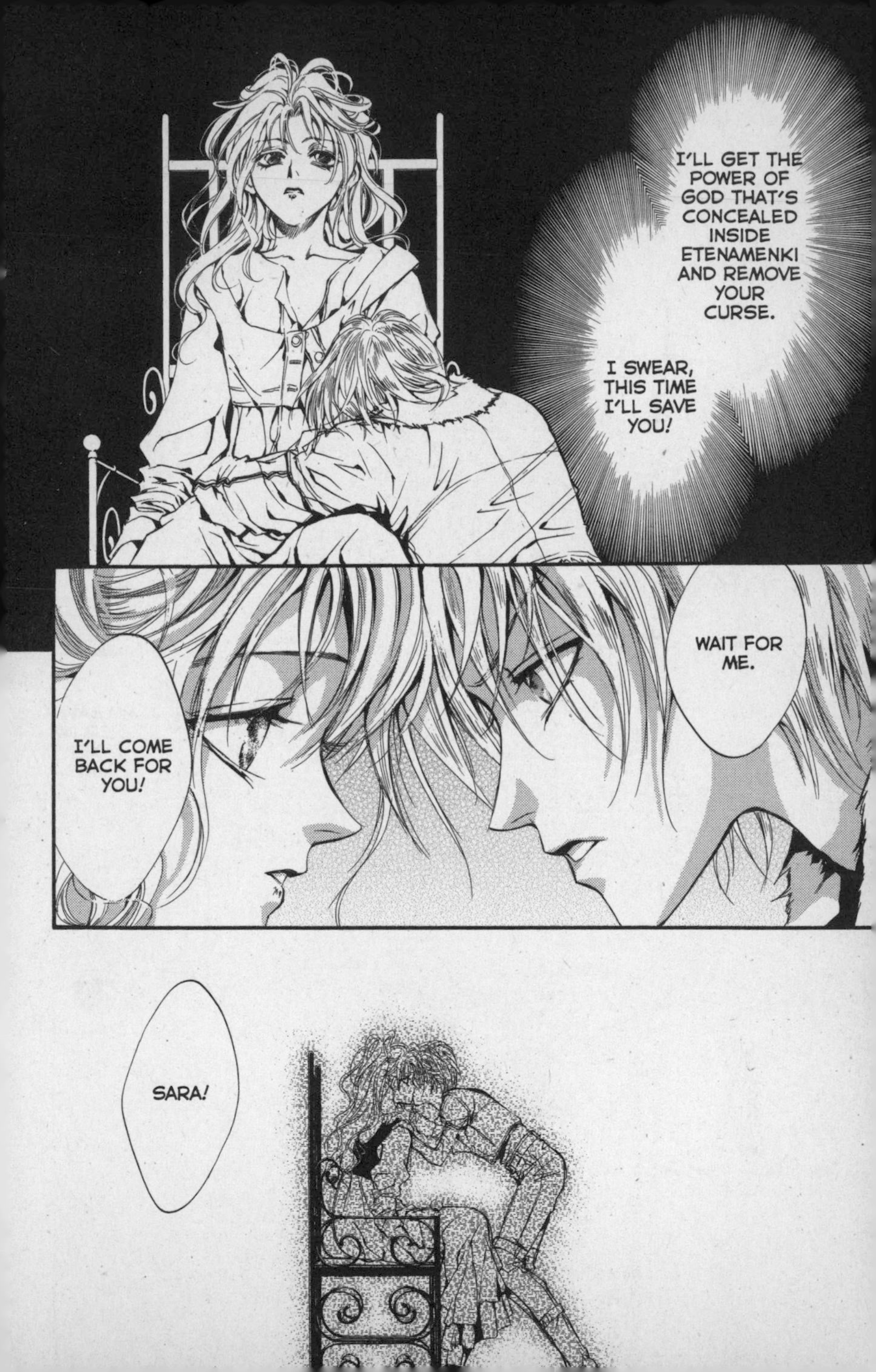
I'LL GET THE POWER OF GOD THAT'S CONCEALED INSIDE ETENAMENKI AND REMOVE YOUR CURSE.
I SWEAR, THIS TIME I'LL SAVE YOU!
WAIT FOR ME.
I'LL COME BACK FOR YOU!
SARA!

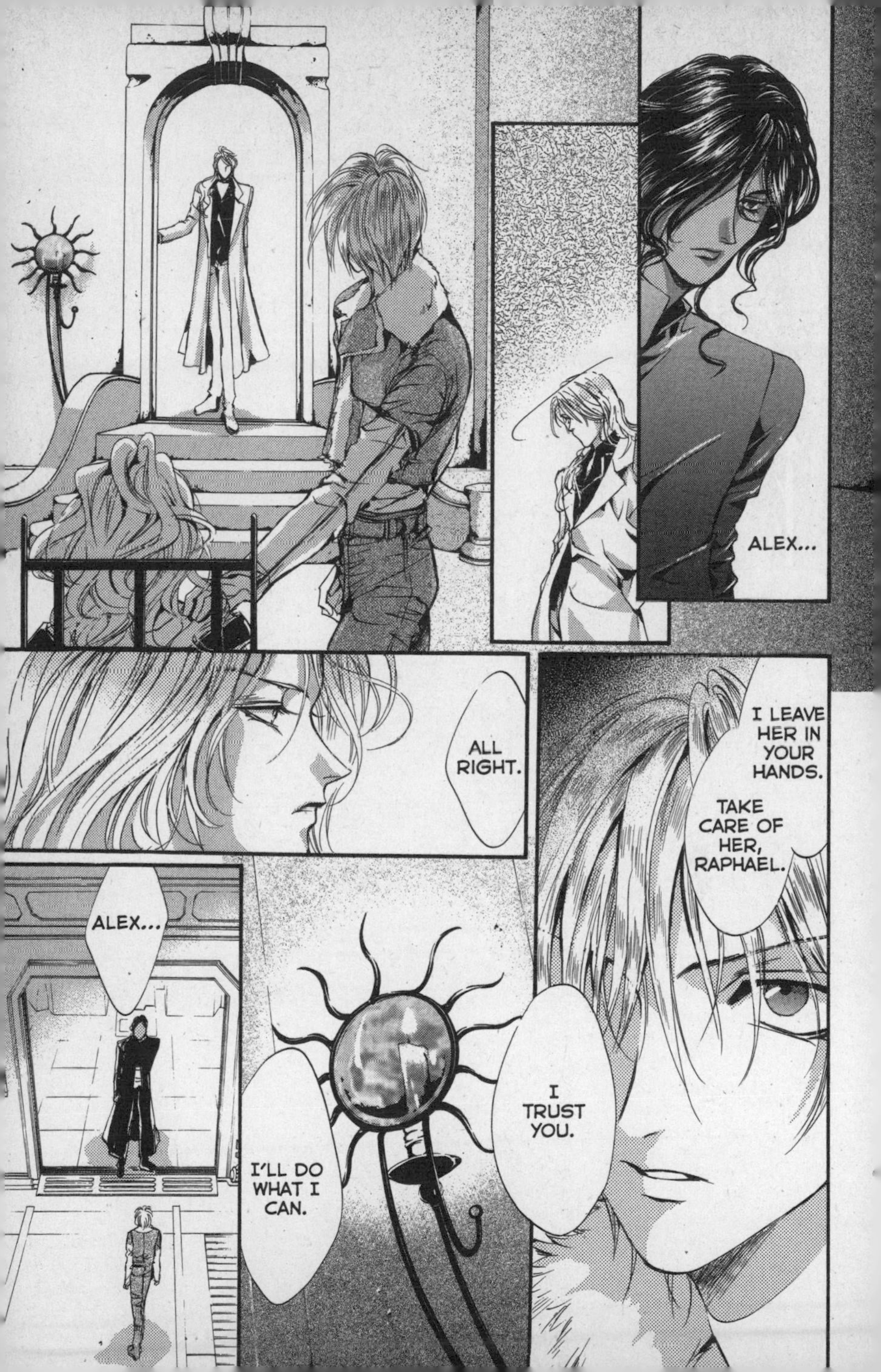
ALEX...
I LEAVE HER IN YOUR HANDS.
TAKE CARE OF HER, RAPHAEL.
I TRUST YOU.
ALL RIGHT.
I'LL DO WHAT I CAN.
ALEX...

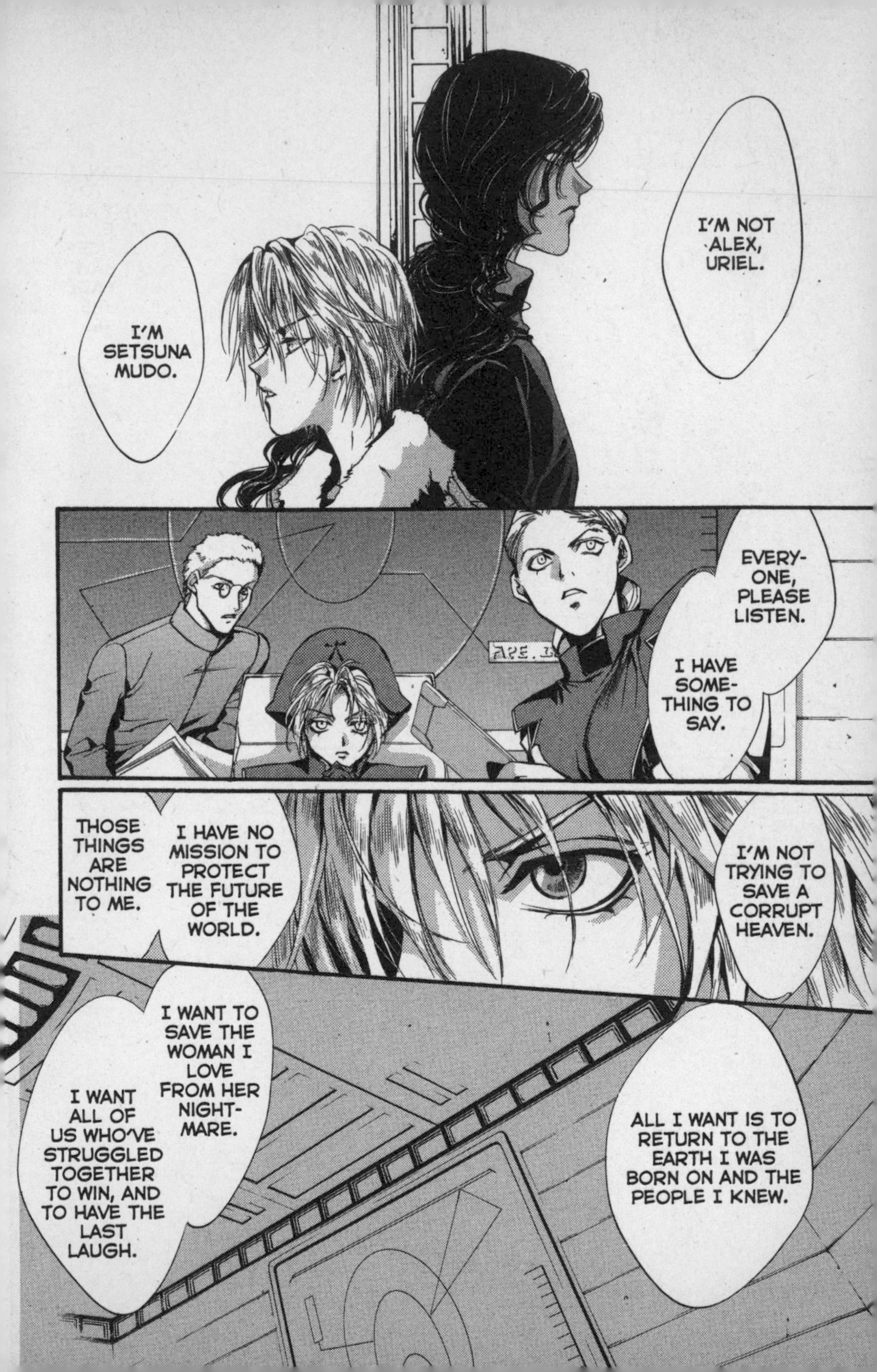
I'M NOT ALEX, URIEL.
I'M SETSUNA MUDO.
EVERY-ONE, PLEASE LISTEN.
I HAVE SOME-THING TO SAY.
I'M NOT TRYING TO SAVE A CORRUPT HEAVEN.
I HAVE NO MISSION TO PROTECT THE FUTURE OF THE WORLD.
THOSE THINGS ARE NOTHING TO ME.
ALL I WANT IS TO RETURN TO THE EARTH I WAS BORN ON AND THE PEOPLE I KNEW.
I WANT TO SAVE THE WOMAN I LOVE FROM HER NIGHT-MARE.
I WANT ALL OF US WHO'VE STRUGGLED TOGETHER TO WIN, AND TO HAVE THE LAST LAUGH.

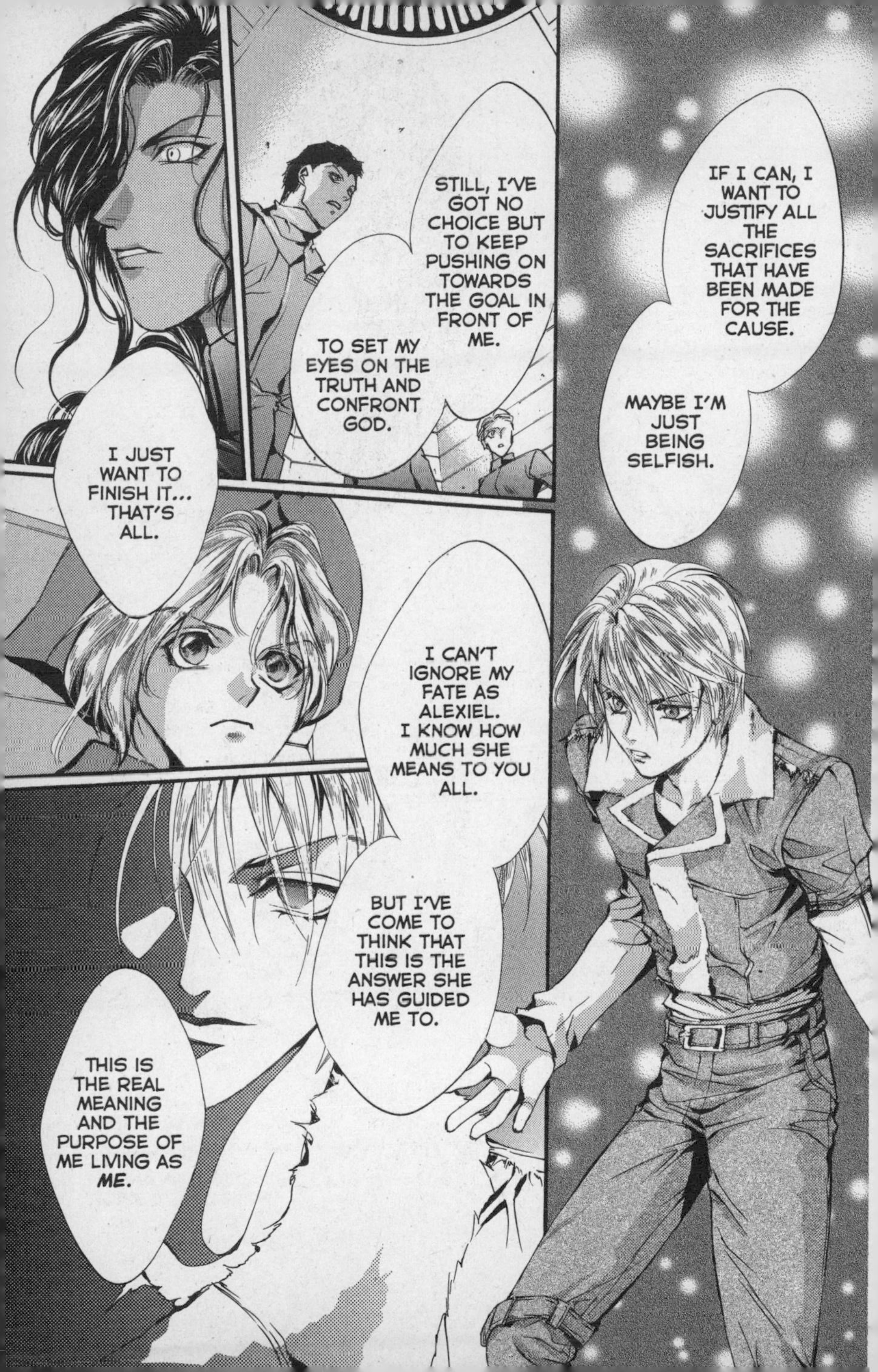
IF I CAN, I WANT TO JUSTIFY ALL THE SACRIFICES THAT HAVE BEEN MADE FOR THE CAUSE.
MAYBE I'M JUST BEING SELFISH.
STILL, I'VE GOT NO CHOICE BUT TO KEEP PUSHING ON TOWARDS THE GOAL IN FRONT OF ME.
TO SET MY EYES ON THE TRUTH AND CONFRONT GOD.
I JUST WANT TO FINISH IT... THAT'S ALL.
I CAN'T IGNORE MY FATE AS ALEXIEL. I KNOW HOW MUCH SHE MEANS TO YOU ALL.
BUT I'VE COME TO THINK THAT THIS IS THE ANSWER SHE HAS GUIDED ME TO.
THIS IS THE REAL MEANING AND THE PURPOSE OF ME LIVING AS *ME*.

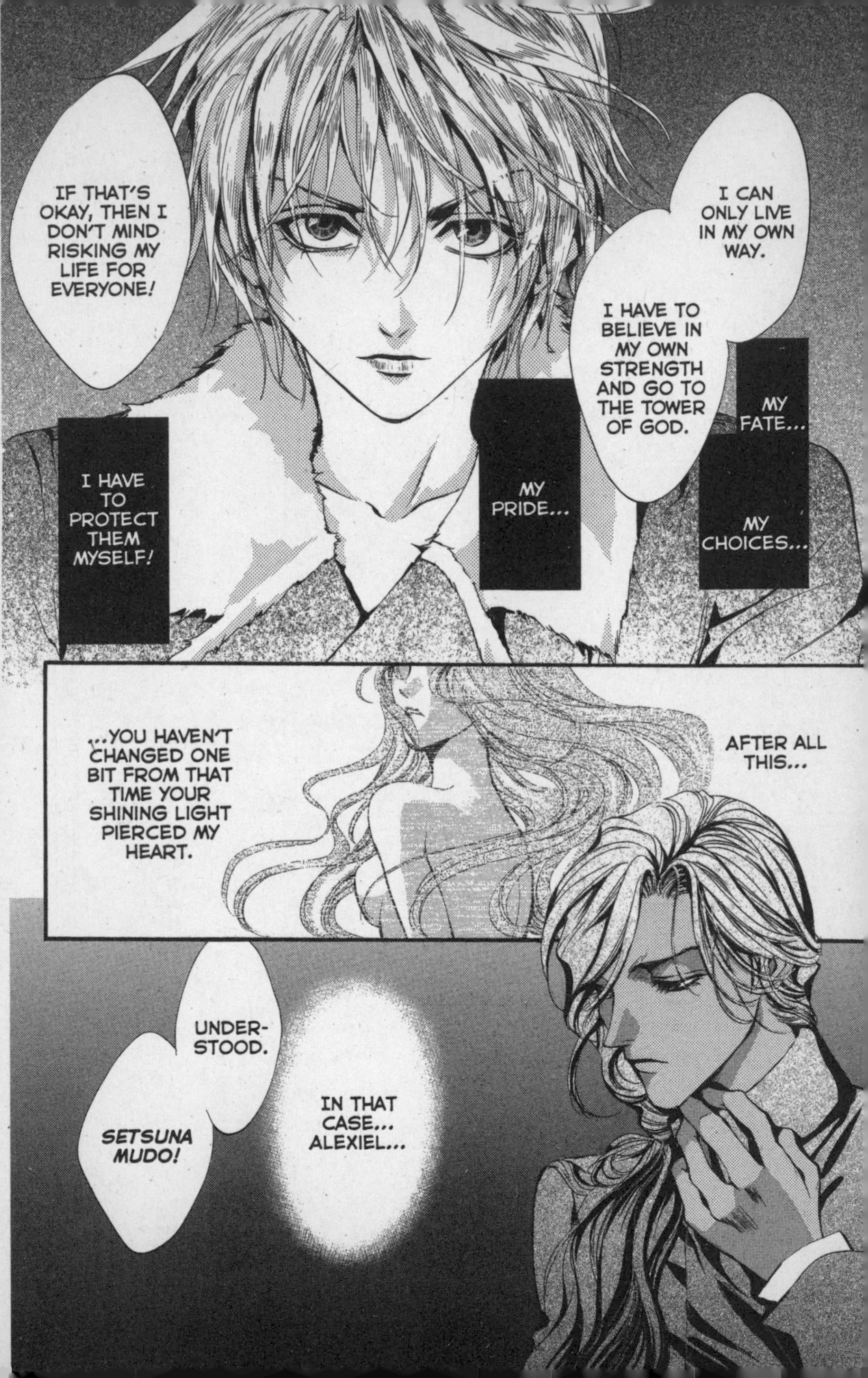
I CAN ONLY LIVE IN MY OWN WAY.
I HAVE TO BELIEVE IN MY OWN STRENGTH AND GO TO THE TOWER OF GOD.
MY FATE...
MY CHOICES...
MY PRIDE...
IF THAT'S OKAY, THEN I DON'T MIND RISKING MY LIFE FOR EVERYONE!
I HAVE TO PROTECT THEM MYSELF!
AFTER ALL THIS...
...YOU HAVEN'T CHANGED ONE BIT FROM THAT TIME YOUR SHINING LIGHT PIERCED MY HEART.
IN THAT CASE... ALEXIEL...
UNDERSTOOD.
SETSUNA MUDO!

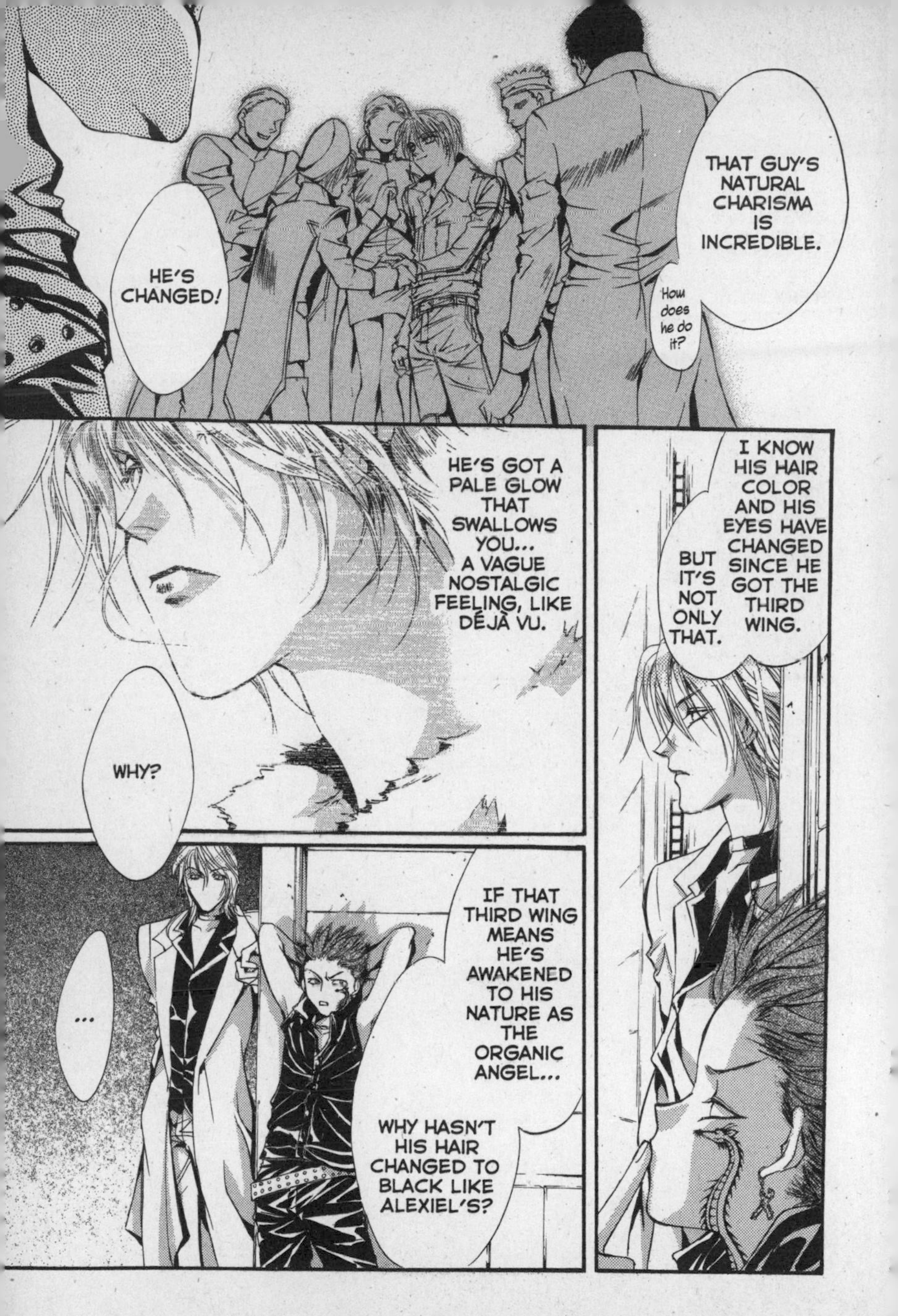
THAT GUY'S NATURAL CHARISMA IS INCREDIBLE.
How does he do it?
HE'S CHANGED!
I KNOW HIS HAIR COLOR AND HIS EYES HAVE CHANGED SINCE HE GOT THE THIRD WING.
BUT IT'S NOT ONLY THAT.
HE'S GOT A PALE GLOW THAT SWALLOWS YOU... A VAGUE NOSTALGIC FEELING, LIKE DÉJÀ VU.
WHY?
IF THAT THIRD WING MEANS HE'S AWAKENED TO HIS NATURE AS THE ORGANIC ANGEL...
WHY HASN'T HIS HAIR CHANGED TO BLACK LIKE ALEXIEL'S?
...

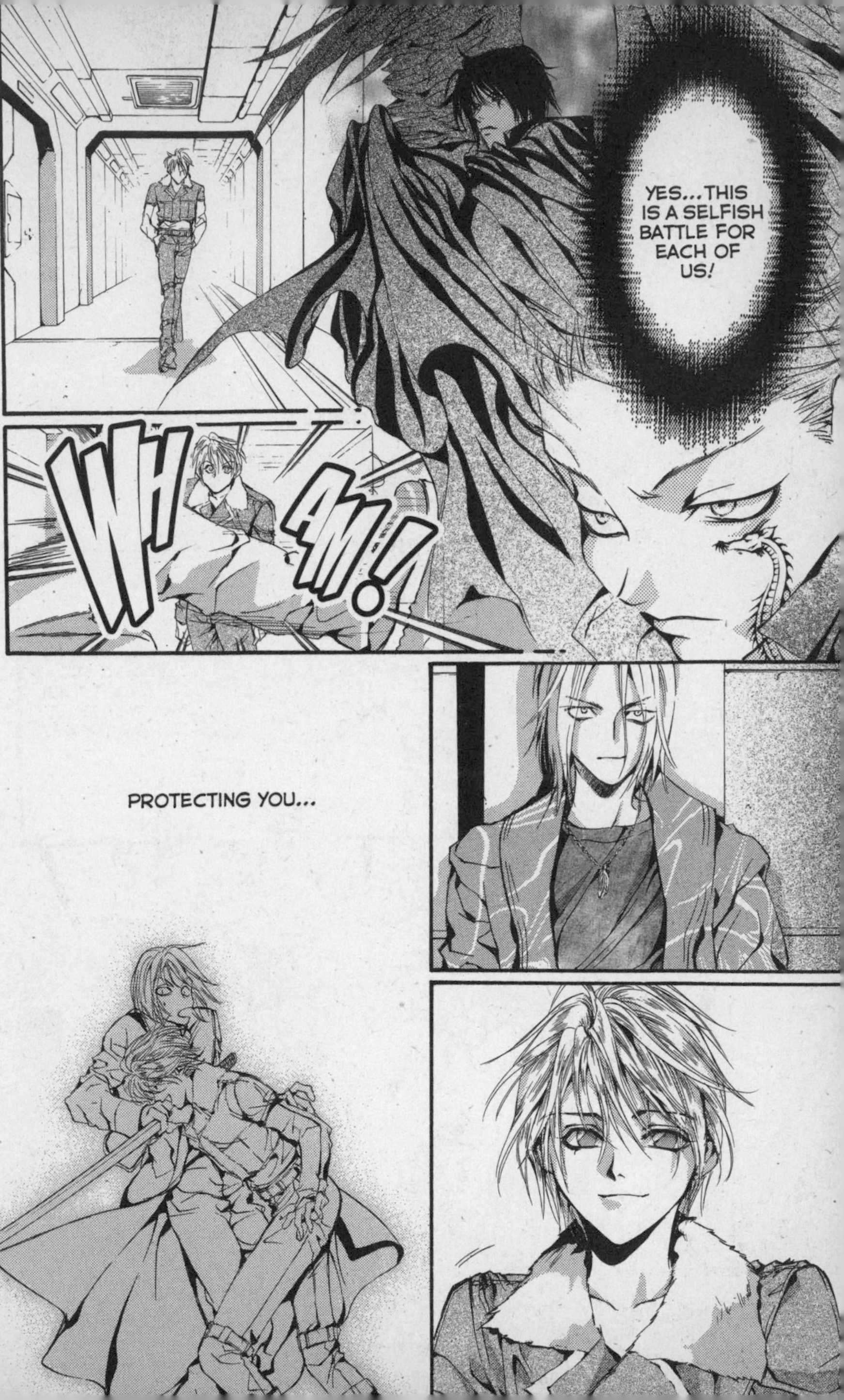
YES...THIS IS A SELFISH BATTLE FOR EACH OF US!
WHAM!
PROTECTING YOU...

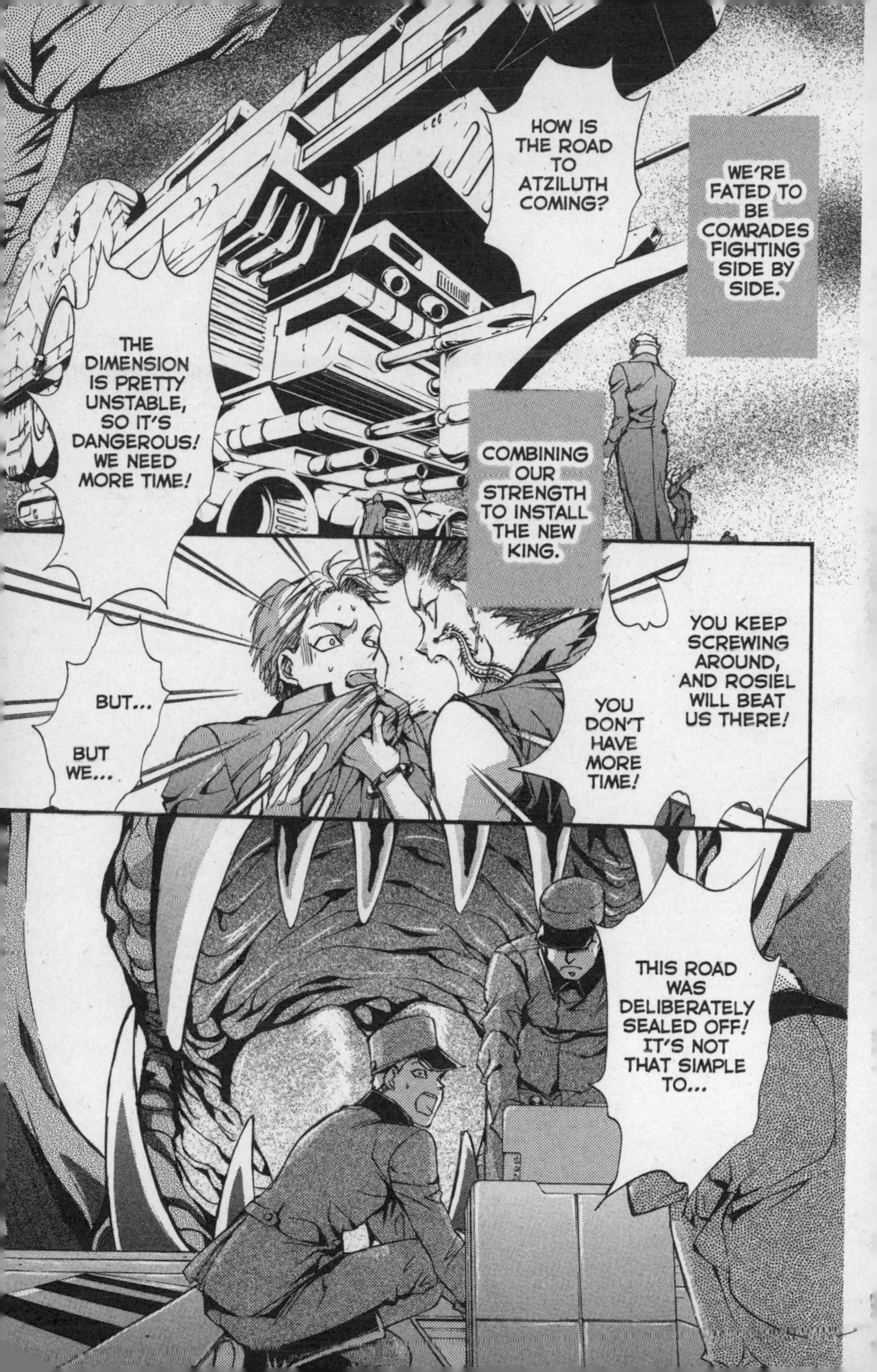
WE'RE FATED TO BE COMRADES FIGHTING SIDE BY SIDE.
HOW IS THE ROAD TO ATZILUTH COMING?
COMBINING OUR STRENGTH TO INSTALL THE NEW KING.
THE DIMENSION IS PRETTY UNSTABLE, SO IT'S DANGEROUS! WE NEED MORE TIME!
YOU KEEP SCREWING AROUND, AND ROSIEL WILL BEAT US THERE!
YOU DON'T HAVE MORE TIME!
BUT...
BUT WE...
THIS ROAD WAS DELIBERATELY SEALED OFF! IT'S NOT THAT SIMPLE TO...

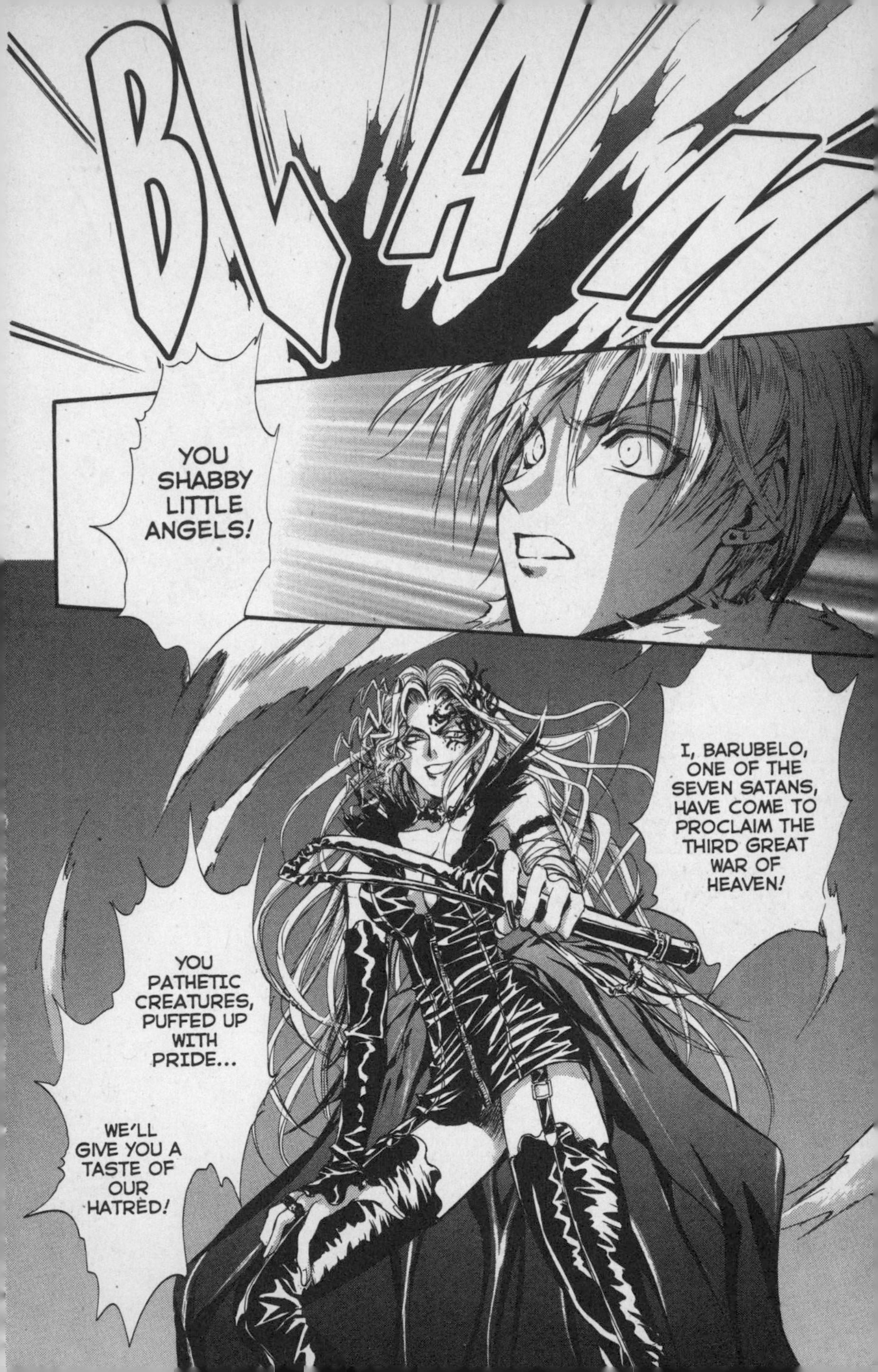
BLAM
YOU SHABBY LITTLE ANGELS!
I, BARUBELO, ONE OF THE SEVEN SATANS, HAVE COME TO PROCLAIM THE THIRD GREAT WAR OF HEAVEN!
YOU PATHETIC CREATURES, PUFFED UP WITH PRIDE...
WE'LL GIVE YOU A TASTE OF OUR HATRED!

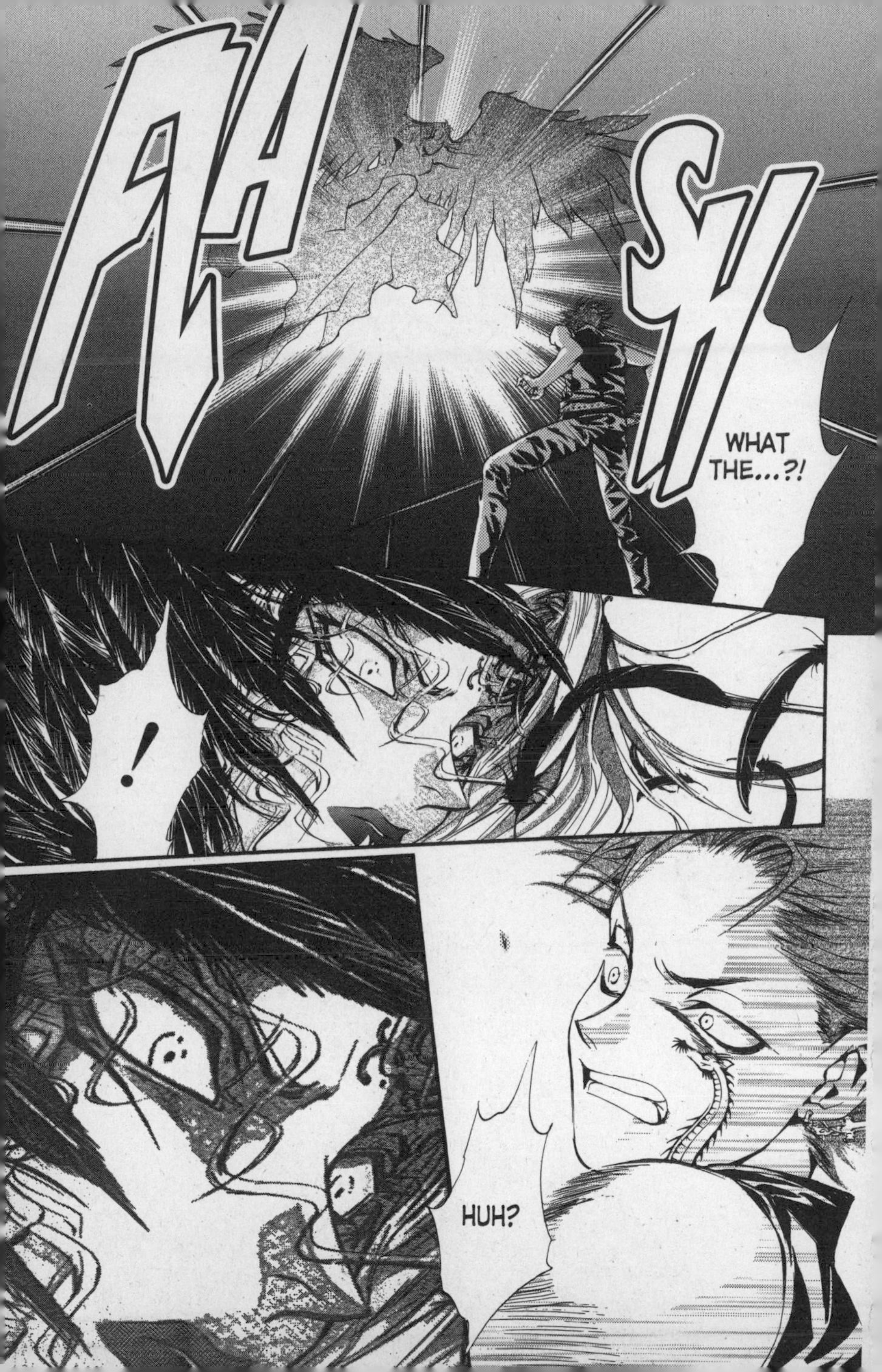
FLASH
WHAT THE...?!
!
HUH?

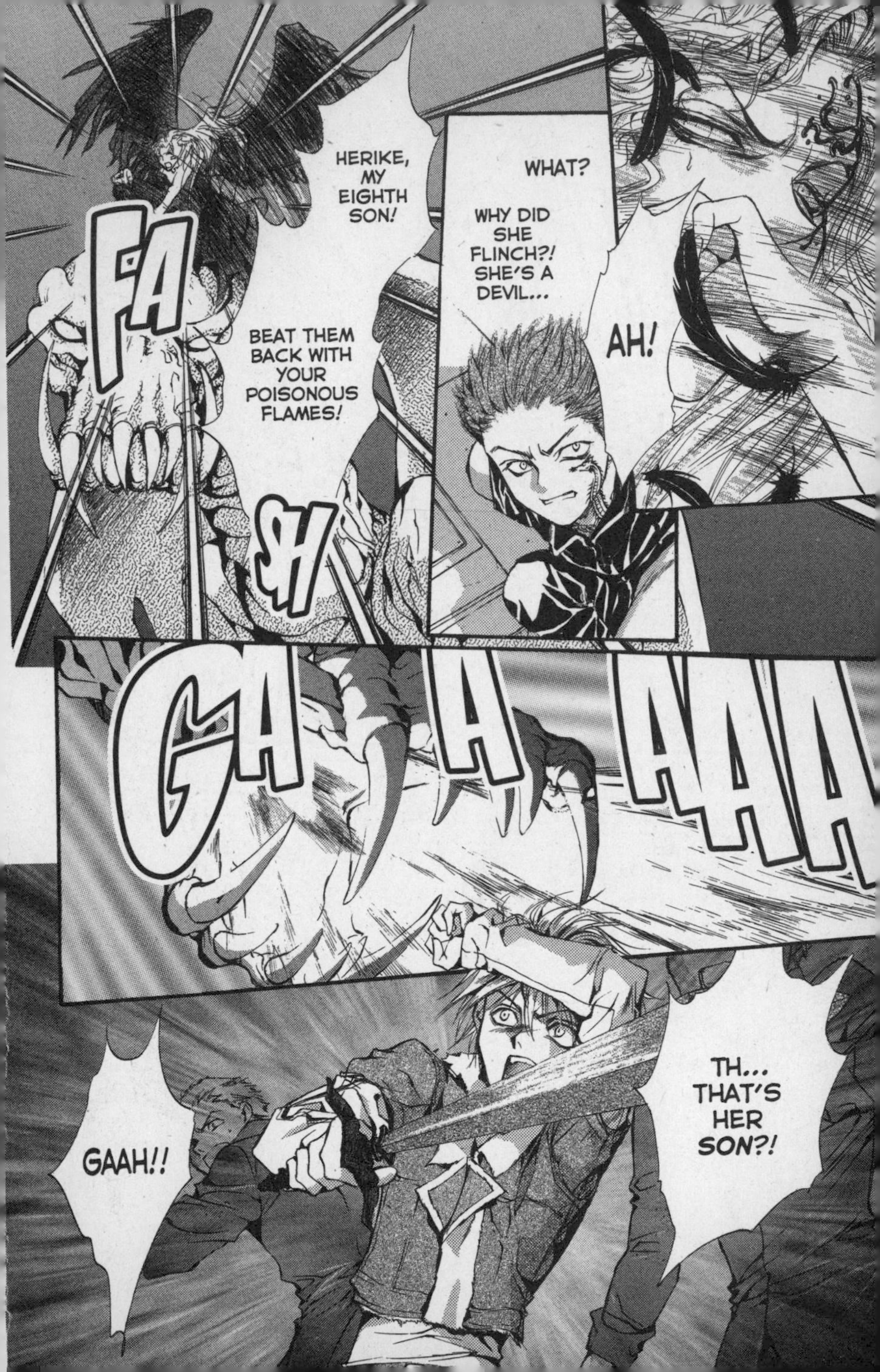
HERIKE, MY EIGHTH SON!
BEAT THEM BACK WITH YOUR POISONOUS FLAMES!
FA
SH
AH!
WHAT?
WHY DID SHE FLINCH?! SHE'S A DEVIL...
GA A AAA
TH... THAT'S HER SON?!
GAAH!!

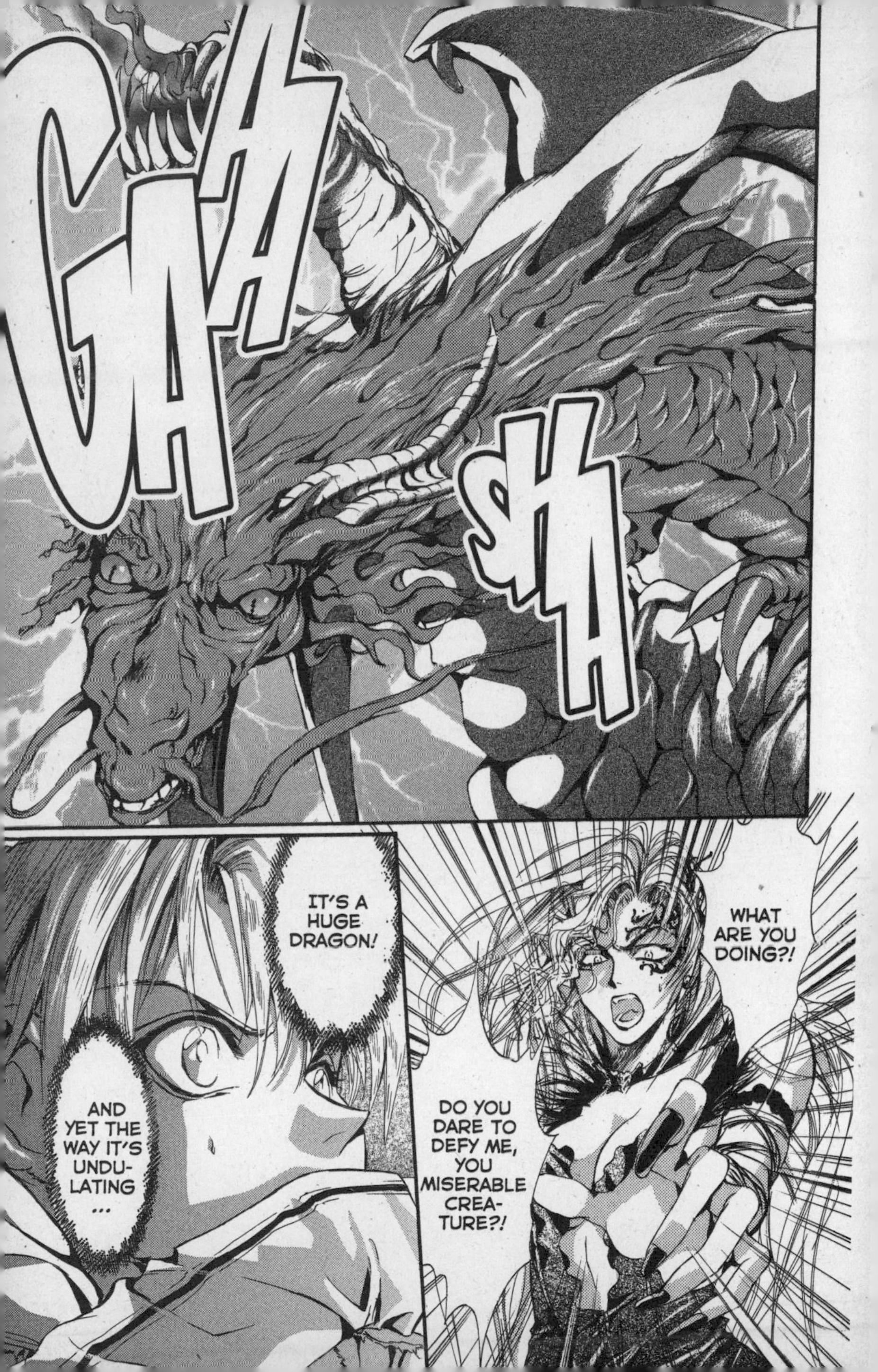
GAA
SHA
WHAT ARE YOU DOING?!
DO YOU DARE TO DEFY ME, YOU MISERABLE CREATURE?!
IT'S A HUGE DRAGON!
AND YET THE WAY IT'S UNDULATING...

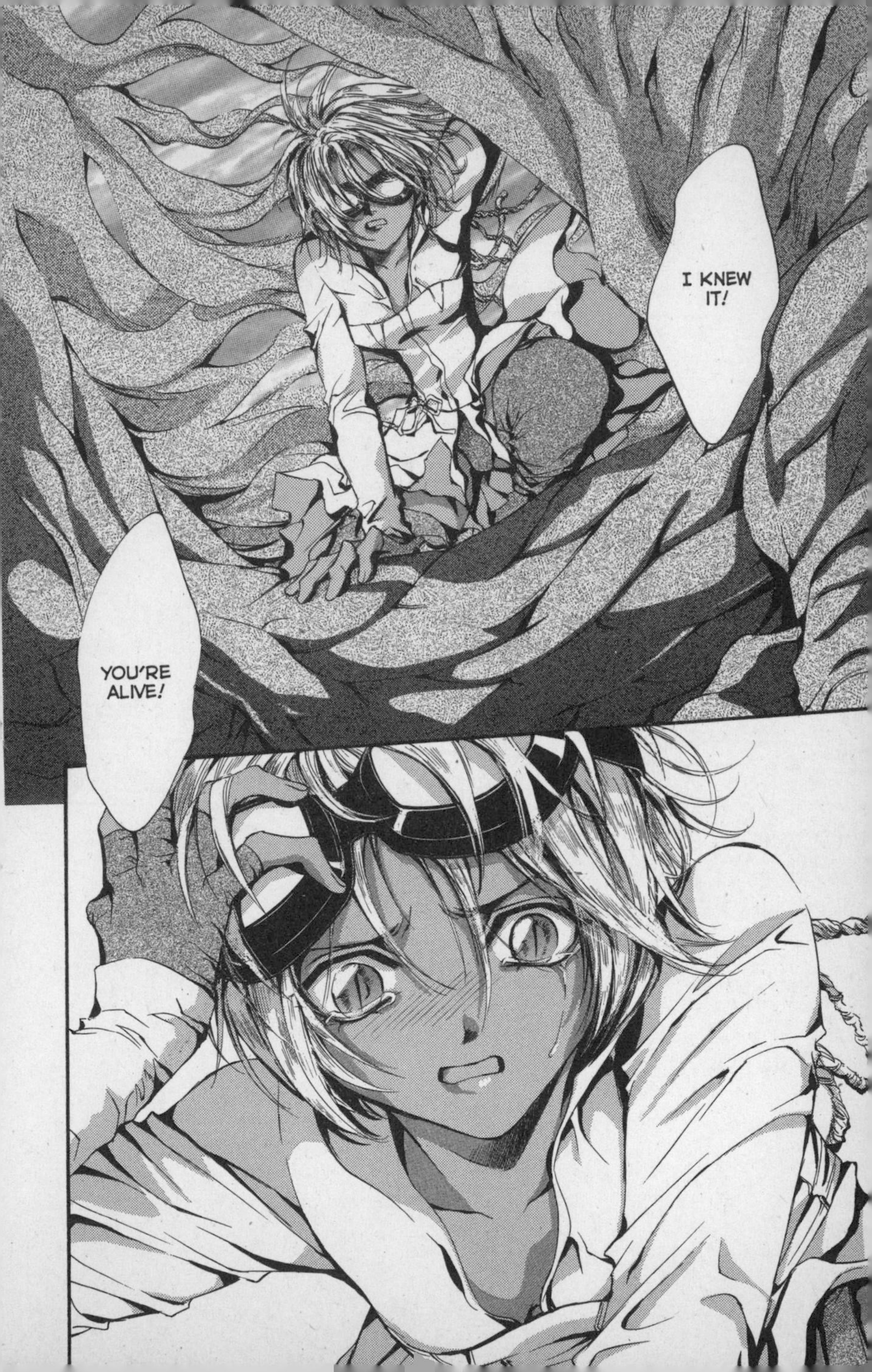
I KNEW IT!
YOU'RE ALIVE!

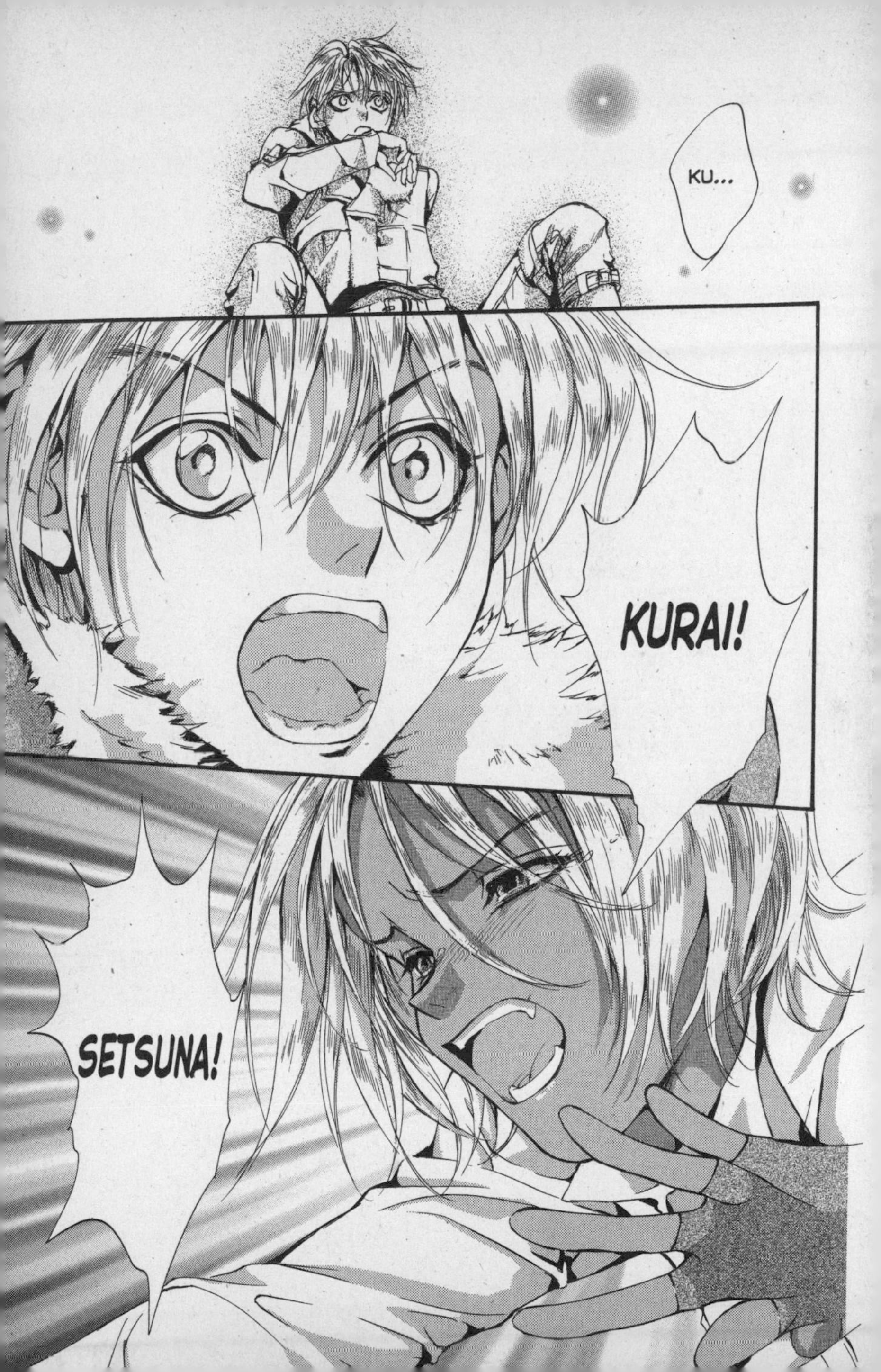
KU...
KURAI!
SETSUNA!

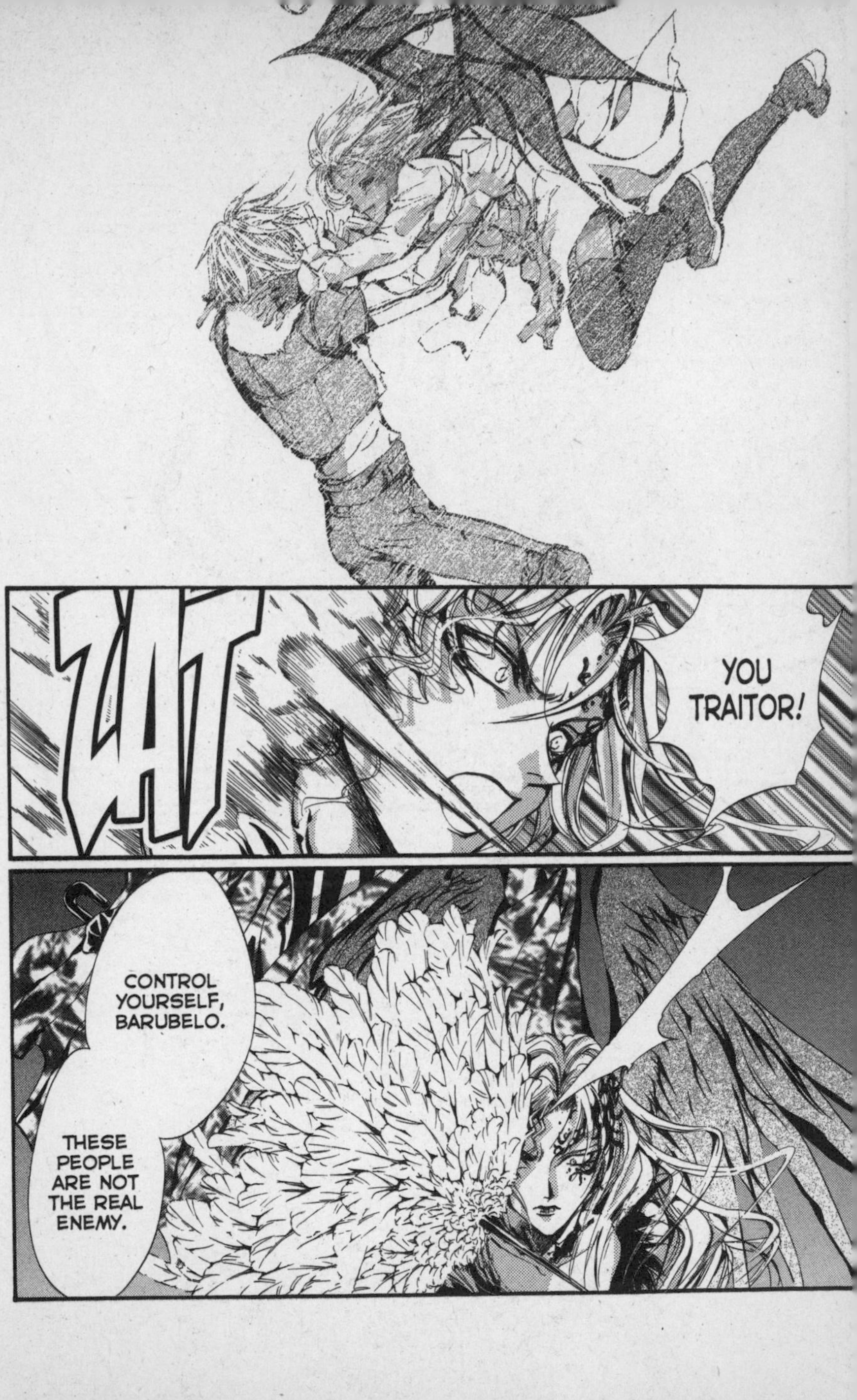
YOU TRAITOR!
ZAT
CONTROL YOURSELF, BARUBELO.
THESE PEOPLE ARE NOT THE REAL ENEMY.

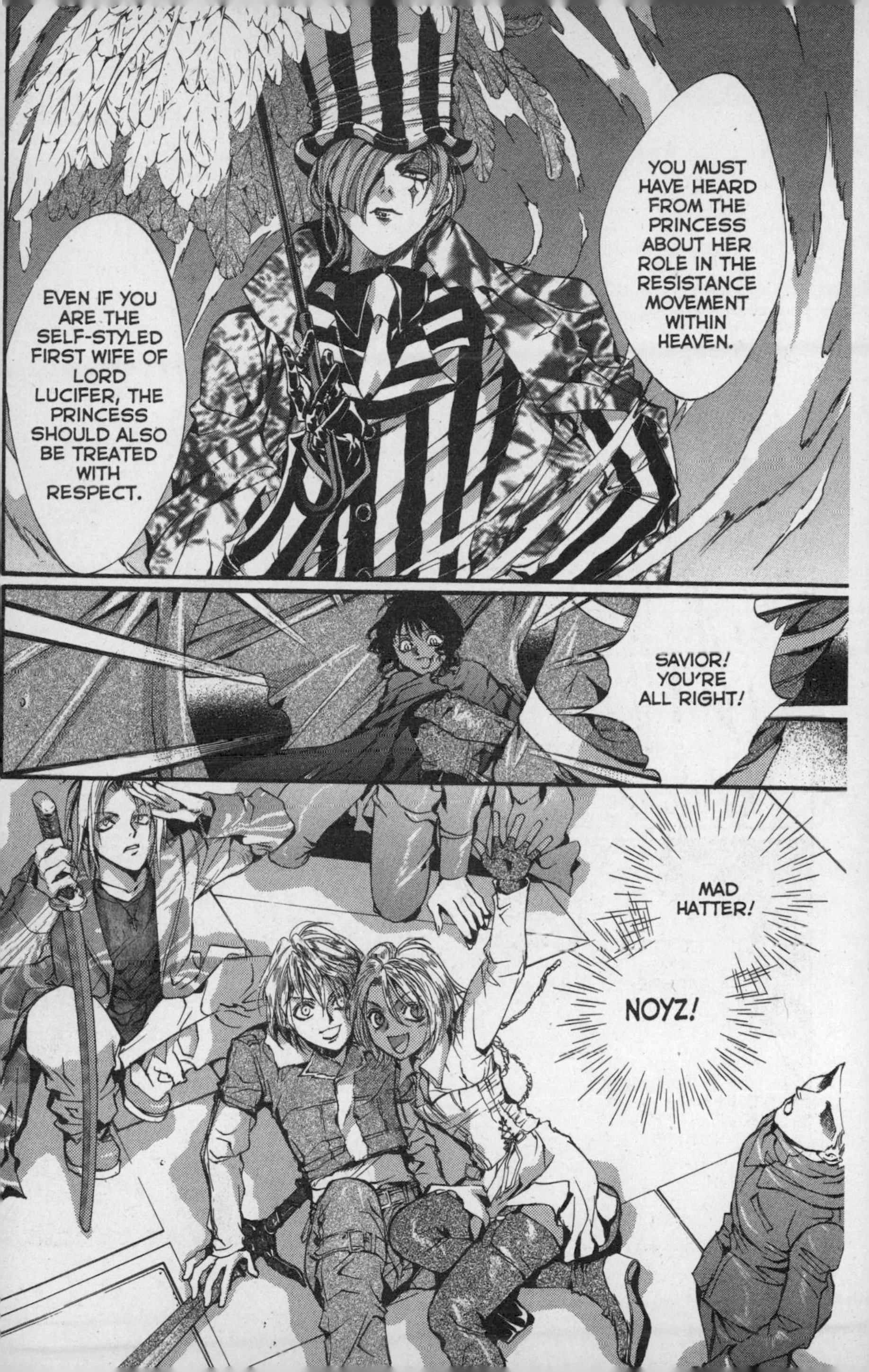
YOU MUST HAVE HEARD FROM THE PRINCESS ABOUT HER ROLE IN THE RESISTANCE MOVEMENT WITHIN HEAVEN.
EVEN IF YOU ARE THE SELF-STYLED FIRST WIFE OF LORD LUCIFER, THE PRINCESS SHOULD ALSO BE TREATED WITH RESPECT.
SAVIOR! YOU'RE ALL RIGHT!
MAD HATTER!
NOYZ!

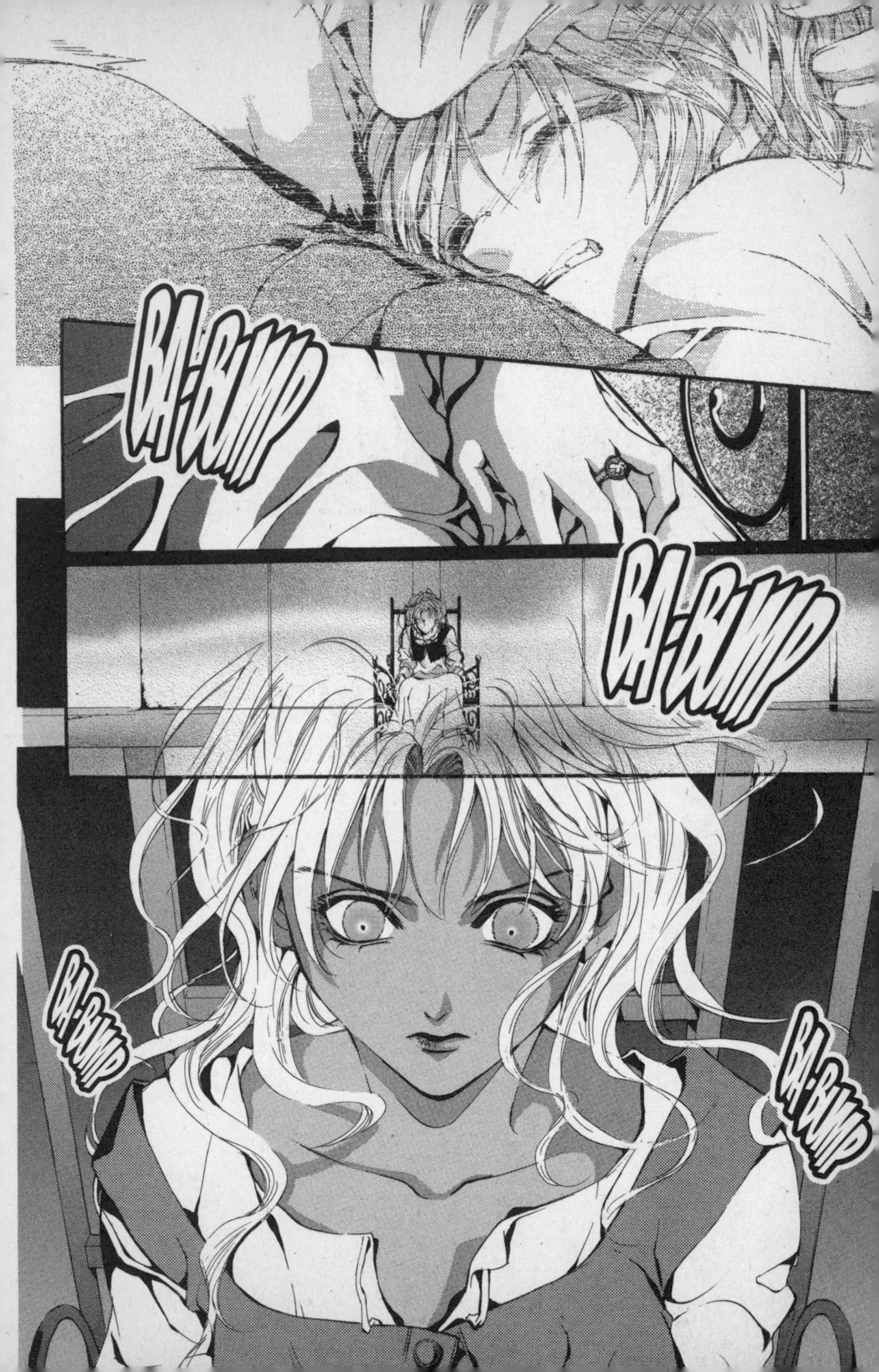
BA-BUMP
BA-BUMP
BA-BUMP
BA-BUMP

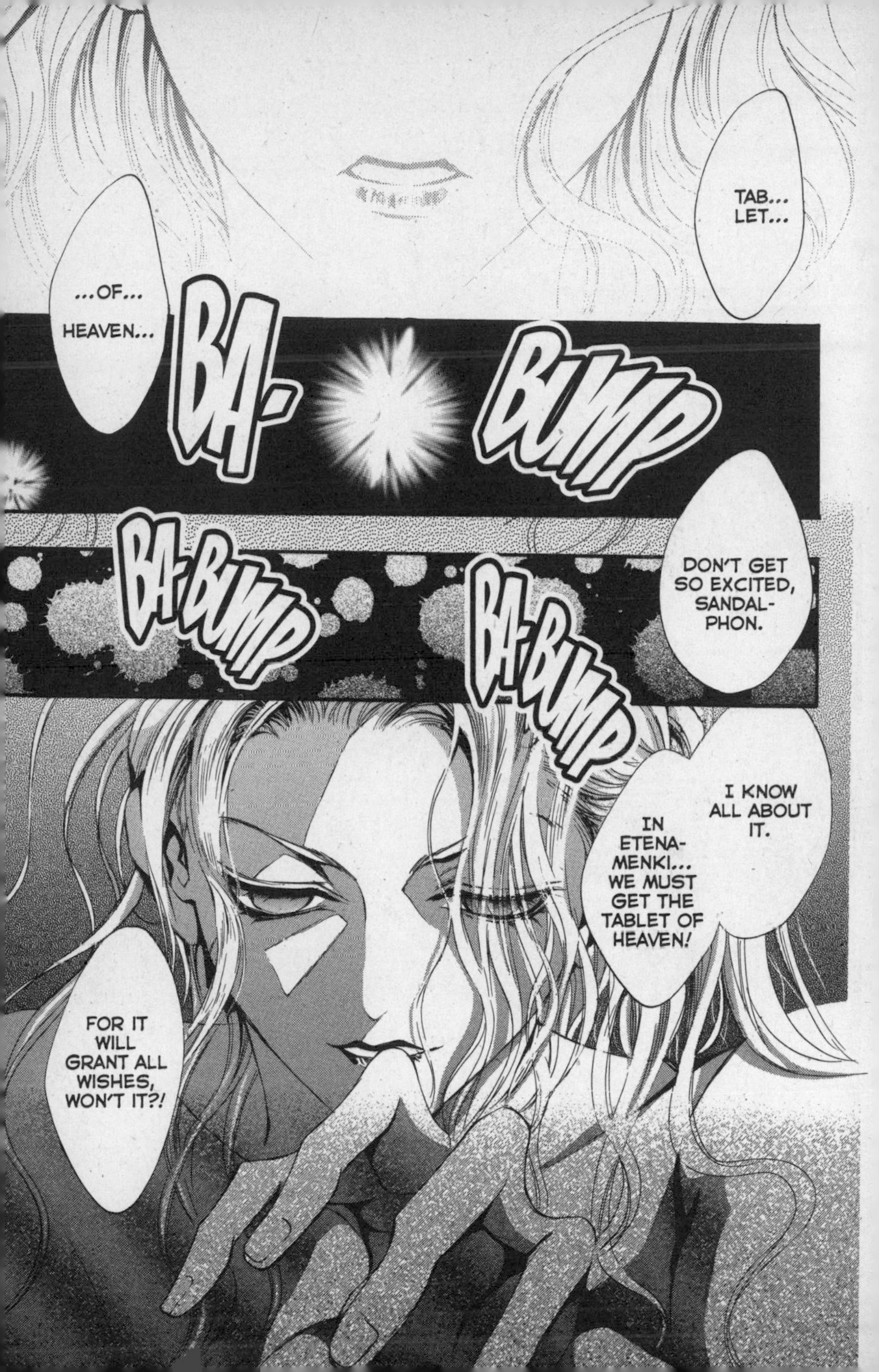
TAB... LET...
...OF... HEAVEN...
BA-BUMP
DON'T GET SO EXCITED, SANDAL-PHON.
BA-BUMP
BA-BUMP
I KNOW ALL ABOUT IT.
IN ETENA-MENKI... WE MUST GET THE TABLET OF HEAVEN!
FOR IT WILL GRANT ALL WISHES, WON'T IT?!

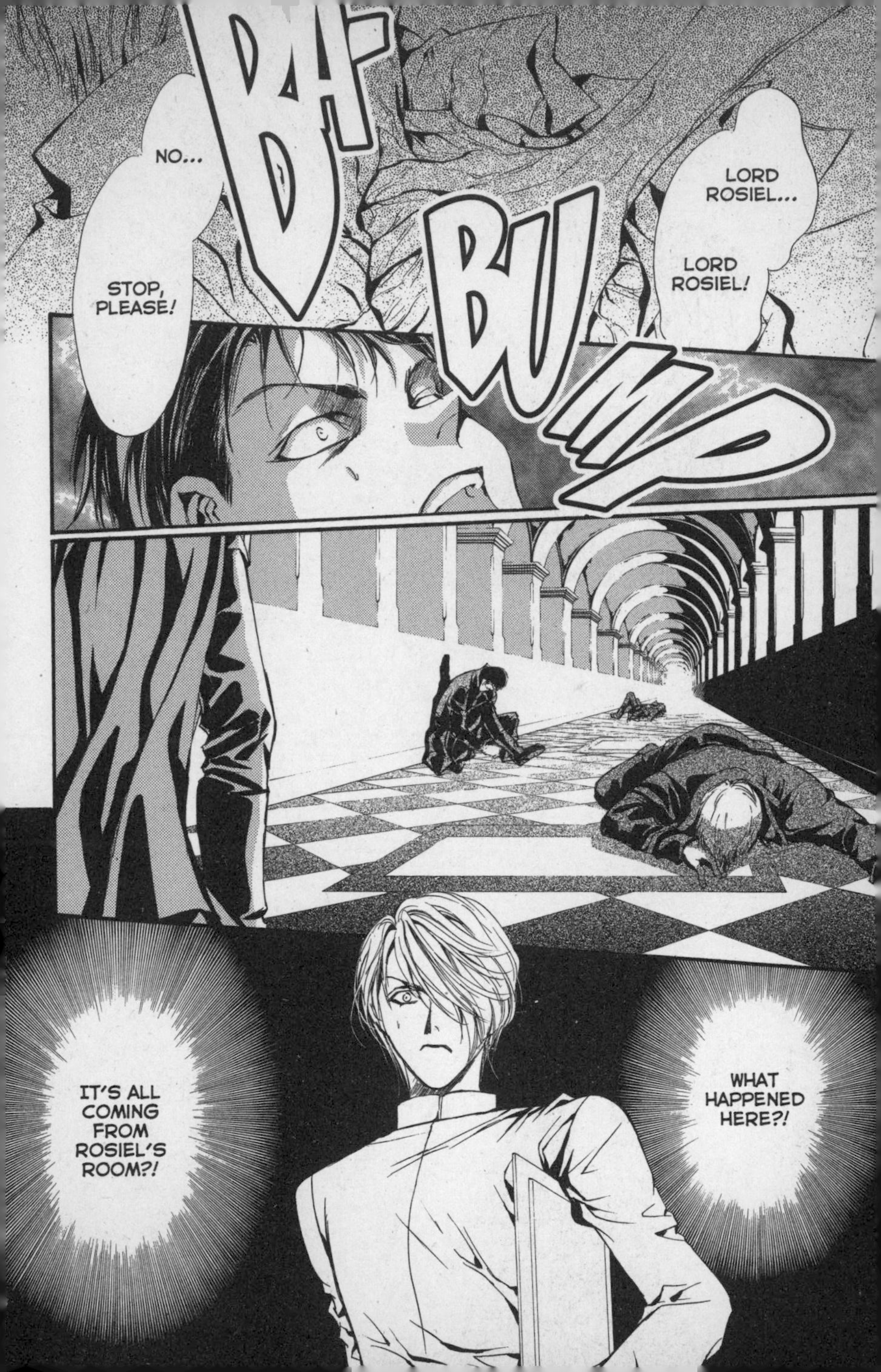

LORD ROSIEL... LORD ROSIEL!
BA-BUMP
NO... STOP, PLEASE!
WHAT HAPPENED HERE?!
IT'S ALL COMING FROM ROSIEL'S ROOM?!

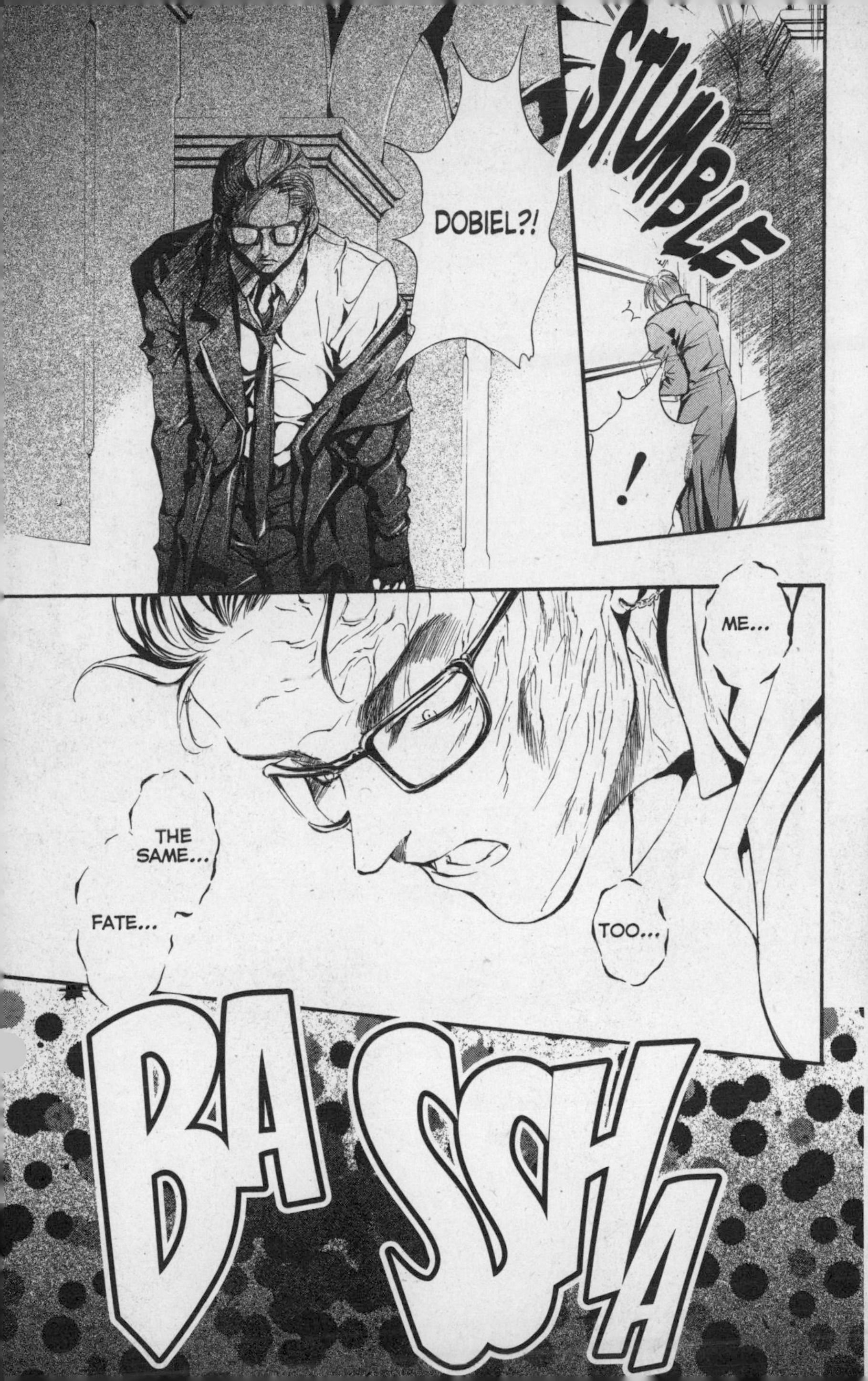
STUMBLE
!
DOBIEL?!
ME...
TOO...
THE SAME...
FATE...
BASCHA

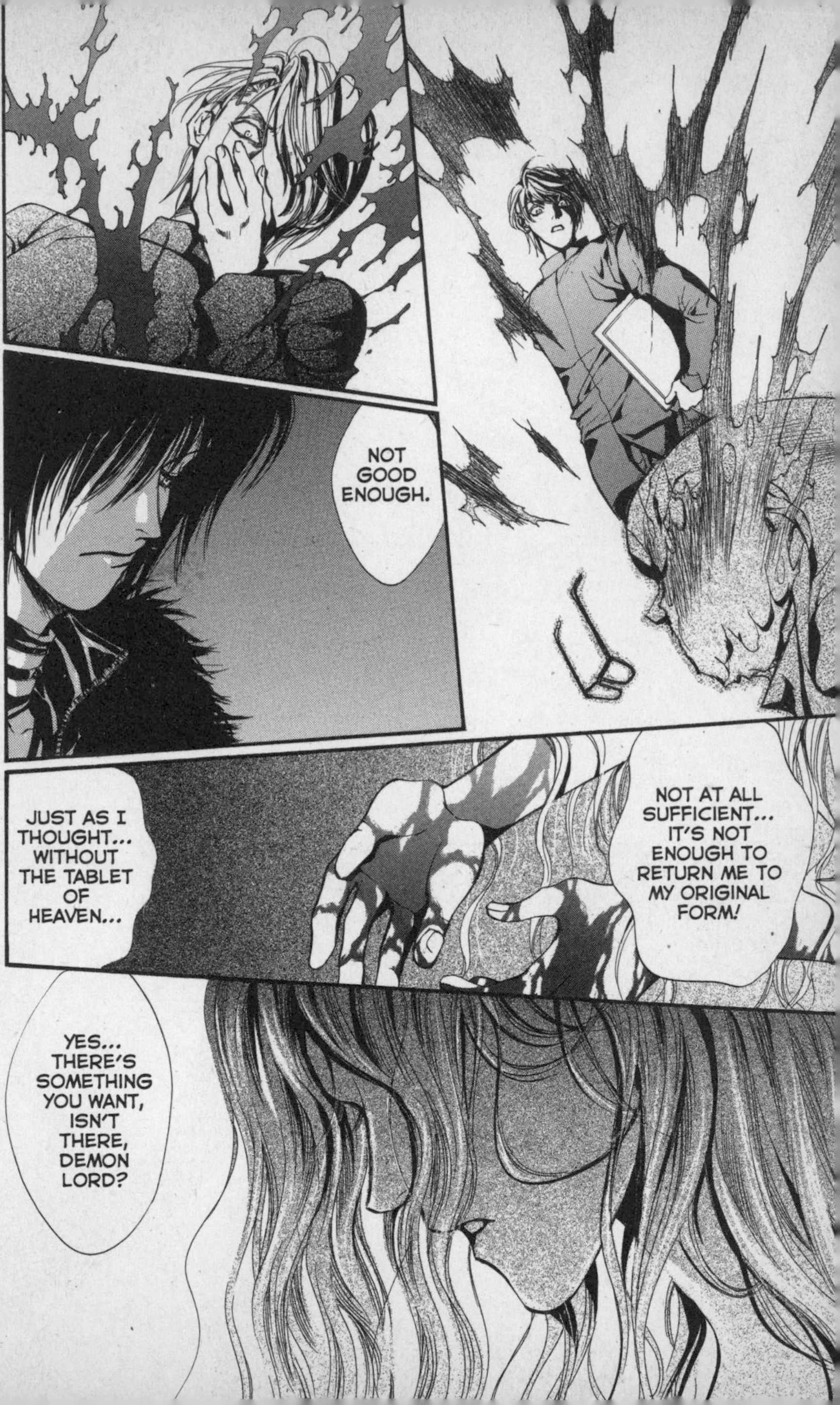
NOT GOOD ENOUGH.
NOT AT ALL SUFFICIENT... IT'S NOT ENOUGH TO RETURN ME TO MY ORIGINAL FORM!
JUST AS I THOUGHT... WITHOUT THE TABLET OF HEAVEN...
YES... THERE'S SOMETHING YOU WANT, ISN'T THERE, DEMON LORD?

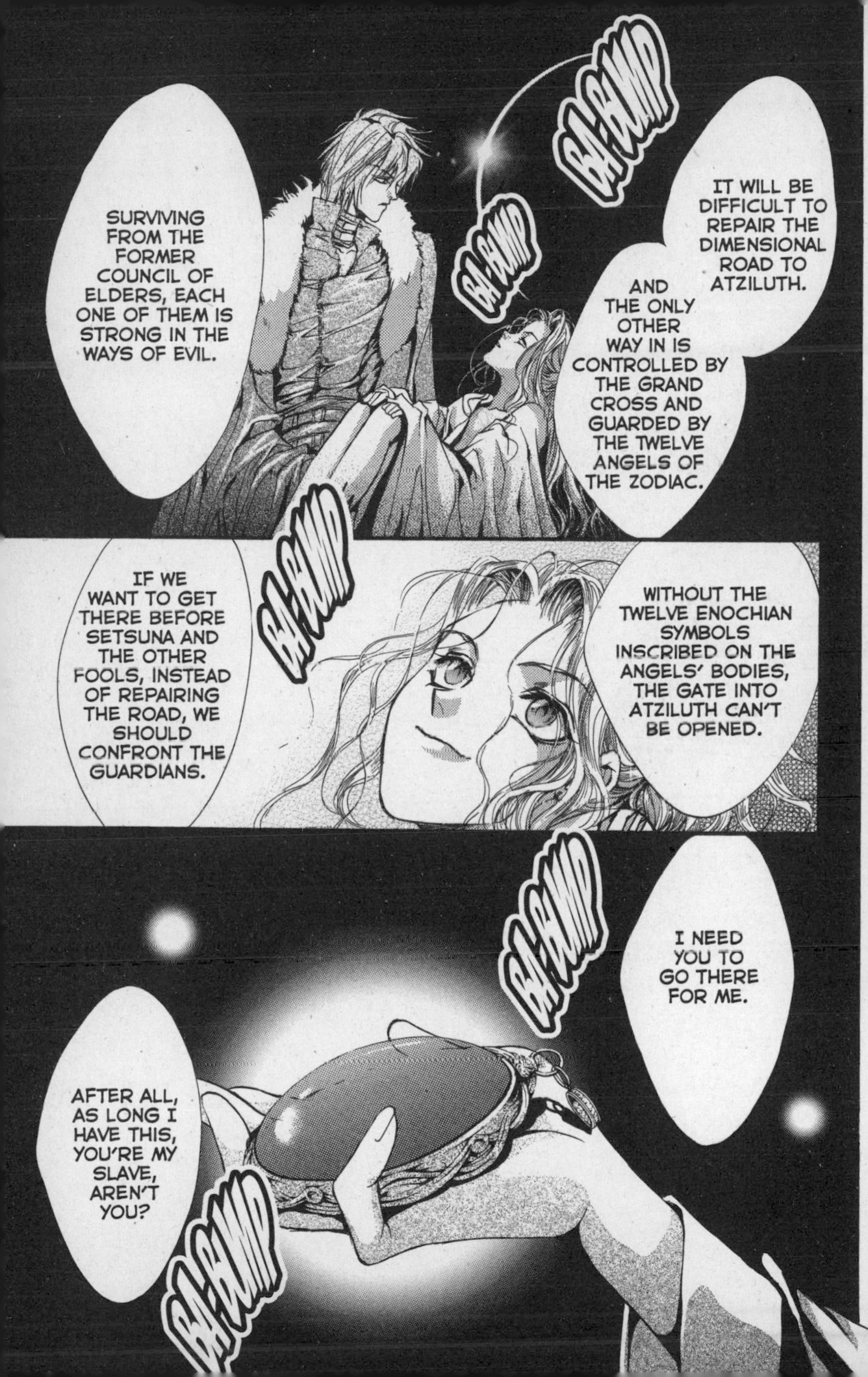
BA-BUMP
BA-BUMP
IT WILL BE DIFFICULT TO REPAIR THE DIMENSIONAL ROAD TO ATZILUTH.
AND THE ONLY OTHER WAY IN IS CONTROLLED BY THE GRAND CROSS AND GUARDED BY THE TWELVE ANGELS OF THE ZODIAC.
SURVIVING FROM THE FORMER COUNCIL OF ELDERS, EACH ONE OF THEM IS STRONG IN THE WAYS OF EVIL.
BA-BUMP
WITHOUT THE TWELVE ENOCHIAN SYMBOLS INSCRIBED ON THE ANGELS' BODIES, THE GATE INTO ATZILUTH CAN'T BE OPENED.
BA-BUMP
IF WE WANT TO GET THERE BEFORE SETSUNA AND THE OTHER FOOLS, INSTEAD OF REPAIRING THE ROAD, WE SHOULD CONFRONT THE GUARDIANS.
I NEED YOU TO GO THERE FOR ME.
BA-BUMP
AFTER ALL, AS LONG I HAVE THIS, YOU'RE MY SLAVE, AREN'T YOU?
BA-BUMP

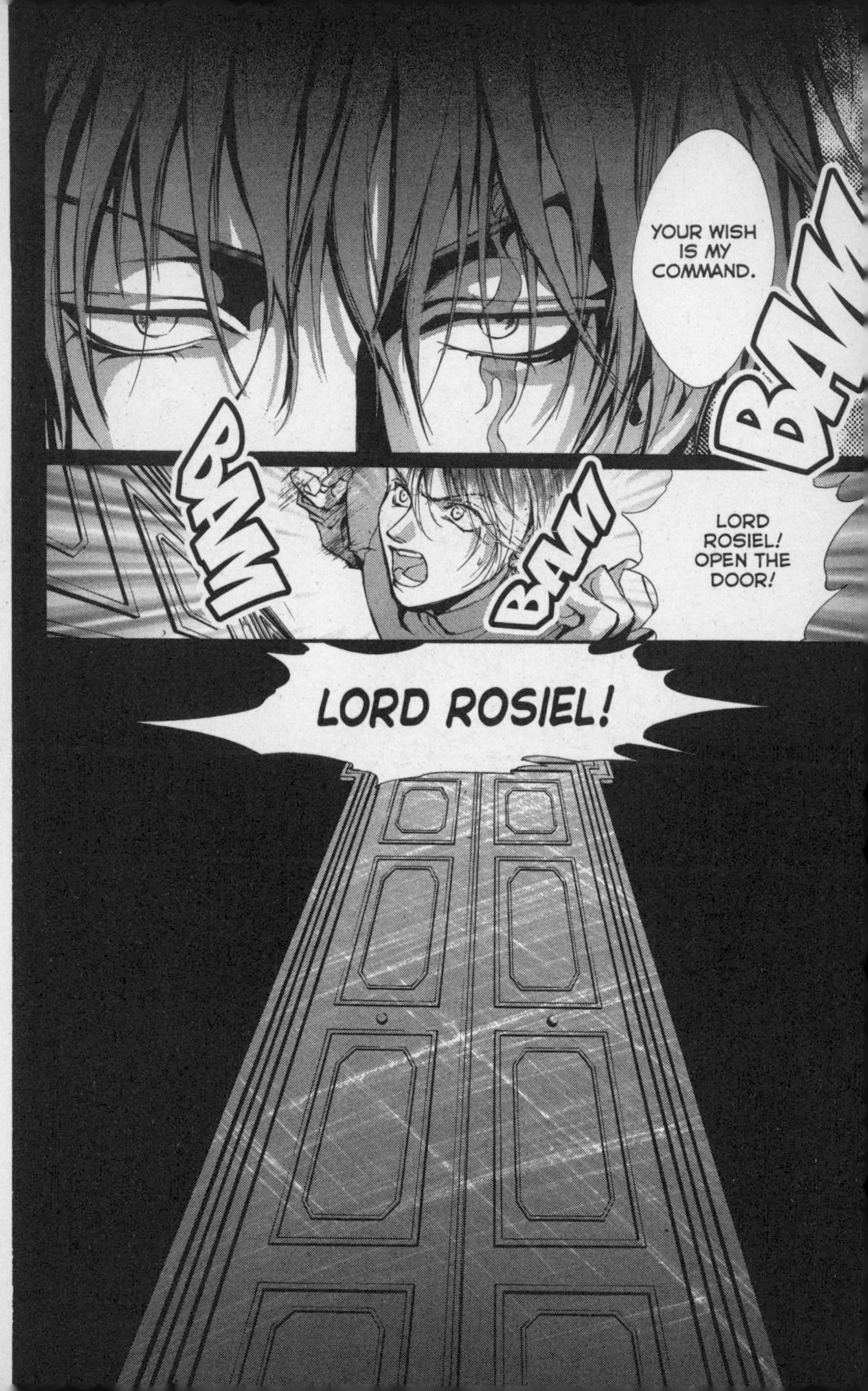
YOUR WISH IS MY COMMAND.
BAM
LORD ROSIEL! OPEN THE DOOR!
BAM
BAM
LORD ROSIEL!

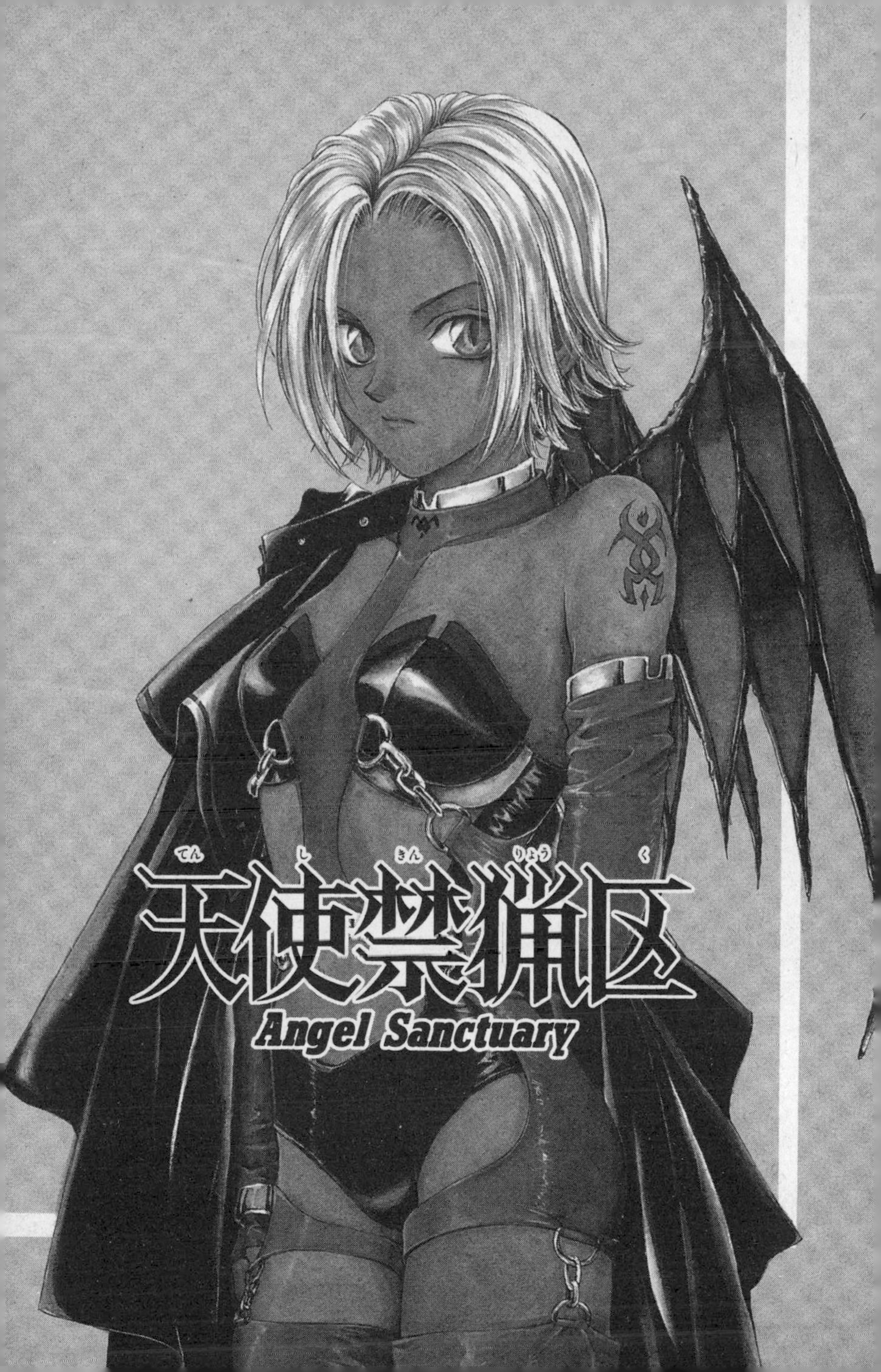
天使禁猟区（てんしきんりょうく）
Angel Sanctuary

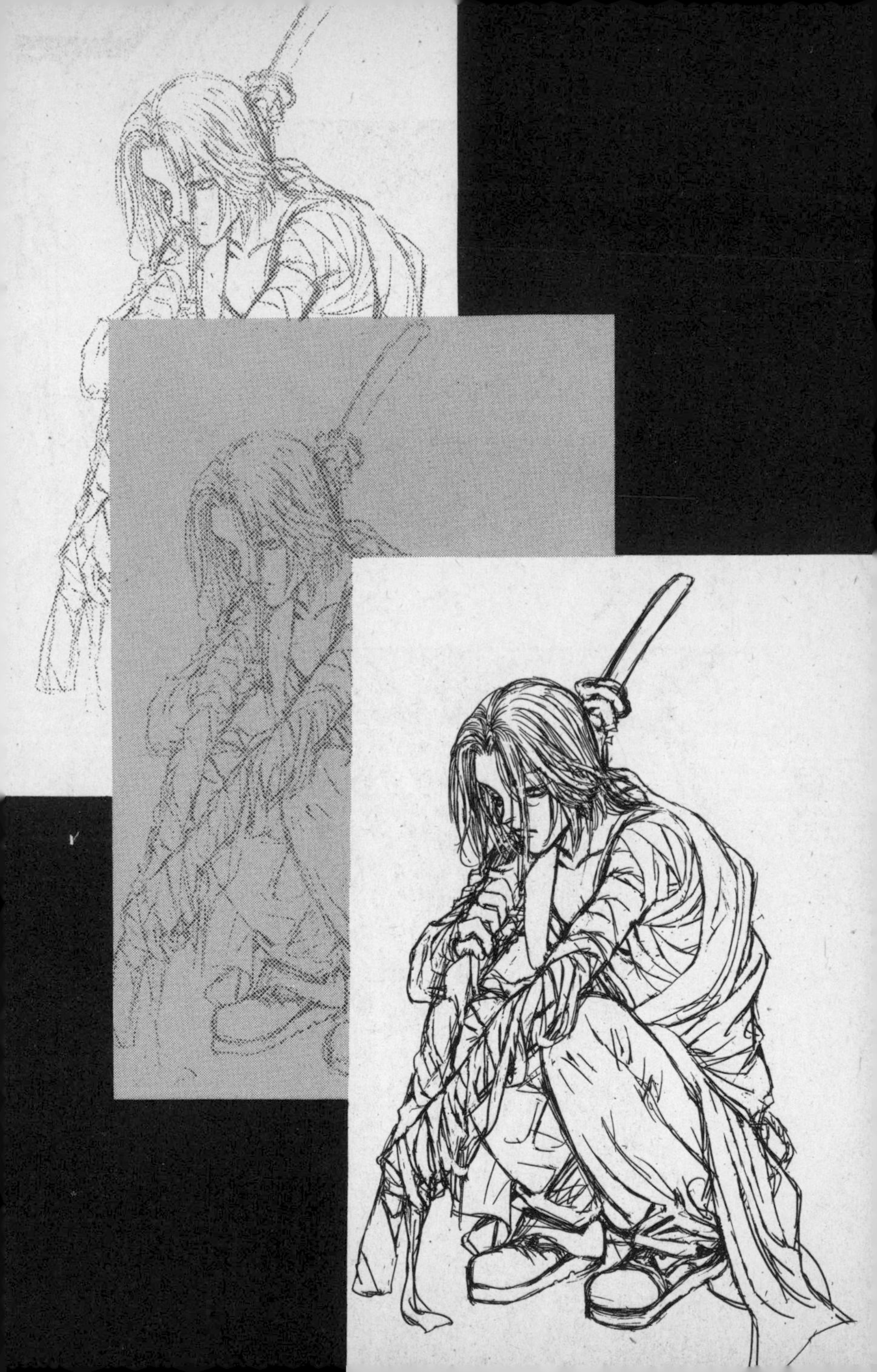

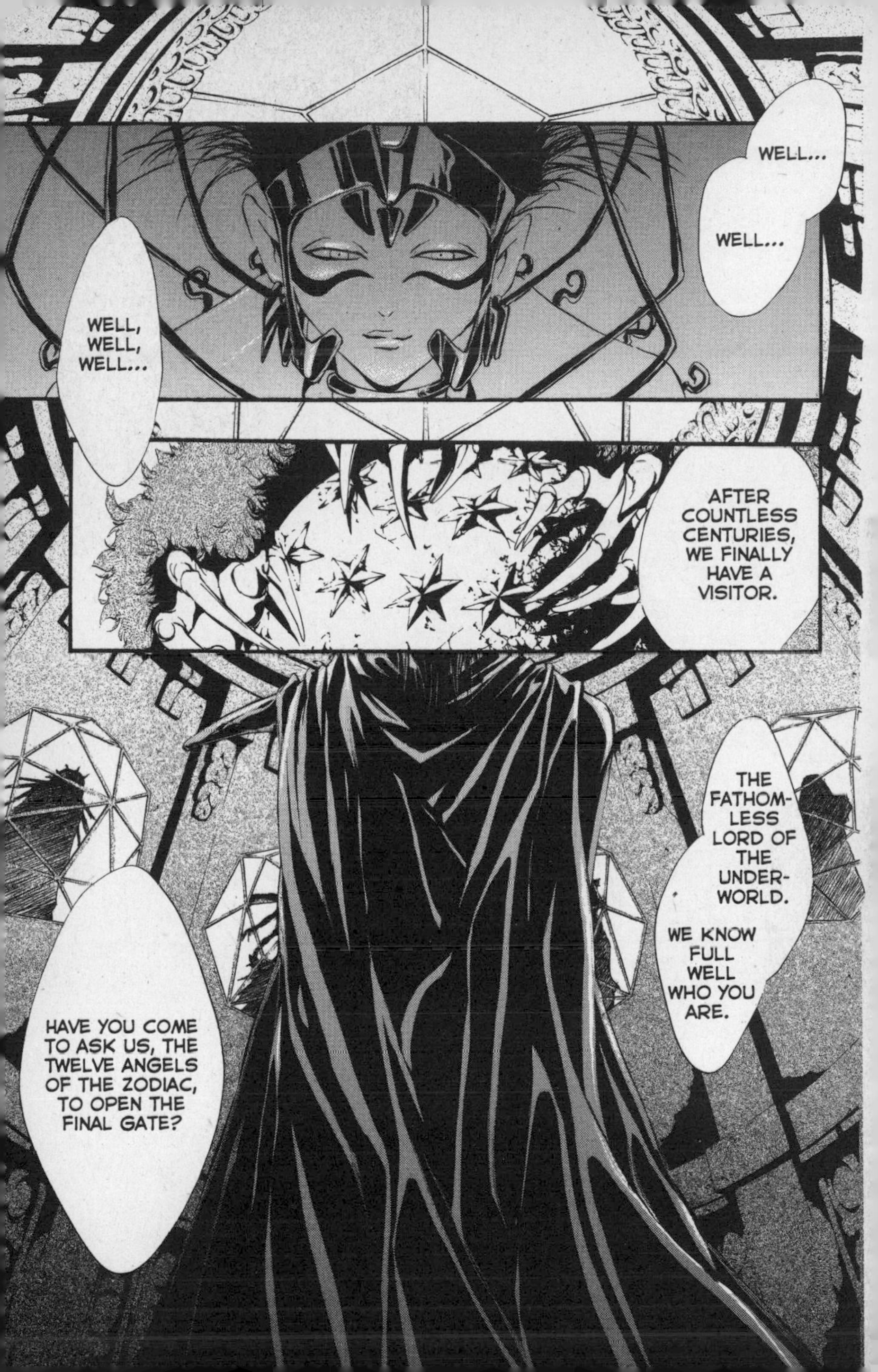
WELL...
WELL...
WELL, WELL, WELL...
AFTER COUNTLESS CENTURIES, WE FINALLY HAVE A VISITOR.
THE FATHOM-LESS LORD OF THE UNDER-WORLD.
WE KNOW FULL WELL WHO YOU ARE.
HAVE YOU COME TO ASK US, THE TWELVE ANGELS OF THE ZODIAC, TO OPEN THE FINAL GATE?

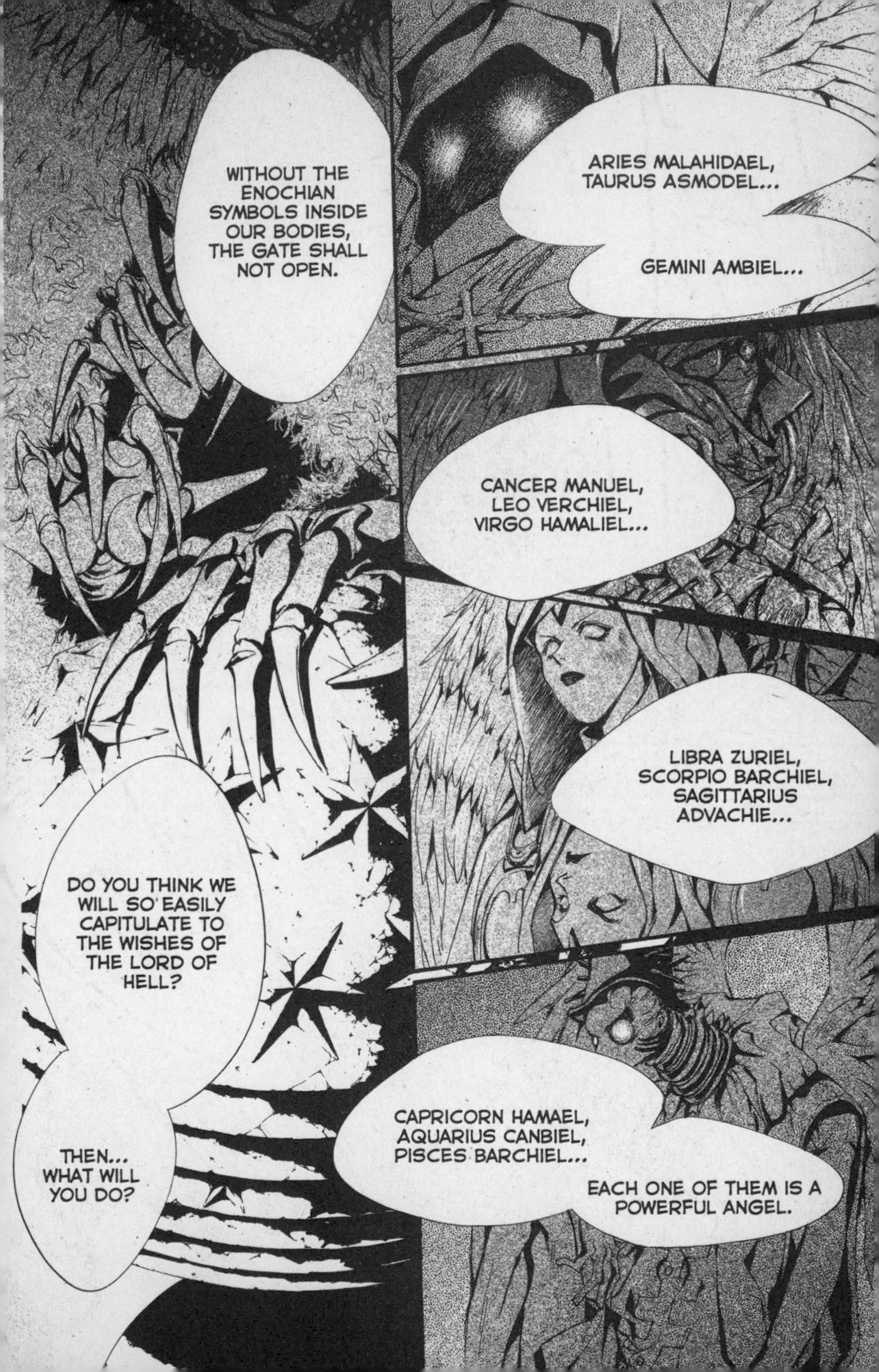
ARIES MALAHIDAEL, TAURUS ASMODEL...
GEMINI AMBIEL...
CANCER MANUEL, LEO VERCHIEL, VIRGO HAMALIEL...
LIBRA ZURIEL, SCORPIO BARCHIEL, SAGITTARIUS ADVACHIE...
CAPRICORN HAMAEL, AQUARIUS CANBIEL, PISCES BARCHIEL...
EACH ONE OF THEM IS A POWERFUL ANGEL.
WITHOUT THE ENOCHIAN SYMBOLS INSIDE OUR BODIES, THE GATE SHALL NOT OPEN.
DO YOU THINK WE WILL SO EASILY CAPITULATE TO THE WISHES OF THE LORD OF HELL?
THEN... WHAT WILL YOU DO?

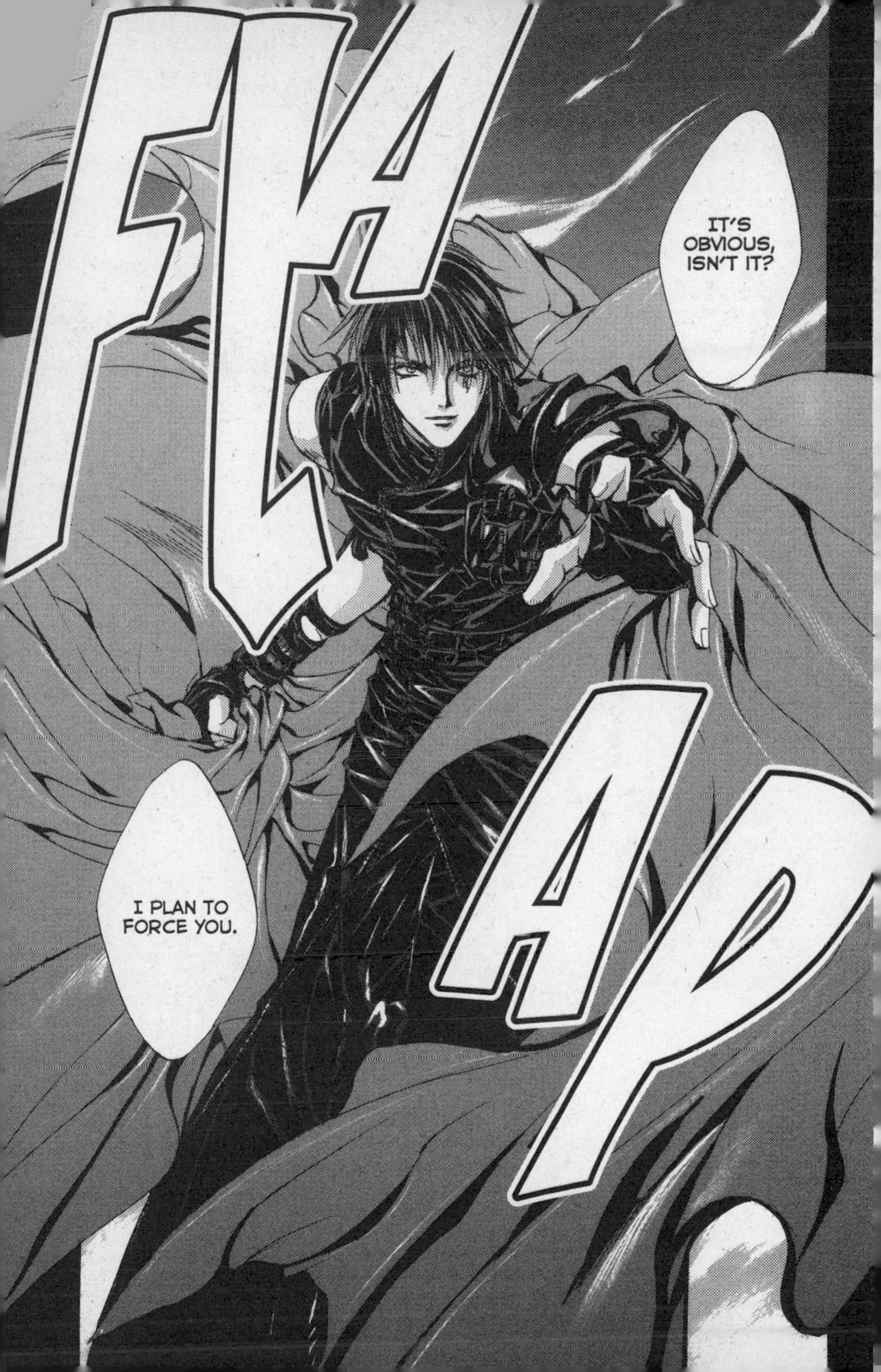
FLA
IT'S OBVIOUS, ISN'T IT?
I PLAN TO FORCE YOU.
AP

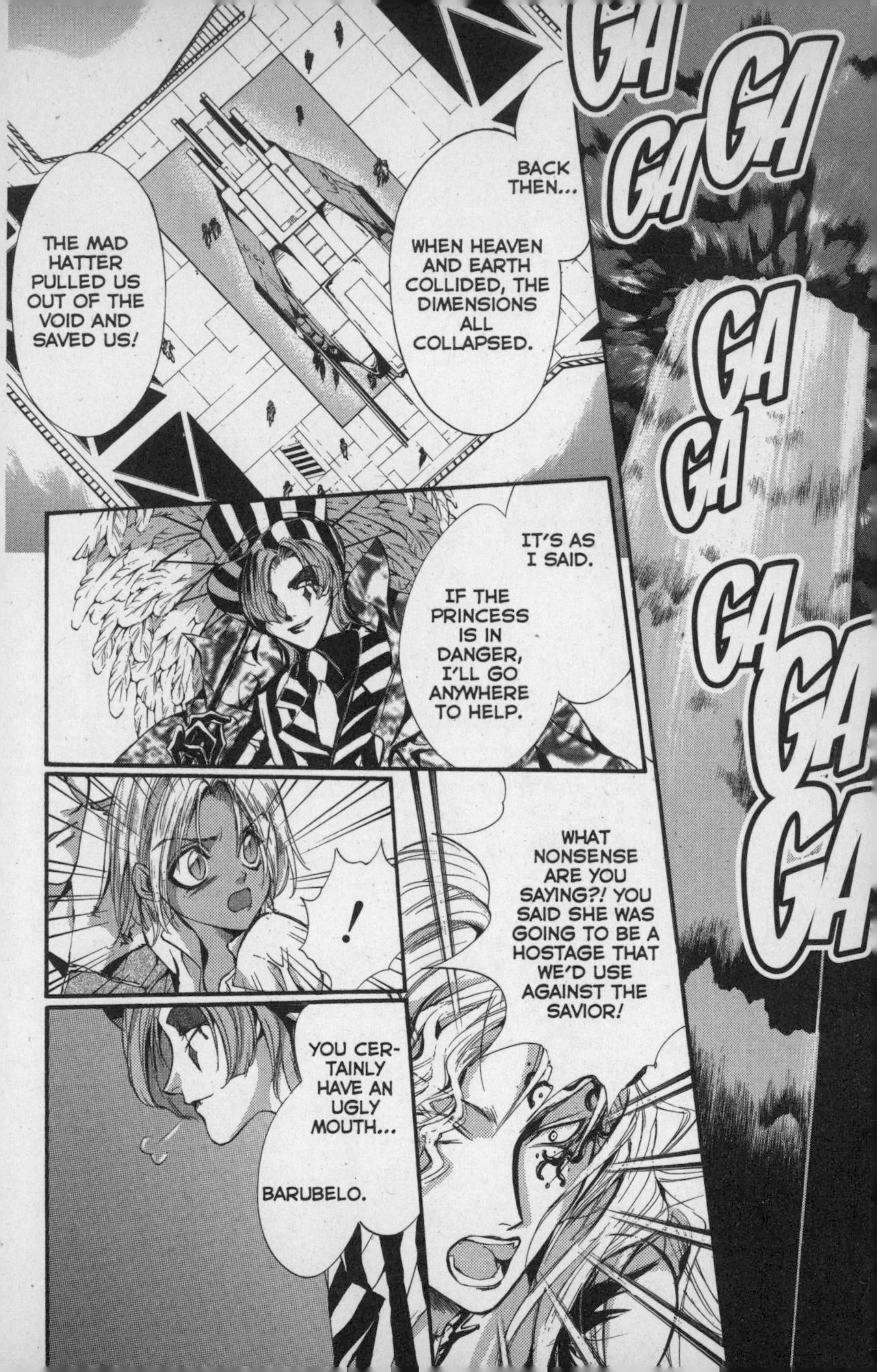
GA
GA GA
GA GA
GA GA GA GA
BACK THEN...
WHEN HEAVEN AND EARTH COLLIDED, THE DIMENSIONS ALL COLLAPSED.
THE MAD HATTER PULLED US OUT OF THE VOID AND SAVED US!
IT'S AS I SAID.
IF THE PRINCESS IS IN DANGER, I'LL GO ANYWHERE TO HELP.
!
WHAT NONSENSE ARE YOU SAYING?! YOU SAID SHE WAS GOING TO BE A HOSTAGE THAT WE'D USE AGAINST THE SAVIOR!
YOU CER-TAINLY HAVE AN UGLY MOUTH...
BARUBELO.

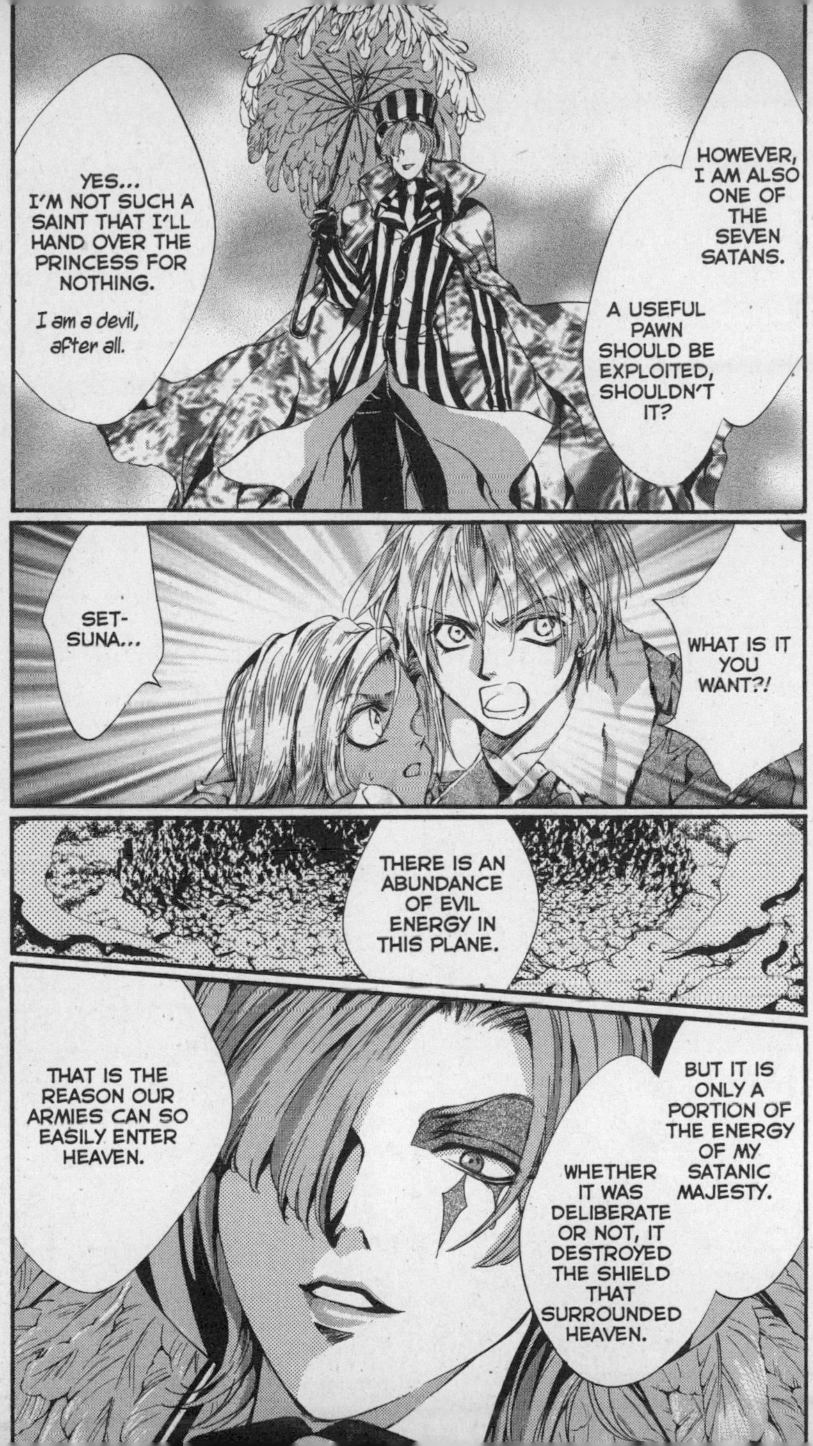
YES... I'M NOT SUCH A SAINT THAT I'LL HAND OVER THE PRINCESS FOR NOTHING.
I am a devil, after all.
HOWEVER, I AM ALSO ONE OF THE SEVEN SATANS.
A USEFUL PAWN SHOULD BE EXPLOITED, SHOULDN'T IT?
WHAT IS IT YOU WANT?!
SET-SUNA...
THERE IS AN ABUNDANCE OF EVIL ENERGY IN THIS PLANE.
THAT IS THE REASON OUR ARMIES CAN SO EASILY ENTER HEAVEN.
BUT IT IS ONLY A PORTION OF THE ENERGY OF MY SATANIC MAJESTY.
WHETHER IT WAS DELIBERATE OR NOT, IT DESTROYED THE SHIELD THAT SURROUNDED HEAVEN.

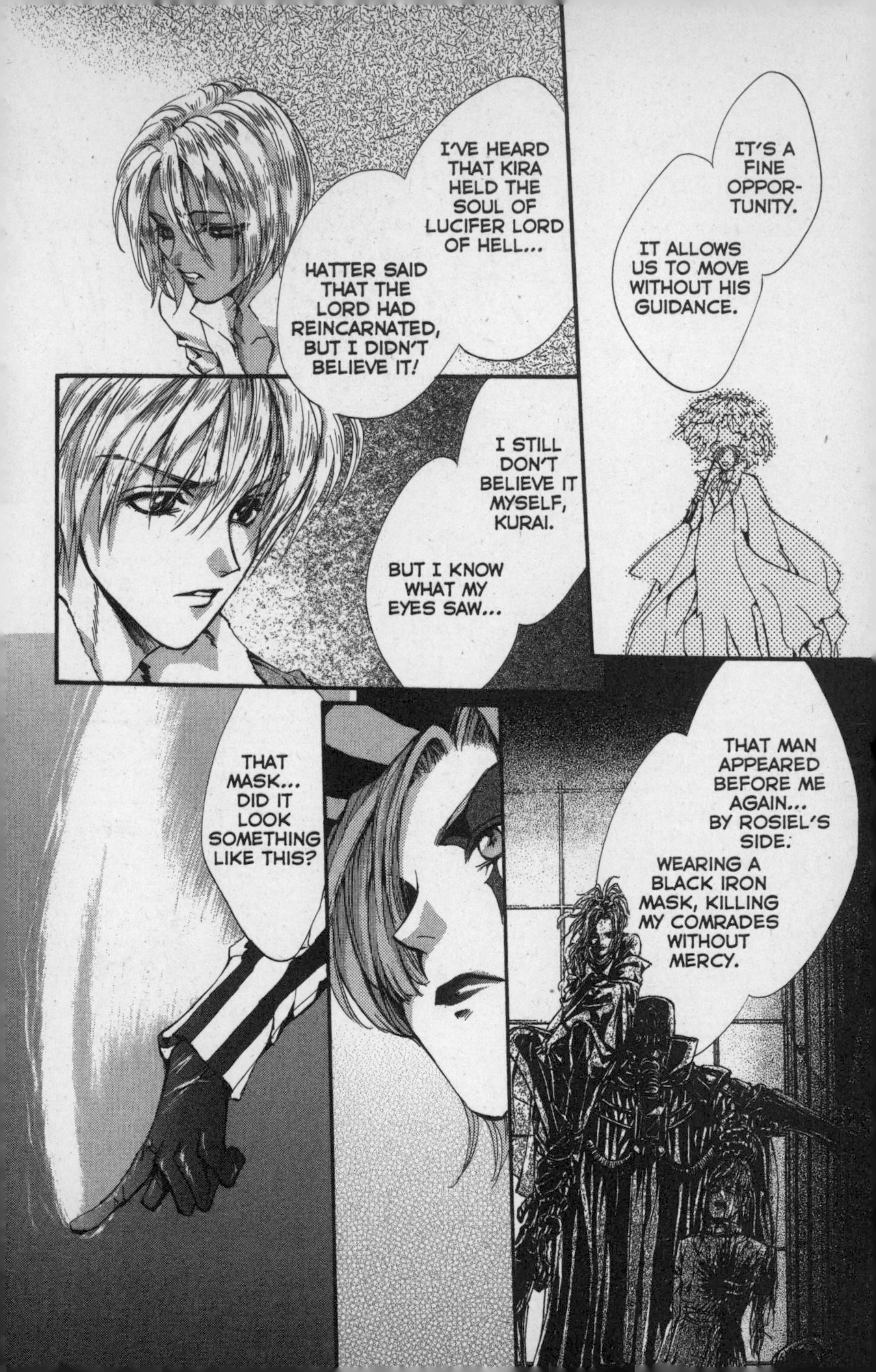
IT'S A FINE OPPORTUNITY.
IT ALLOWS US TO MOVE WITHOUT HIS GUIDANCE.
I'VE HEARD THAT KIRA HELD THE SOUL OF LUCIFER LORD OF HELL...
HATTER SAID THAT THE LORD HAD REINCARNATED, BUT I DIDN'T BELIEVE IT!
I STILL DON'T BELIEVE IT MYSELF, KURAI.
BUT I KNOW WHAT MY EYES SAW...
THAT MAN APPEARED BEFORE ME AGAIN... BY ROSIEL'S SIDE.
WEARING A BLACK IRON MASK, KILLING MY COMRADES WITHOUT MERCY.
THAT MASK... DID IT LOOK SOMETHING LIKE THIS?

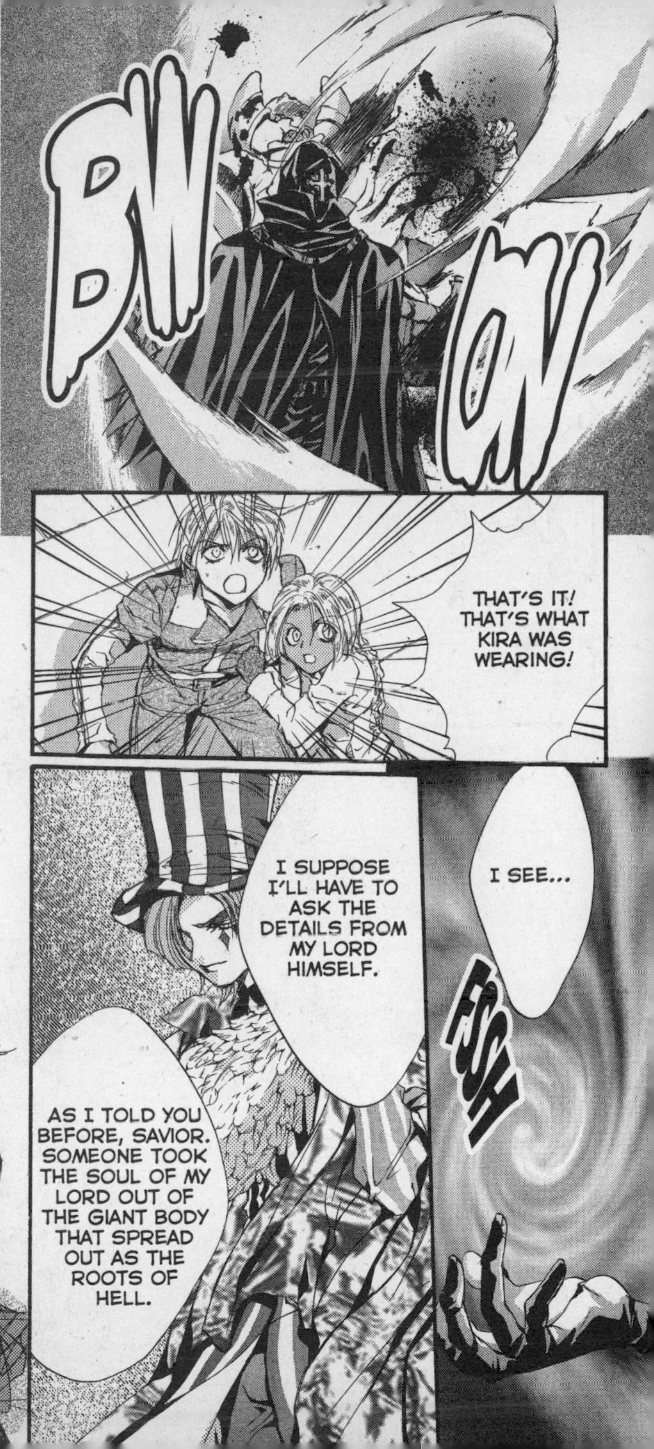
THAT'S IT! THAT'S WHAT KIRA WAS WEARING!
I SEE...
FSSH
I SUPPOSE I'LL HAVE TO ASK THE DETAILS FROM MY LORD HIMSELF.
AS I TOLD YOU BEFORE, SAVIOR. SOMEONE TOOK THE SOUL OF MY LORD OUT OF THE GIANT BODY THAT SPREAD OUT AS THE ROOTS OF HELL.

It's been a long time since we saw Kurai! So long, there are some panels where I forgot what tone her clothes were. She looks like she's gotten just a little older...can you tell? Everyone had expected her to reappear as an adult. But for me, Kurai looks good as a girl, so I didn't change her. Two people guessed that Mad Hatter would save her. The cover I drew this time was a little erotic, and I almost junked it. But I didn't have time for anything else, so here it is. I'm a little embarrassed. The drawing below is Kurai, in sort of a high school girl pose. Dobiel got killed right after he made his reappearance. Too bad!

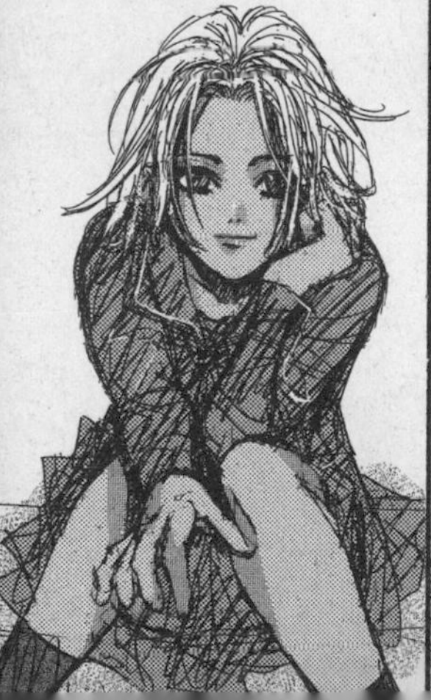

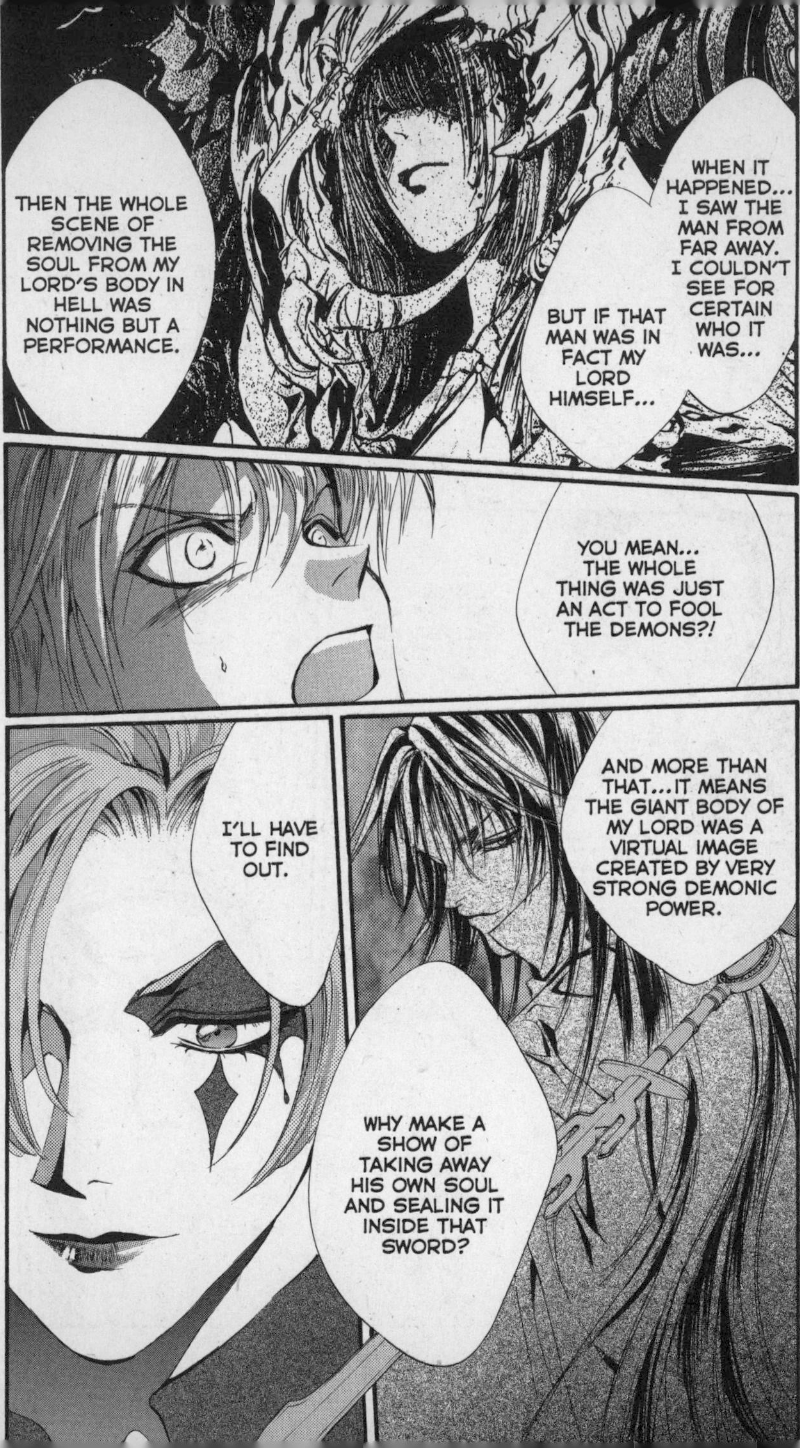
WHEN IT HAPPENED... I SAW THE MAN FROM FAR AWAY. I COULDN'T SEE FOR CERTAIN WHO IT WAS...
BUT IF THAT MAN WAS IN FACT MY LORD HIMSELF...
THEN THE WHOLE SCENE OF REMOVING THE SOUL FROM MY LORD'S BODY IN HELL WAS NOTHING BUT A PERFORMANCE.
YOU MEAN... THE WHOLE THING WAS JUST AN ACT TO FOOL THE DEMONS?!
AND MORE THAN THAT...IT MEANS THE GIANT BODY OF MY LORD WAS A VIRTUAL IMAGE CREATED BY VERY STRONG DEMONIC POWER.
WHY MAKE A SHOW OF TAKING AWAY HIS OWN SOUL AND SEALING IT INSIDE THAT SWORD?
I'LL HAVE TO FIND OUT.

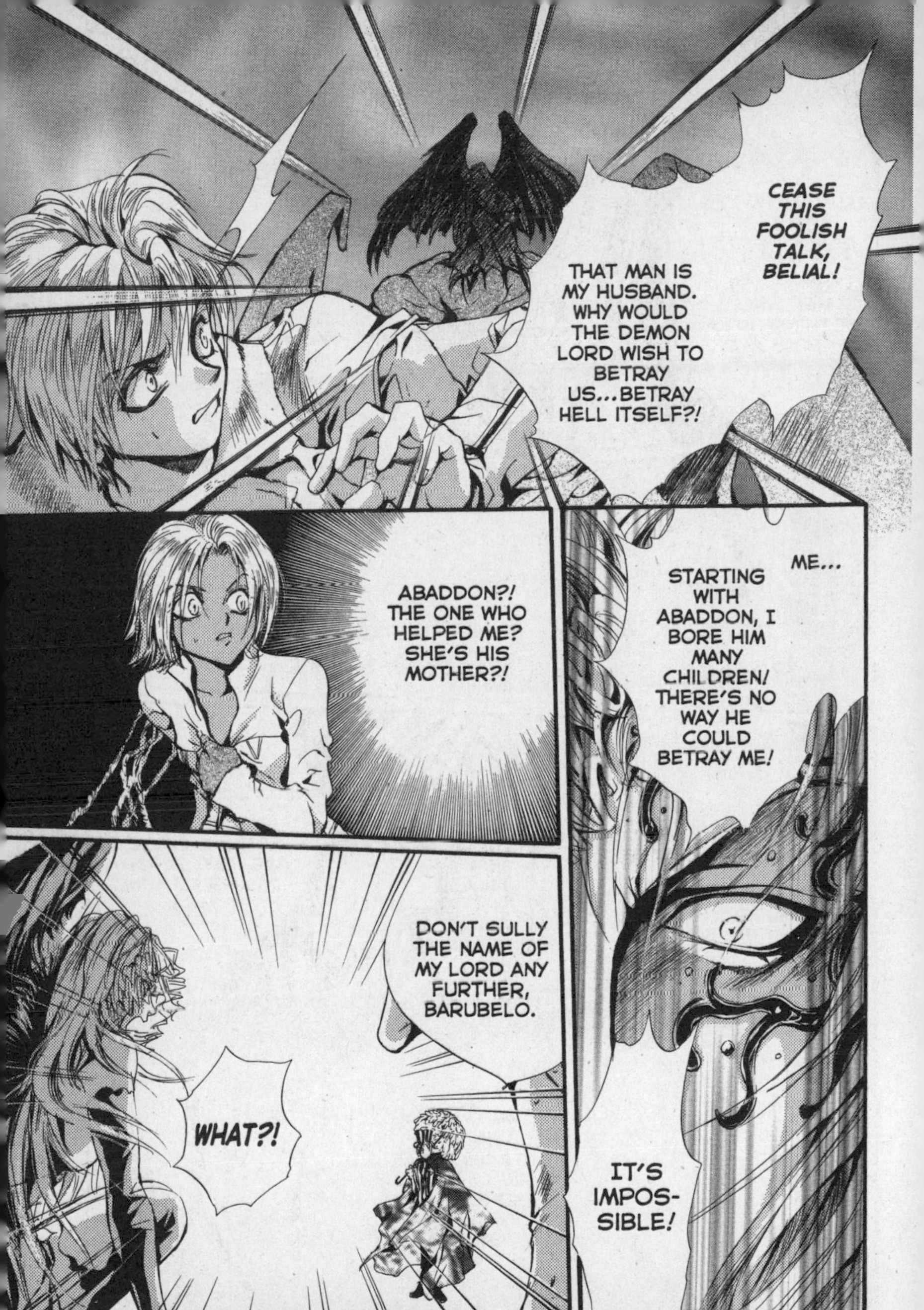
CEASE THIS FOOLISH TALK, BELIAL!
THAT MAN IS MY HUSBAND. WHY WOULD THE DEMON LORD WISH TO BETRAY US...BETRAY HELL ITSELF?!
ME...
STARTING WITH ABADDON, I BORE HIM MANY CHILDREN! THERE'S NO WAY HE COULD BETRAY ME!
IT'S IMPOSSIBLE!
ABADDON?! THE ONE WHO HELPED ME? SHE'S HIS MOTHER?!
DON'T SULLY THE NAME OF MY LORD ANY FURTHER, BARUBELO.
WHAT?!

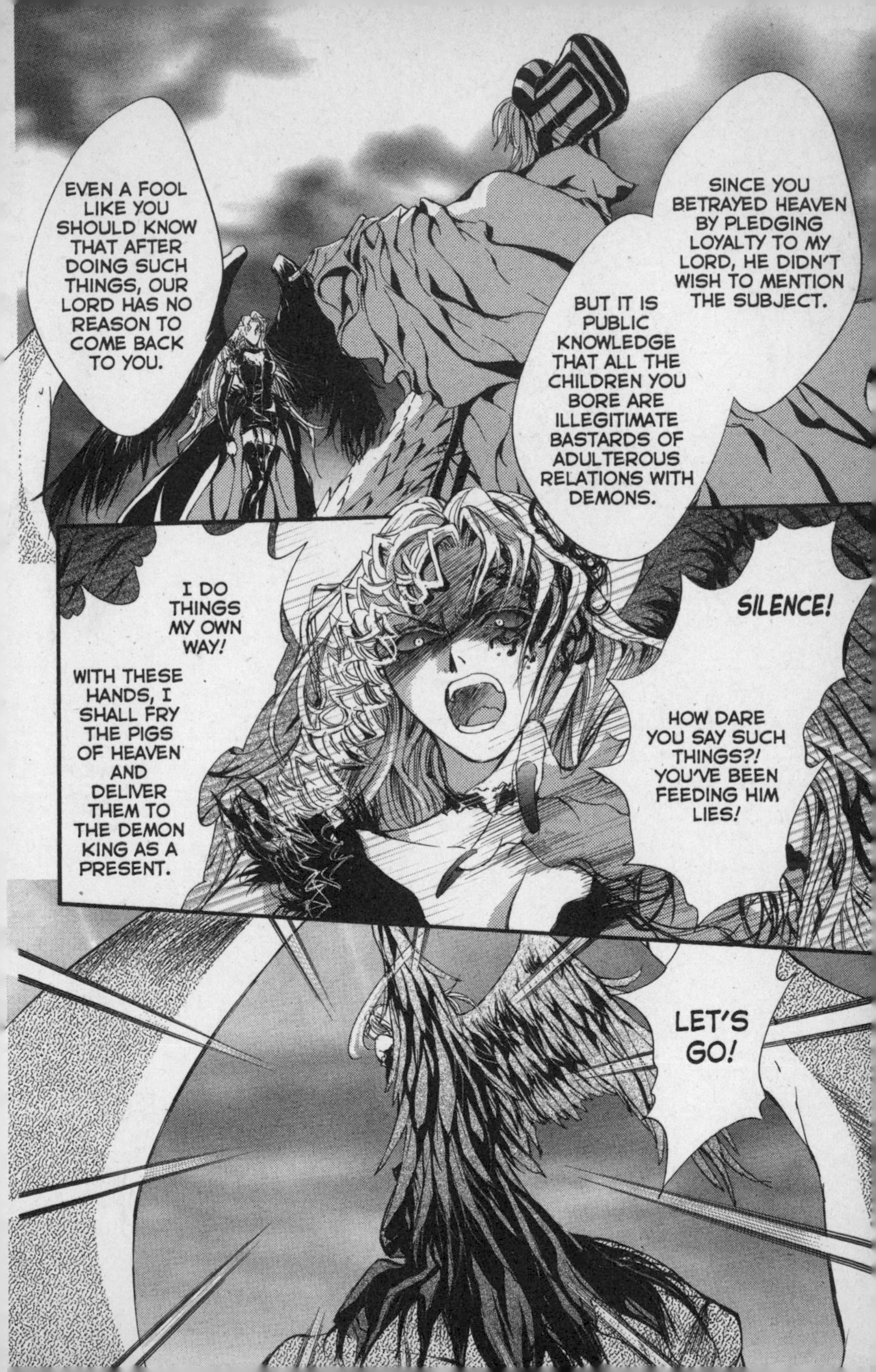
SINCE YOU BETRAYED HEAVEN BY PLEDGING LOYALTY TO MY LORD, HE DIDN'T WISH TO MENTION THE SUBJECT.
BUT IT IS PUBLIC KNOWLEDGE THAT ALL THE CHILDREN YOU BORE ARE ILLEGITIMATE BASTARDS OF ADULTEROUS RELATIONS WITH DEMONS.
EVEN A FOOL LIKE YOU SHOULD KNOW THAT AFTER DOING SUCH THINGS, OUR LORD HAS NO REASON TO COME BACK TO YOU.
SILENCE!
HOW DARE YOU SAY SUCH THINGS?! YOU'VE BEEN FEEDING HIM LIES!
I DO THINGS MY OWN WAY!
WITH THESE HANDS, I SHALL FRY THE PIGS OF HEAVEN AND DELIVER THEM TO THE DEMON KING AS A PRESENT.
LET'S GO!

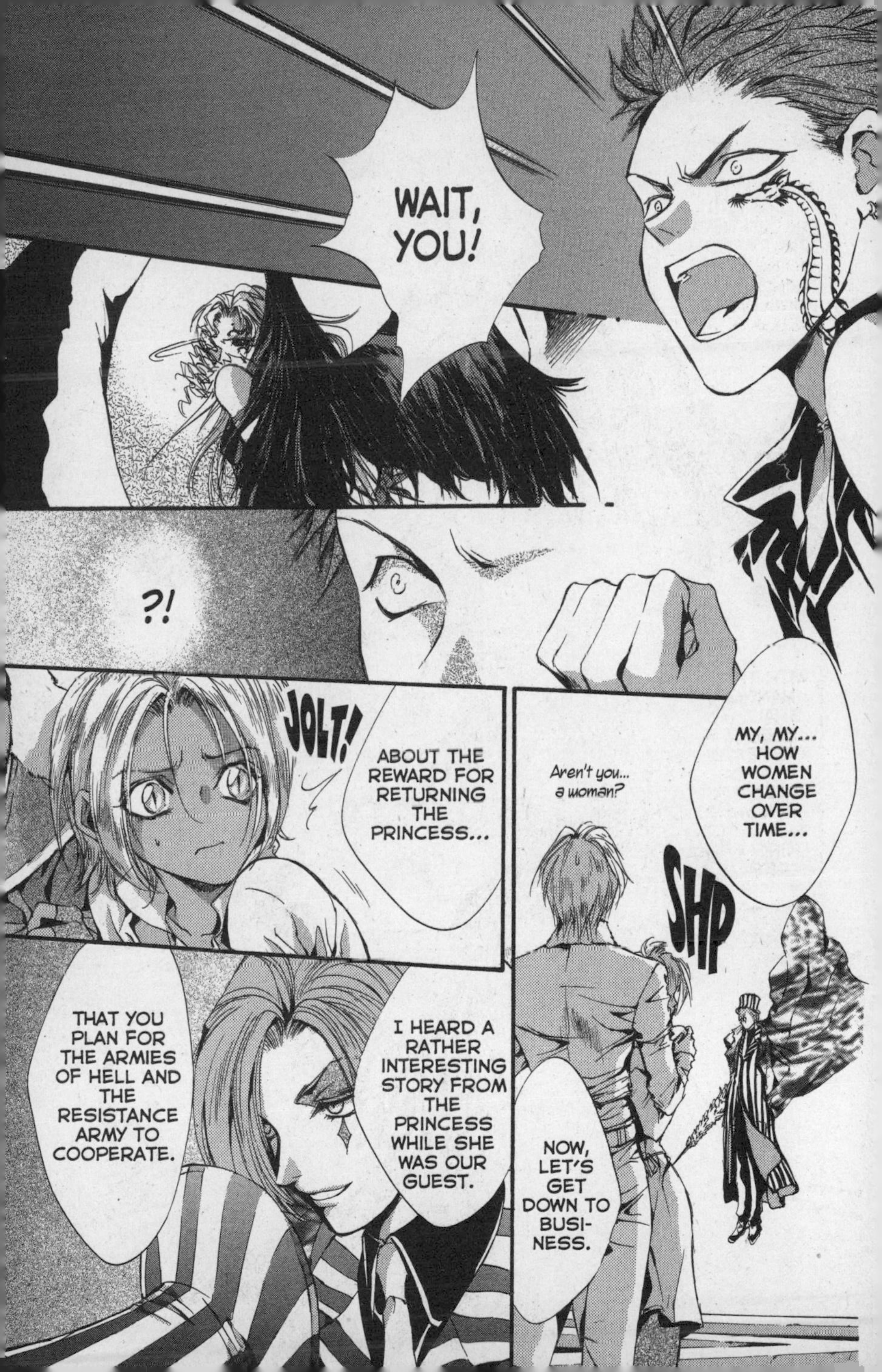
WAIT, YOU!
?!
MY, MY... HOW WOMEN CHANGE OVER TIME...
Aren't you... a woman?
SHP
NOW, LET'S GET DOWN TO BUSINESS.
JOLT!
ABOUT THE REWARD FOR RETURNING THE PRINCESS...
I HEARD A RATHER INTERESTING STORY FROM THE PRINCESS WHILE SHE WAS OUR GUEST.
THAT YOU PLAN FOR THE ARMIES OF HELL AND THE RESISTANCE ARMY TO COOPERATE.

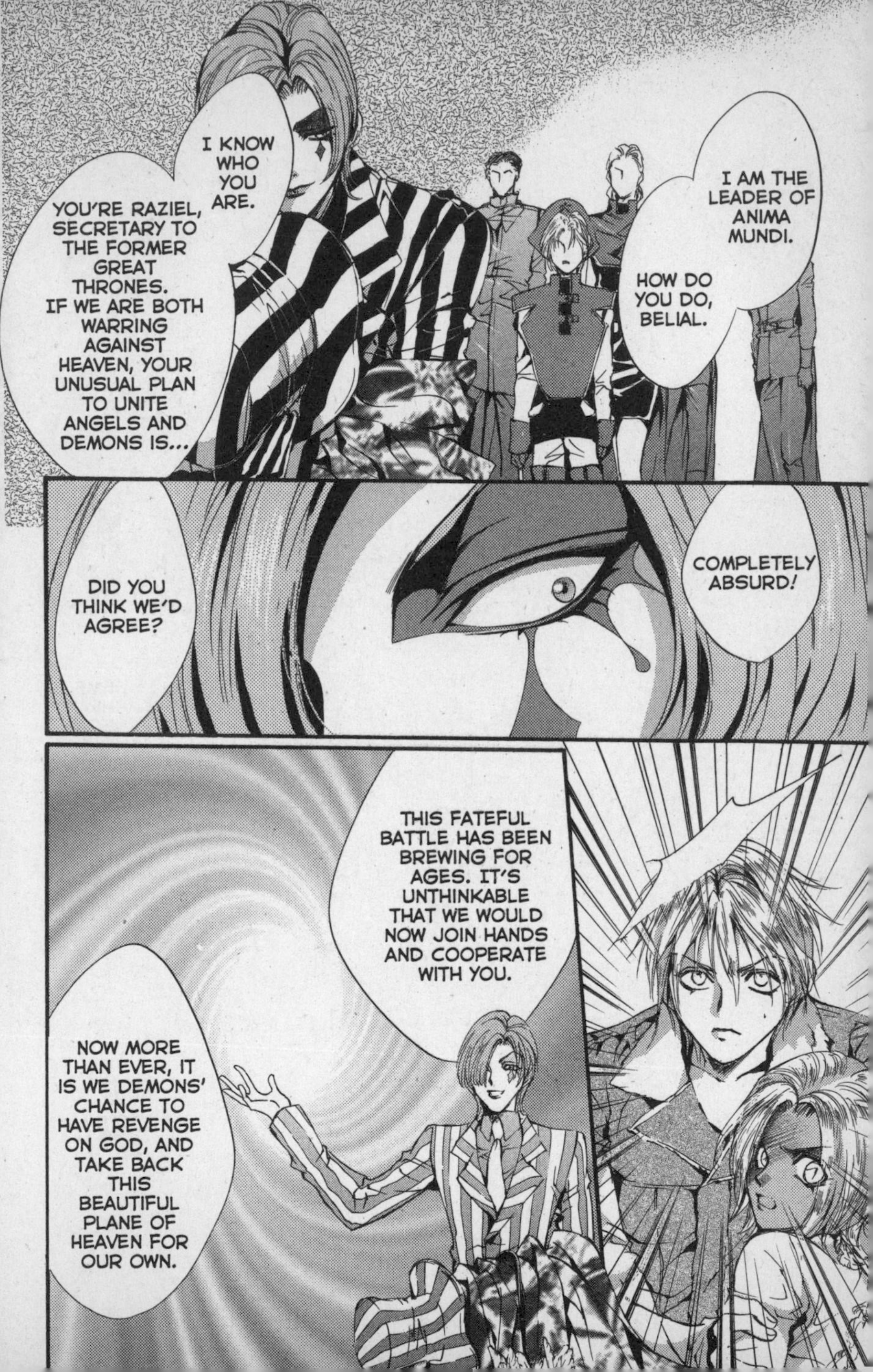
I AM THE LEADER OF ANIMA MUNDI.
HOW DO YOU DO, BELIAL.
I KNOW WHO YOU ARE.
YOU'RE RAZIEL, SECRETARY TO THE FORMER GREAT THRONES. IF WE ARE BOTH WARRING AGAINST HEAVEN, YOUR UNUSUAL PLAN TO UNITE ANGELS AND DEMONS IS...
COMPLETELY ABSURD!
DID YOU THINK WE'D AGREE?
THIS FATEFUL BATTLE HAS BEEN BREWING FOR AGES. IT'S UNTHINKABLE THAT WE WOULD NOW JOIN HANDS AND COOPERATE WITH YOU.
NOW MORE THAN EVER, IT IS WE DEMONS' CHANCE TO HAVE REVENGE ON GOD, AND TAKE BACK THIS BEAUTIFUL PLANE OF HEAVEN FOR OUR OWN.

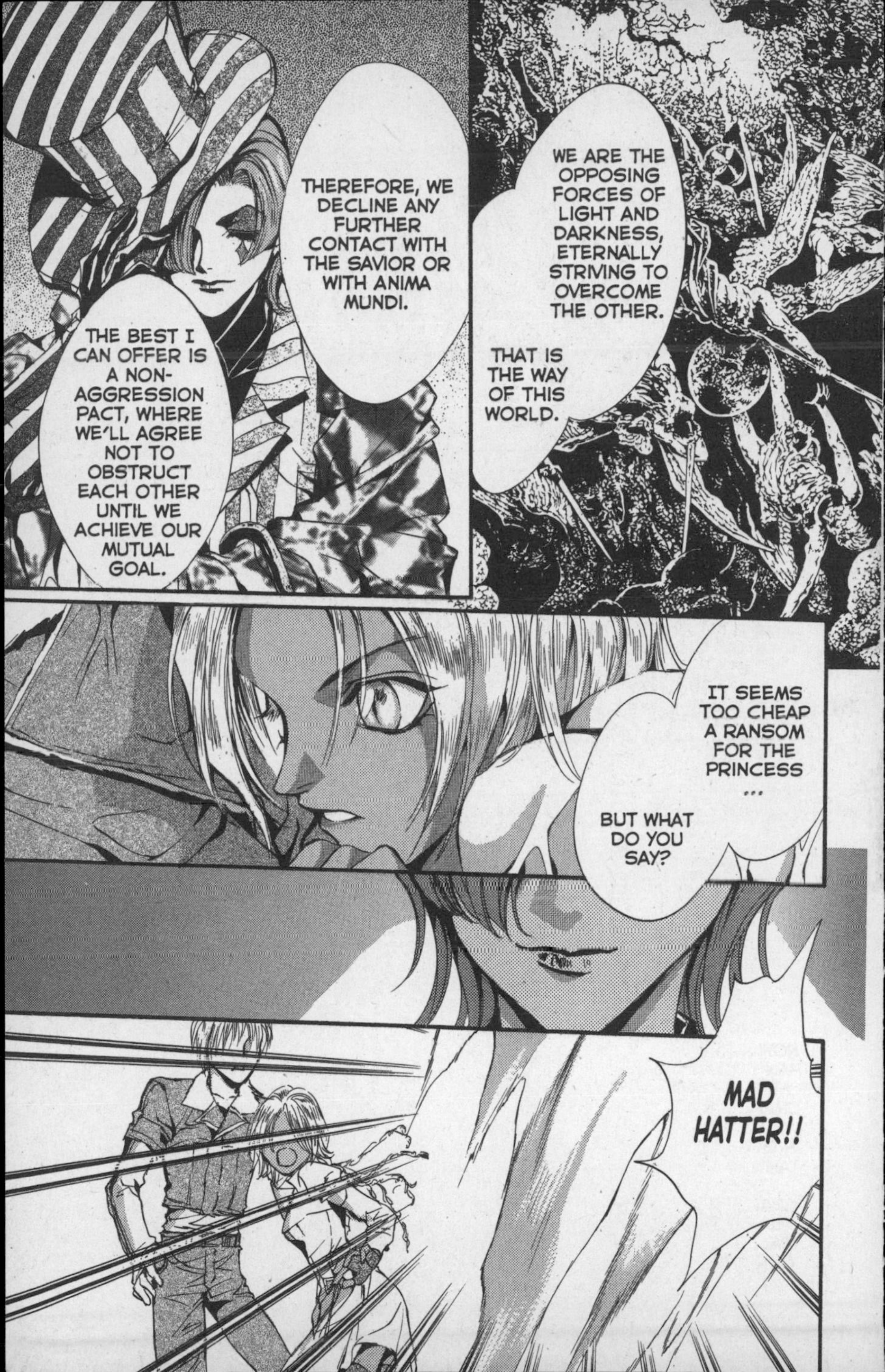
WE ARE THE OPPOSING FORCES OF LIGHT AND DARKNESS, ETERNALLY STRIVING TO OVERCOME THE OTHER.
THAT IS THE WAY OF THIS WORLD.
THEREFORE, WE DECLINE ANY FURTHER CONTACT WITH THE SAVIOR OR WITH ANIMA MUNDI.
THE BEST I CAN OFFER IS A NON-AGGRESSION PACT, WHERE WE'LL AGREE NOT TO OBSTRUCT EACH OTHER UNTIL WE ACHIEVE OUR MUTUAL GOAL.
IT SEEMS TOO CHEAP A RANSOM FOR THE PRINCESS...
BUT WHAT DO YOU SAY?
MAD HATTER!!

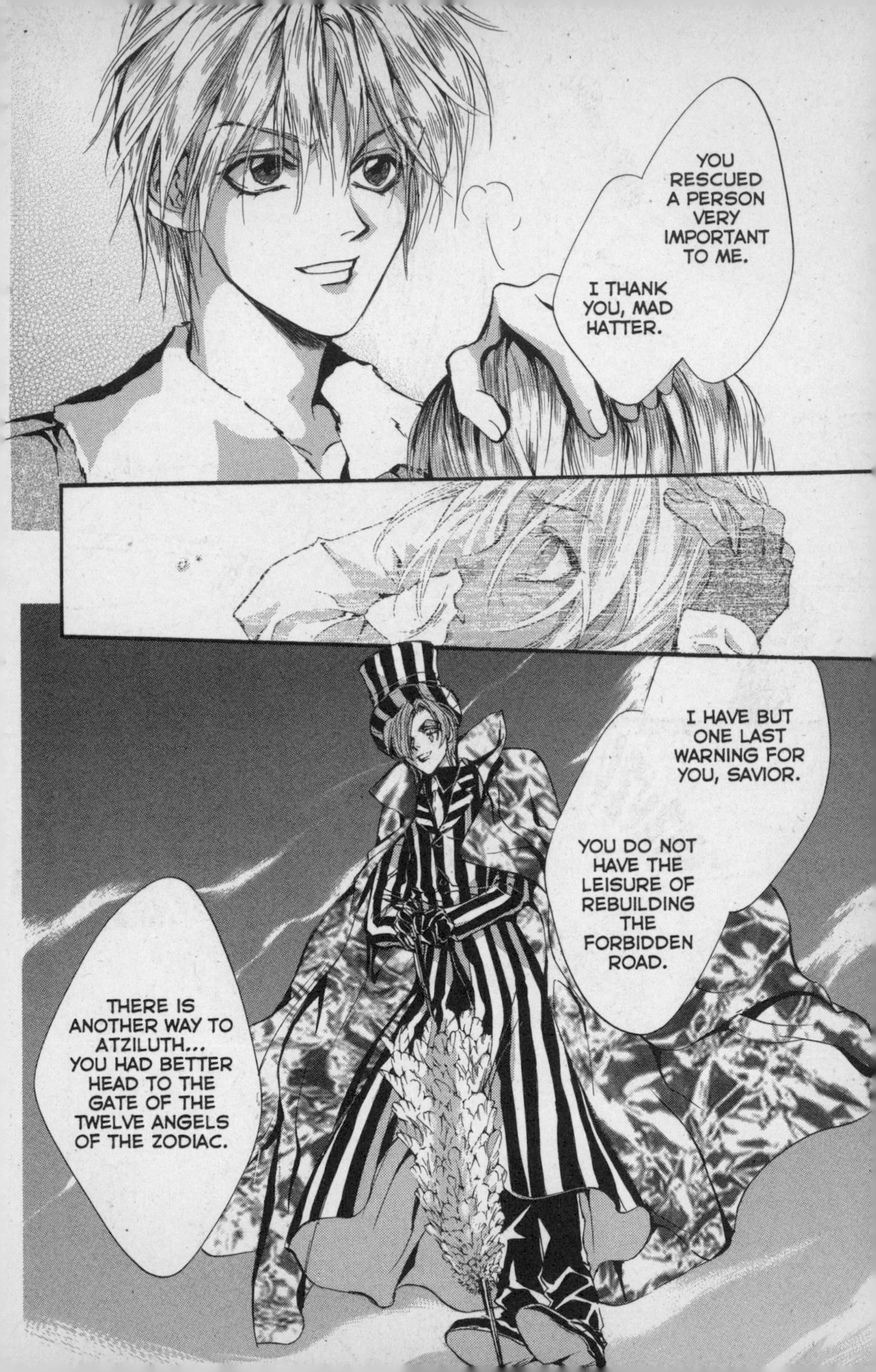
YOU RESCUED A PERSON VERY IMPORTANT TO ME.
I THANK YOU, MAD HATTER.
I HAVE BUT ONE LAST WARNING FOR YOU, SAVIOR.
YOU DO NOT HAVE THE LEISURE OF REBUILDING THE FORBIDDEN ROAD.
THERE IS ANOTHER WAY TO ATZILUTH... YOU HAD BETTER HEAD TO THE GATE OF THE TWELVE ANGELS OF THE ZODIAC.

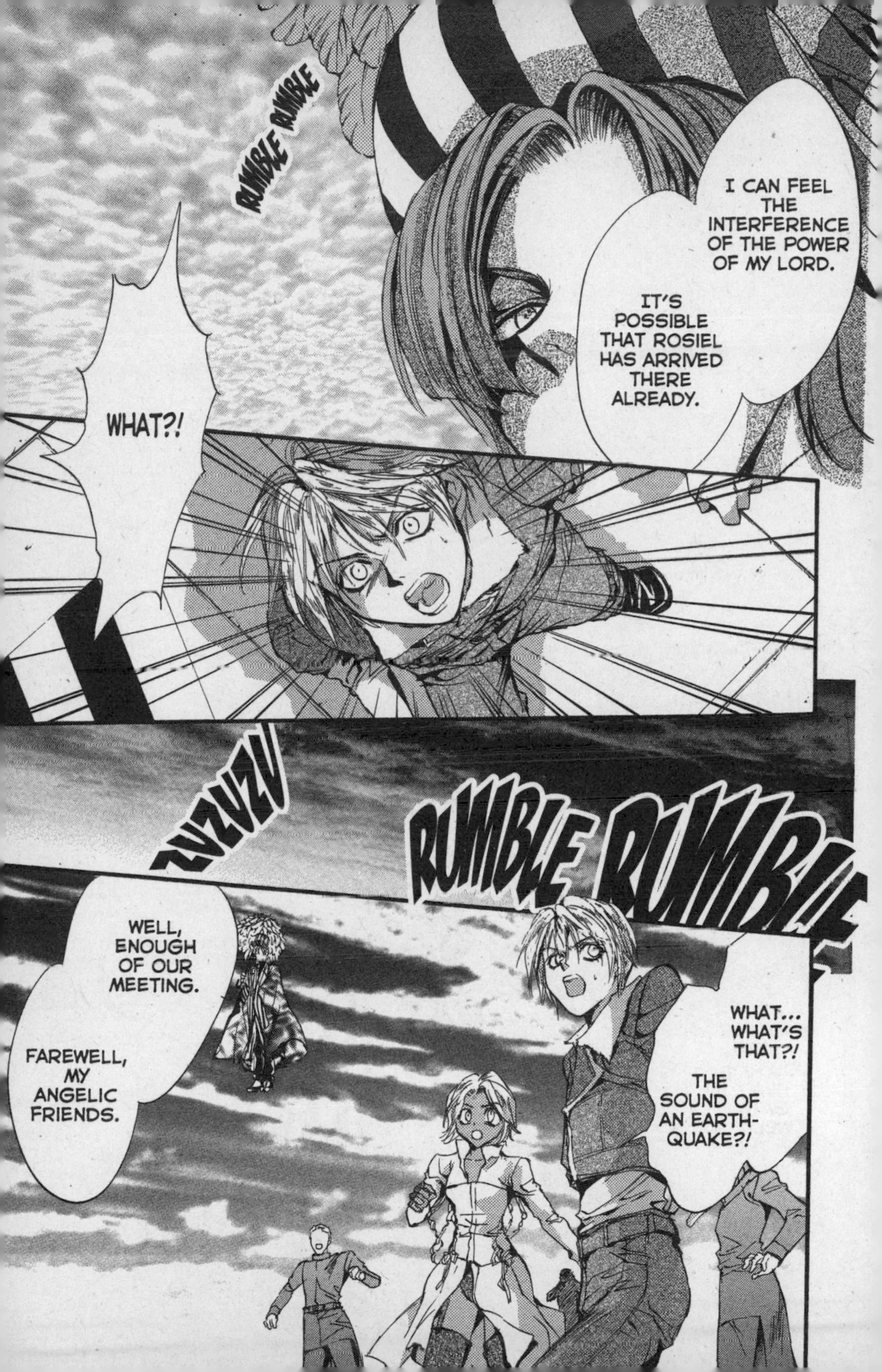
I CAN FEEL THE INTERFERENCE OF THE POWER OF MY LORD.
IT'S POSSIBLE THAT ROSIEL HAS ARRIVED THERE ALREADY.
RUMBLE RUMBLE
WHAT?!
ZVZVZV
RUMBLE RUMBLE
WHAT... WHAT'S THAT?!
THE SOUND OF AN EARTH-QUAKE?!
WELL, ENOUGH OF OUR MEETING.
FAREWELL, MY ANGELIC FRIENDS.

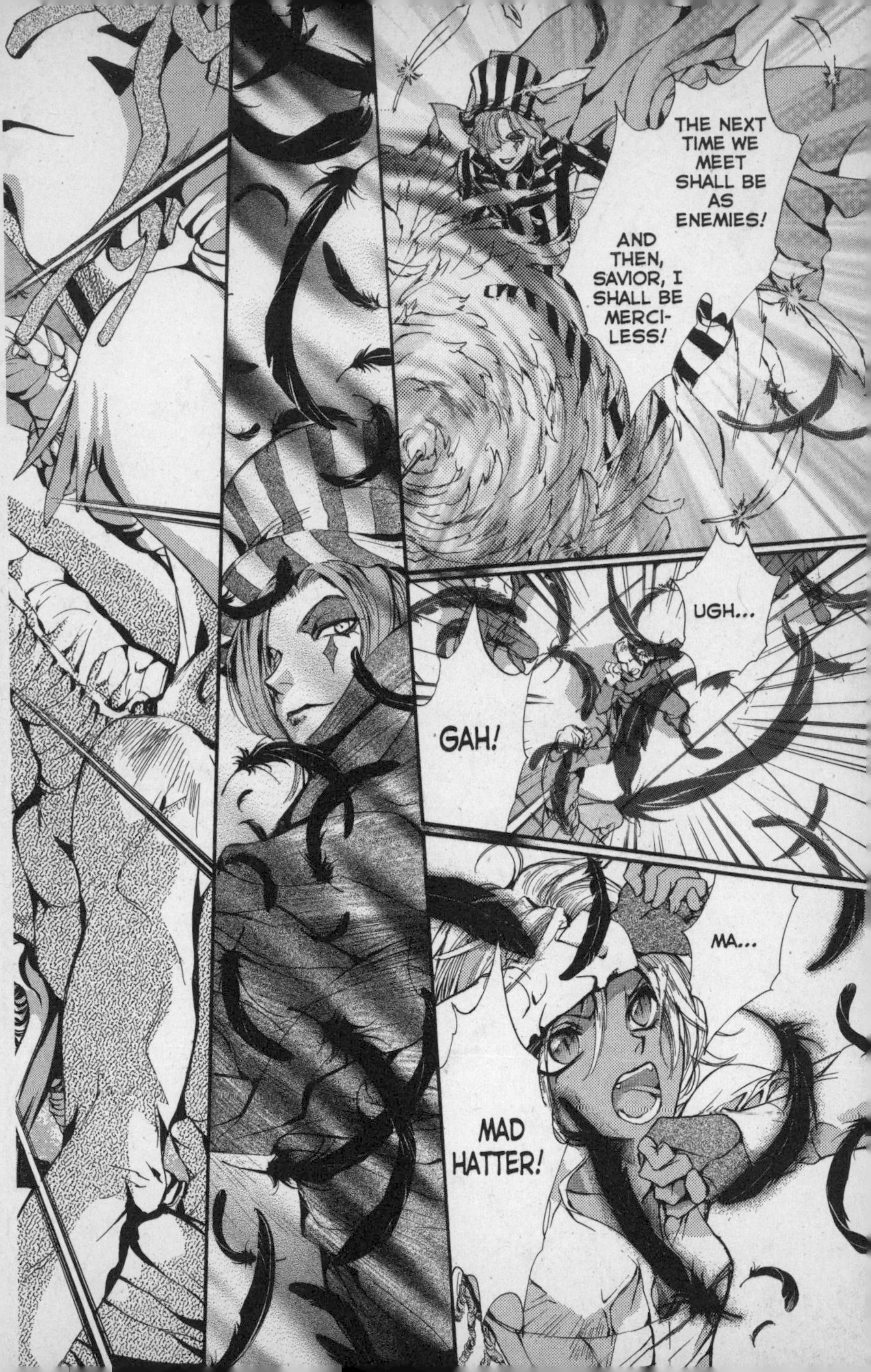
THE NEXT TIME WE MEET SHALL BE AS ENEMIES!
AND THEN, SAVIOR, I SHALL BE MERCILESS!
UGH...
GAH!
MA...
MAD HATTER!

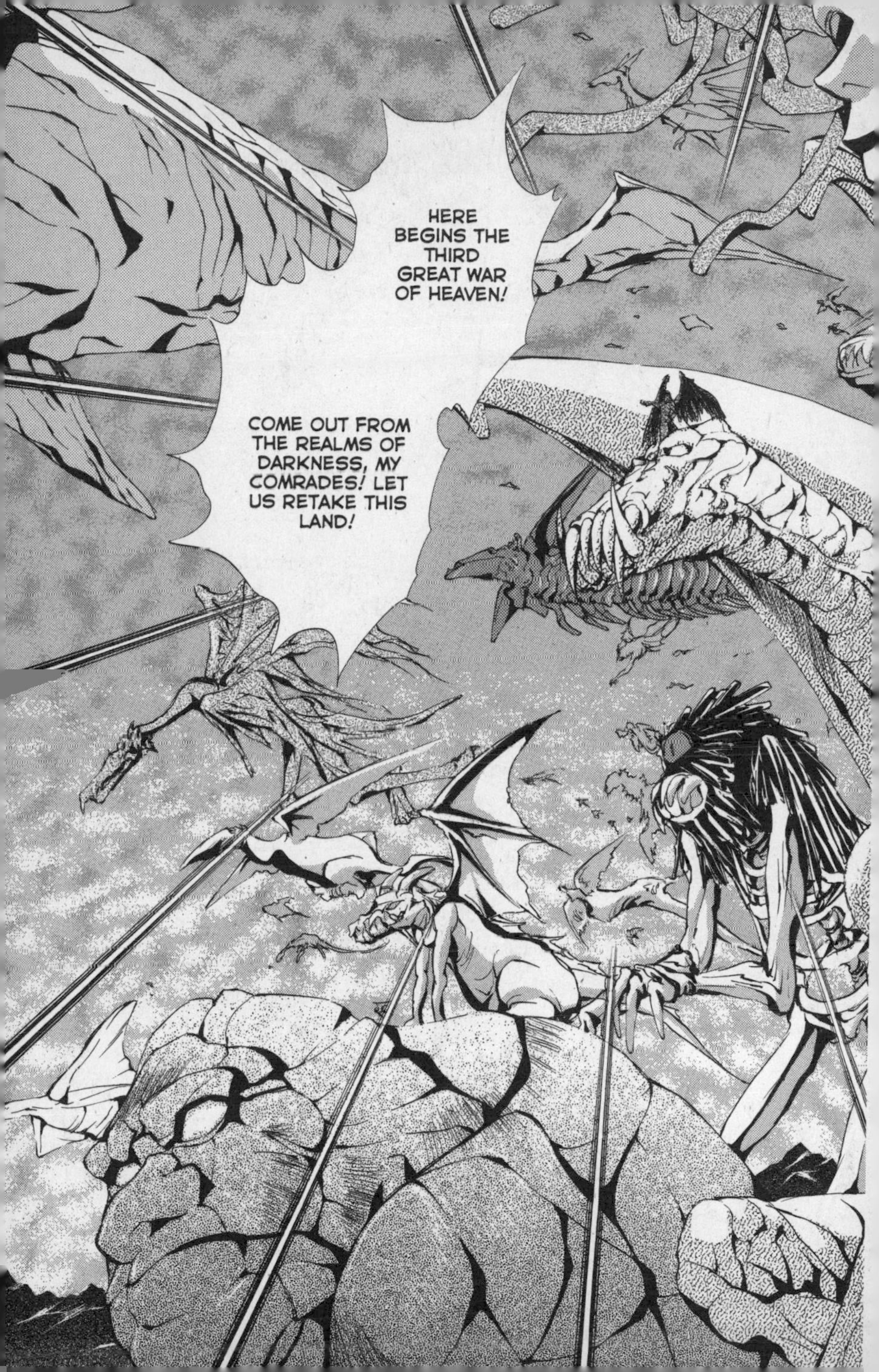
HERE BEGINS THE THIRD GREAT WAR OF HEAVEN!
COME OUT FROM THE REALMS OF DARKNESS, MY COMRADES! LET US RETAKE THIS LAND!

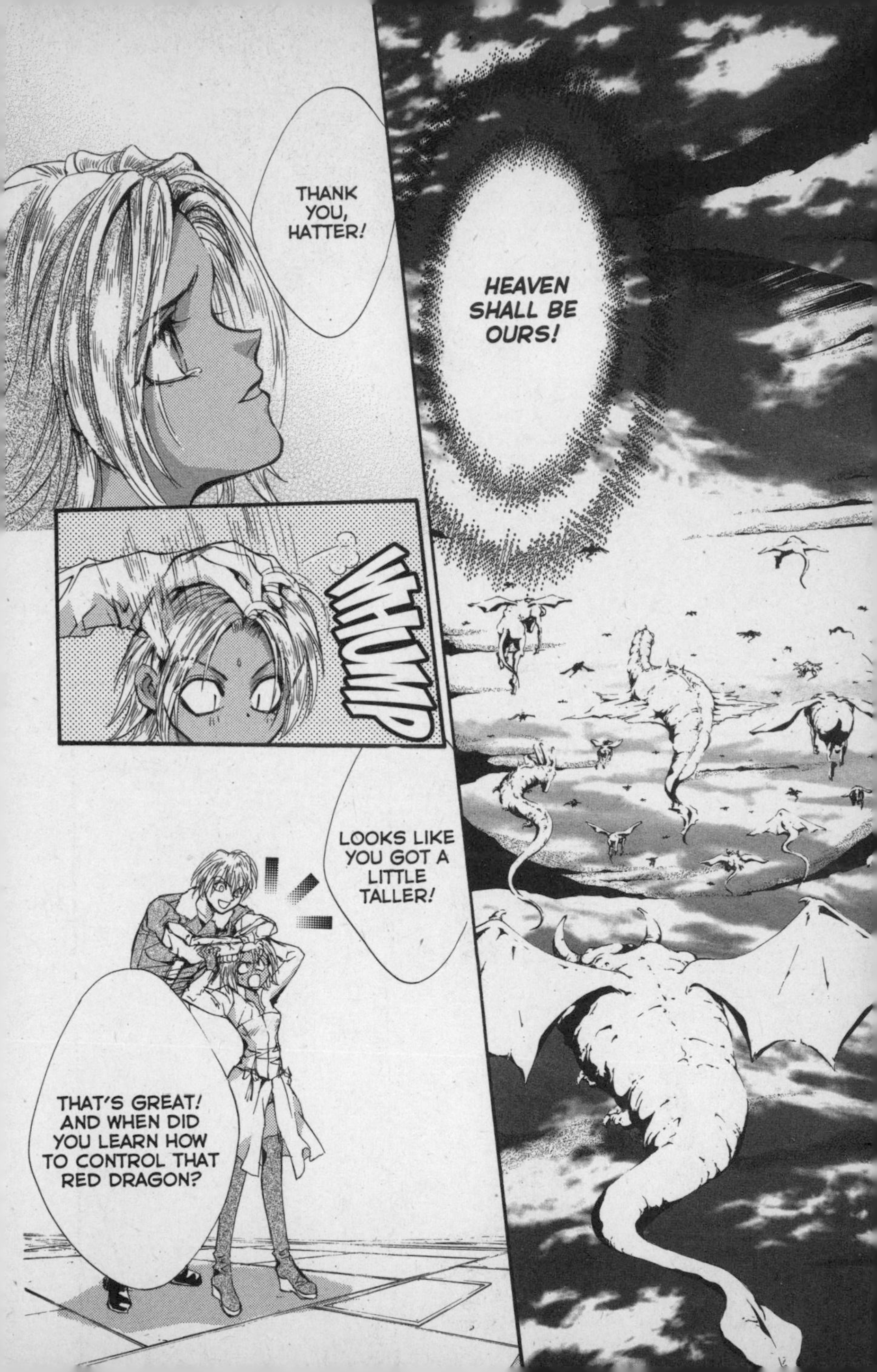
HEAVEN SHALL BE OURS!
THANK YOU, HATTER!
WHUMP
LOOKS LIKE YOU GOT A LITTLE TALLER!
THAT'S GREAT! AND WHEN DID YOU LEARN HOW TO CONTROL THAT RED DRAGON?

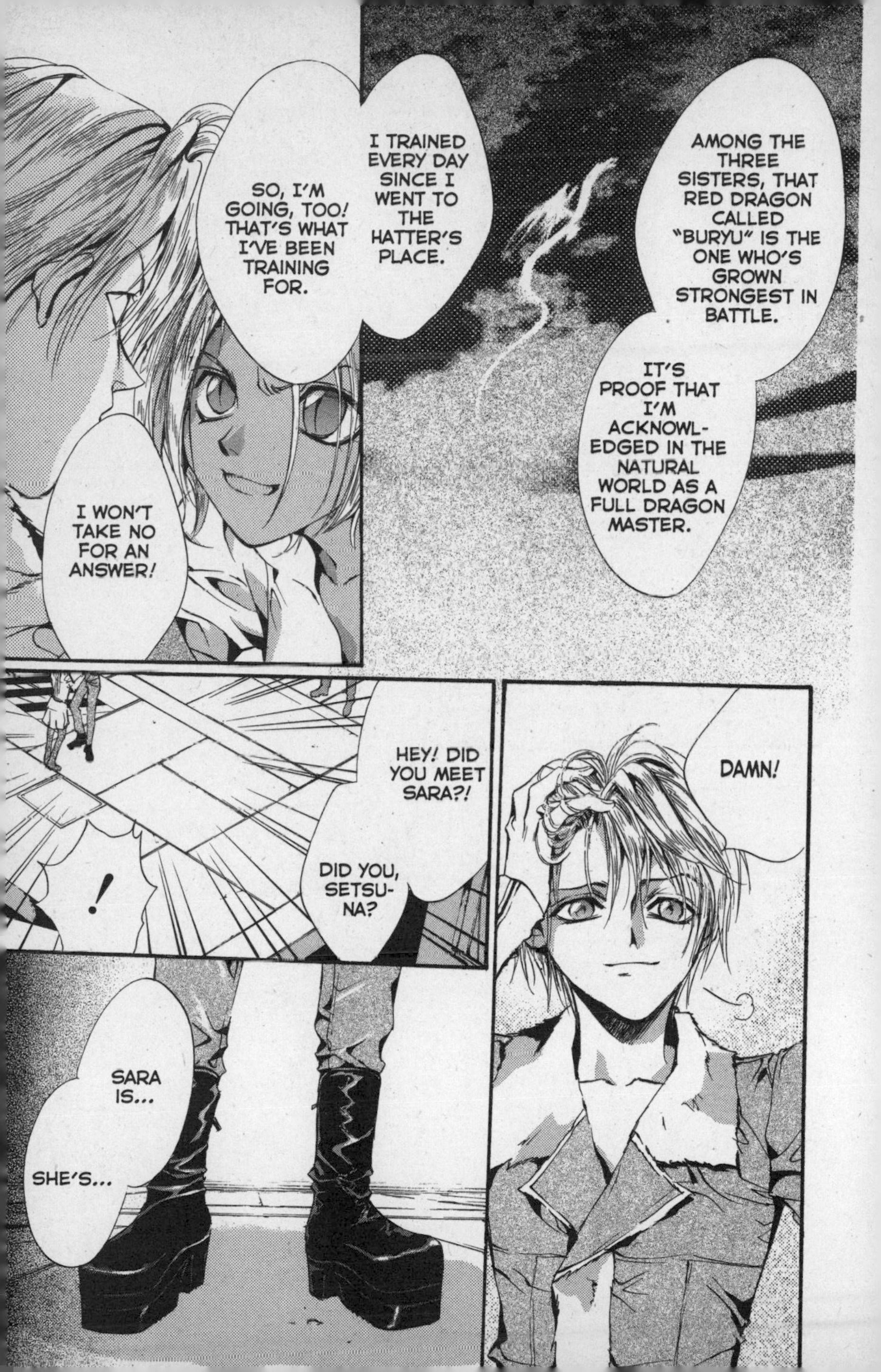
AMONG THE THREE SISTERS, THAT RED DRAGON CALLED "BURYU" IS THE ONE WHO'S GROWN STRONGEST IN BATTLE.
IT'S PROOF THAT I'M ACKNOWL-EDGED IN THE NATURAL WORLD AS A FULL DRAGON MASTER.
I TRAINED EVERY DAY SINCE I WENT TO THE HATTER'S PLACE.
SO, I'M GOING, TOO! THAT'S WHAT I'VE BEEN TRAINING FOR.
I WON'T TAKE NO FOR AN ANSWER!
DAMN!
HEY! DID YOU MEET SARA?!
DID YOU, SETSU-NA?
!
SARA IS...
SHE'S...

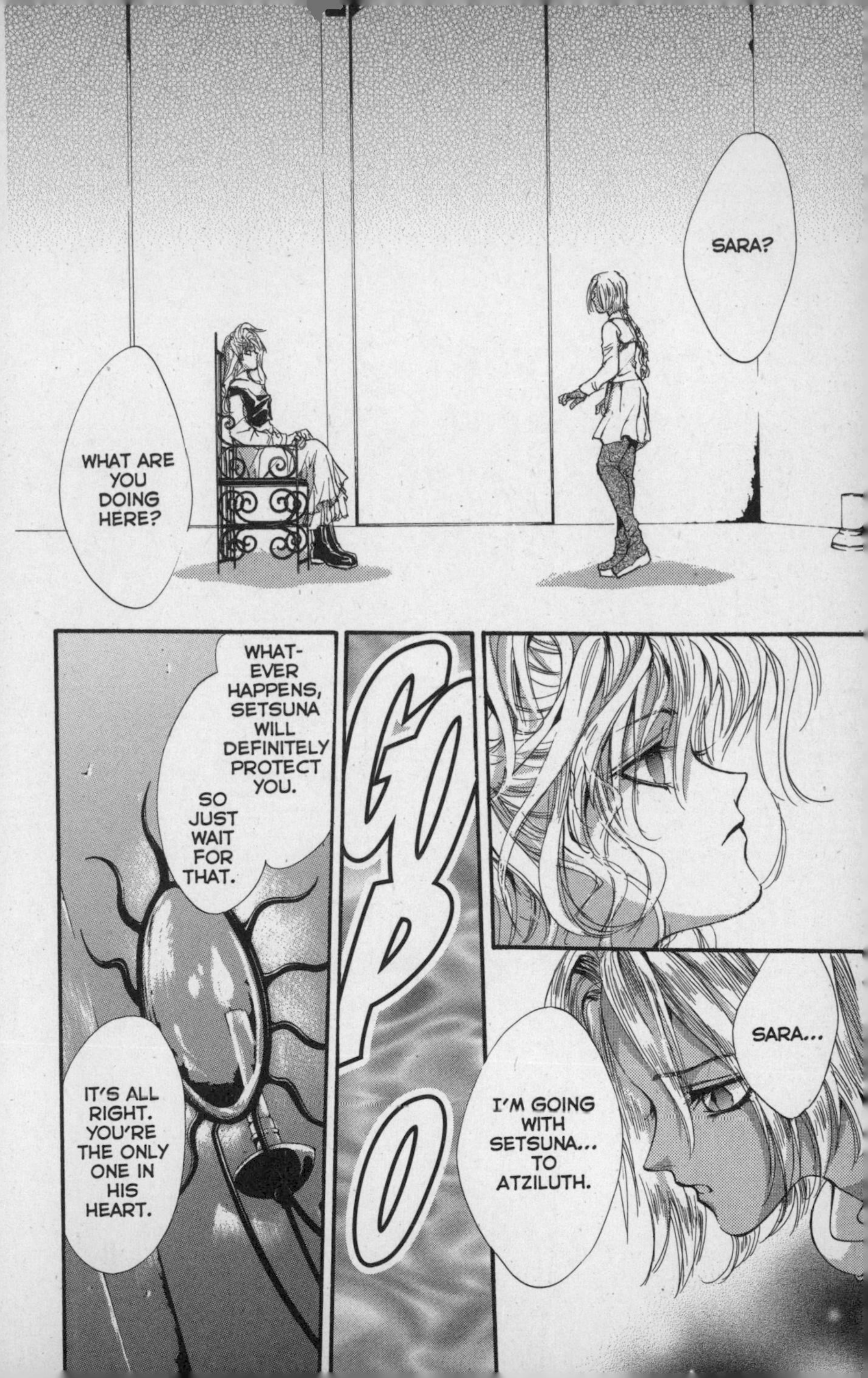
SARA?
WHAT ARE YOU DOING HERE?
SARA...
I'M GOING WITH SETSUNA... TO ATZILUTH.
WHAT-EVER HAPPENS, SETSUNA WILL DEFINITELY PROTECT YOU.
SO JUST WAIT FOR THAT.
IT'S ALL RIGHT. YOU'RE THE ONLY ONE IN HIS HEART.

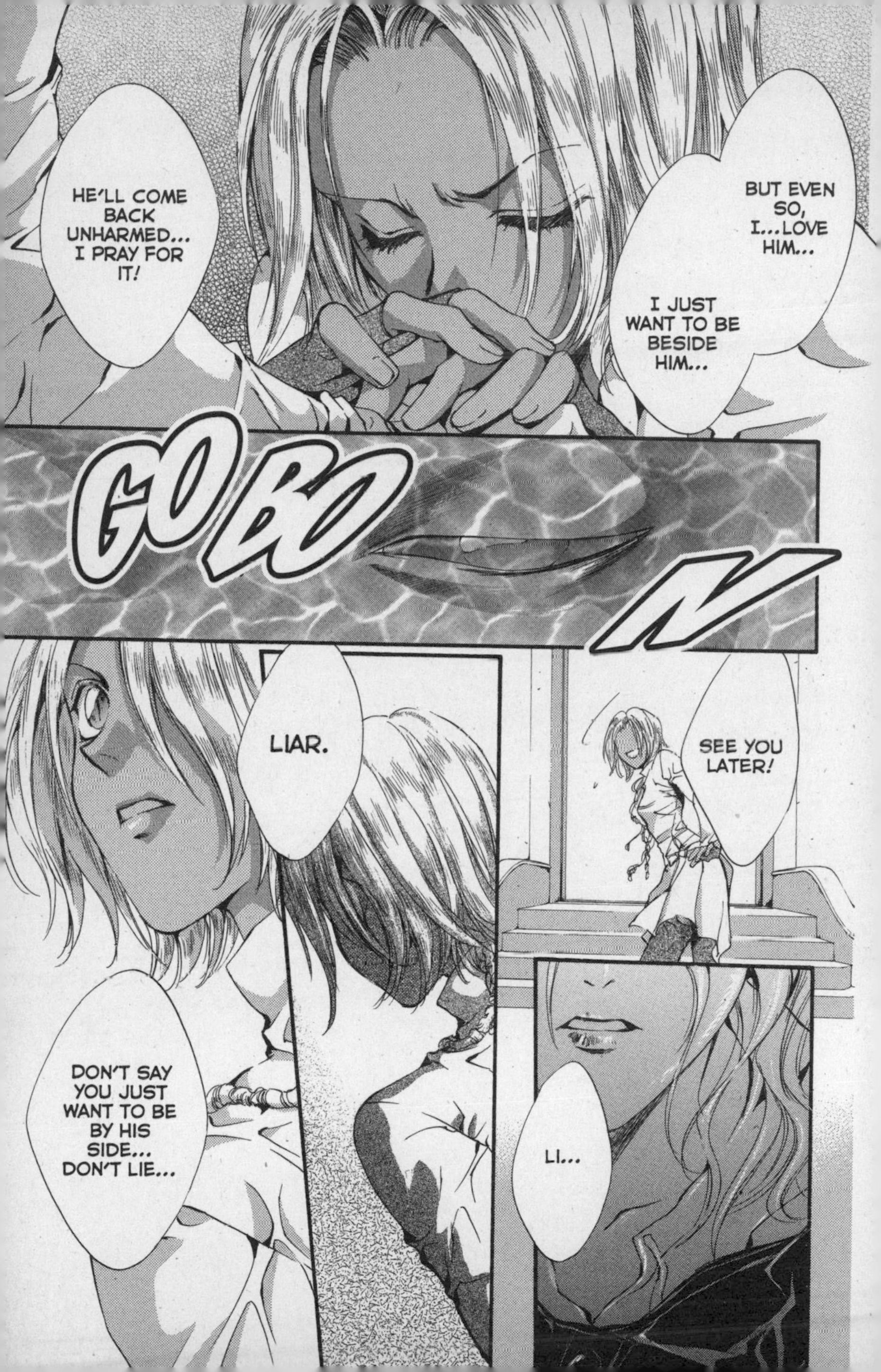
BUT EVEN SO, I...LOVE HIM...
I JUST WANT TO BE BESIDE HIM...
HE'LL COME BACK UNHARMED... I PRAY FOR IT!
GOBON
SEE YOU LATER!
LI...
LIAR.
DON'T SAY YOU JUST WANT TO BE BY HIS SIDE... DON'T LIE...

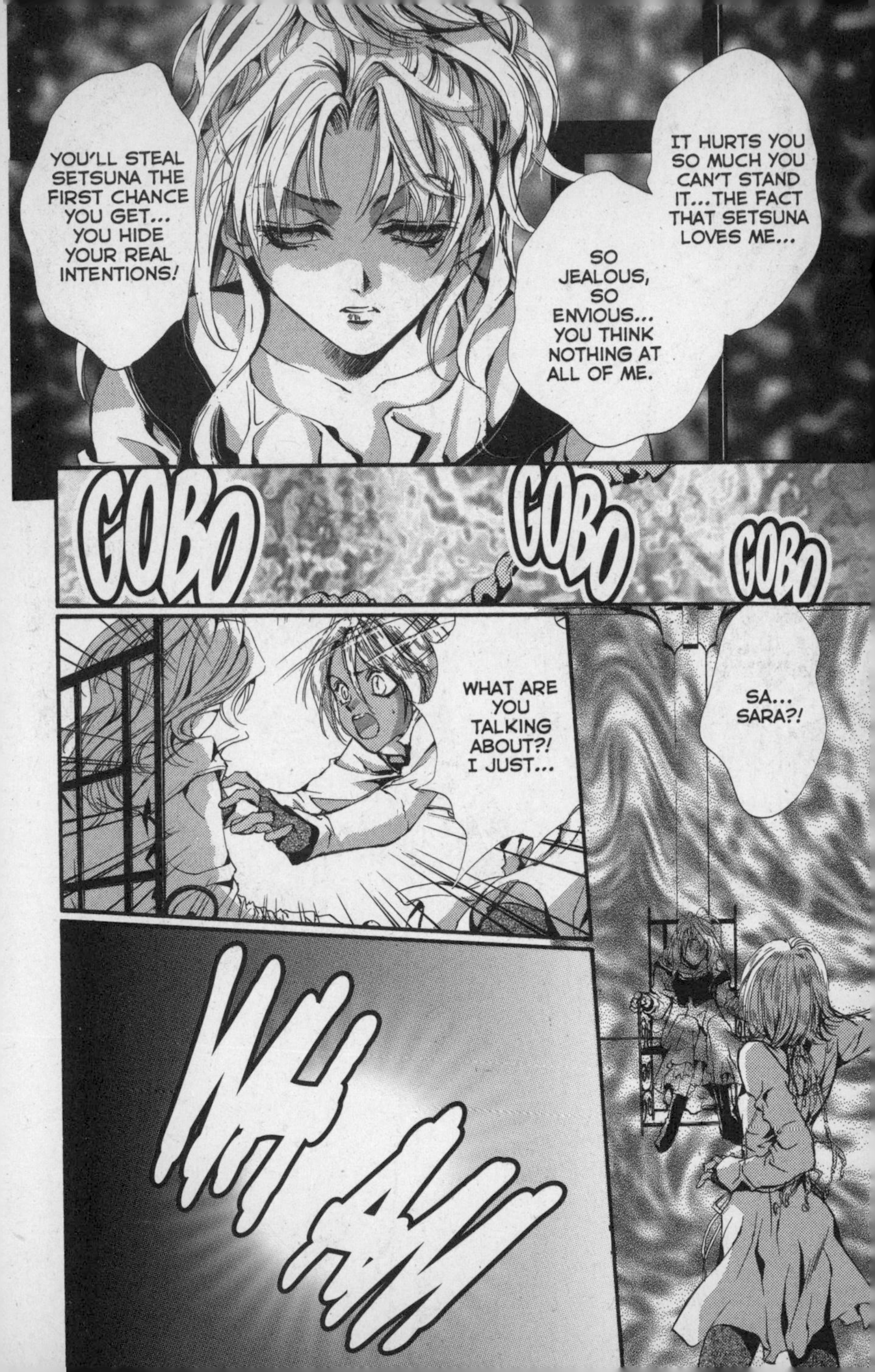
IT HURTS YOU SO MUCH YOU CAN'T STAND IT...THE FACT THAT SETSUNA LOVES ME...
SO JEALOUS, SO ENVIOUS... YOU THINK NOTHING AT ALL OF ME.
YOU'LL STEAL SETSUNA THE FIRST CHANCE YOU GET... YOU HIDE YOUR REAL INTENTIONS!
GOBO
GOBO
GOBO
SA... SARA?!
WHAT ARE YOU TALKING ABOUT?! I JUST...
WHAM

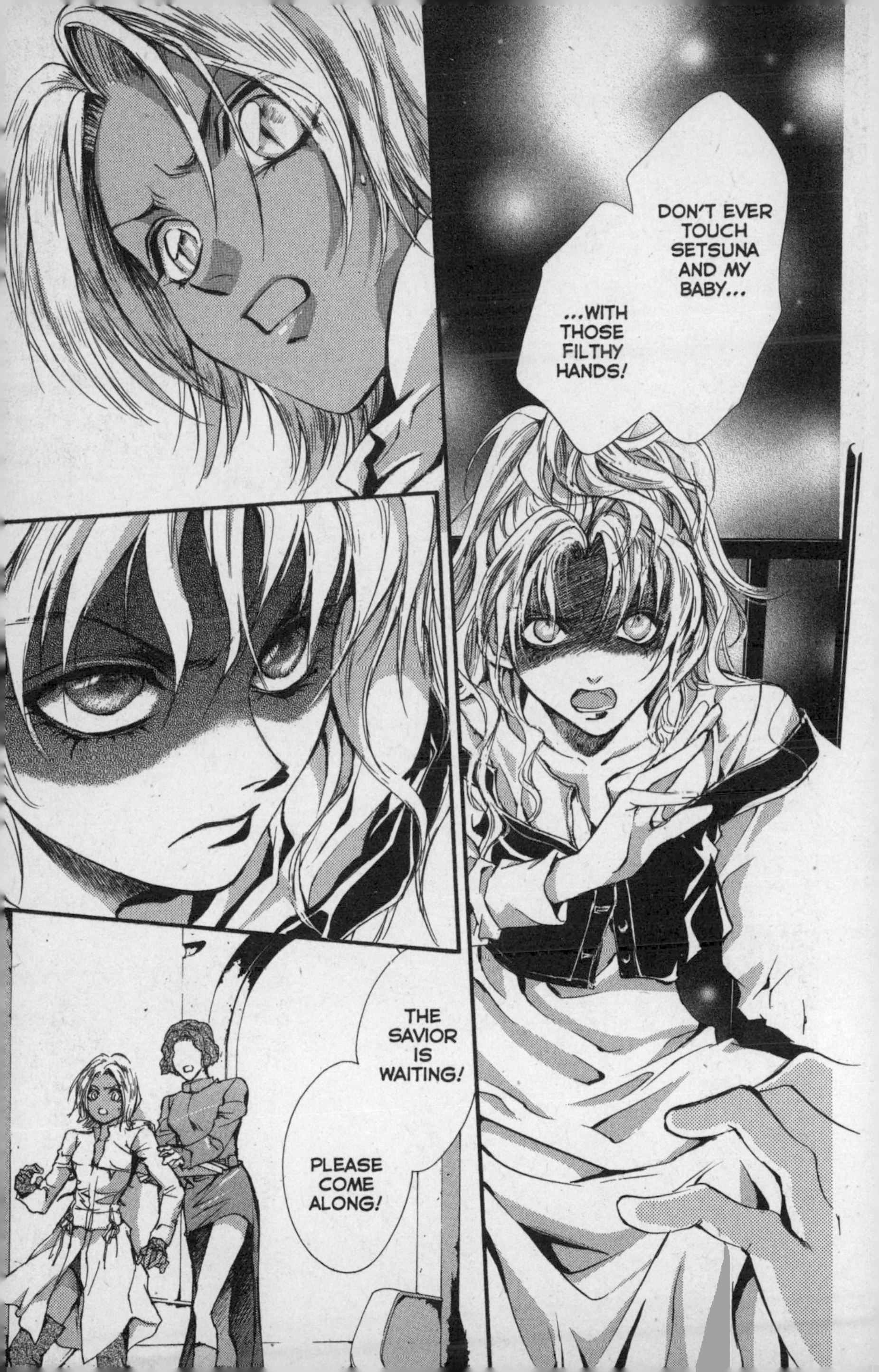
DON'T EVER TOUCH SETSUNA AND MY BABY...
...WITH THOSE FILTHY HANDS!
THE SAVIOR IS WAITING!
PLEASE COME ALONG!

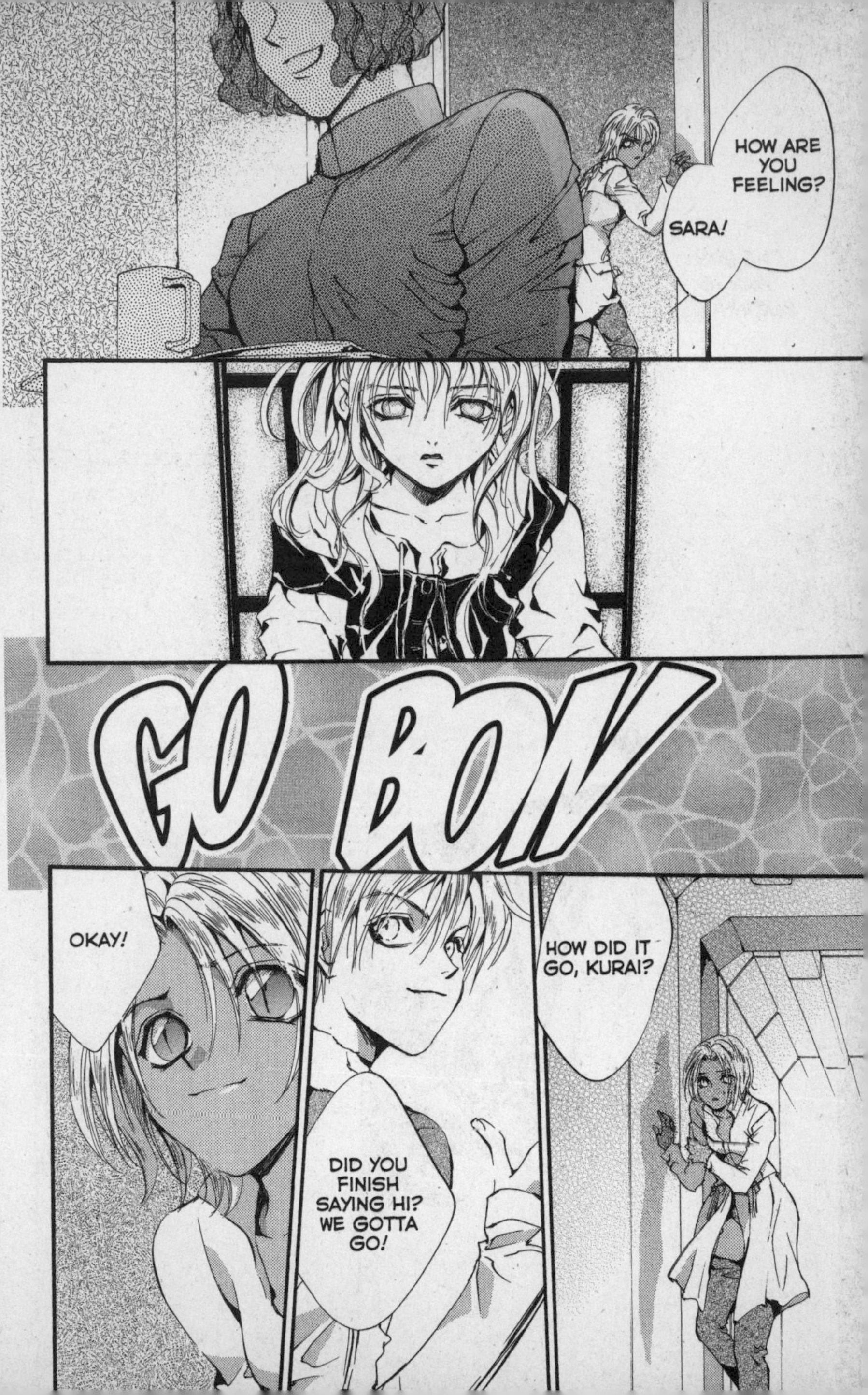
HOW ARE YOU FEELING?
SARA!
GO BON
HOW DID IT GO, KURAI?
DID YOU FINISH SAYING HI? WE GOTTA GO!
OKAY!

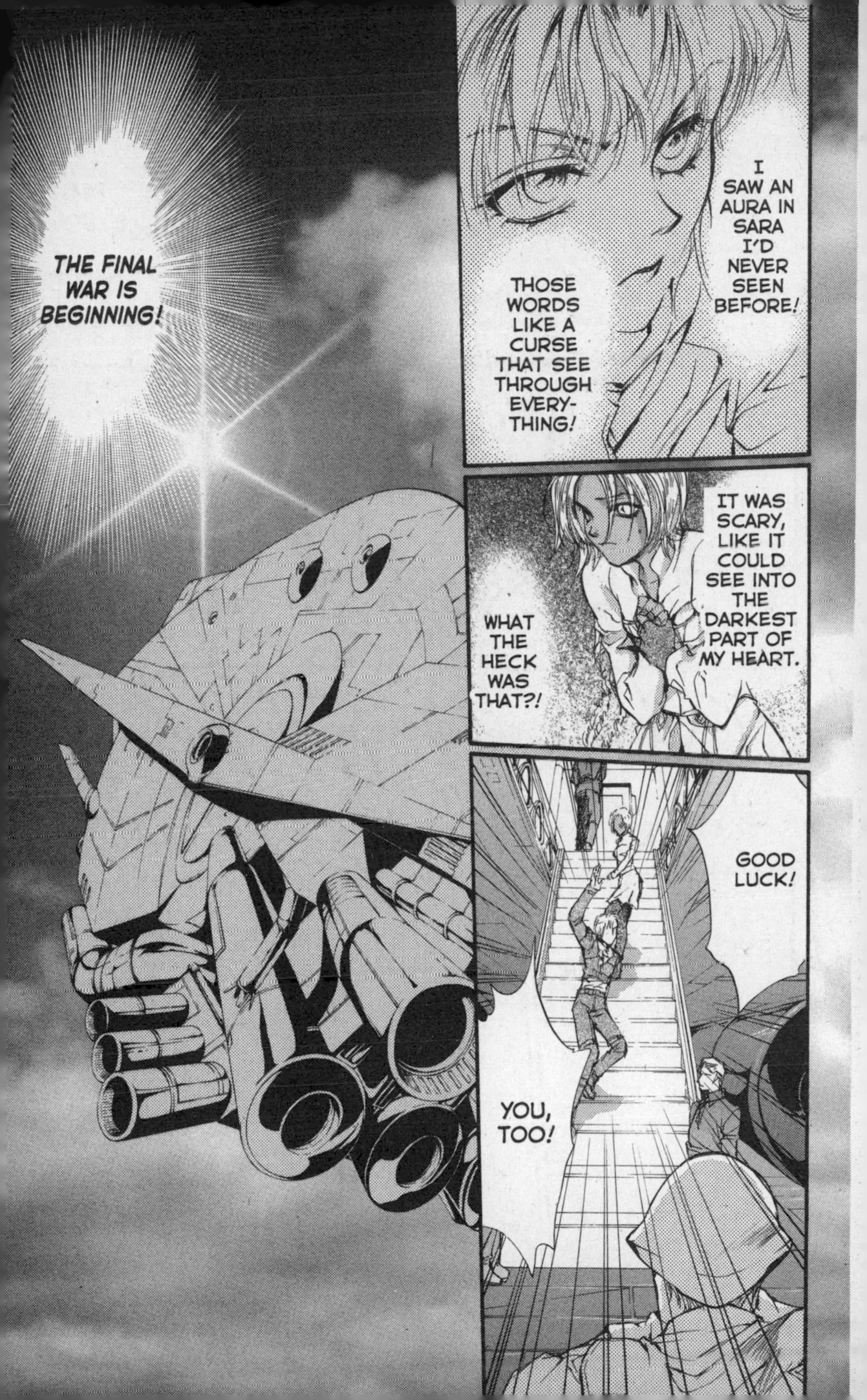
I SAW AN AURA IN SARA I'D NEVER SEEN BEFORE!
THOSE WORDS LIKE A CURSE THAT SEE THROUGH EVERY-THING!
IT WAS SCARY, LIKE IT COULD SEE INTO THE DARKEST PART OF MY HEART.
WHAT THE HECK WAS THAT?!
GOOD LUCK!
YOU, TOO!
THE FINAL WAR IS BEGINNING!

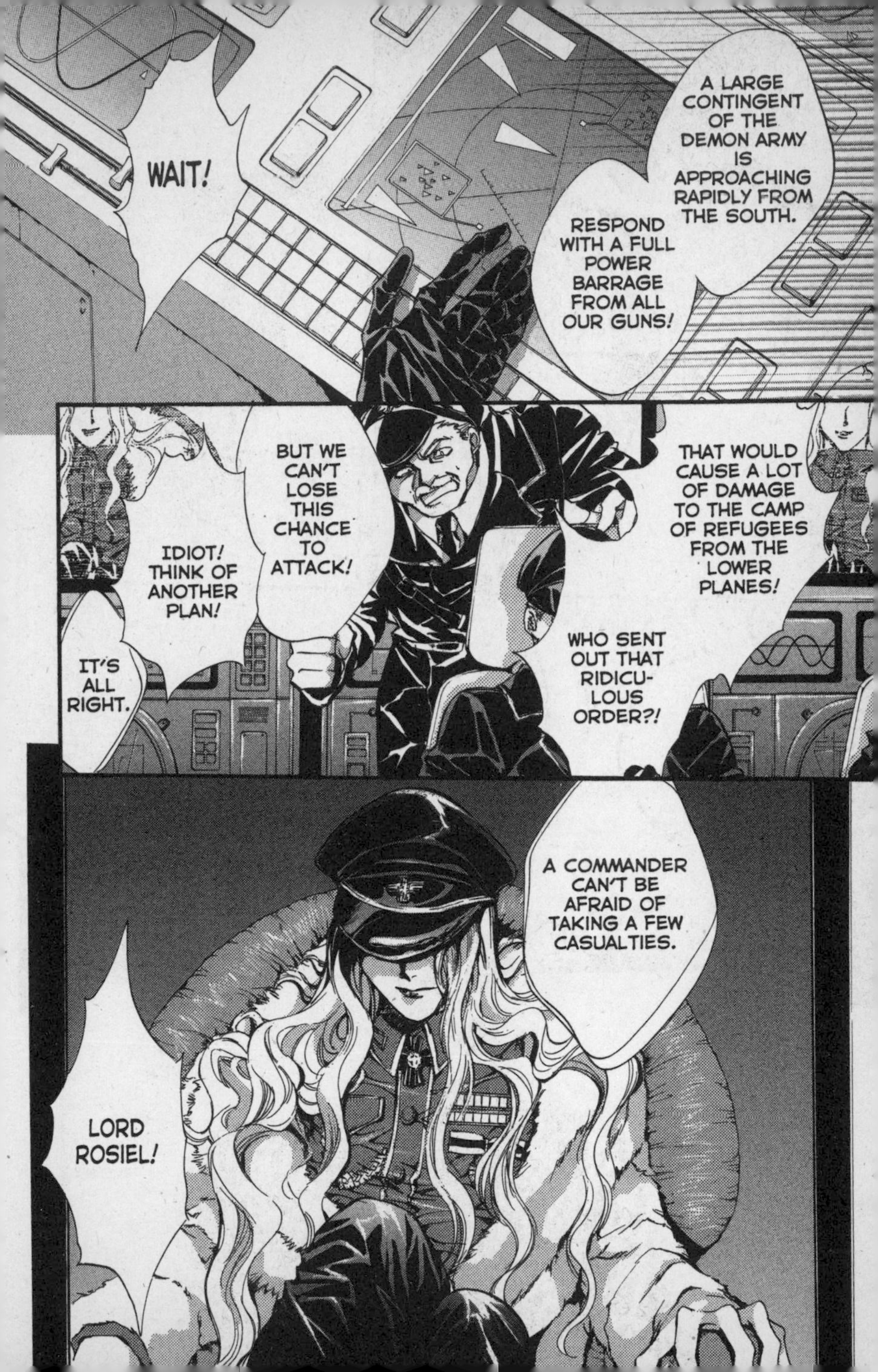
A LARGE CONTINGENT OF THE DEMON ARMY IS APPROACHING RAPIDLY FROM THE SOUTH.
RESPOND WITH A FULL POWER BARRAGE FROM ALL OUR GUNS!
WAIT!
THAT WOULD CAUSE A LOT OF DAMAGE TO THE CAMP OF REFUGEES FROM THE LOWER PLANES!
BUT WE CAN'T LOSE THIS CHANCE TO ATTACK!
IDIOT! THINK OF ANOTHER PLAN!
WHO SENT OUT THAT RIDICU-LOUS ORDER?!
IT'S ALL RIGHT.
A COMMANDER CAN'T BE AFRAID OF TAKING A FEW CASUALTIES.
LORD ROSIEL!

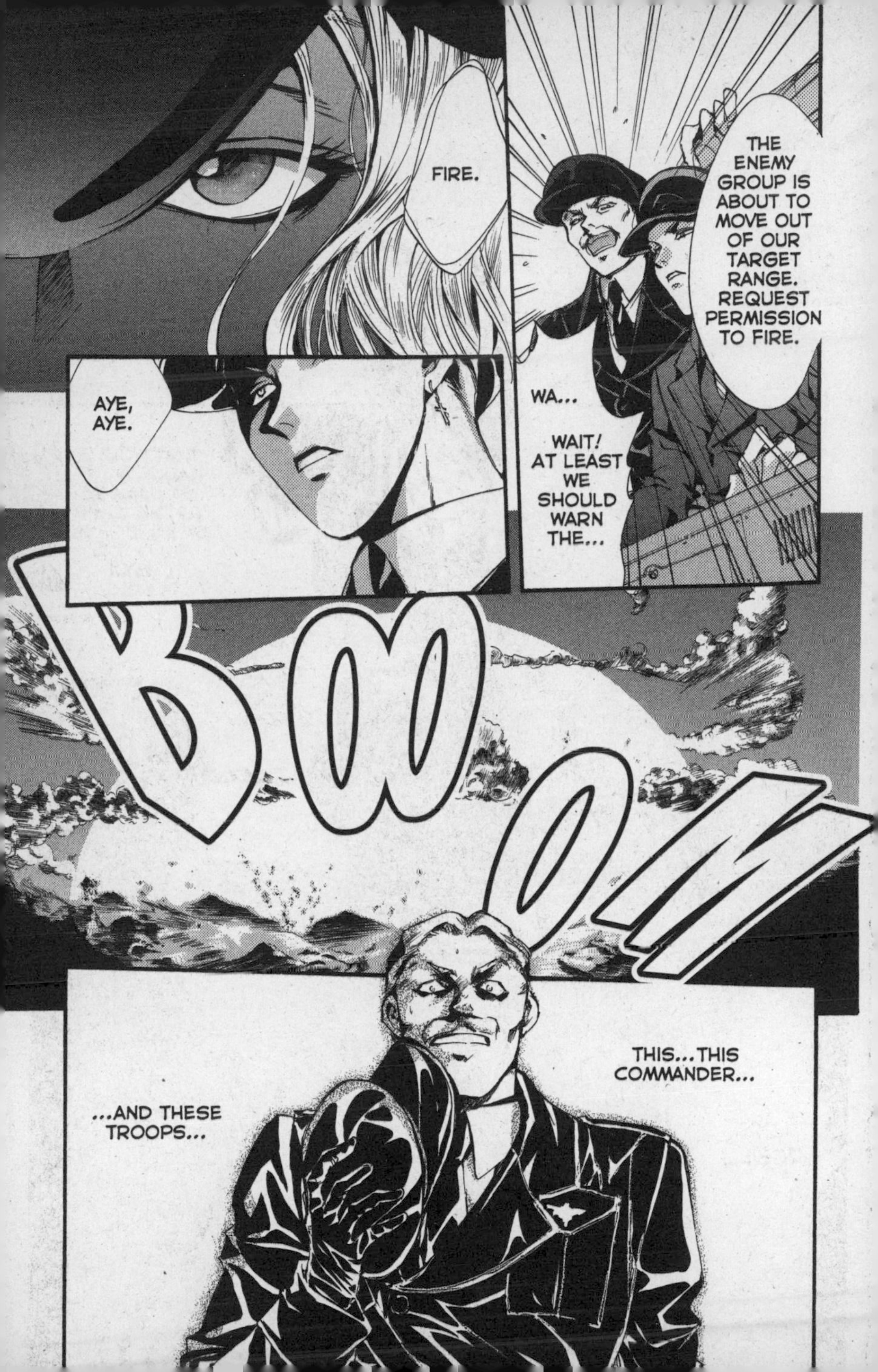
THE ENEMY GROUP IS ABOUT TO MOVE OUT OF OUR TARGET RANGE. REQUEST PERMISSION TO FIRE.
WA...
WAIT! AT LEAST WE SHOULD WARN THE...
FIRE.
AYE, AYE.
BOOOM
THIS...THIS COMMANDER...
...AND THESE TROOPS...

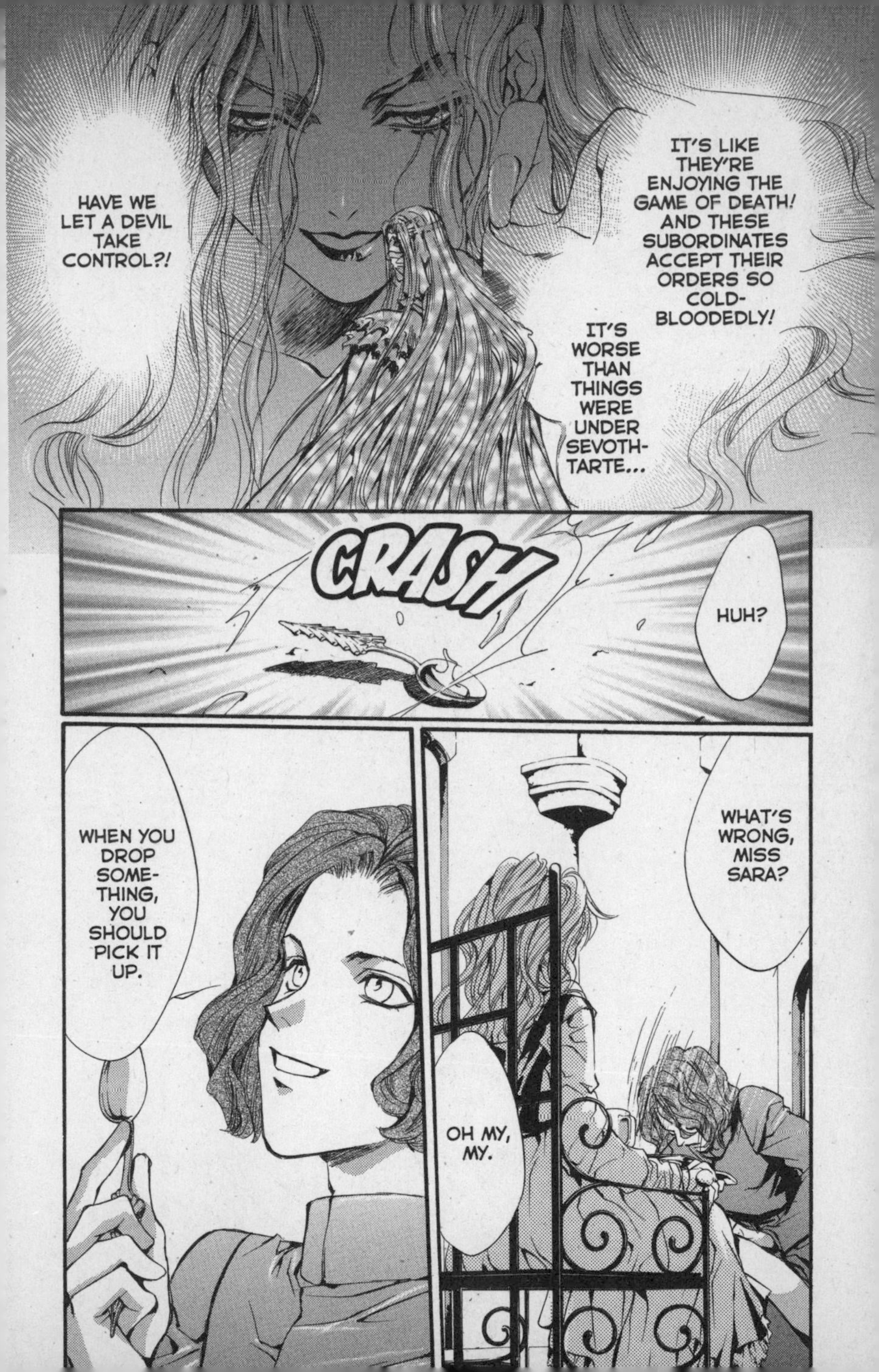
IT'S LIKE THEY'RE ENJOYING THE GAME OF DEATH! AND THESE SUBORDINATES ACCEPT THEIR ORDERS SO COLD-BLOODEDLY!
IT'S WORSE THAN THINGS WERE UNDER SEVOTH-TARTE...
HAVE WE LET A DEVIL TAKE CONTROL?!
CRASH
HUH?
WHAT'S WRONG, MISS SARA?
OH MY, MY.
WHEN YOU DROP SOME-THING, YOU SHOULD PICK IT UP.

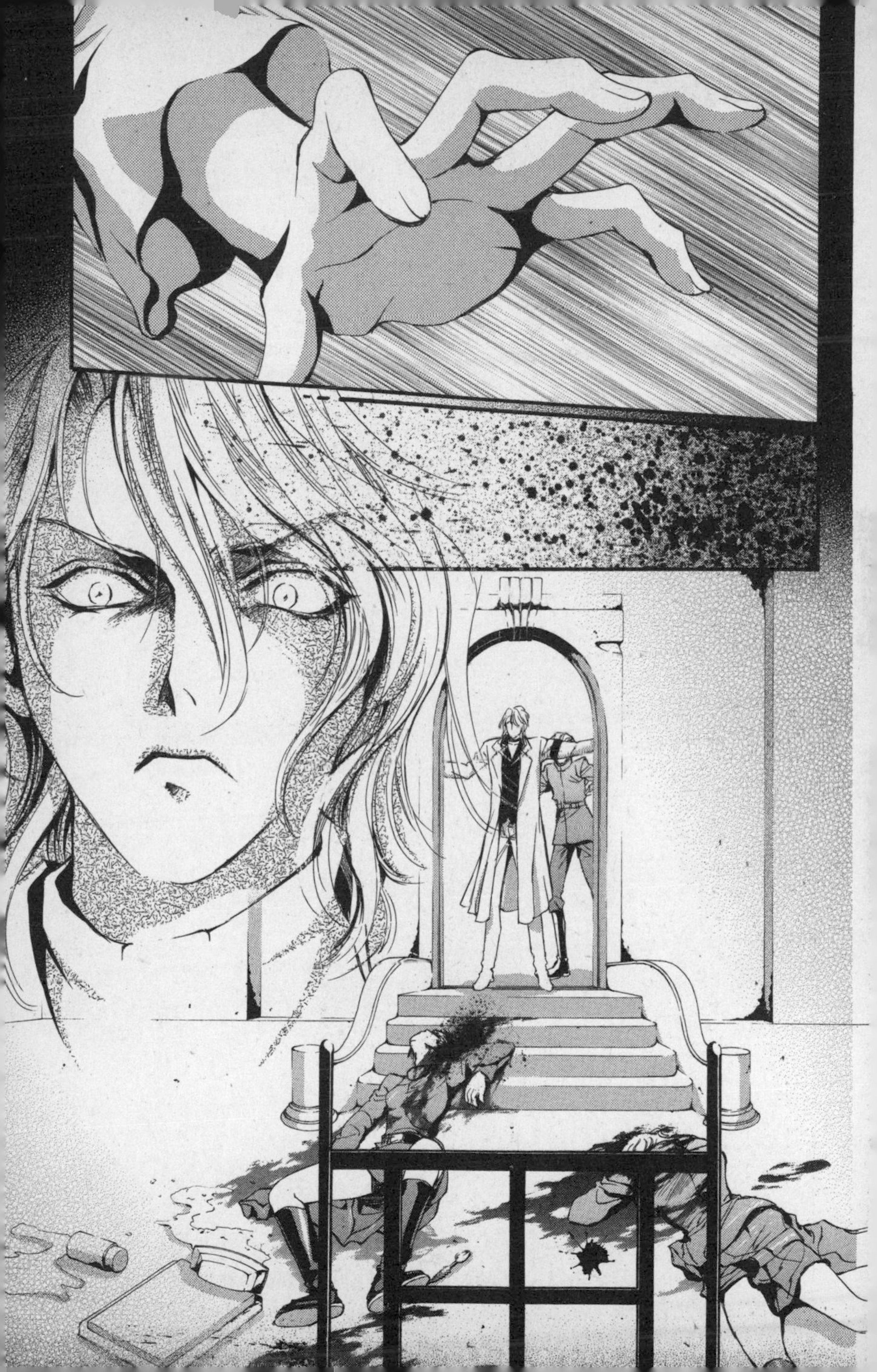

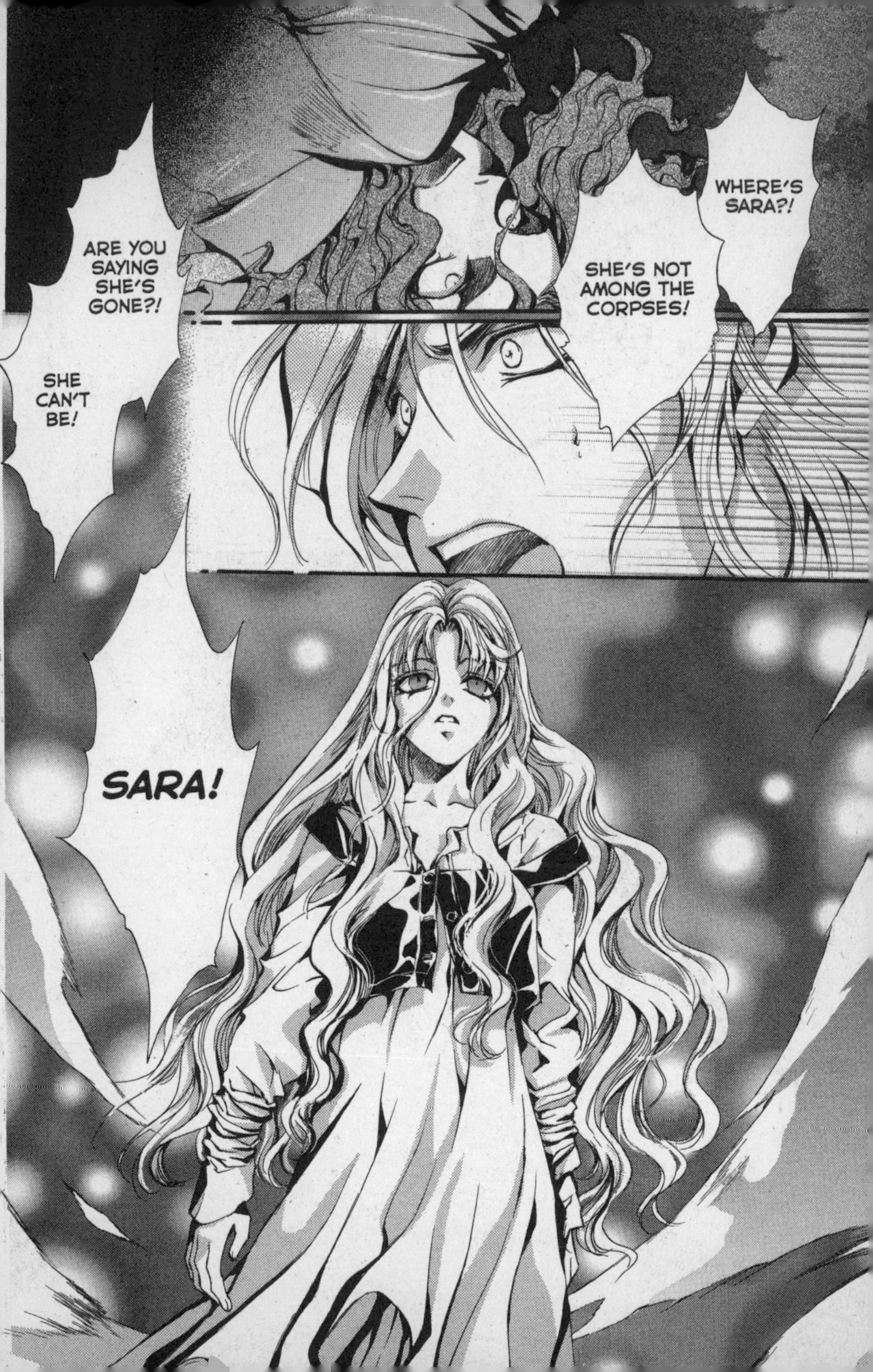
WHERE'S SARA?!
SHE'S NOT AMONG THE CORPSES!
ARE YOU SAYING SHE'S GONE?!
SHE CAN'T BE!
SARA!

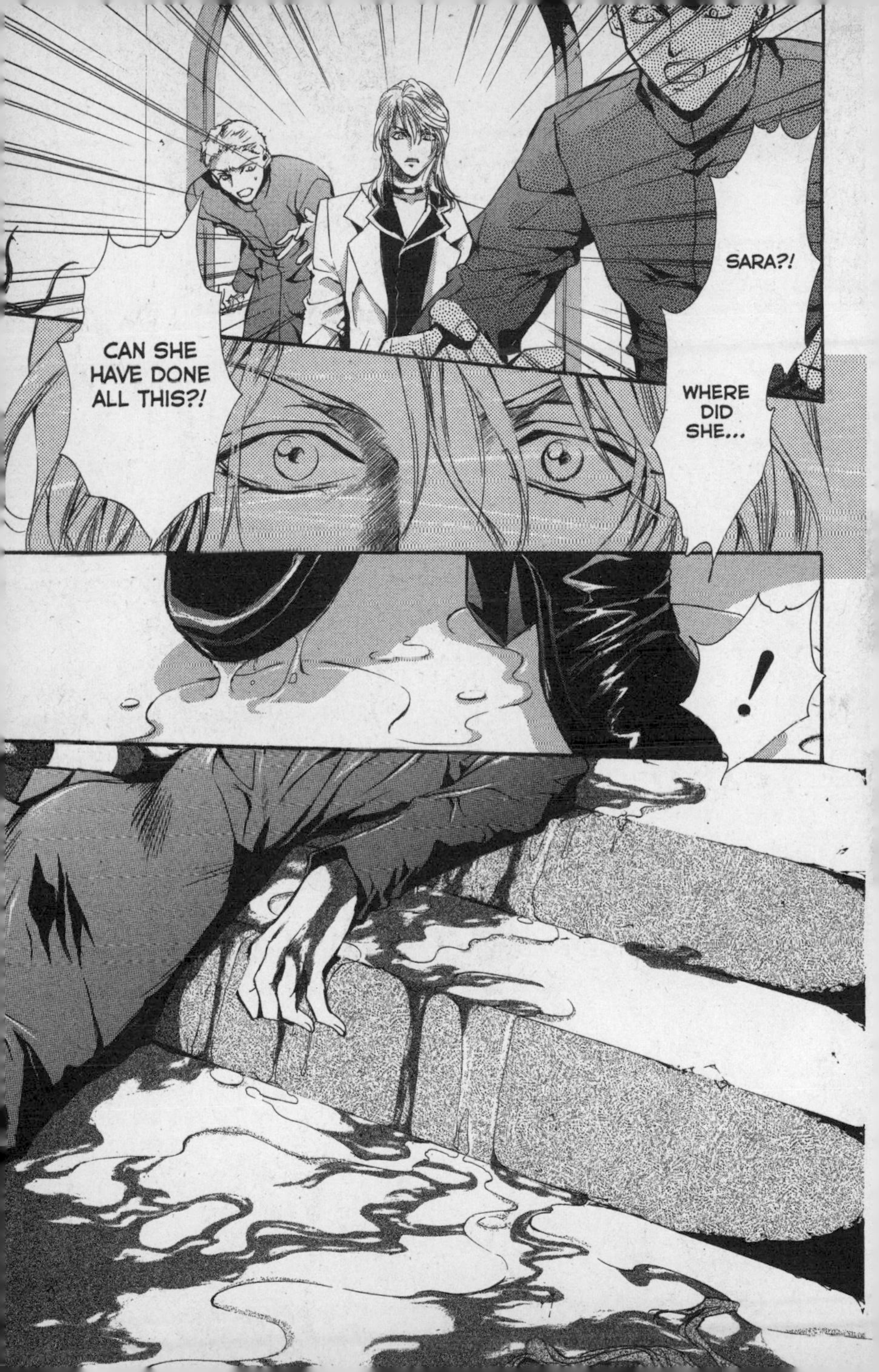
SARA?!
CAN SHE HAVE DONE ALL THIS?!
WHERE DID SHE...
!

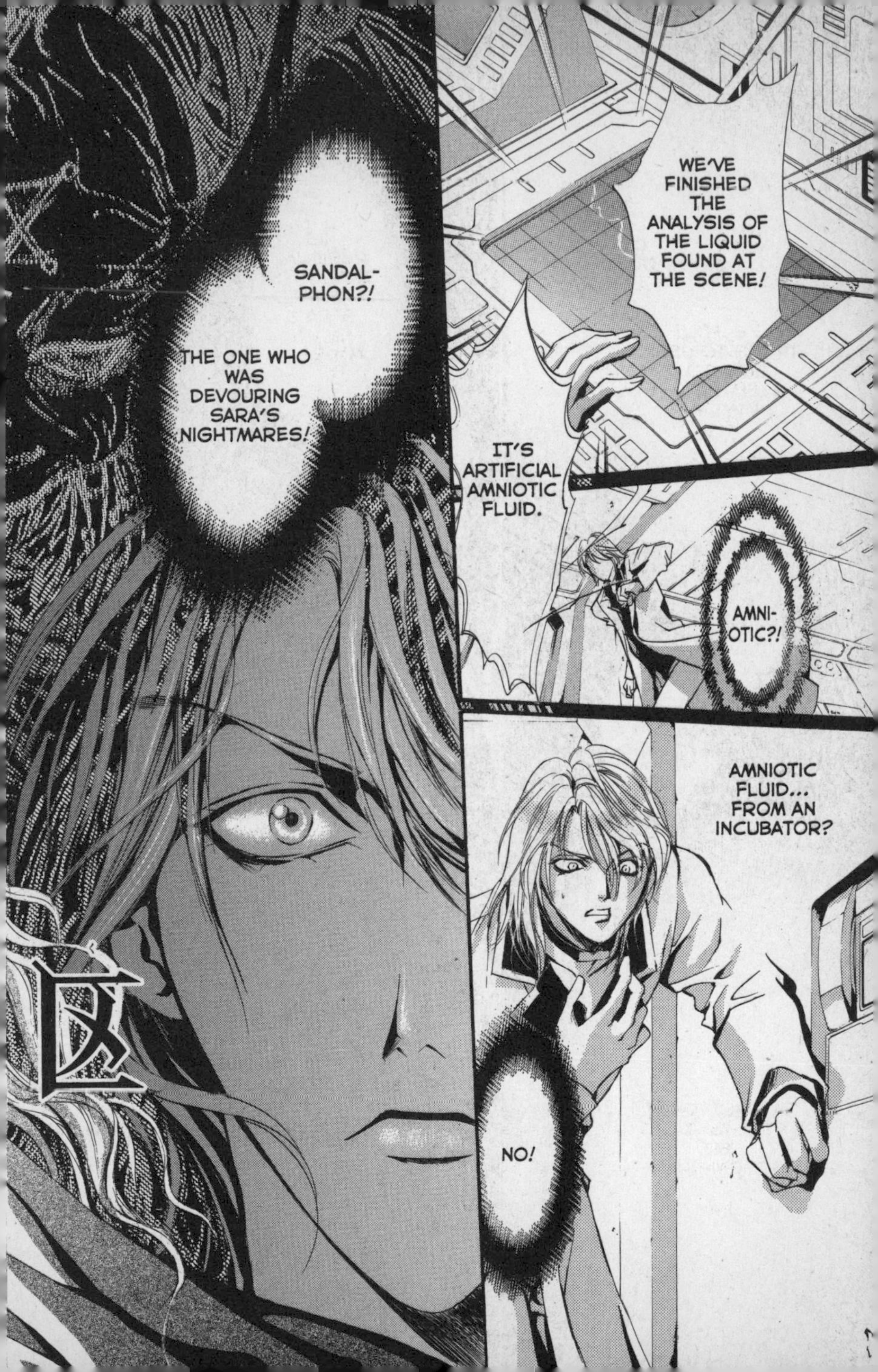
WE'VE FINISHED THE ANALYSIS OF THE LIQUID FOUND AT THE SCENE!
IT'S ARTIFICIAL AMNIOTIC FLUID.
AMNI-OTIC?!
AMNIOTIC FLUID... FROM AN INCUBATOR?
NO!
SANDAL-PHON?!
THE ONE WHO WAS DEVOURING SARA'S NIGHTMARES!

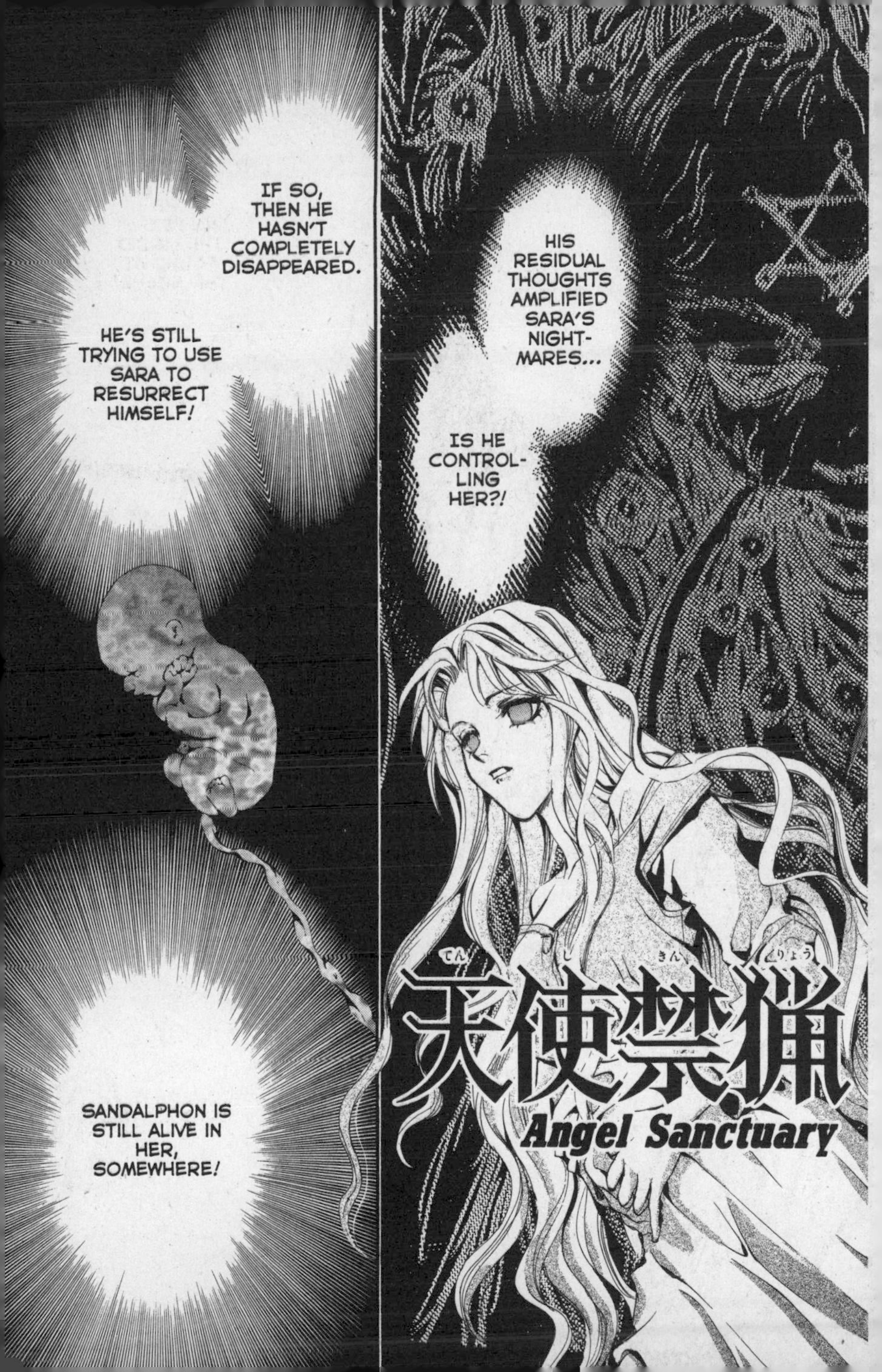
HIS RESIDUAL THOUGHTS AMPLIFIED SARA'S NIGHTMARES...
IS HE CONTROLLING HER?!
天使禁猟
Angel Sanctuary
IF SO, THEN HE HASN'T COMPLETELY DISAPPEARED.
HE'S STILL TRYING TO USE SARA TO RESURRECT HIMSELF!
SANDALPHON IS STILL ALIVE IN HER, SOMEWHERE!

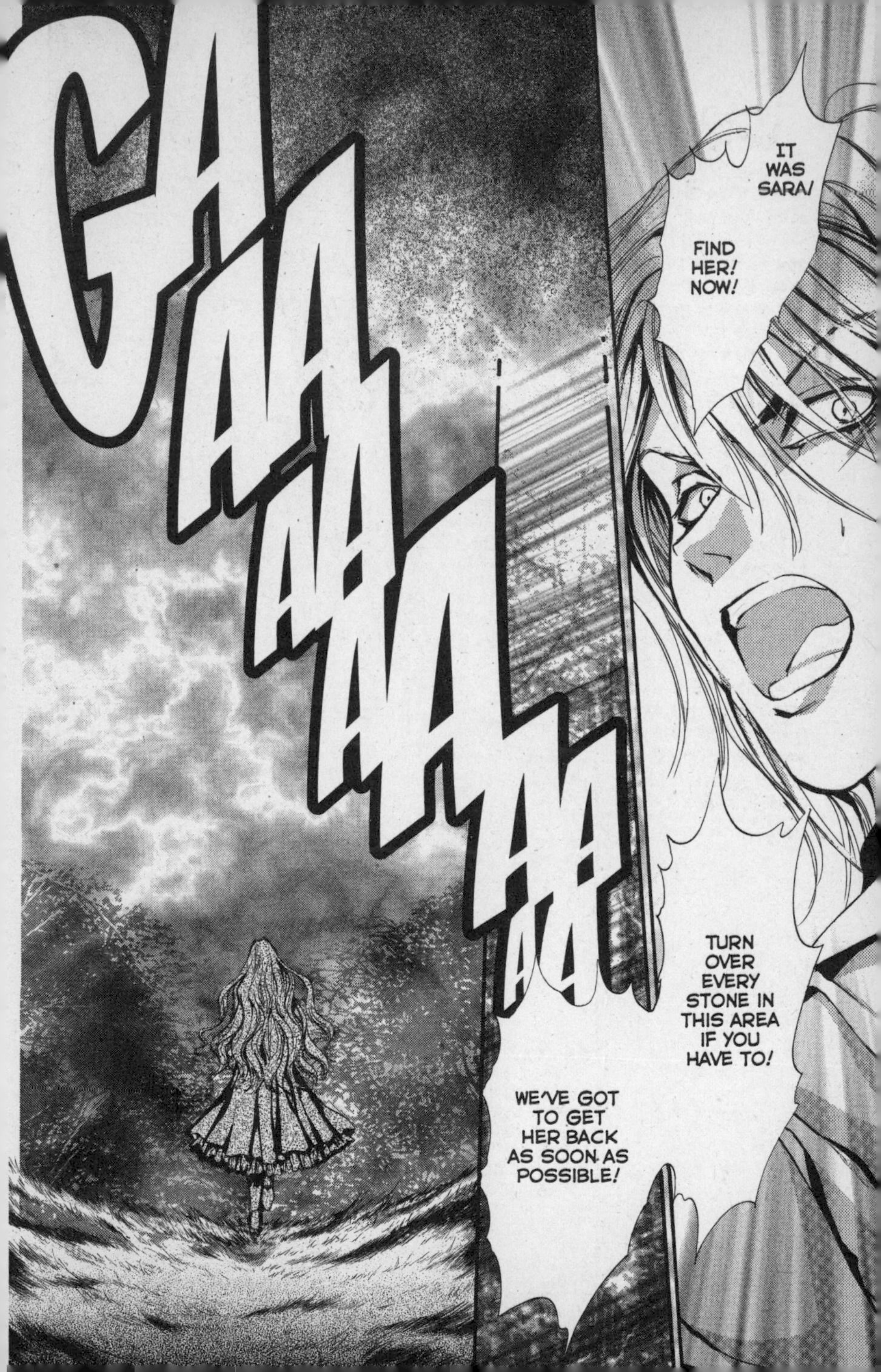
IT WAS SARA!
FIND HER! NOW!
TURN OVER EVERY STONE IN THIS AREA IF YOU HAVE TO!
WE'VE GOT TO GET HER BACK AS SOON AS POSSIBLE!
GAAAAAAA

When I was drawing Kato's mechanical arm, I was reminded of Tetsuo in "Akira." A long time ago, I was commenting about "Akira" on television, and said, "it was incredible when Akira grew into a giant blob!" But it wasn't Akira who did that, it was Tetsuo. I also thought of the mechanical arm scene in "Terminator 2," although that had a totally different feel to it. I wish I'd drawn mine to look a little brawnier...oh well. It's already done. Now the 12 Angels of the Zodiac have appeared. I can't design that many characters! I had always wanted to use them somewhere. I'm still reflecting on how I'll use them from here.

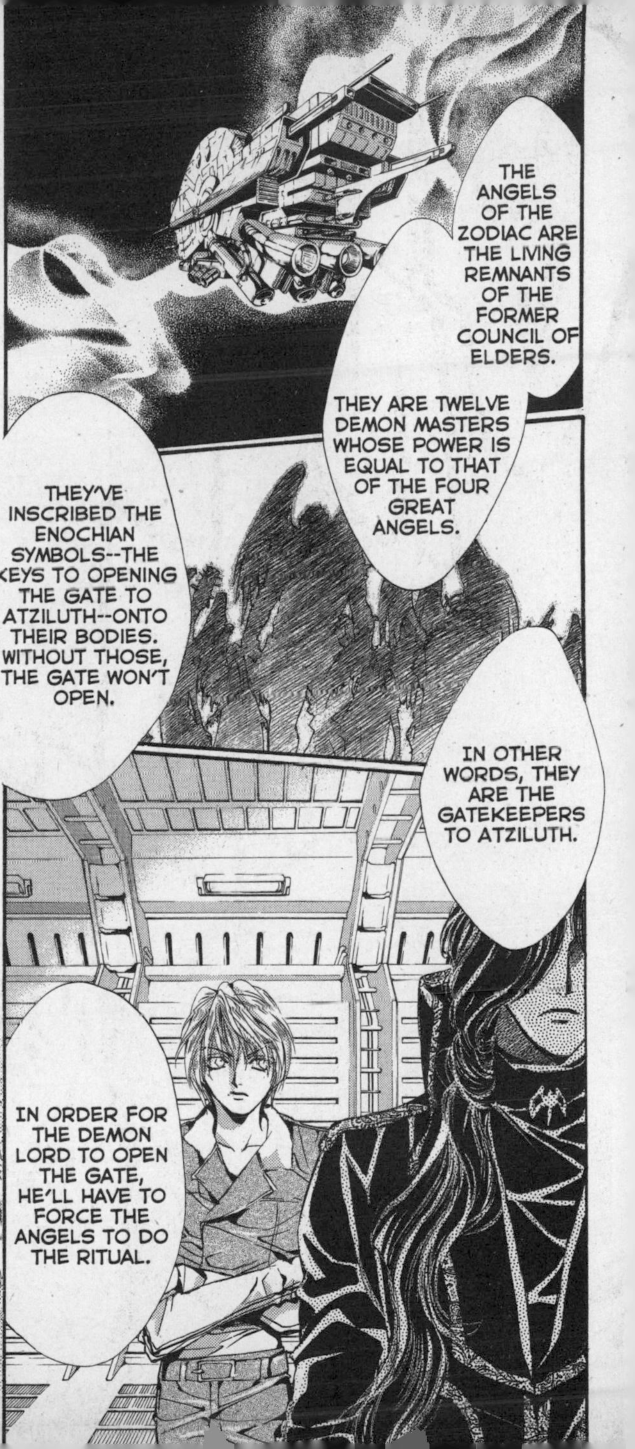
THE ANGELS OF THE ZODIAC ARE THE LIVING REMNANTS OF THE FORMER COUNCIL OF ELDERS.
THEY ARE TWELVE DEMON MASTERS WHOSE POWER IS EQUAL TO THAT OF THE FOUR GREAT ANGELS.
THEY'VE INSCRIBED THE ENOCHIAN SYMBOLS--THE KEYS TO OPENING THE GATE TO ATZILUTH--ONTO THEIR BODIES. WITHOUT THOSE, THE GATE WON'T OPEN.
IN OTHER WORDS, THEY ARE THE GATEKEEPERS TO ATZILUTH.
IN ORDER FOR THE DEMON LORD TO OPEN THE GATE, HE'LL HAVE TO FORCE THE ANGELS TO DO THE RITUAL.

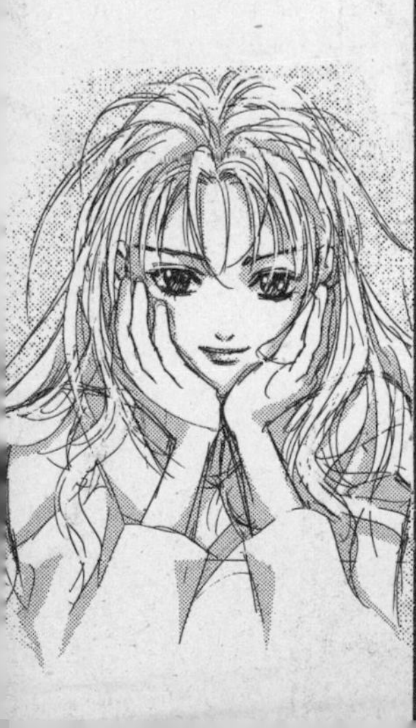

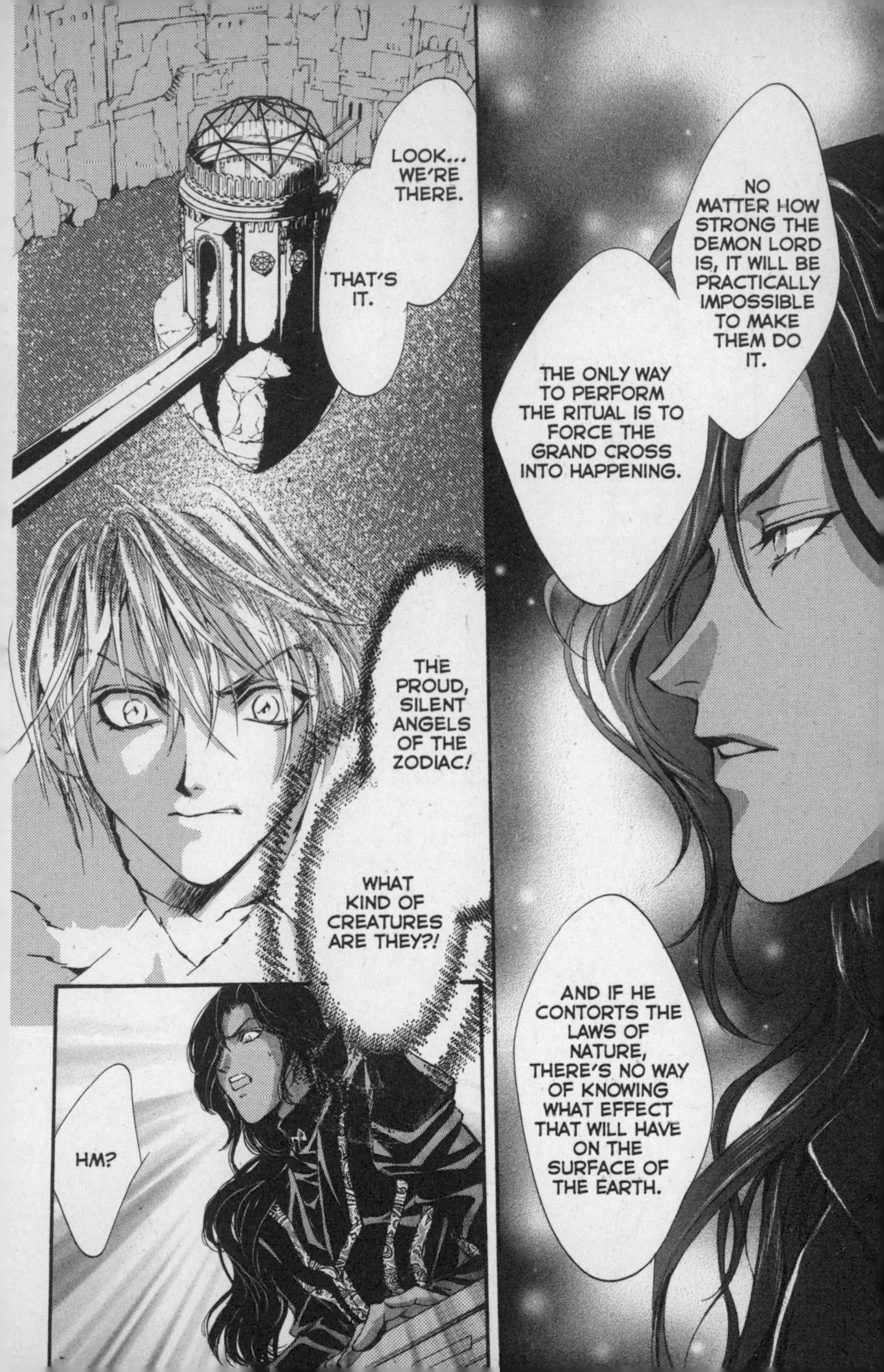
NO MATTER HOW STRONG THE DEMON LORD IS, IT WILL BE PRACTICALLY IMPOSSIBLE TO MAKE THEM DO IT.
THE ONLY WAY TO PERFORM THE RITUAL IS TO FORCE THE GRAND CROSS INTO HAPPENING.
AND IF HE CONTORTS THE LAWS OF NATURE, THERE'S NO WAY OF KNOWING WHAT EFFECT THAT WILL HAVE ON THE SURFACE OF THE EARTH.
LOOK... WE'RE THERE.
THAT'S IT.
THE PROUD, SILENT ANGELS OF THE ZODIAC!
WHAT KIND OF CREATURES ARE THEY?!
HM?

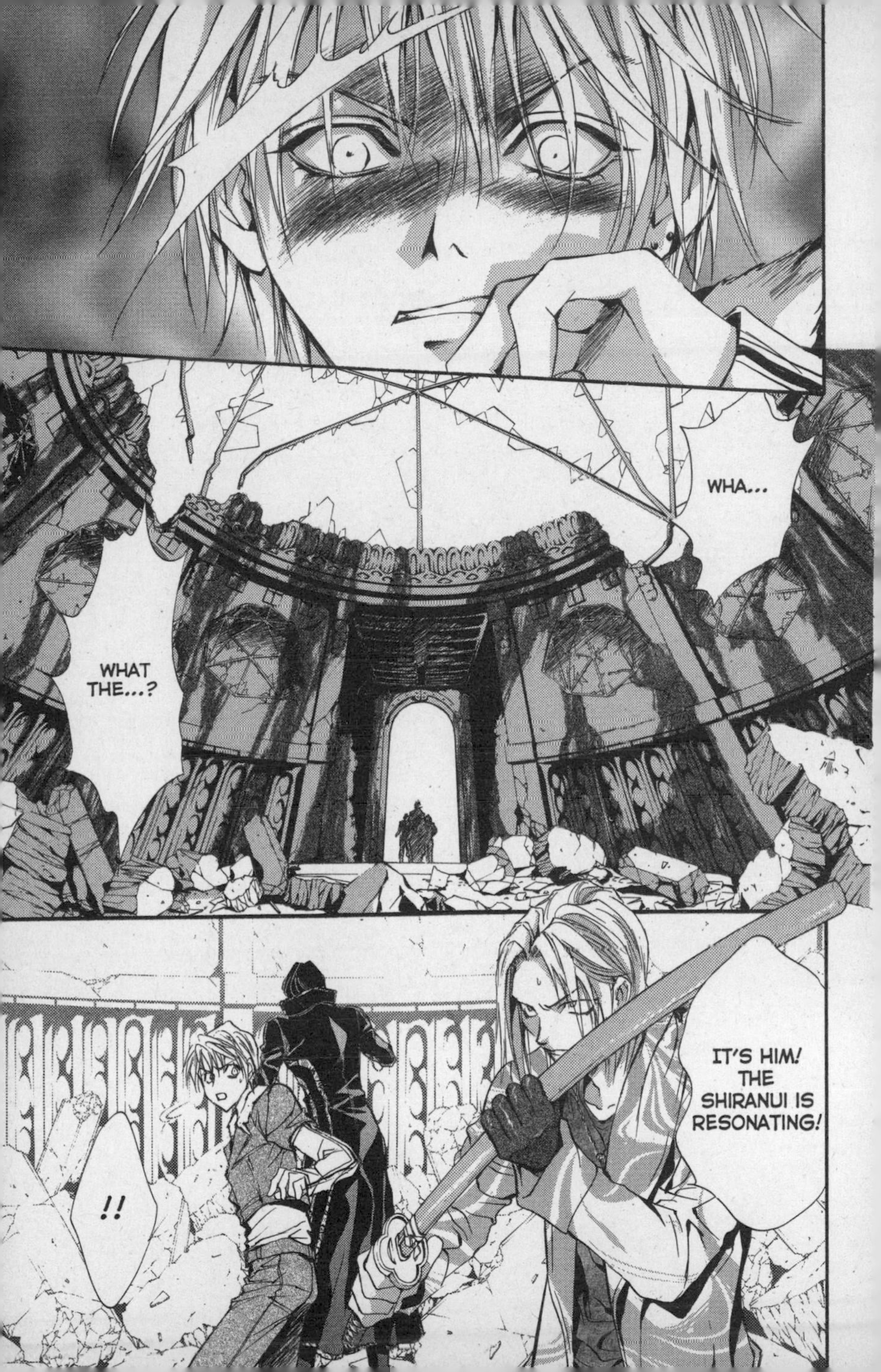
WHA...
WHAT THE...?
IT'S HIM! THE SHIRANUI IS RESONATING!
!!

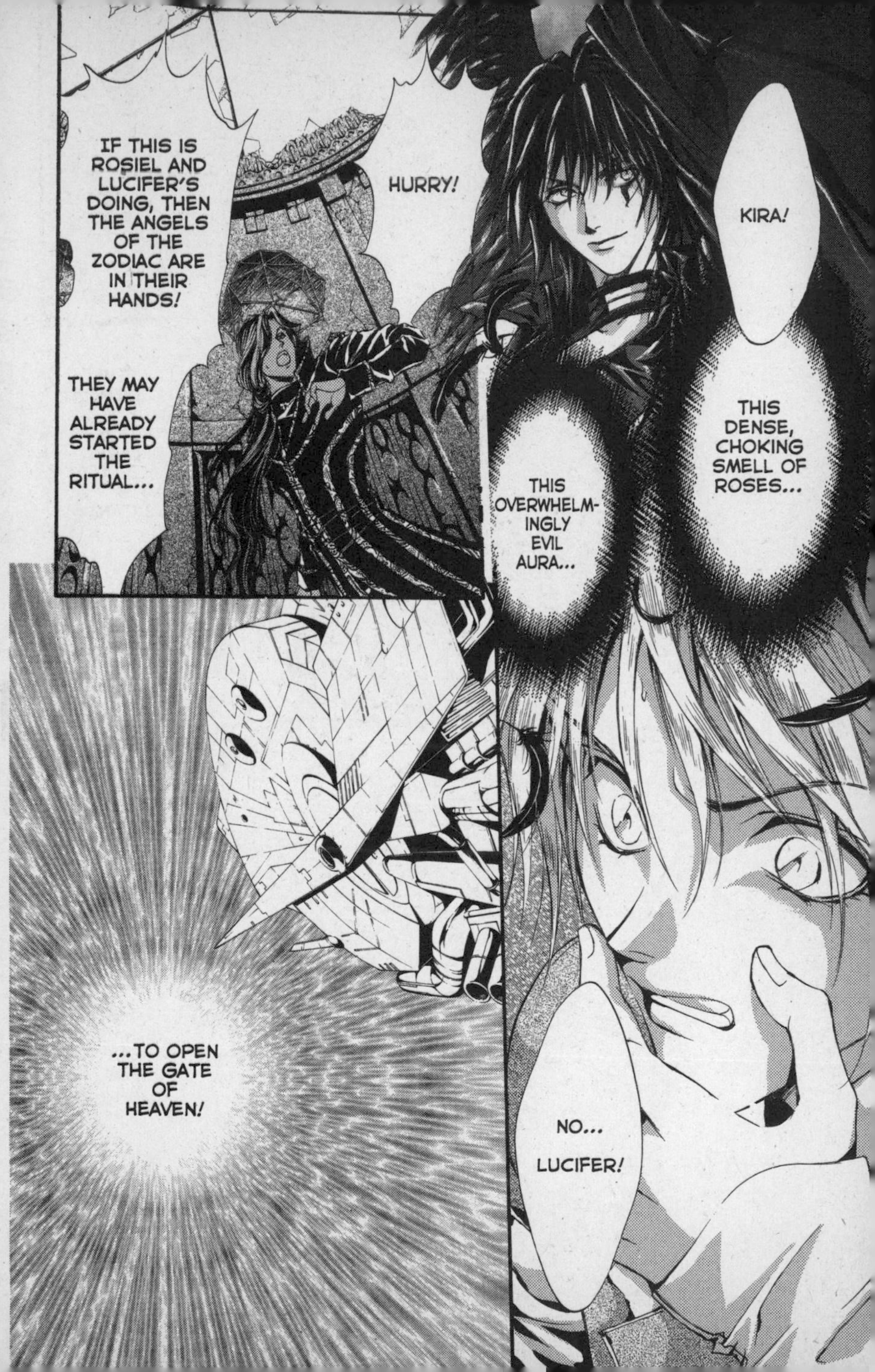
KIRA!
THIS DENSE, CHOKING SMELL OF ROSES...
THIS OVERWHELMINGLY EVIL AURA...
IF THIS IS ROSIEL AND LUCIFER'S DOING, THEN THE ANGELS OF THE ZODIAC ARE IN THEIR HANDS!
HURRY!
THEY MAY HAVE ALREADY STARTED THE RITUAL...
NO... LUCIFER!
...TO OPEN THE GATE OF HEAVEN!

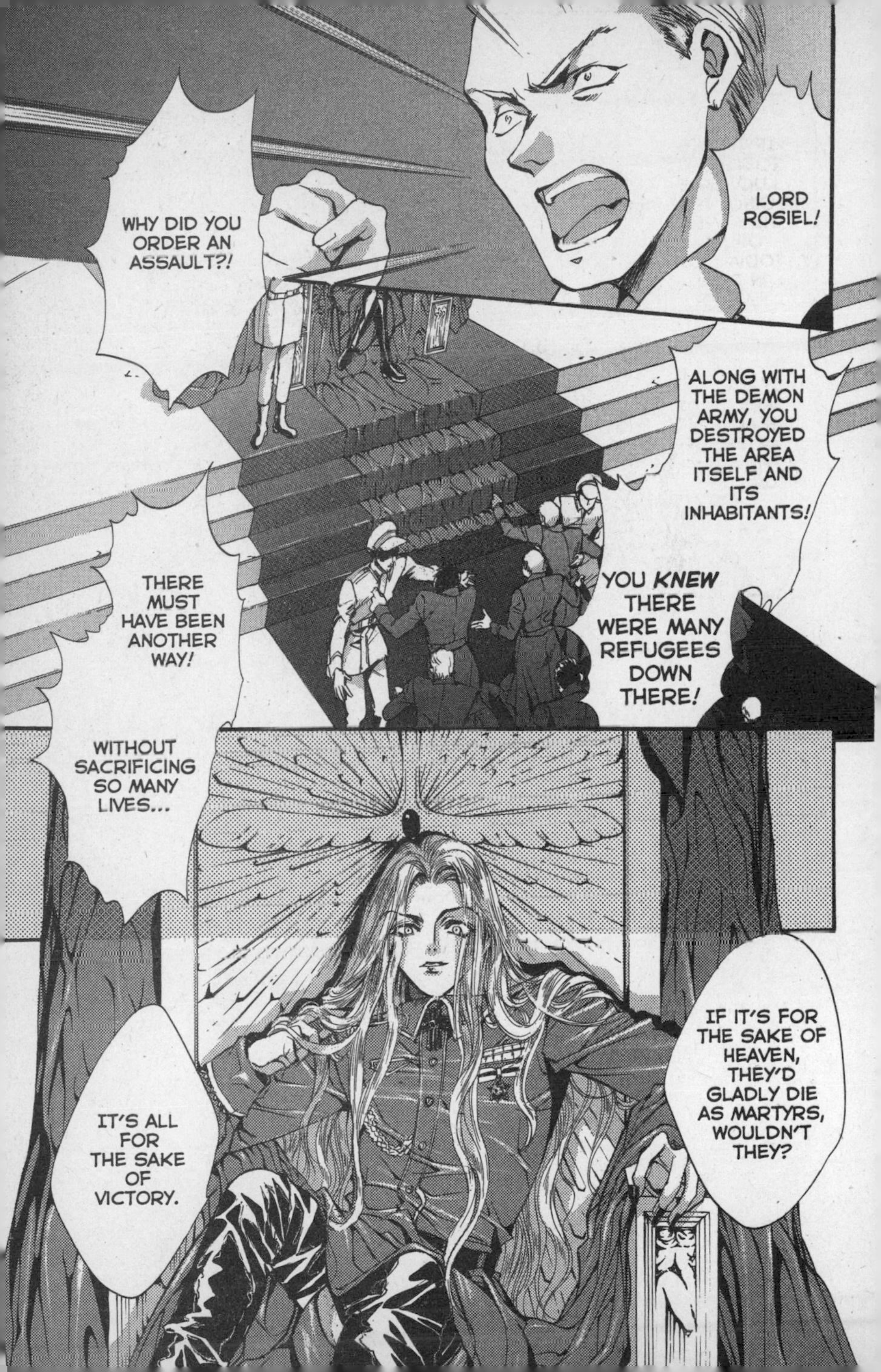
LORD ROSIEL!
WHY DID YOU ORDER AN ASSAULT?!
ALONG WITH THE DEMON ARMY, YOU DESTROYED THE AREA ITSELF AND ITS INHABITANTS!
YOU *KNEW* THERE WERE MANY REFUGEES DOWN THERE!
THERE MUST HAVE BEEN ANOTHER WAY!
WITHOUT SACRIFICING SO MANY LIVES...
IF IT'S FOR THE SAKE OF HEAVEN, THEY'D GLADLY DIE AS MARTYRS, WOULDN'T THEY?
IT'S ALL FOR THE SAKE OF VICTORY.

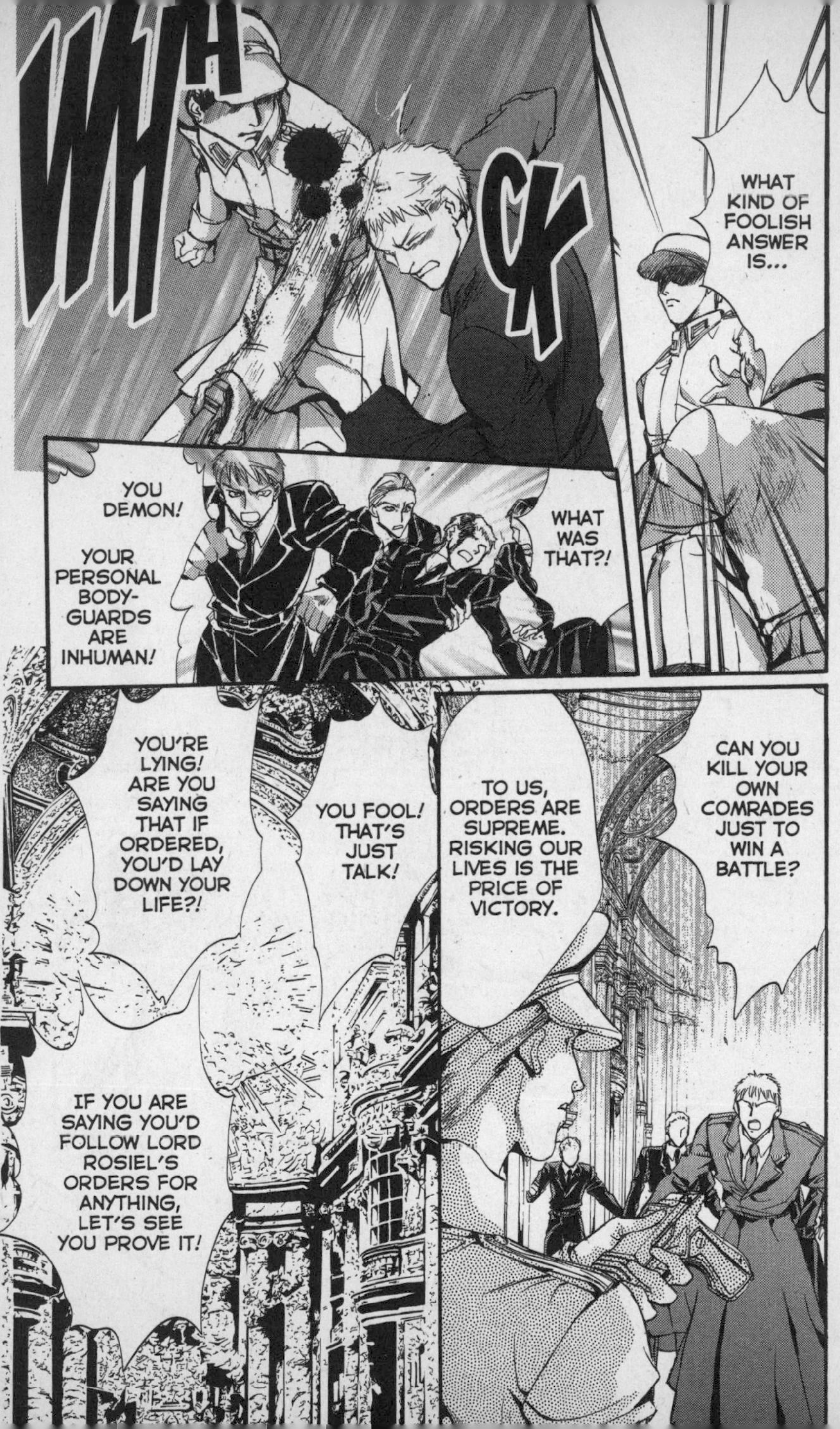
WHAT KIND OF FOOLISH ANSWER IS...
WHA
CK
WHAT WAS THAT?!
YOU DEMON!
YOUR PERSONAL BODY-GUARDS ARE INHUMAN!
CAN YOU KILL YOUR OWN COMRADES JUST TO WIN A BATTLE?
TO US, ORDERS ARE SUPREME. RISKING OUR LIVES IS THE PRICE OF VICTORY.
YOU FOOL! THAT'S JUST TALK!
YOU'RE LYING! ARE YOU SAYING THAT IF ORDERED, YOU'D LAY DOWN YOUR LIFE?!
IF YOU ARE SAYING YOU'D FOLLOW LORD ROSIEL'S ORDERS FOR ANYTHING, LET'S SEE YOU PROVE IT!

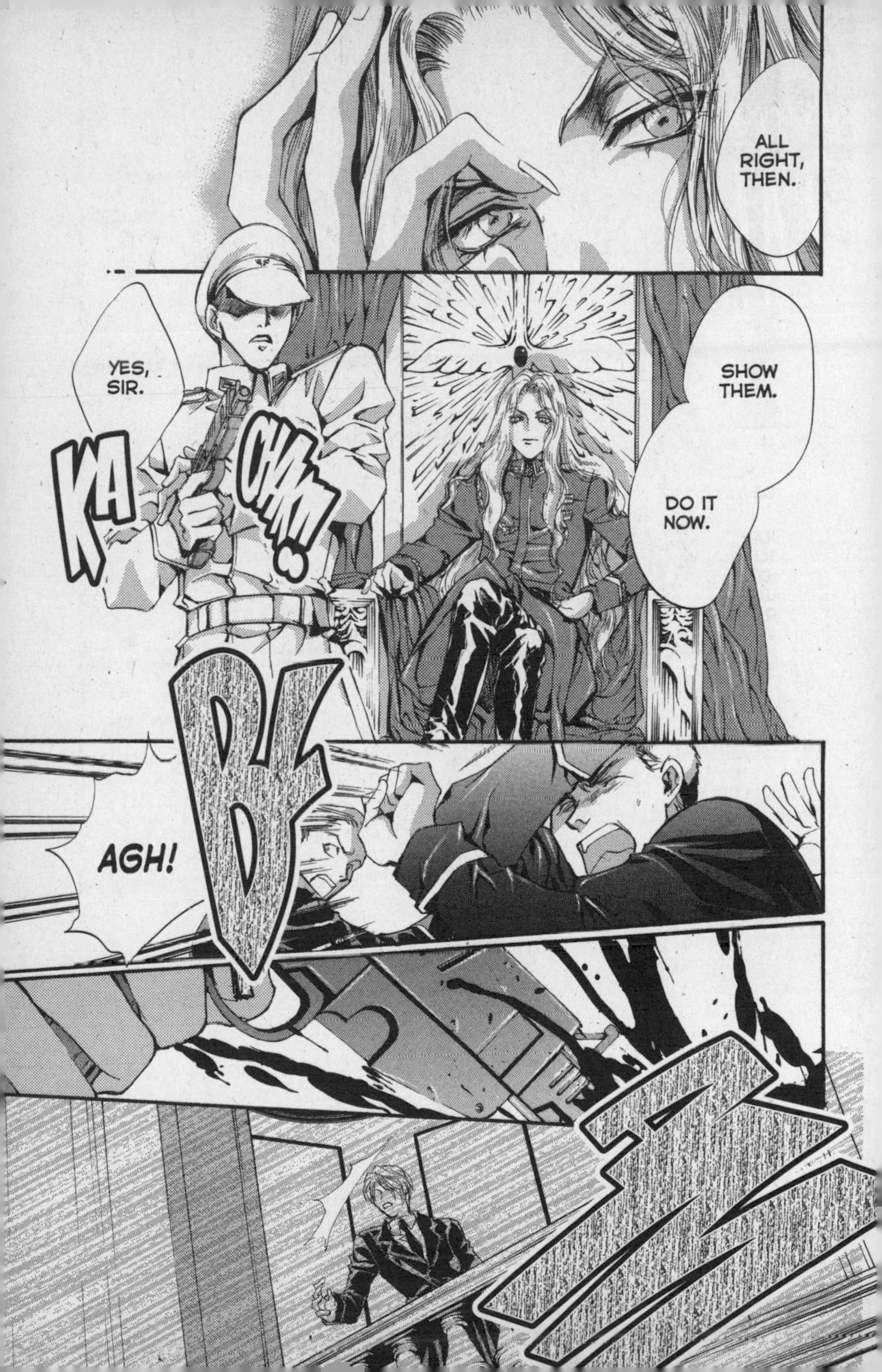
ALL RIGHT, THEN.
SHOW THEM.
DO IT NOW.
YES, SIR.
KA
CHK!
AGH!

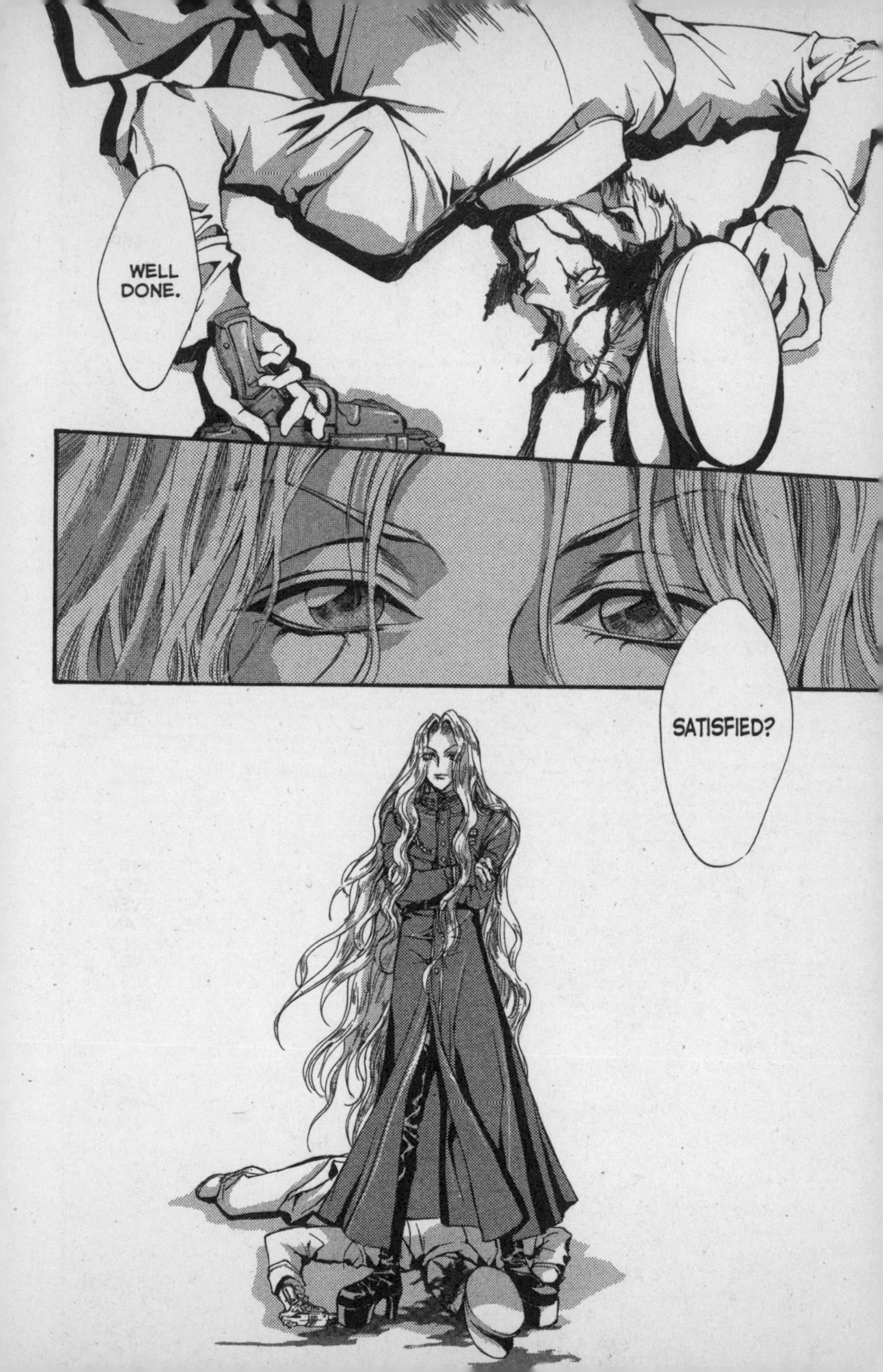
WELL DONE.
SATISFIED?

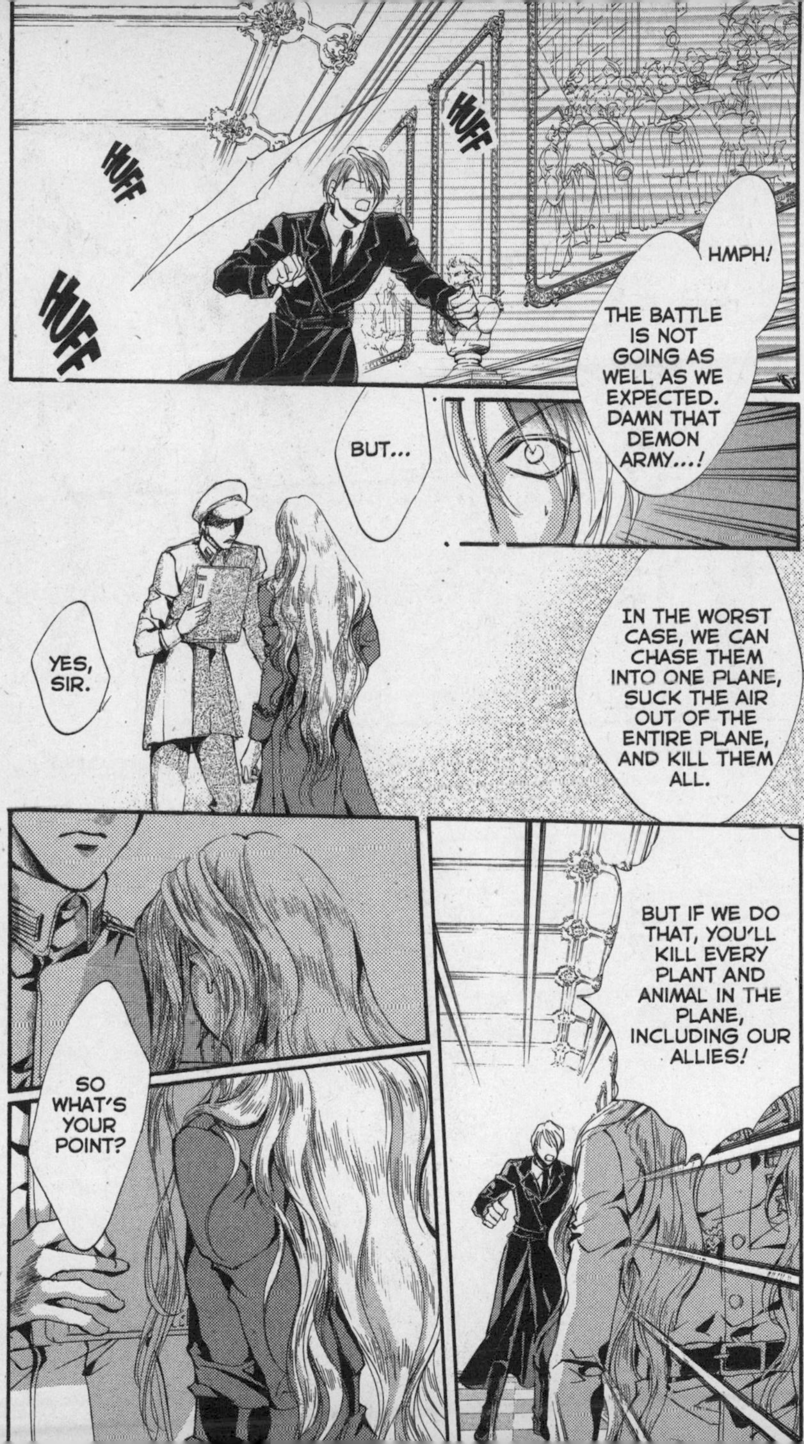
HUFF
HUFF
HUFF
HMPH!
THE BATTLE IS NOT GOING AS WELL AS WE EXPECTED. DAMN THAT DEMON ARMY...!
BUT...
IN THE WORST CASE, WE CAN CHASE THEM INTO ONE PLANE, SUCK THE AIR OUT OF THE ENTIRE PLANE, AND KILL THEM ALL.
YES, SIR.
BUT IF WE DO THAT, YOU'LL KILL EVERY PLANT AND ANIMAL IN THE PLANE, INCLUDING OUR ALLIES!
SO WHAT'S YOUR POINT?

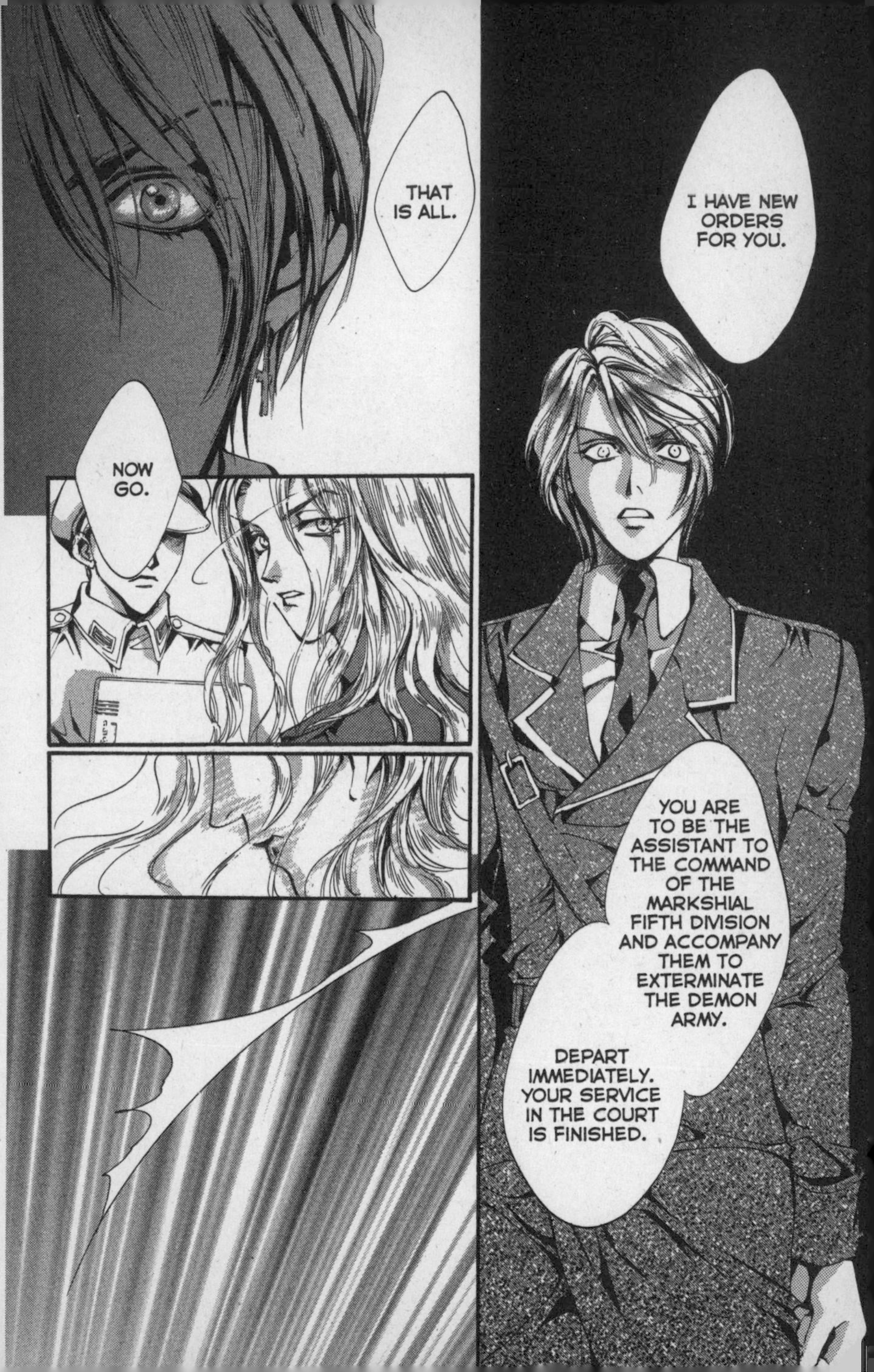
I HAVE NEW ORDERS FOR YOU.
YOU ARE TO BE THE ASSISTANT TO THE COMMAND OF THE MARKSHIAL FIFTH DIVISION AND ACCOMPANY THEM TO EXTERMINATE THE DEMON ARMY.
DEPART IMMEDIATELY. YOUR SERVICE IN THE COURT IS FINISHED.
THAT IS ALL.
NOW GO.

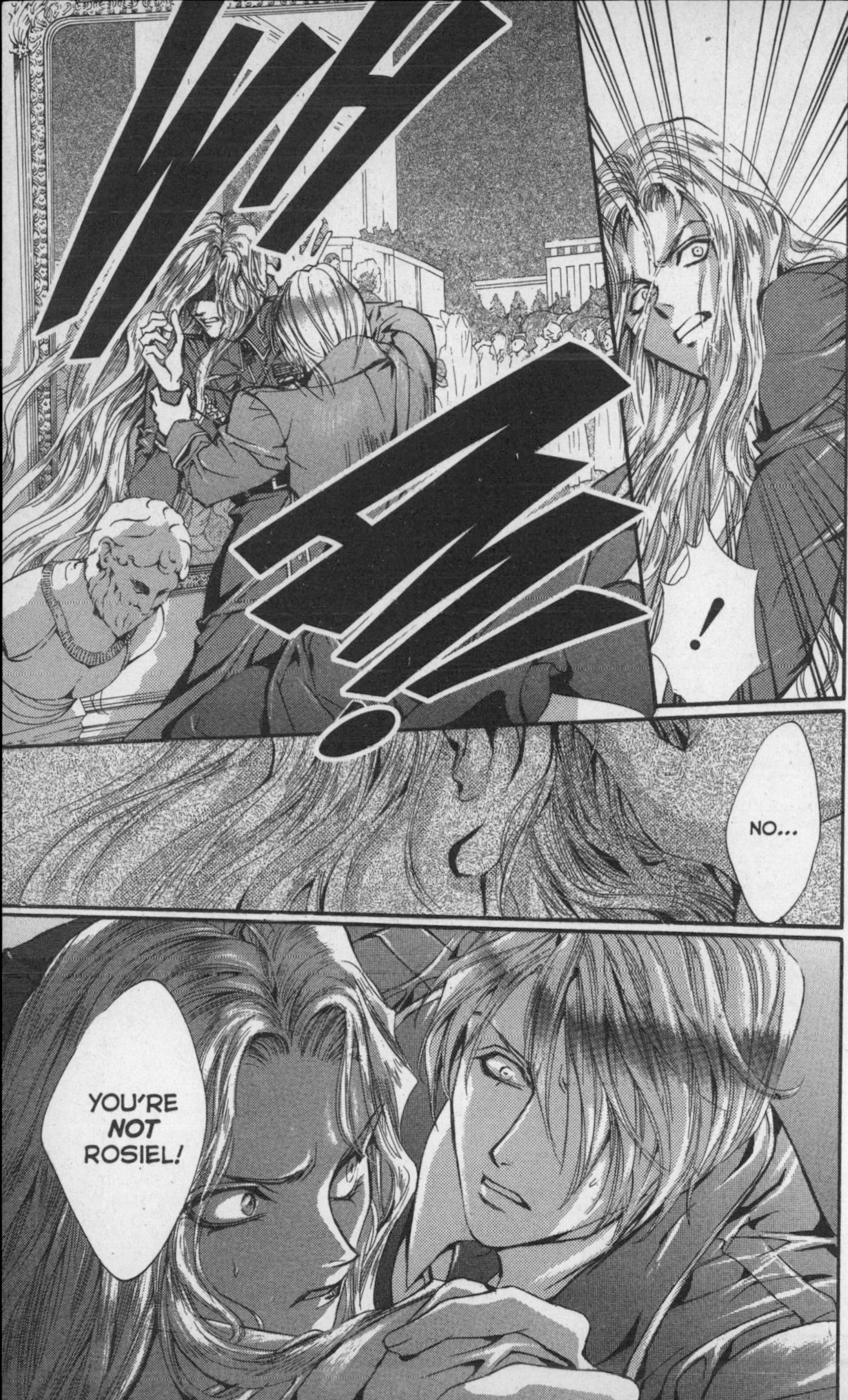
!
NO...
YOU'RE *NOT* ROSIEL!

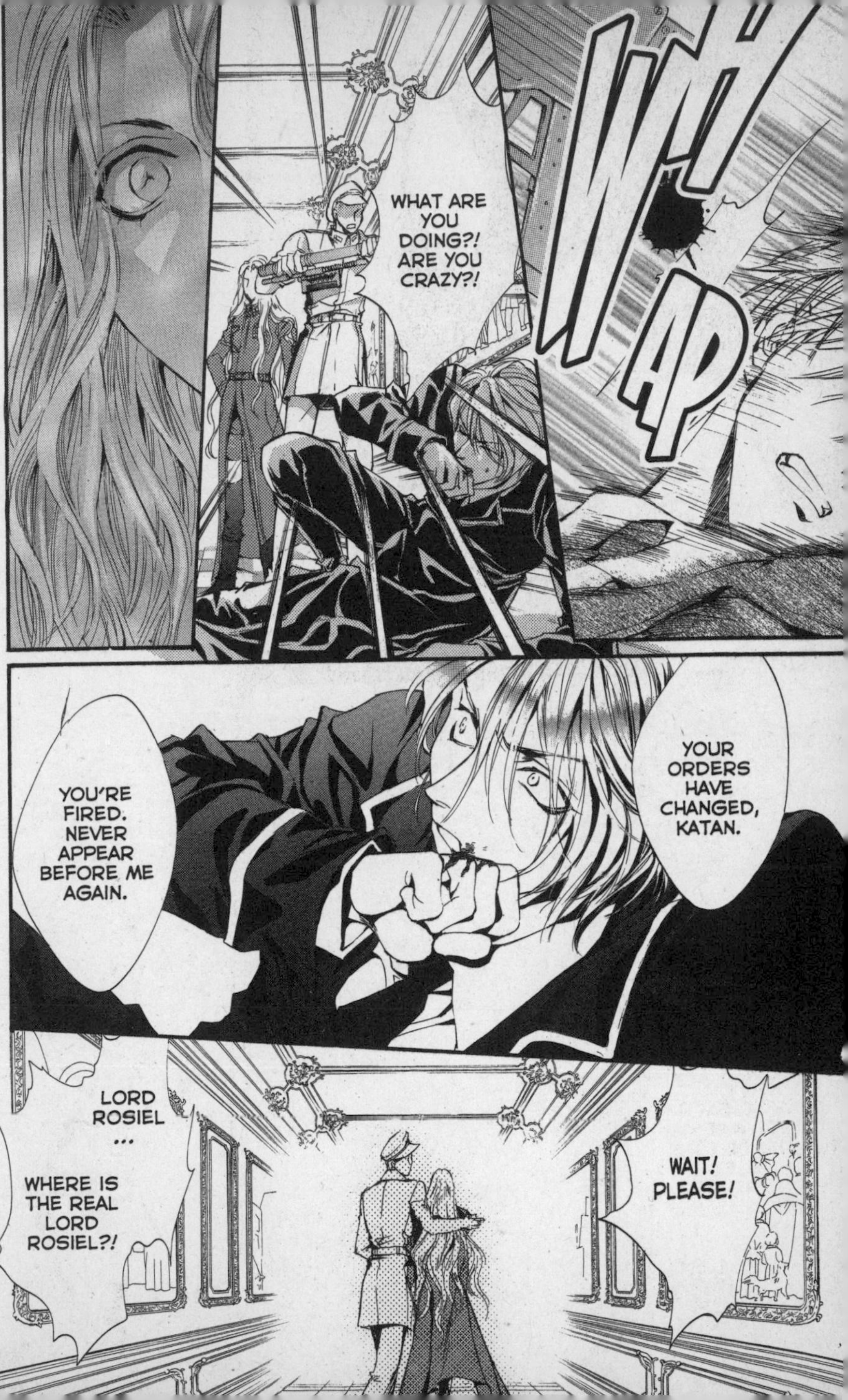
WHAP
WHAT ARE YOU DOING?! ARE YOU CRAZY?!
YOUR ORDERS HAVE CHANGED, KATAN.
YOU'RE FIRED. NEVER APPEAR BEFORE ME AGAIN.
WAIT! PLEASE!
LORD ROSIEL ...
WHERE IS THE REAL LORD ROSIEL?!

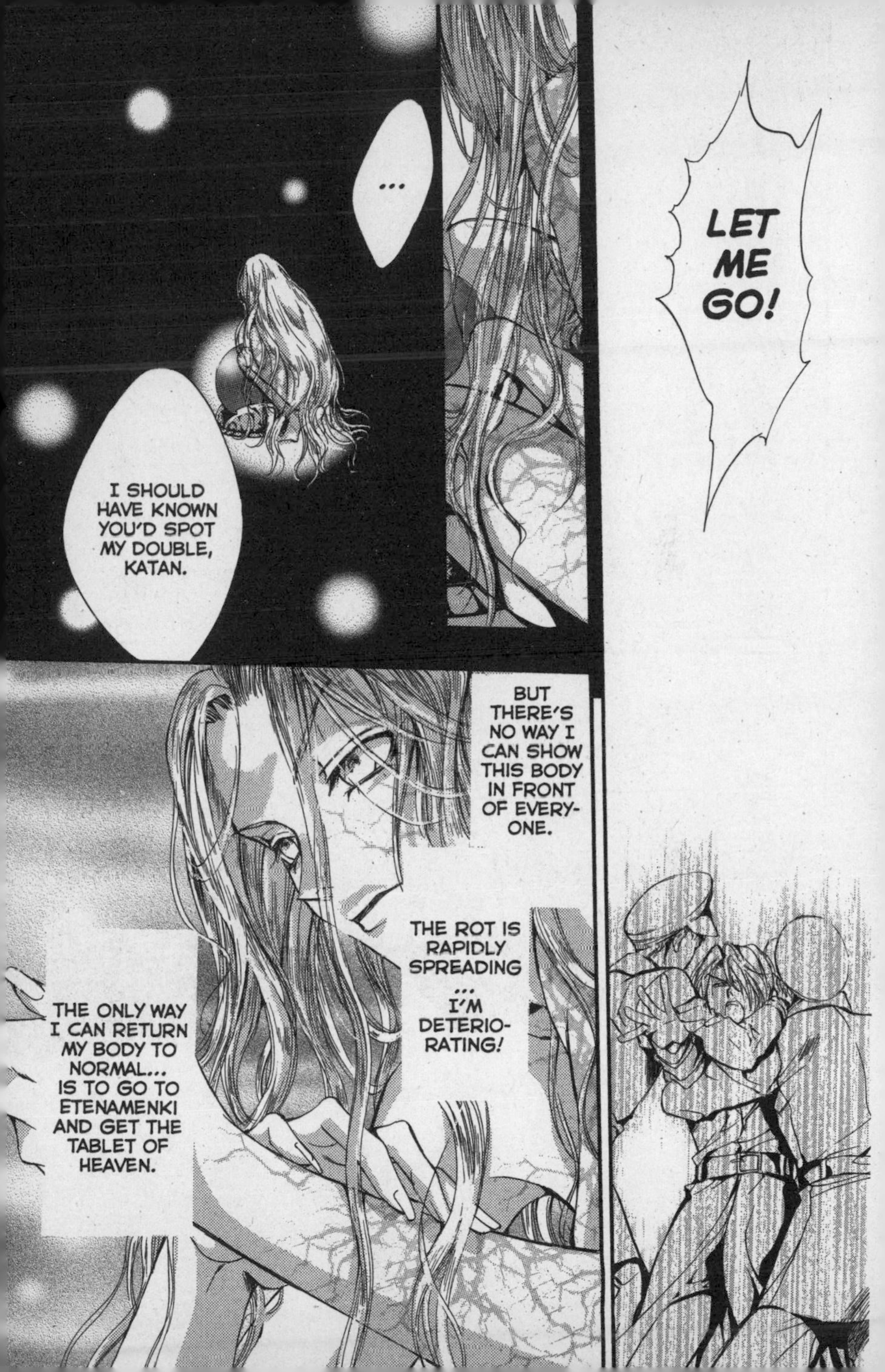
LET ME GO!
...
I SHOULD HAVE KNOWN YOU'D SPOT MY DOUBLE, KATAN.
BUT THERE'S NO WAY I CAN SHOW THIS BODY IN FRONT OF EVERY-ONE.
THE ROT IS RAPIDLY SPREADING ... I'M DETERIO-RATING!
THE ONLY WAY I CAN RETURN MY BODY TO NORMAL... IS TO GO TO ETENAMENKI AND GET THE TABLET OF HEAVEN.

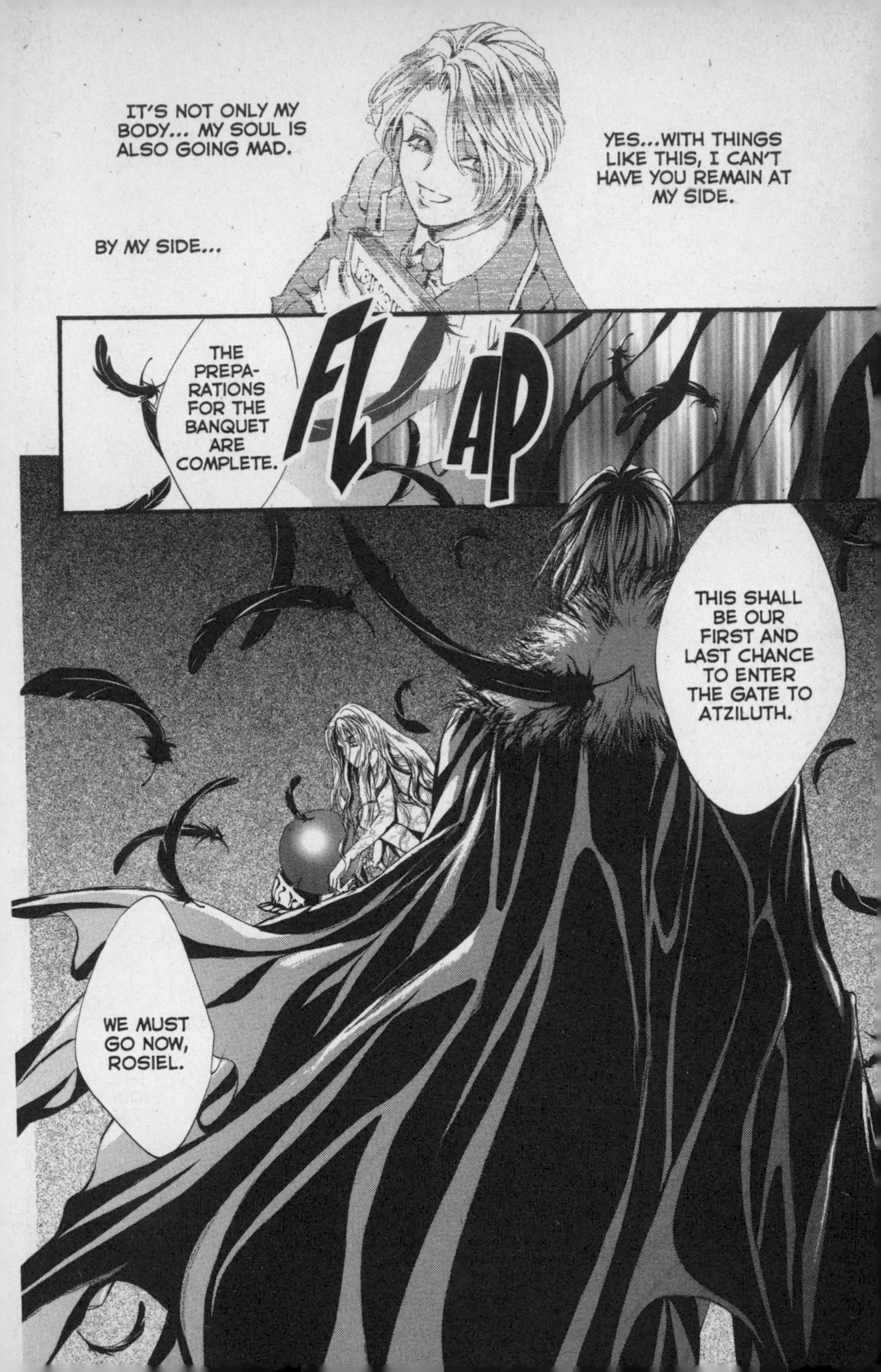
YES...WITH THINGS LIKE THIS, I CAN'T HAVE YOU REMAIN AT MY SIDE.
IT'S NOT ONLY MY BODY... MY SOUL IS ALSO GOING MAD.
BY MY SIDE...
FLAP
THE PREPA-RATIONS FOR THE BANQUET ARE COMPLETE.
THIS SHALL BE OUR FIRST AND LAST CHANCE TO ENTER THE GATE TO ATZILUTH.
WE MUST GO NOW, ROSIEL.

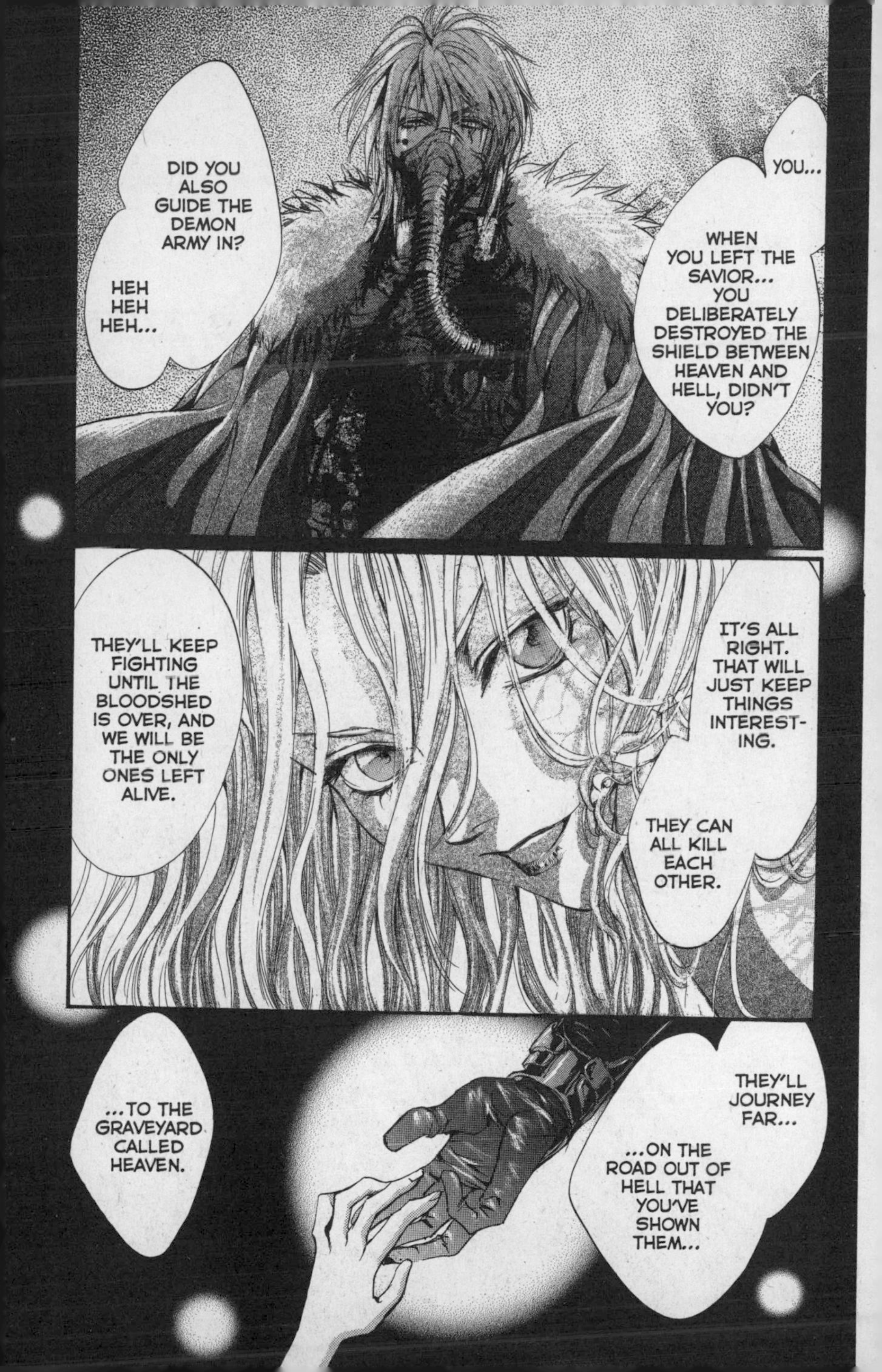
YOU...
WHEN YOU LEFT THE SAVIOR... YOU DELIBERATELY DESTROYED THE SHIELD BETWEEN HEAVEN AND HELL, DIDN'T YOU?
DID YOU ALSO GUIDE THE DEMON ARMY IN?
HEH HEH HEH...
IT'S ALL RIGHT. THAT WILL JUST KEEP THINGS INTEREST-ING.
THEY CAN ALL KILL EACH OTHER.
THEY'LL KEEP FIGHTING UNTIL THE BLOODSHED IS OVER, AND WE WILL BE THE ONLY ONES LEFT ALIVE.
THEY'LL JOURNEY FAR...
...ON THE ROAD OUT OF HELL THAT YOU'VE SHOWN THEM...
...TO THE GRAVEYARD CALLED HEAVEN.

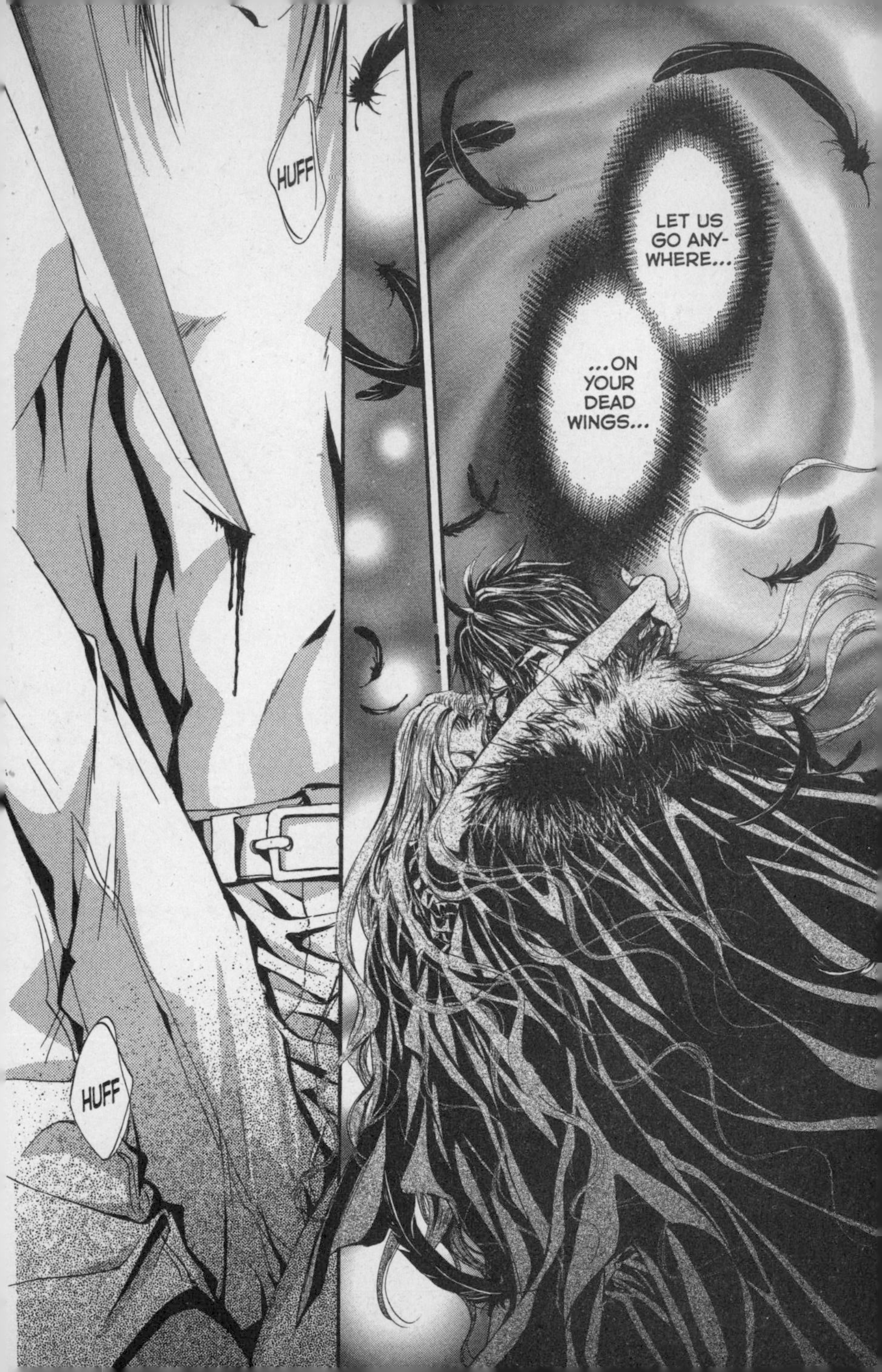
LET US GO ANY-WHERE...
...ON YOUR DEAD WINGS...
HUFF
HUFF

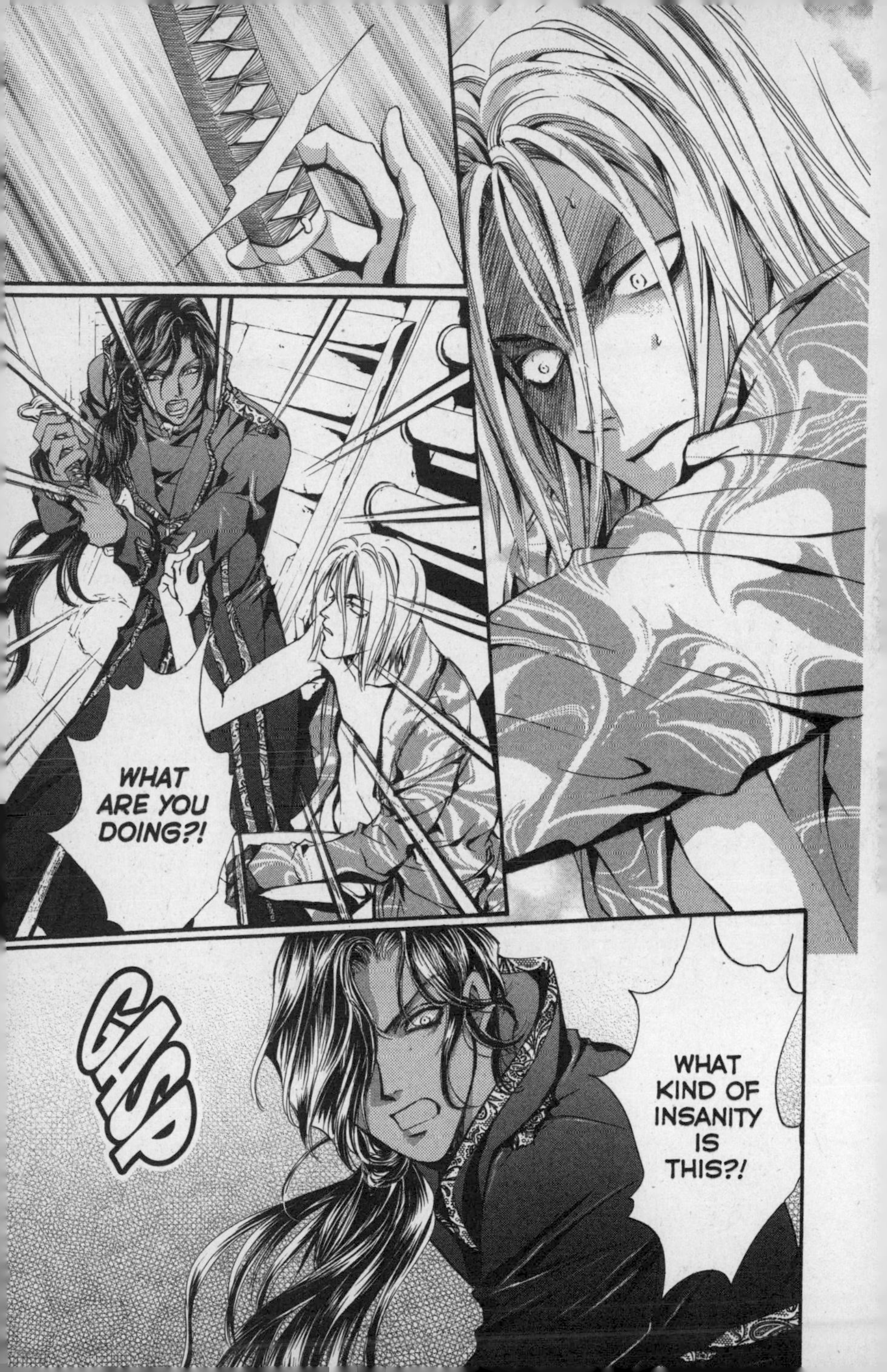
WHAT ARE YOU DOING?!
WHAT KIND OF INSANITY IS THIS?!
GASP

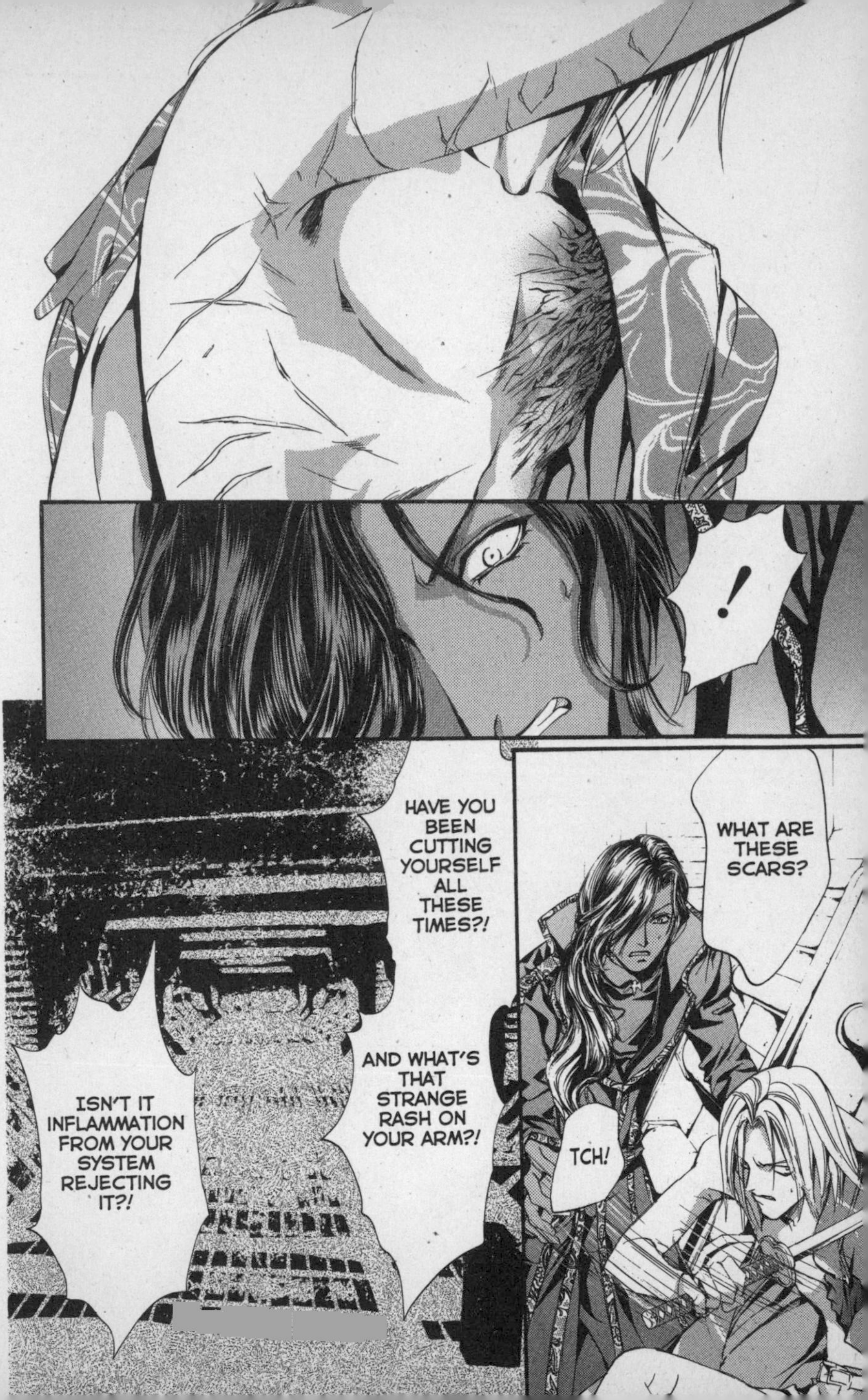
!
WHAT ARE THESE SCARS?
TCH!
HAVE YOU BEEN CUTTING YOURSELF ALL THESE TIMES?!
AND WHAT'S THAT STRANGE RASH ON YOUR ARM?!
ISN'T IT INFLAMMATION FROM YOUR SYSTEM REJECTING IT?!

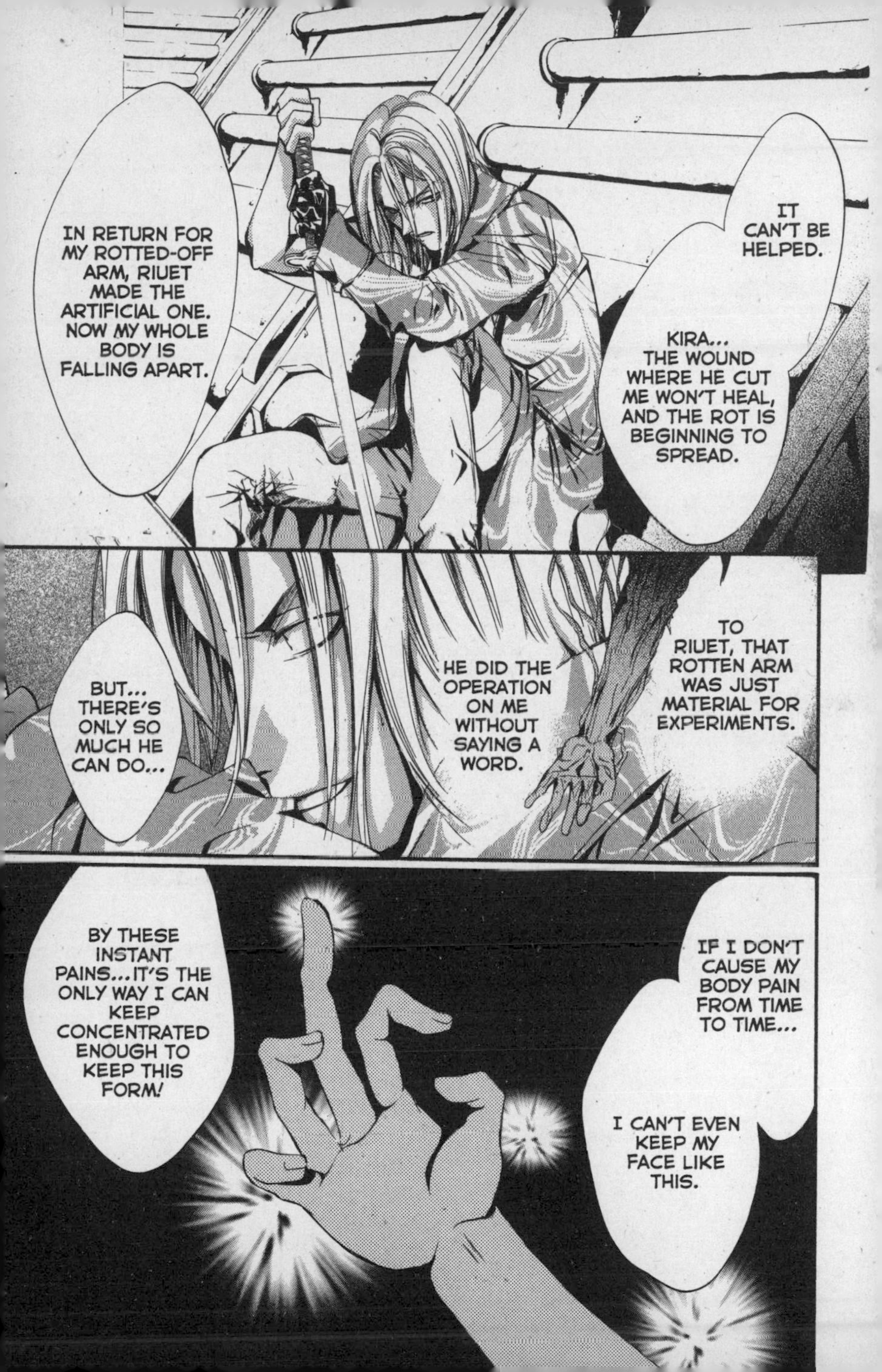
IT CAN'T BE HELPED.
KIRA... THE WOUND WHERE HE CUT ME WON'T HEAL, AND THE ROT IS BEGINNING TO SPREAD.
IN RETURN FOR MY ROTTED-OFF ARM, RIUET MADE THE ARTIFICIAL ONE. NOW MY WHOLE BODY IS FALLING APART.
TO RIUET, THAT ROTTEN ARM WAS JUST MATERIAL FOR EXPERIMENTS.
HE DID THE OPERATION ON ME WITHOUT SAYING A WORD.
BUT... THERE'S ONLY SO MUCH HE CAN DO...
IF I DON'T CAUSE MY BODY PAIN FROM TIME TO TIME...
I CAN'T EVEN KEEP MY FACE LIKE THIS.
BY THESE INSTANT PAINS...IT'S THE ONLY WAY I CAN KEEP CONCENTRATED ENOUGH TO KEEP THIS FORM!

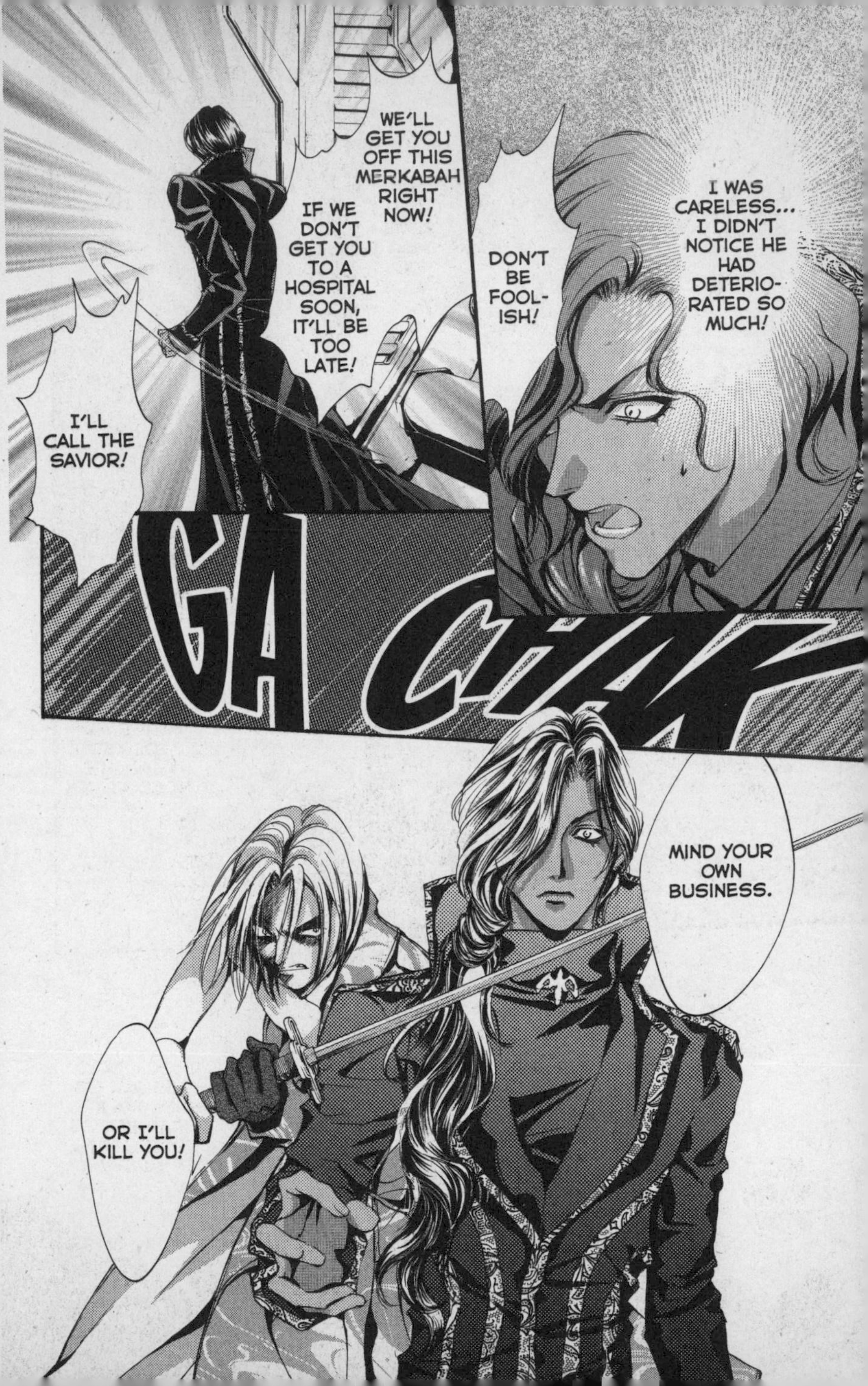
I WAS CARELESS... I DIDN'T NOTICE HE HAD DETERIO-RATED SO MUCH!
DON'T BE FOOL-ISH!
WE'LL GET YOU OFF THIS MERKABAH RIGHT NOW!
IF WE DON'T GET YOU TO A HOSPITAL SOON, IT'LL BE TOO LATE!
I'LL CALL THE SAVIOR!
GA
MIND YOUR OWN BUSINESS.
OR I'LL KILL YOU!

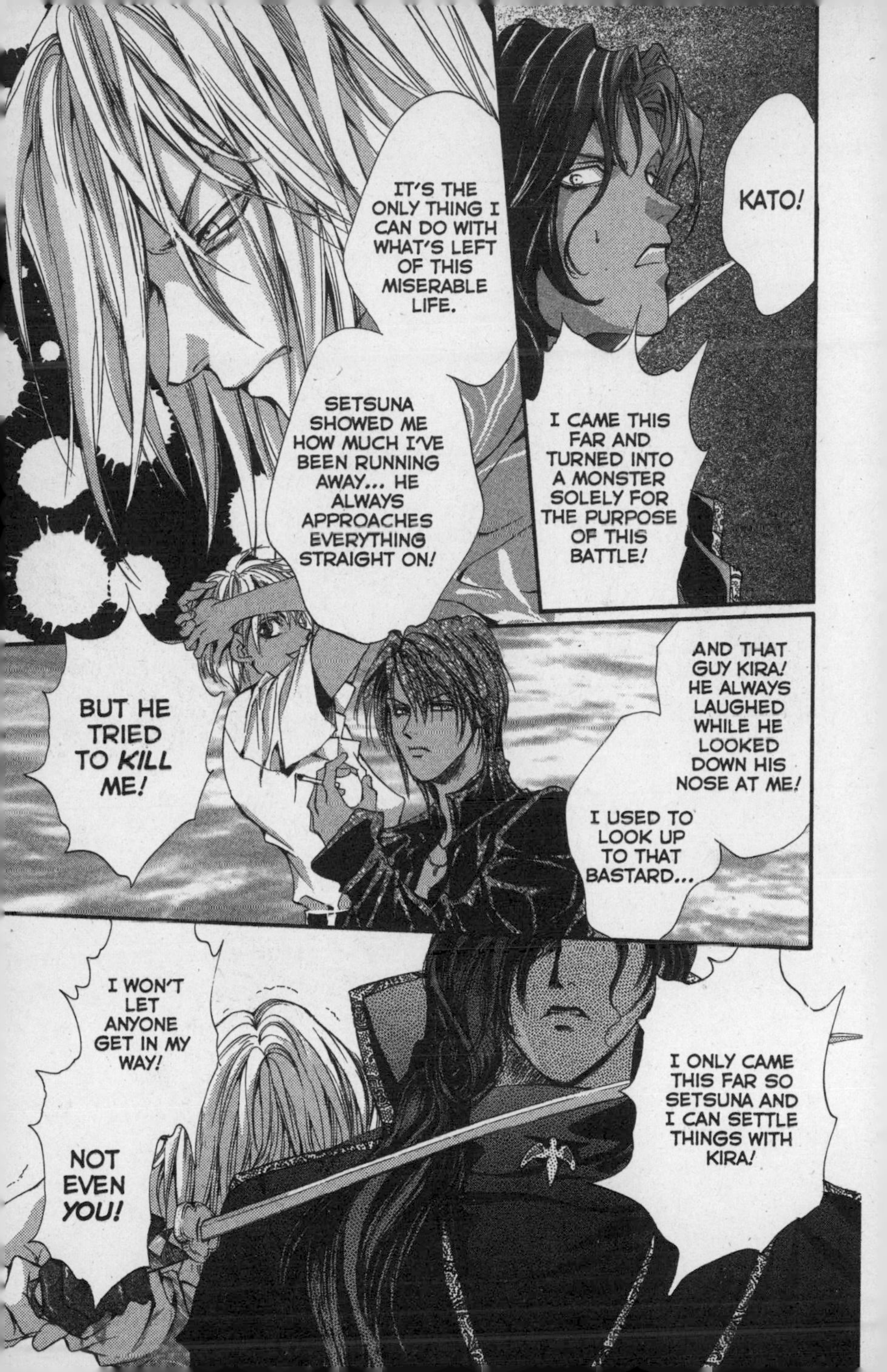
KATO!
I CAME THIS FAR AND TURNED INTO A MONSTER SOLELY FOR THE PURPOSE OF THIS BATTLE!
IT'S THE ONLY THING I CAN DO WITH WHAT'S LEFT OF THIS MISERABLE LIFE.
SETSUNA SHOWED ME HOW MUCH I'VE BEEN RUNNING AWAY... HE ALWAYS APPROACHES EVERYTHING STRAIGHT ON!
AND THAT GUY KIRA! HE ALWAYS LAUGHED WHILE HE LOOKED DOWN HIS NOSE AT ME!
I USED TO LOOK UP TO THAT BASTARD...
BUT HE TRIED TO *KILL* ME!
I ONLY CAME THIS FAR SO SETSUNA AND I CAN SETTLE THINGS WITH KIRA!
I WON'T LET ANYONE GET IN MY WAY!
NOT EVEN *YOU*!

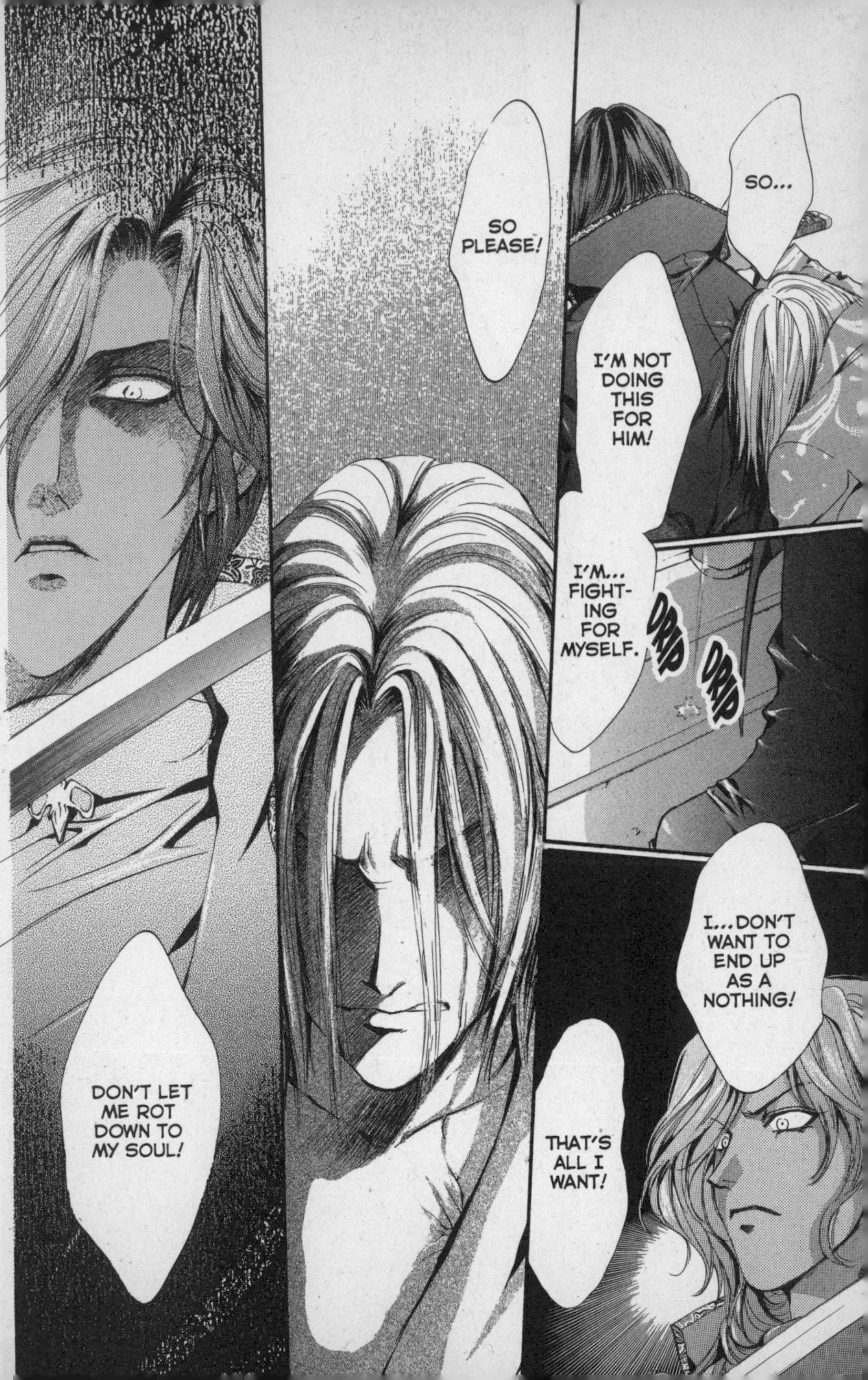
SO...
I'M NOT DOING THIS FOR HIM!
I'M... FIGHTING FOR MYSELF.
DRIP
DRIP
I...DON'T WANT TO END UP AS A NOTHING!
THAT'S ALL I WANT!
SO PLEASE!
DON'T LET ME ROT DOWN TO MY SOUL!

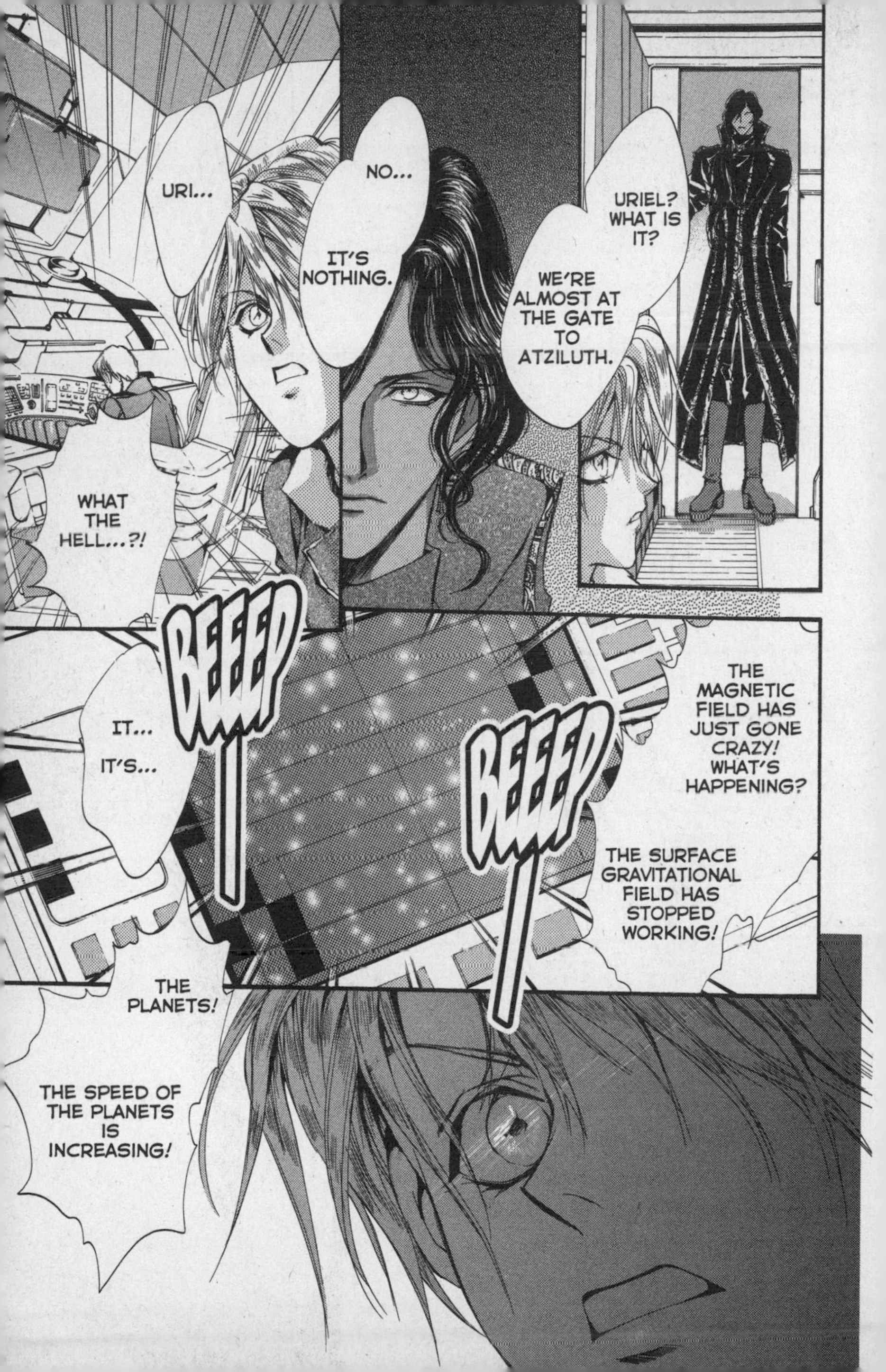
URIEL? WHAT IS IT?
WE'RE ALMOST AT THE GATE TO ATZILUTH.
NO...
IT'S NOTHING.
URI...
WHAT THE HELL...?!
THE MAGNETIC FIELD HAS JUST GONE CRAZY! WHAT'S HAPPENING?
THE SURFACE GRAVITATIONAL FIELD HAS STOPPED WORKING!
BEEEP
BEEEP
IT...
IT'S...
THE PLANETS!
THE SPEED OF THE PLANETS IS INCREASING!

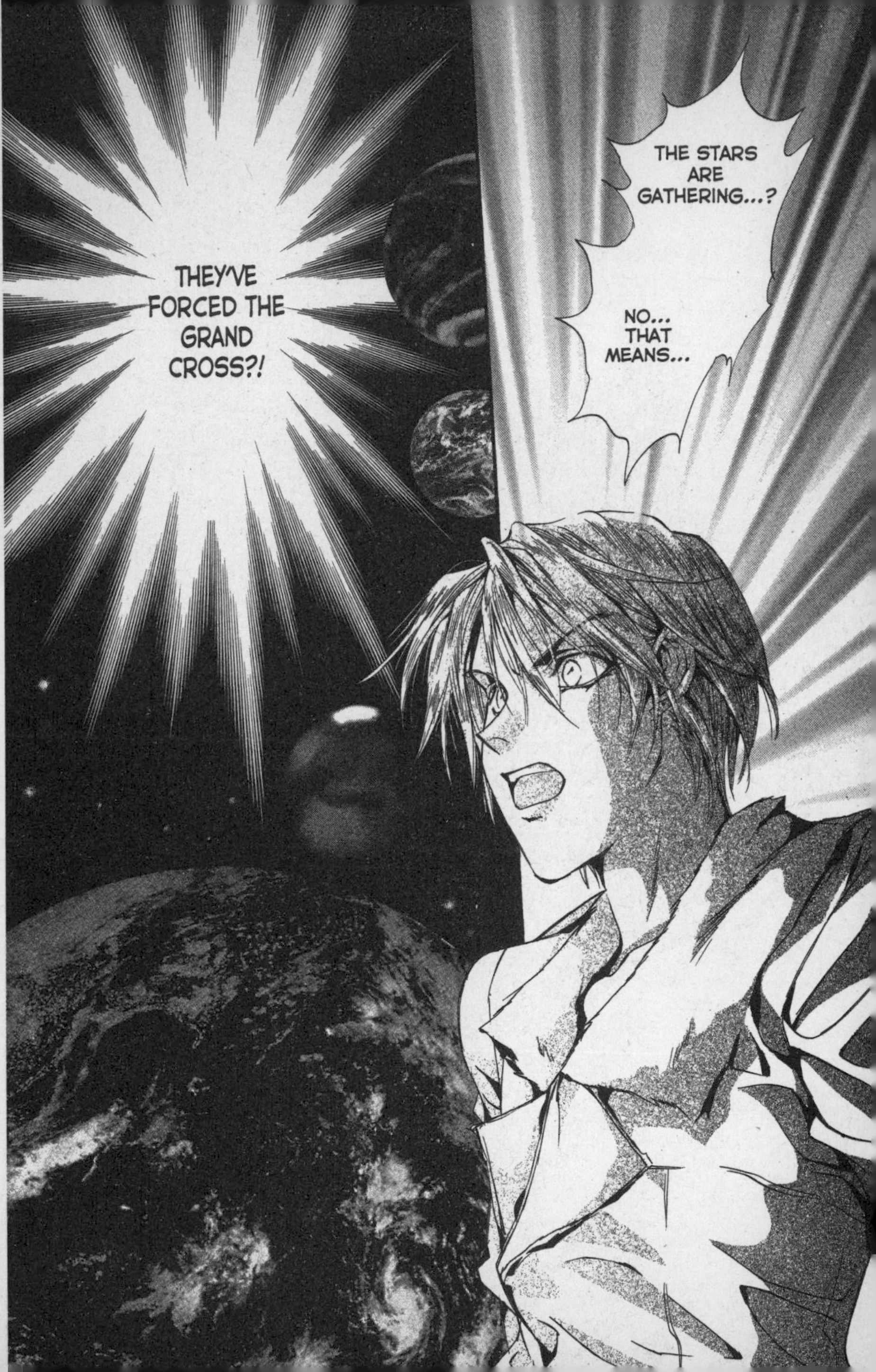
THE STARS ARE GATHERING...?
NO... THAT MEANS...
THEY'VE FORCED THE GRAND CROSS?!

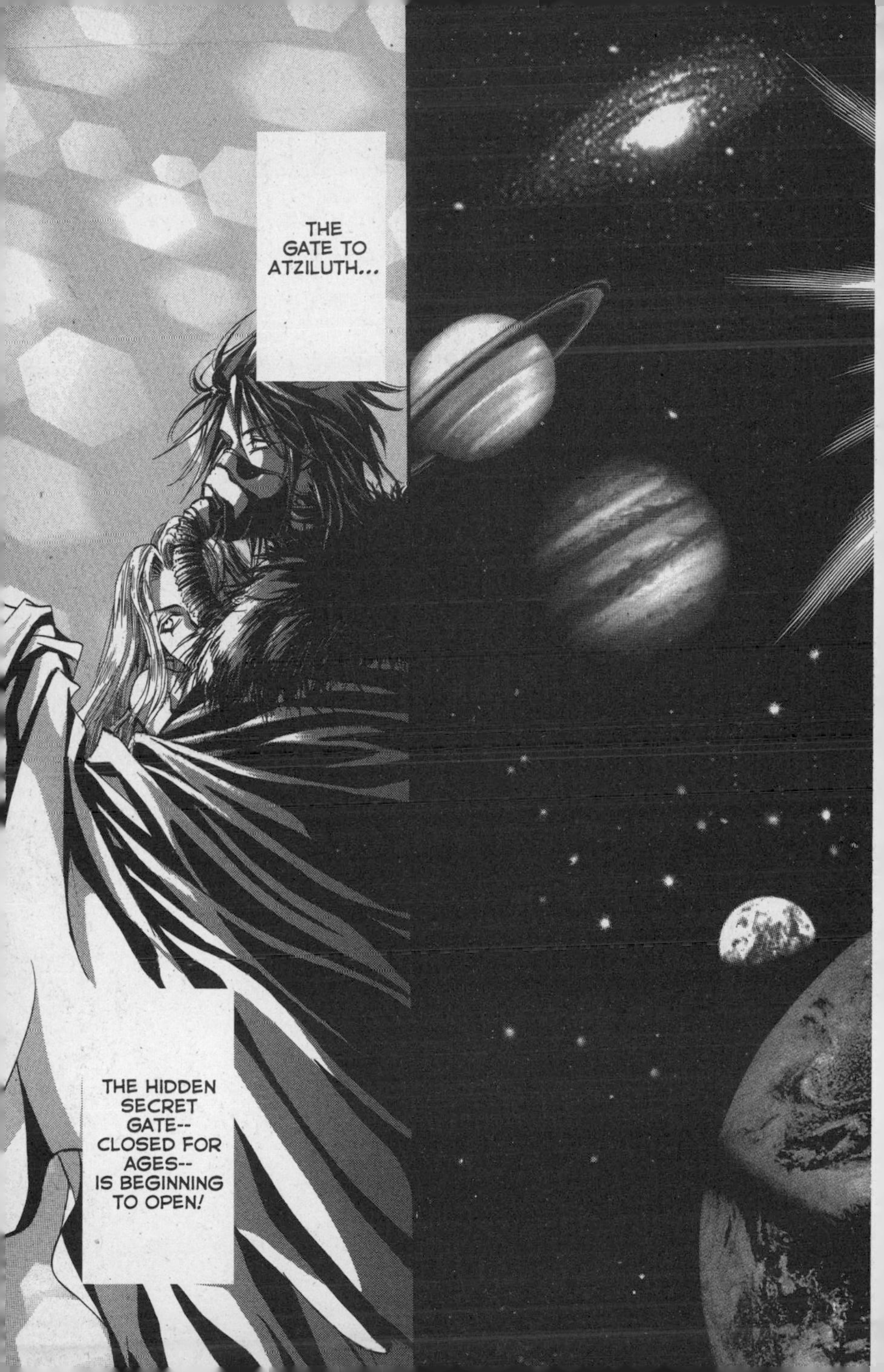
THE GATE TO ATZILUTH...
THE HIDDEN SECRET GATE-- CLOSED FOR AGES-- IS BEGINNING TO OPEN!

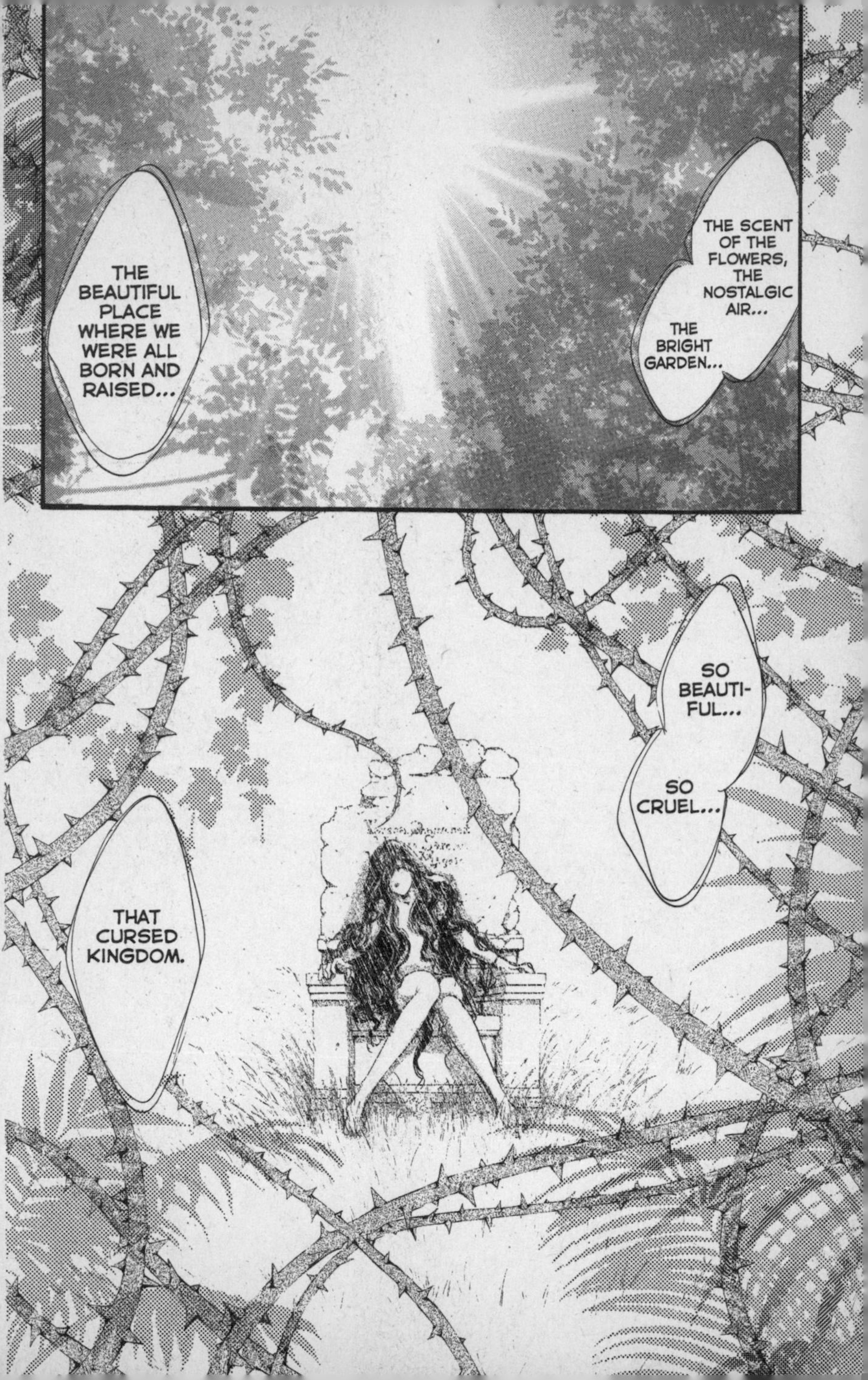
THE SCENT OF THE FLOWERS, THE NOSTALGIC AIR...
THE BRIGHT GARDEN...
THE BEAUTIFUL PLACE WHERE WE WERE ALL BORN AND RAISED...
SO BEAUTI-FUL...
SO CRUEL...
THAT CURSED KINGDOM.

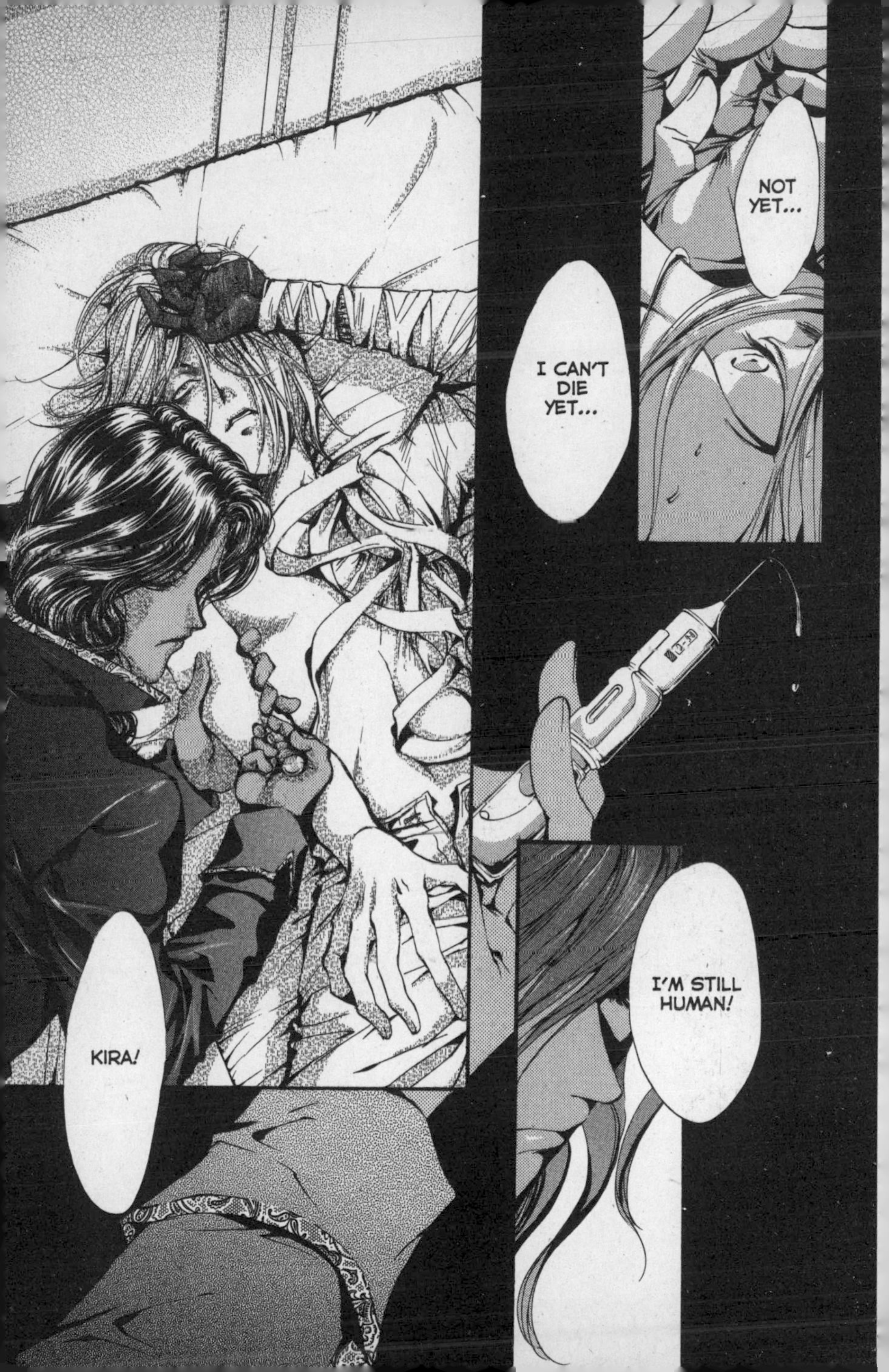
NOT YET...
I CAN'T DIE YET...
I'M STILL HUMAN!
KIRA!

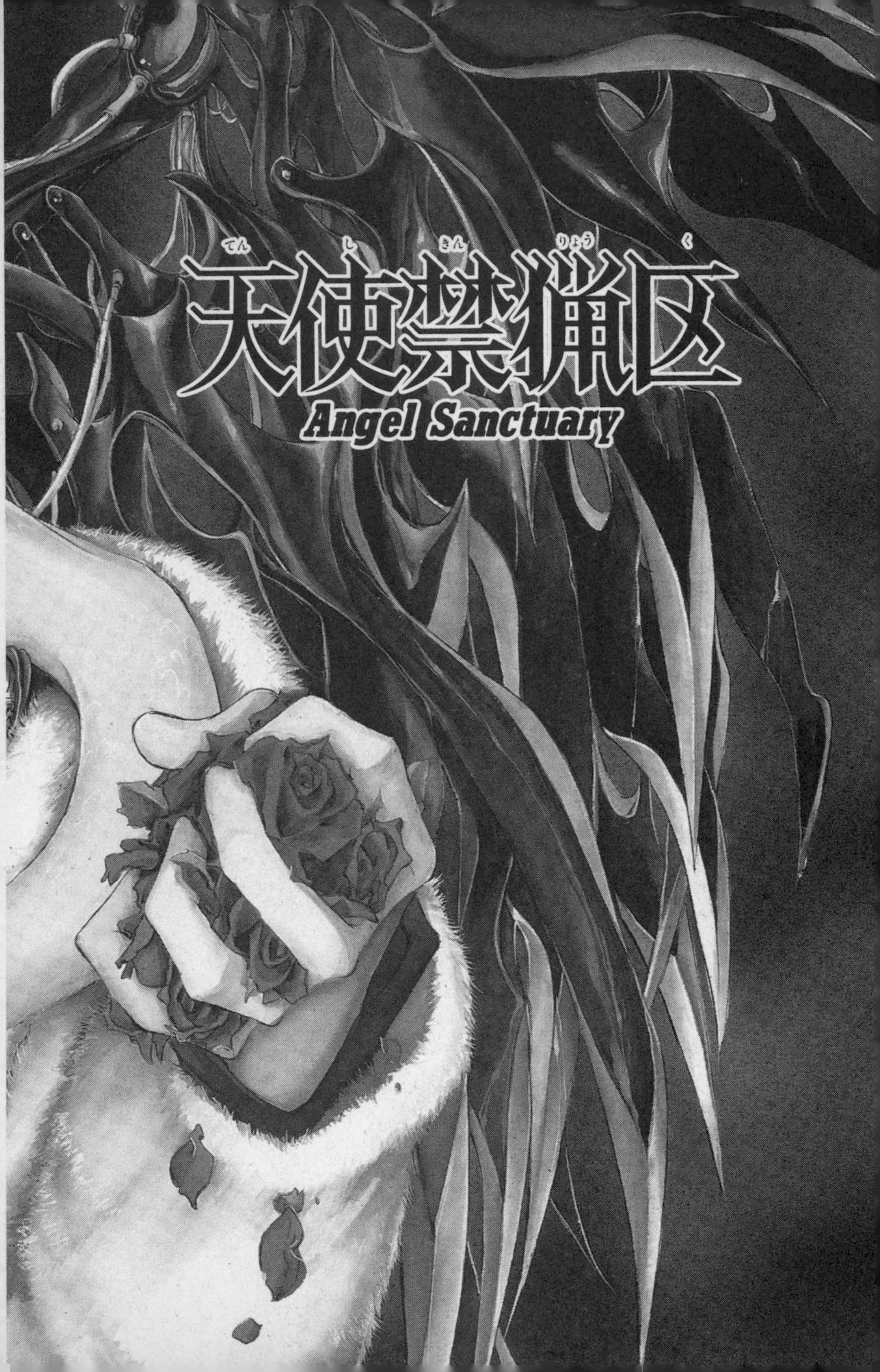
天使禁猟区
Angel Sanctuary

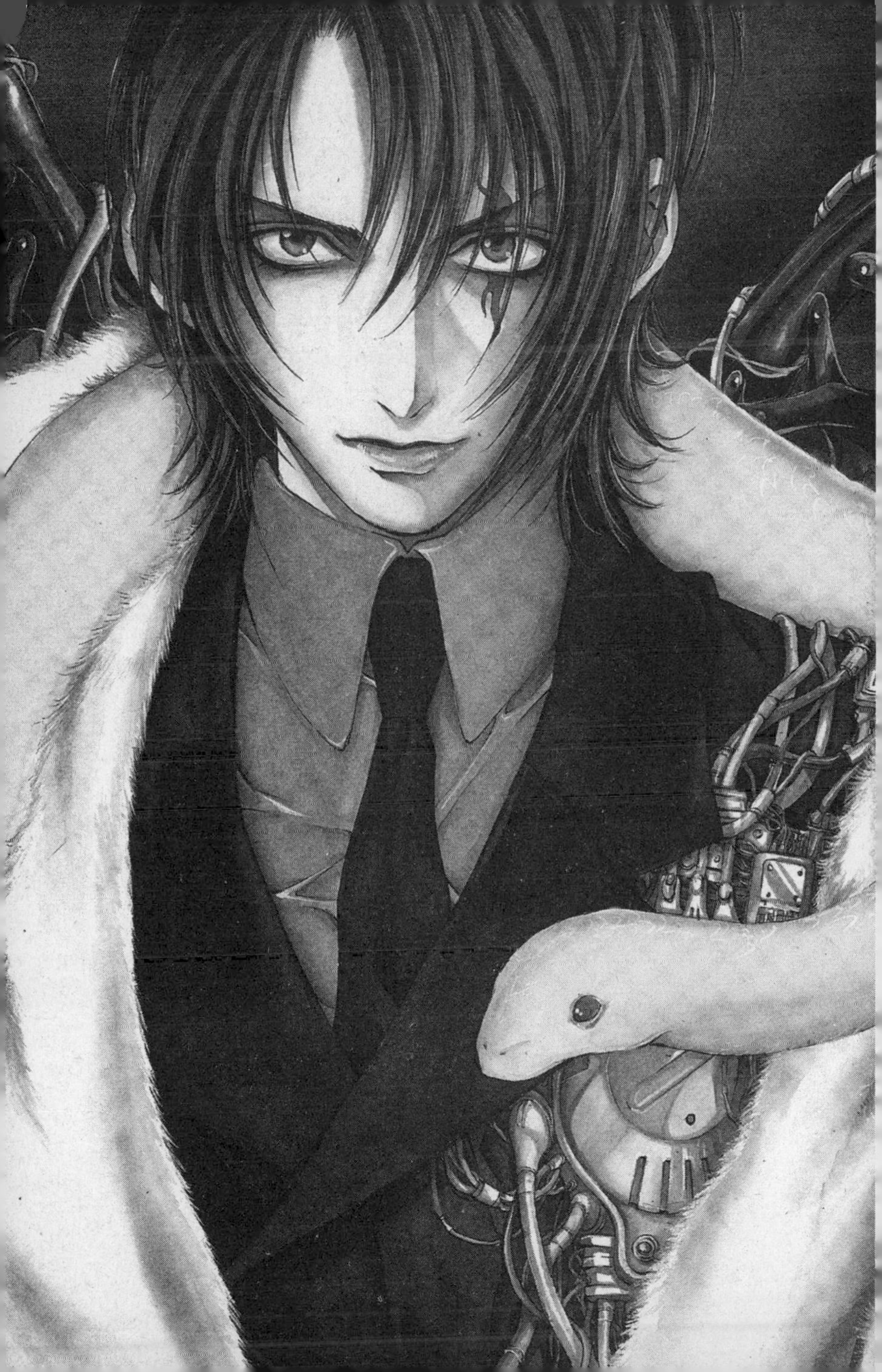

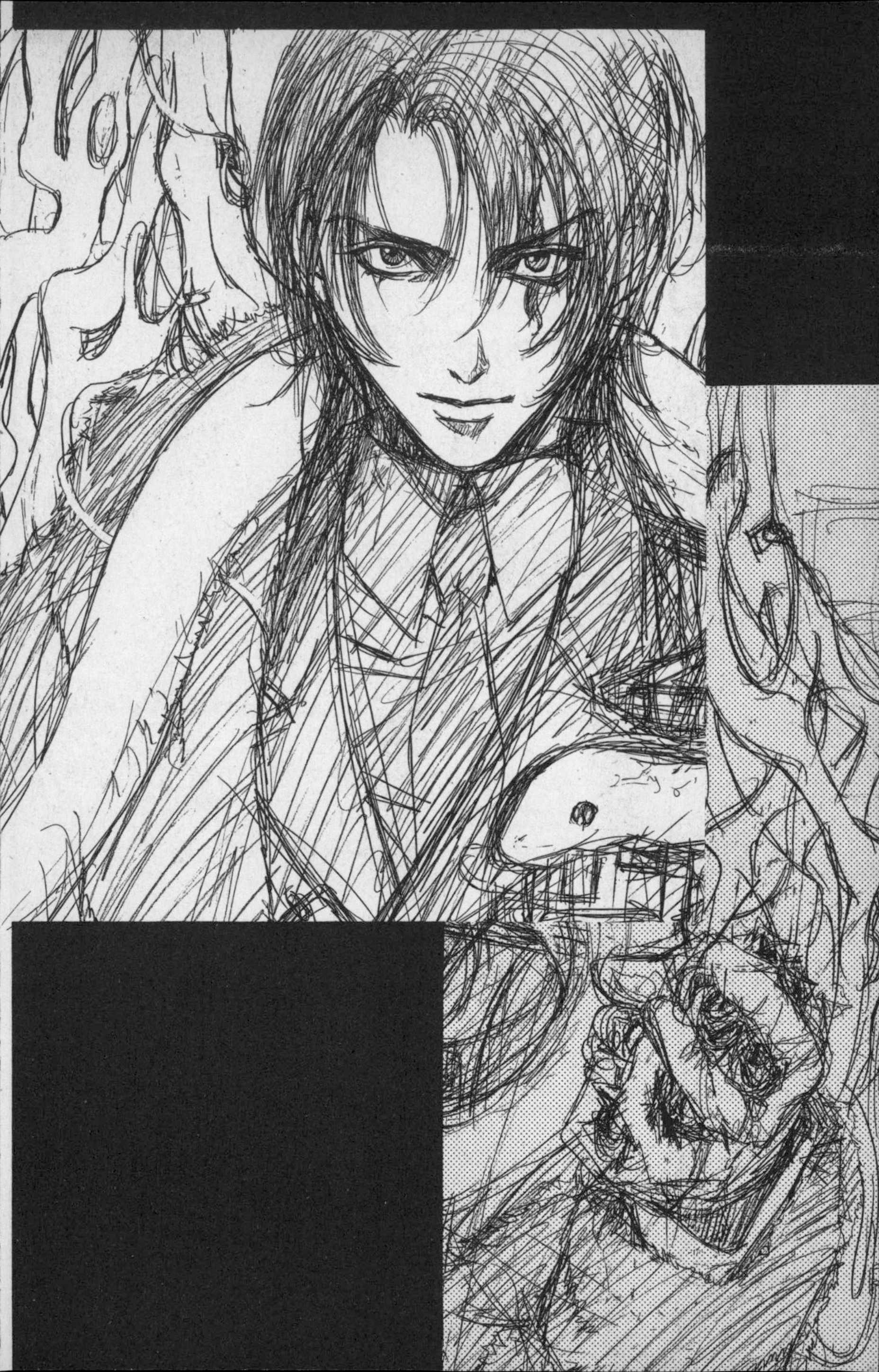

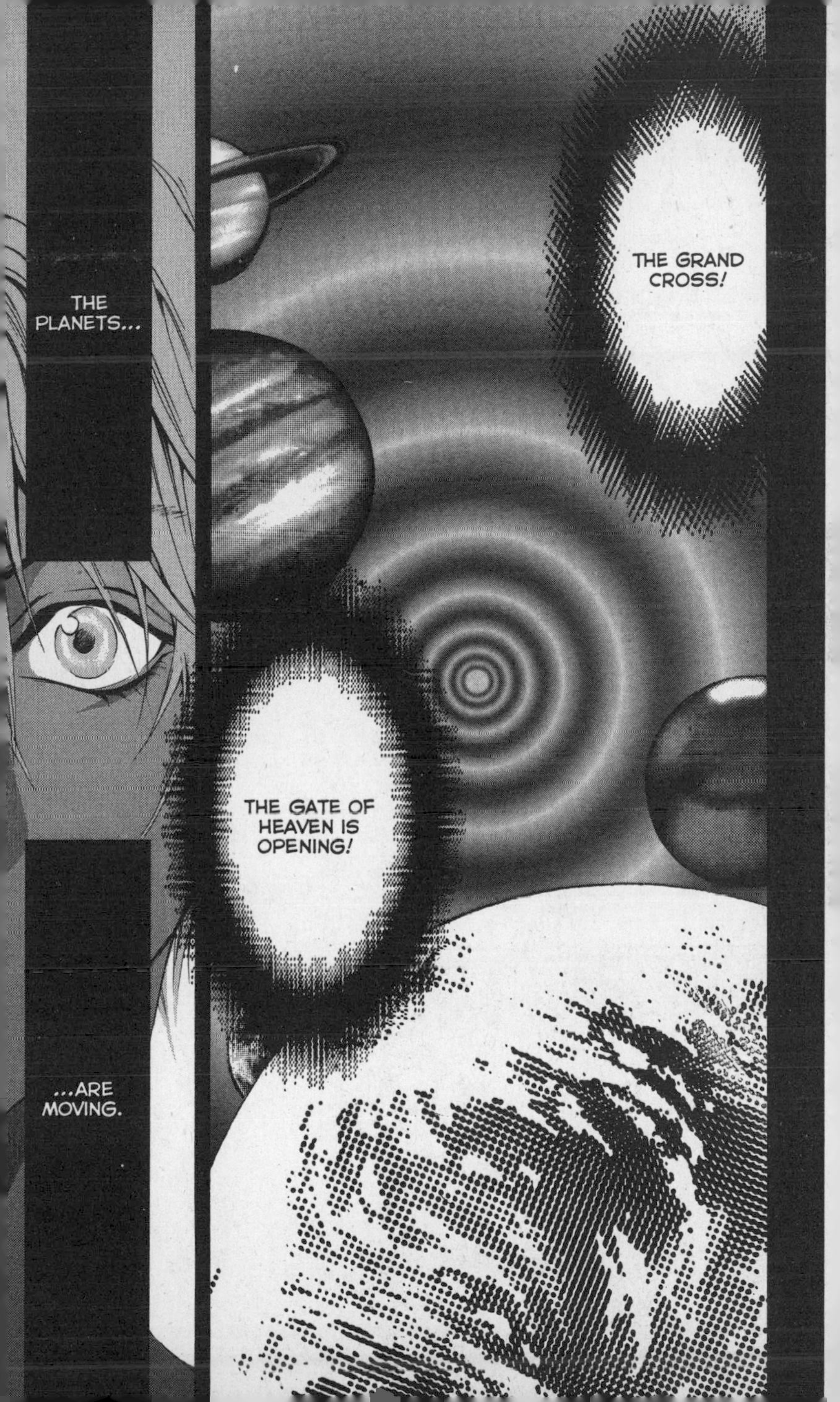
THE GRAND CROSS!
THE GATE OF HEAVEN IS OPENING!
THE PLANETS...
...ARE MOVING.

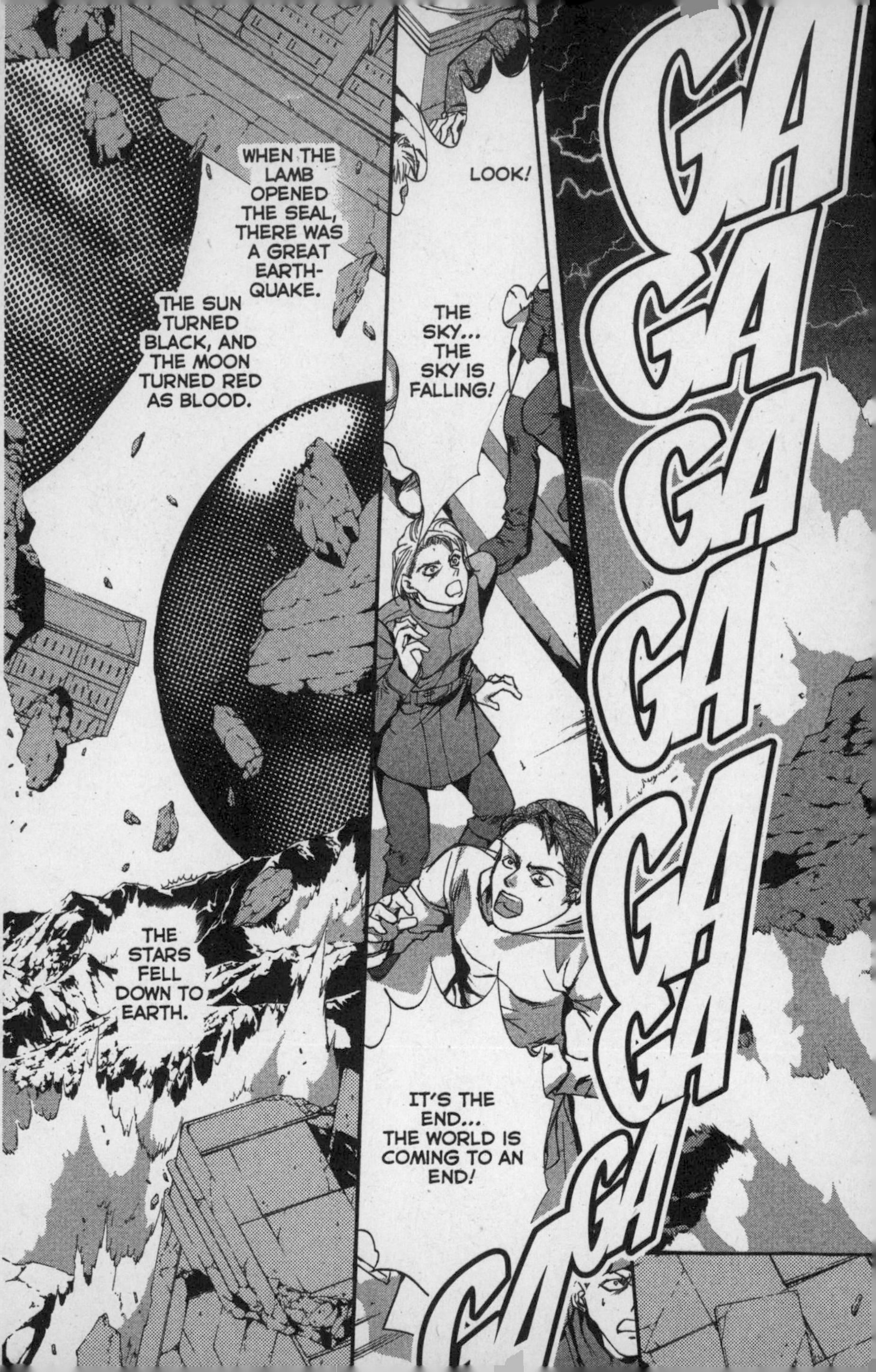
GA GA GA GA GA GA GA GA
LOOK!
THE SKY... THE SKY IS FALLING!
IT'S THE END... THE WORLD IS COMING TO AN END!
WHEN THE LAMB OPENED THE SEAL, THERE WAS A GREAT EARTH-QUAKE.
THE SUN TURNED BLACK, AND THE MOON TURNED RED AS BLOOD.
THE STARS FELL DOWN TO EARTH.

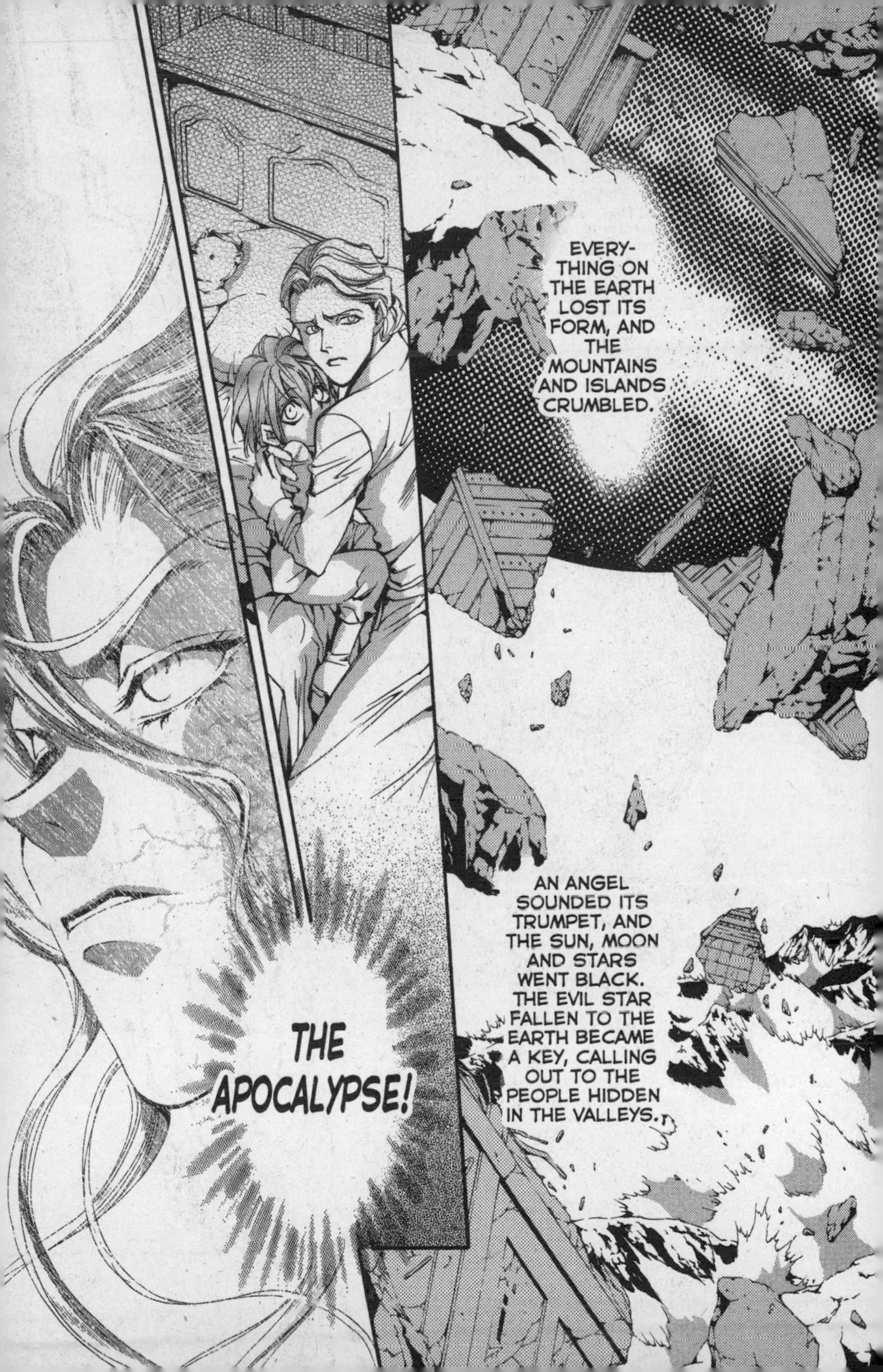
EVERYTHING ON THE EARTH LOST ITS FORM, AND THE MOUNTAINS AND ISLANDS CRUMBLED.
AN ANGEL SOUNDED ITS TRUMPET, AND THE SUN, MOON AND STARS WENT BLACK. THE EVIL STAR FALLEN TO THE EARTH BECAME A KEY, CALLING OUT TO THE PEOPLE HIDDEN IN THE VALLEYS.
THE APOCALYPSE!

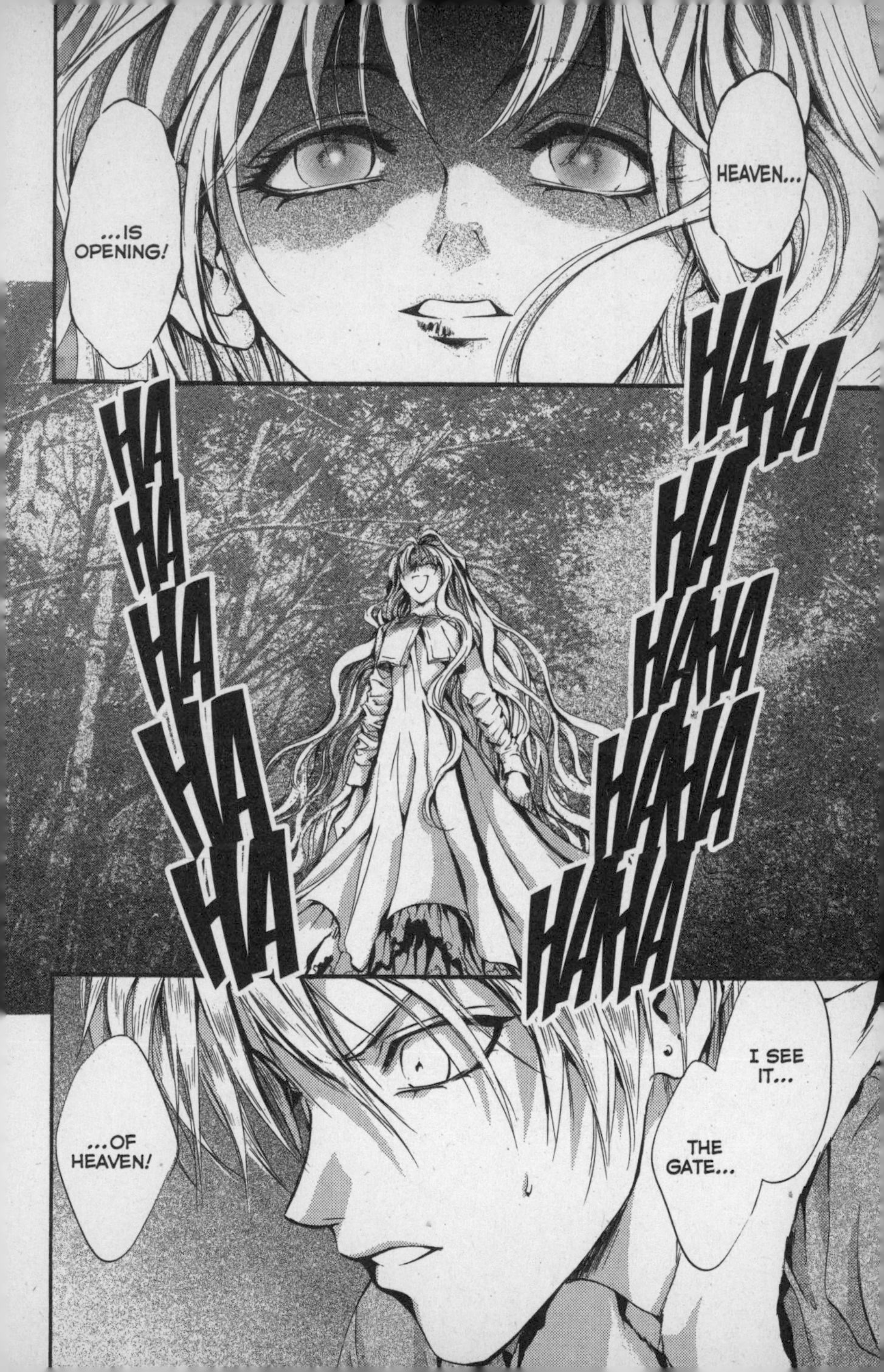
HEAVEN...
...IS OPENING!
HAHA HA HAHA HAHA HAHA
HA HA HA HA HA HA
I SEE IT...
THE GATE...
...OF HEAVEN!

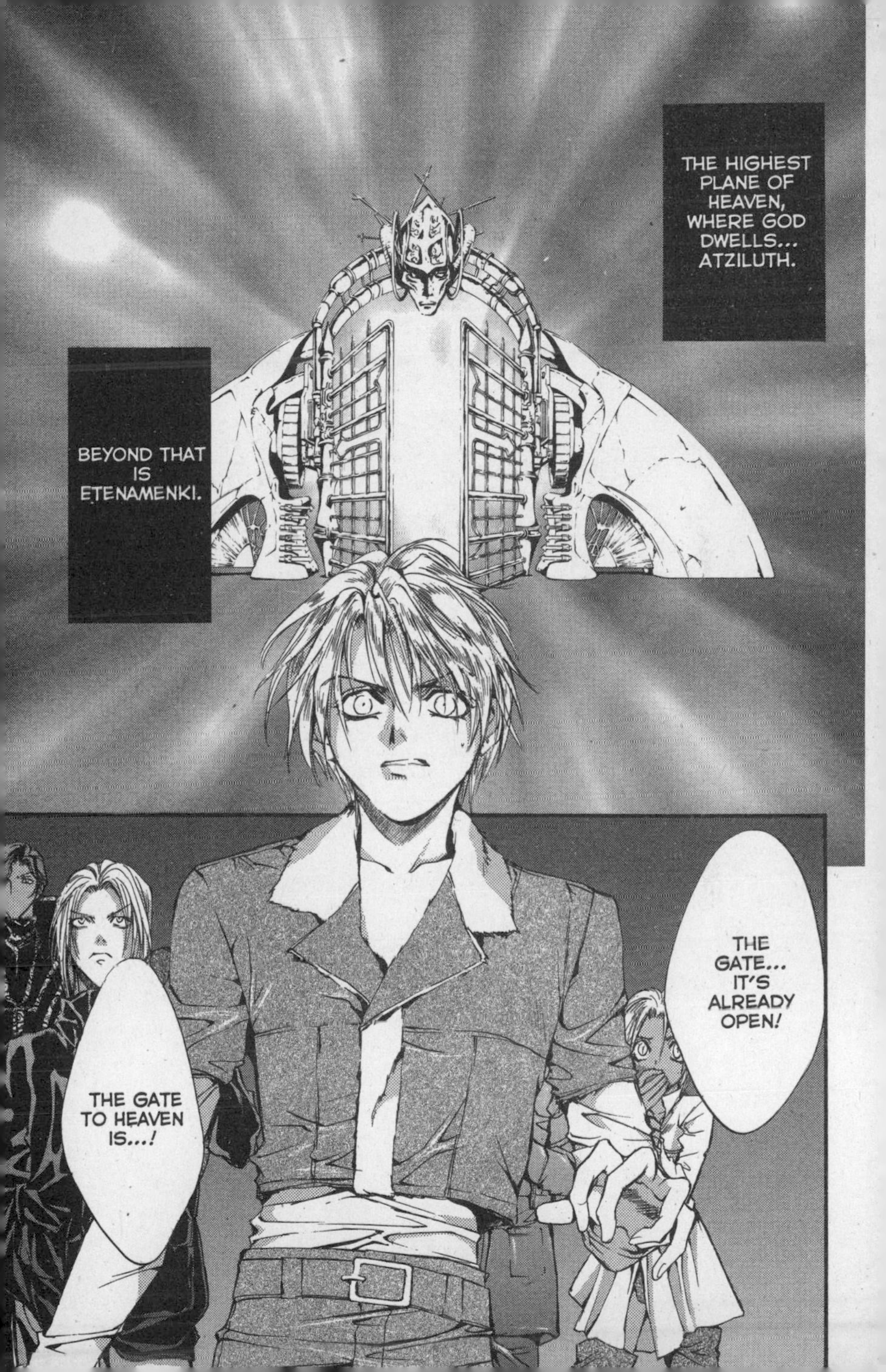
THE HIGHEST PLANE OF HEAVEN, WHERE GOD DWELLS... ATZILUTH.
BEYOND THAT IS ETENAMENKI.
THE GATE... IT'S ALREADY OPEN!
THE GATE TO HEAVEN IS...!

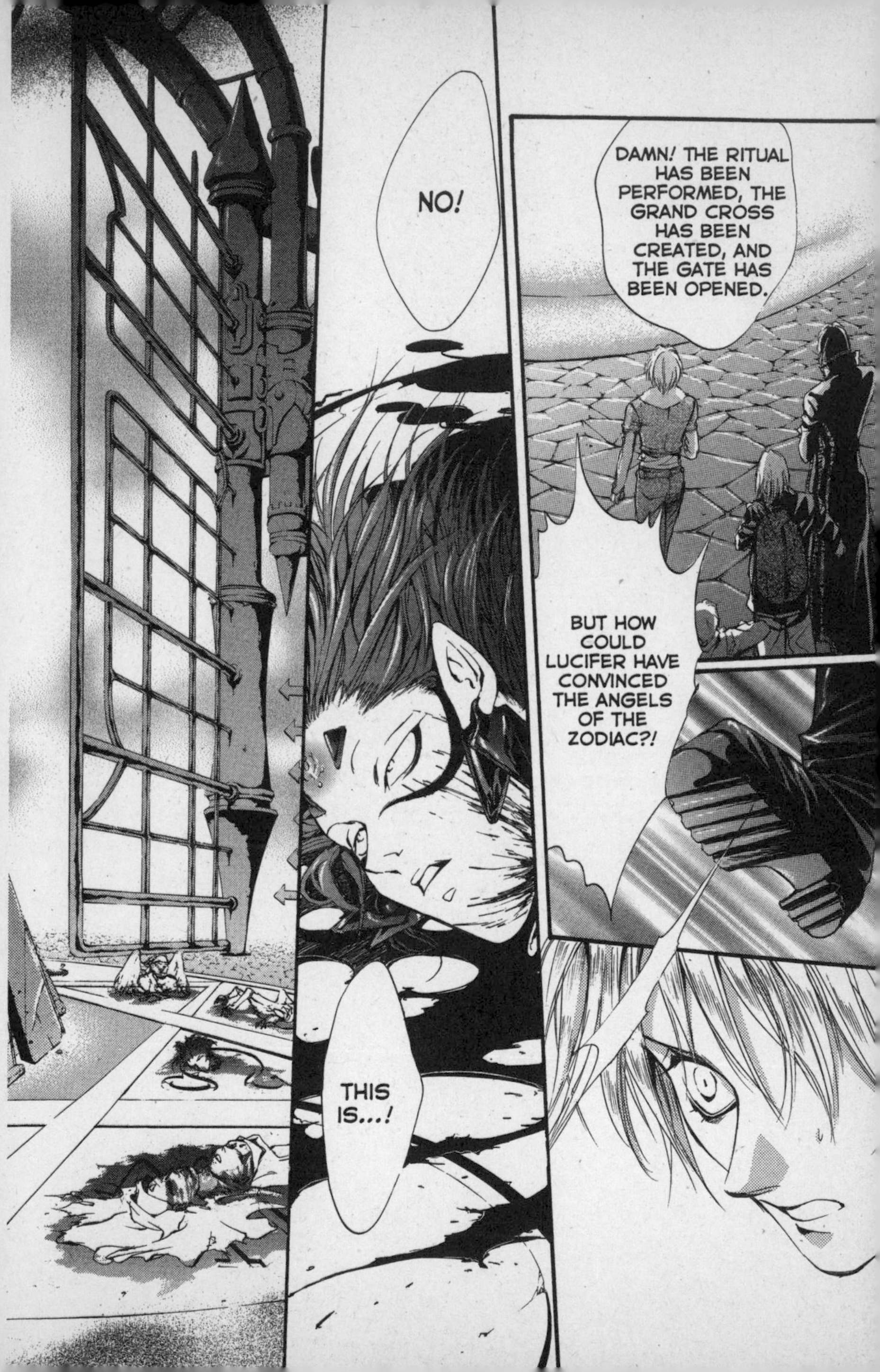
DAMN! THE RITUAL HAS BEEN PERFORMED, THE GRAND CROSS HAS BEEN CREATED, AND THE GATE HAS BEEN OPENED.
BUT HOW COULD LUCIFER HAVE CONVINCED THE ANGELS OF THE ZODIAC?!
NO!
THIS IS...!

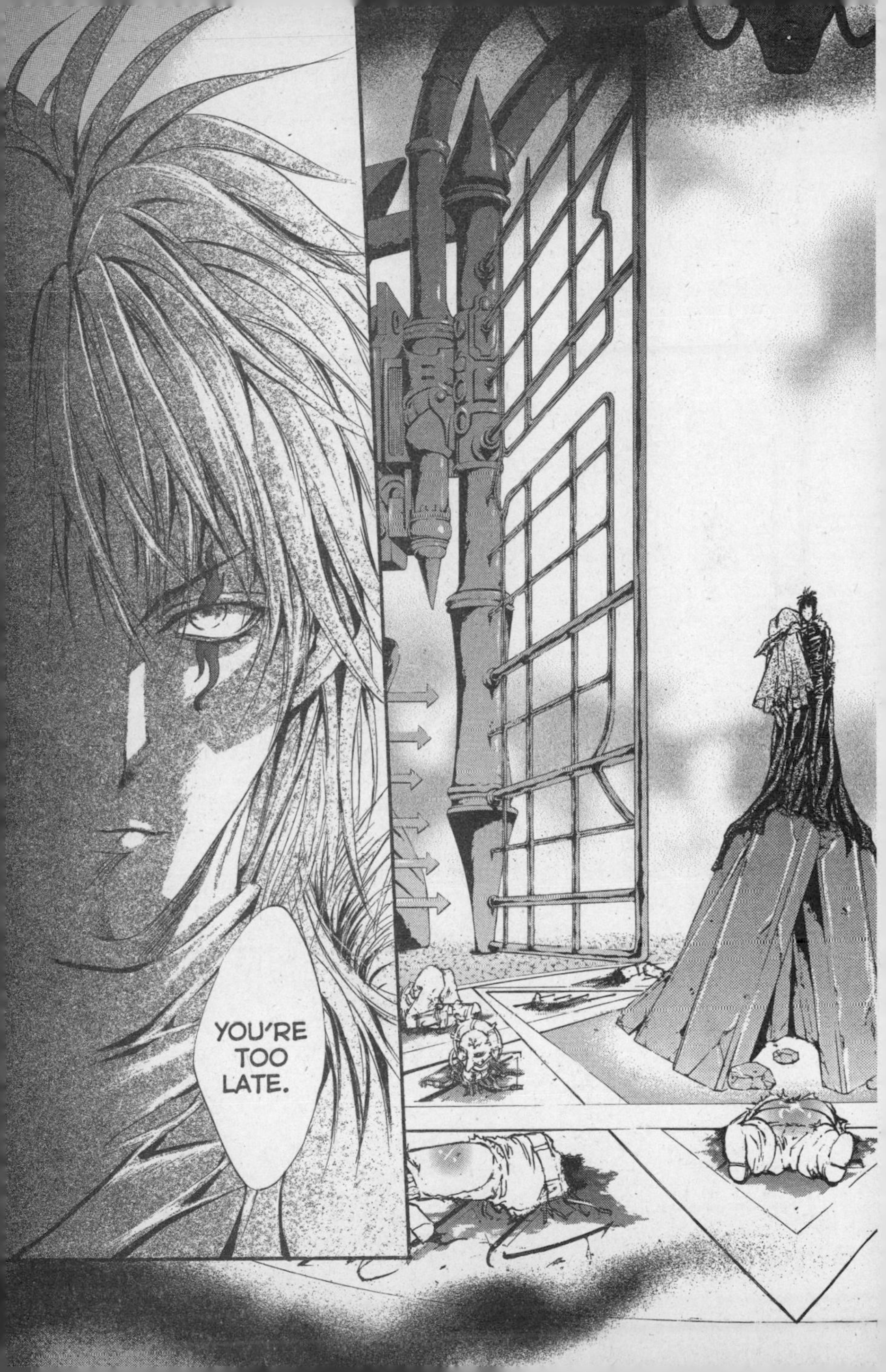
YOU'RE TOO LATE.

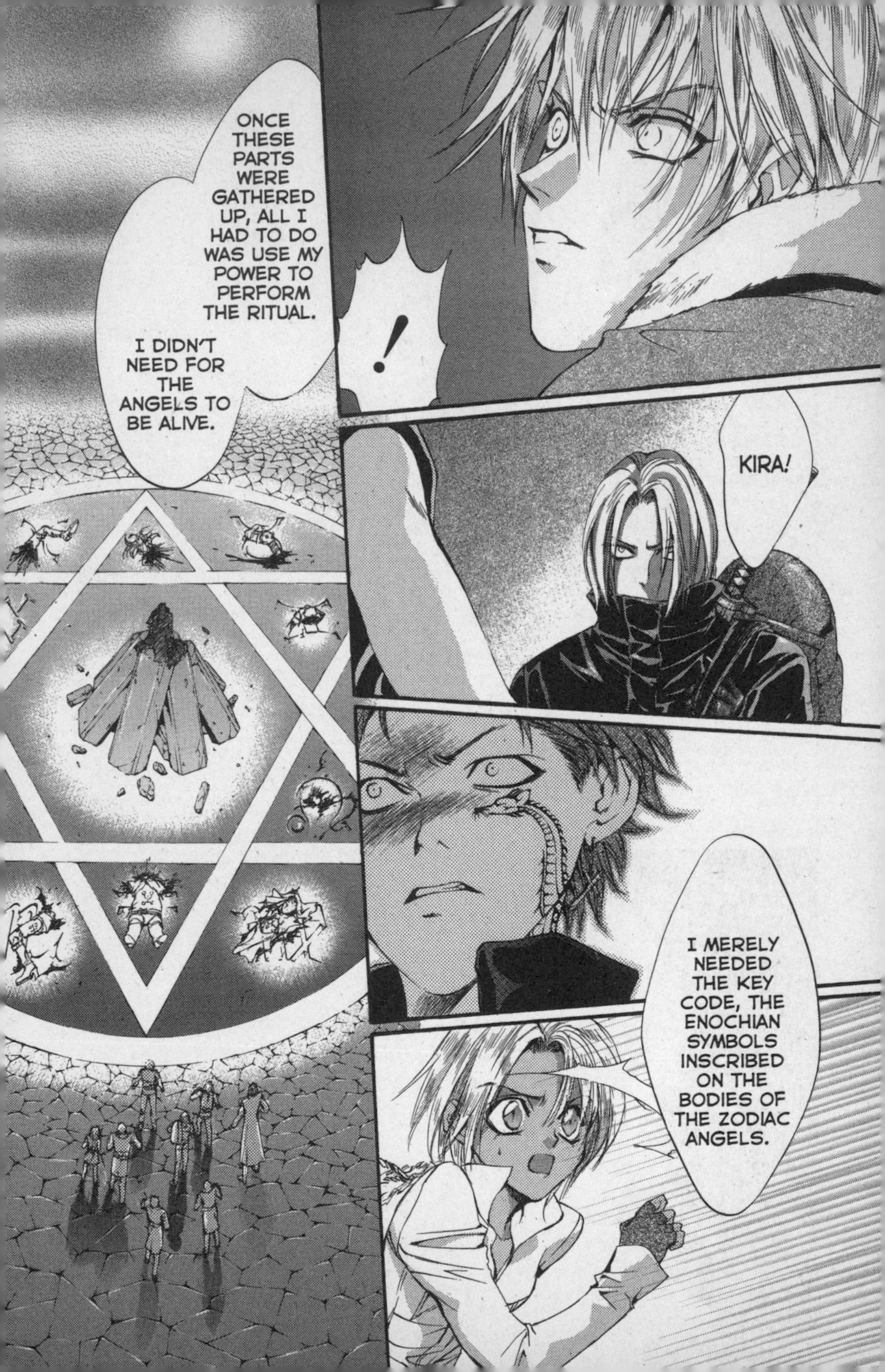
!
KIRA!
I MERELY NEEDED THE KEY CODE, THE ENOCHIAN SYMBOLS INSCRIBED ON THE BODIES OF THE ZODIAC ANGELS.
ONCE THESE PARTS WERE GATHERED UP, ALL I HAD TO DO WAS USE MY POWER TO PERFORM THE RITUAL.
I DIDN'T NEED FOR THE ANGELS TO BE ALIVE.

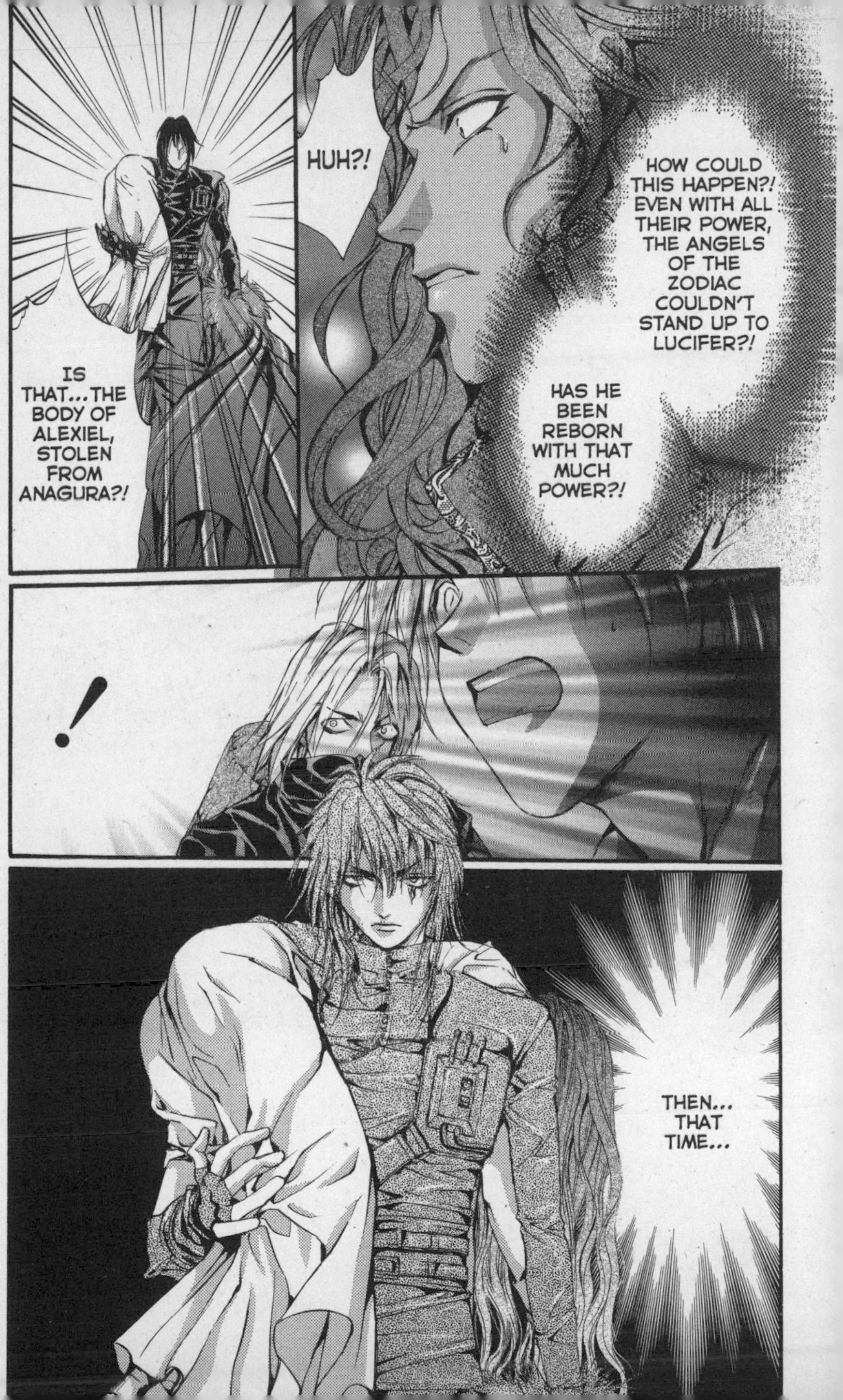
HOW COULD THIS HAPPEN?! EVEN WITH ALL THEIR POWER, THE ANGELS OF THE ZODIAC COULDN'T STAND UP TO LUCIFER?!
HAS HE BEEN REBORN WITH THAT MUCH POWER?!
HUH?!
IS THAT...THE BODY OF ALEXIEL, STOLEN FROM ANAGURA?!
!
THEN... THAT TIME...

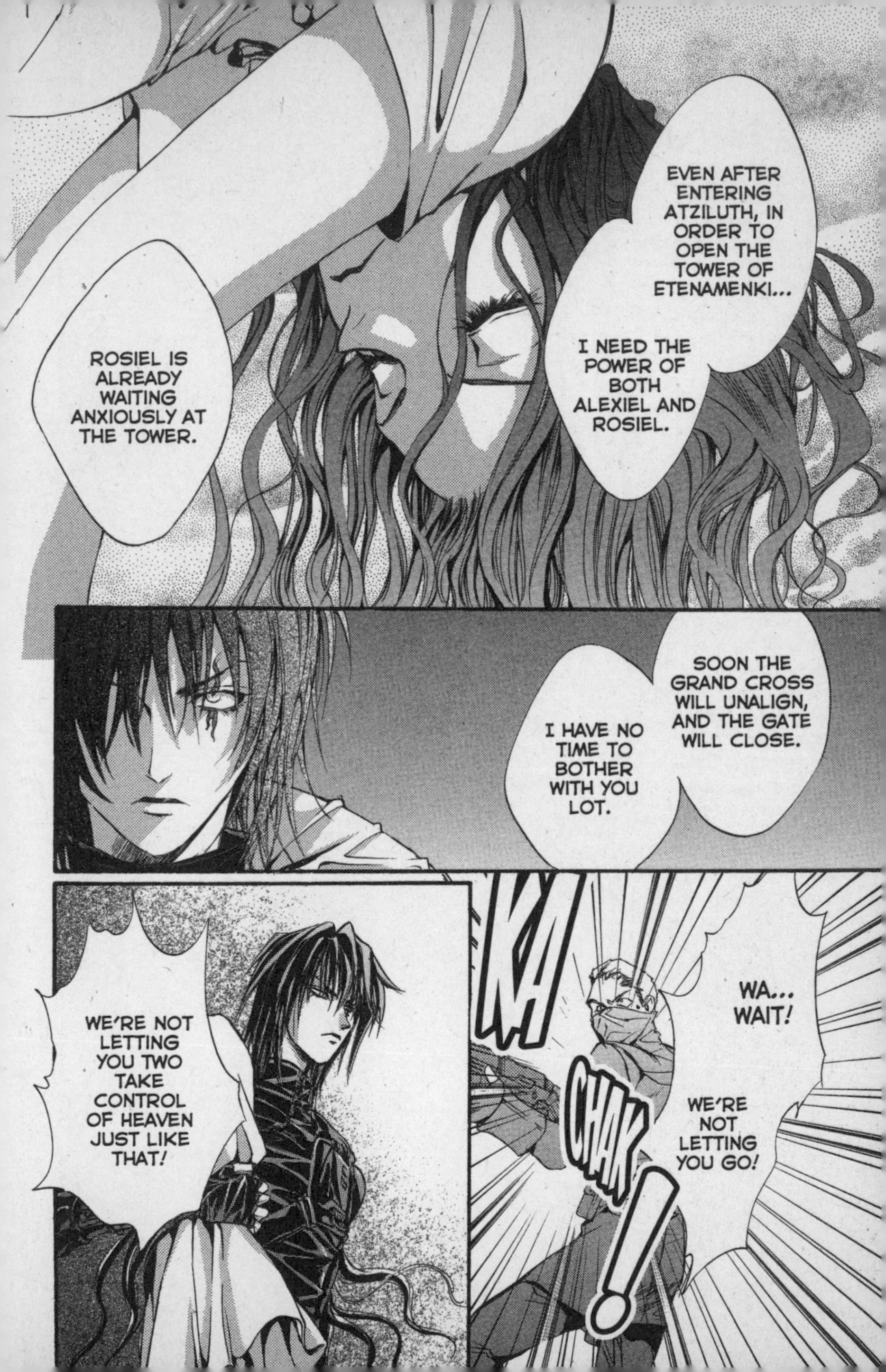
EVEN AFTER ENTERING ATZILUTH, IN ORDER TO OPEN THE TOWER OF ETENAMENKI...
I NEED THE POWER OF BOTH ALEXIEL AND ROSIEL.
ROSIEL IS ALREADY WAITING ANXIOUSLY AT THE TOWER.
SOON THE GRAND CROSS WILL UNALIGN, AND THE GATE WILL CLOSE.
I HAVE NO TIME TO BOTHER WITH YOU LOT.
WA... WAIT!
KA
WE'RE NOT LETTING YOU GO!
CHAK!
WE'RE NOT LETTING YOU TWO TAKE CONTROL OF HEAVEN JUST LIKE THAT!

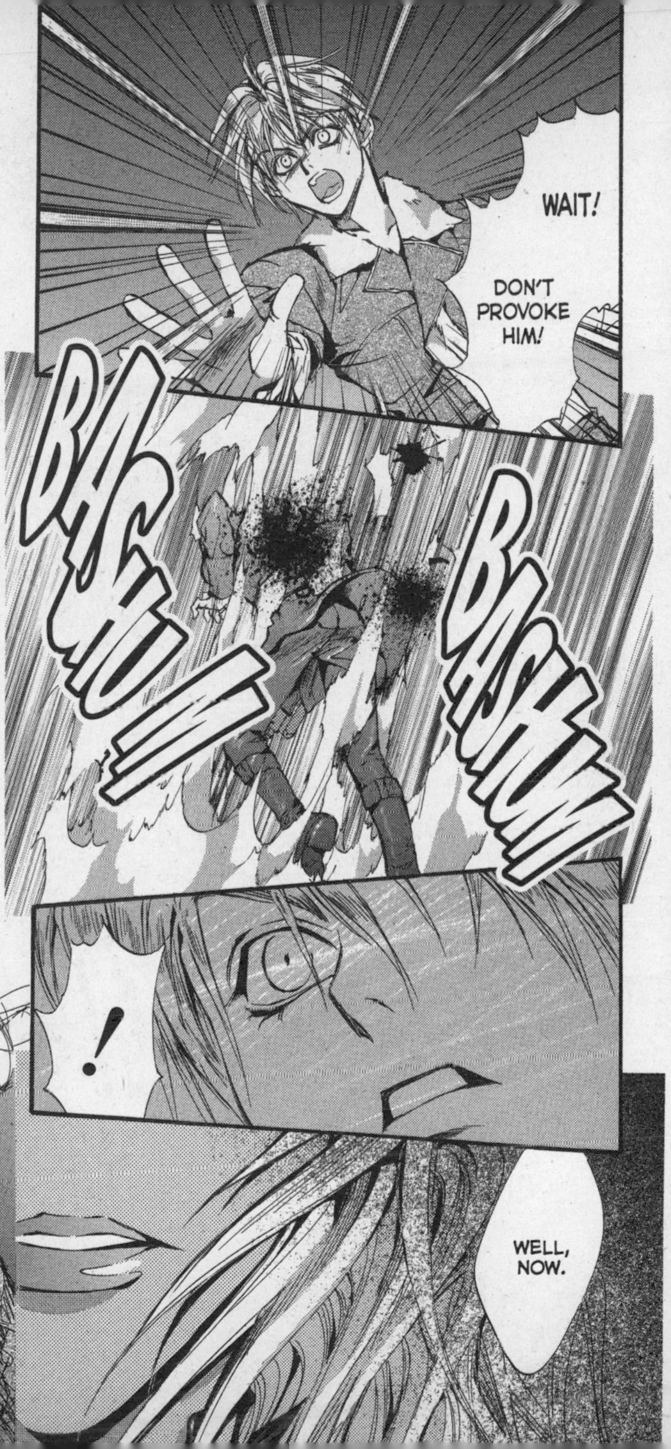
WAIT!
DON'T PROVOKE HIM!
BASHUM!
BACHU!
!
WELL, NOW.

The Grand Cross! It really isn't much like a cross. The more you look into it, the more it doesn't make sense. Can't say it's a "cross," really. I guess it doesn't matter so much. But when I searched the Web, I found "Life at the time of great cataclysm after the Grand Cross." It's good nothing like that happened. Sorry about the Twelve Angels of the Zodiac. I couldn't draw them all. That picture in the last scene of the previous section of a girl sleeping on a throne is Alexiel when she was young. Some people thought it was Sara or Doll. But why? Sara's hair color is totally different.

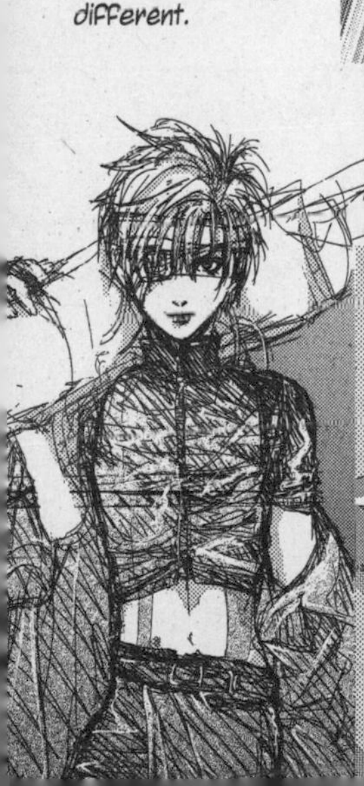

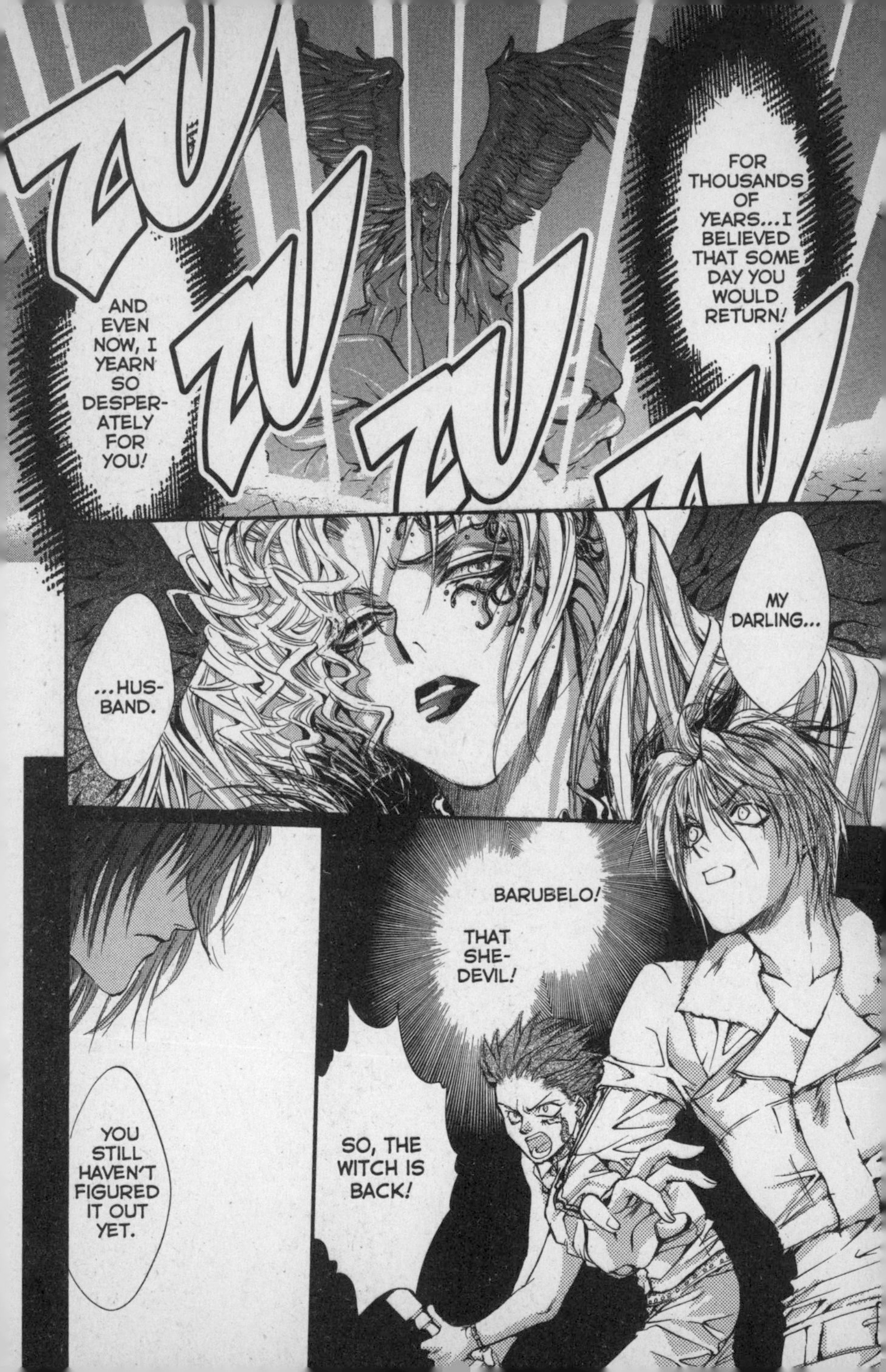
FOR THOUSANDS OF YEARS...I BELIEVED THAT SOME DAY YOU WOULD RETURN!
ZU ZU ZU ZU
AND EVEN NOW, I YEARN SO DESPERATELY FOR YOU!
MY DARLING...
...HUSBAND.
BARUBELO!
THAT SHE-DEVIL!
SO, THE WITCH IS BACK!
YOU STILL HAVEN'T FIGURED IT OUT YET.

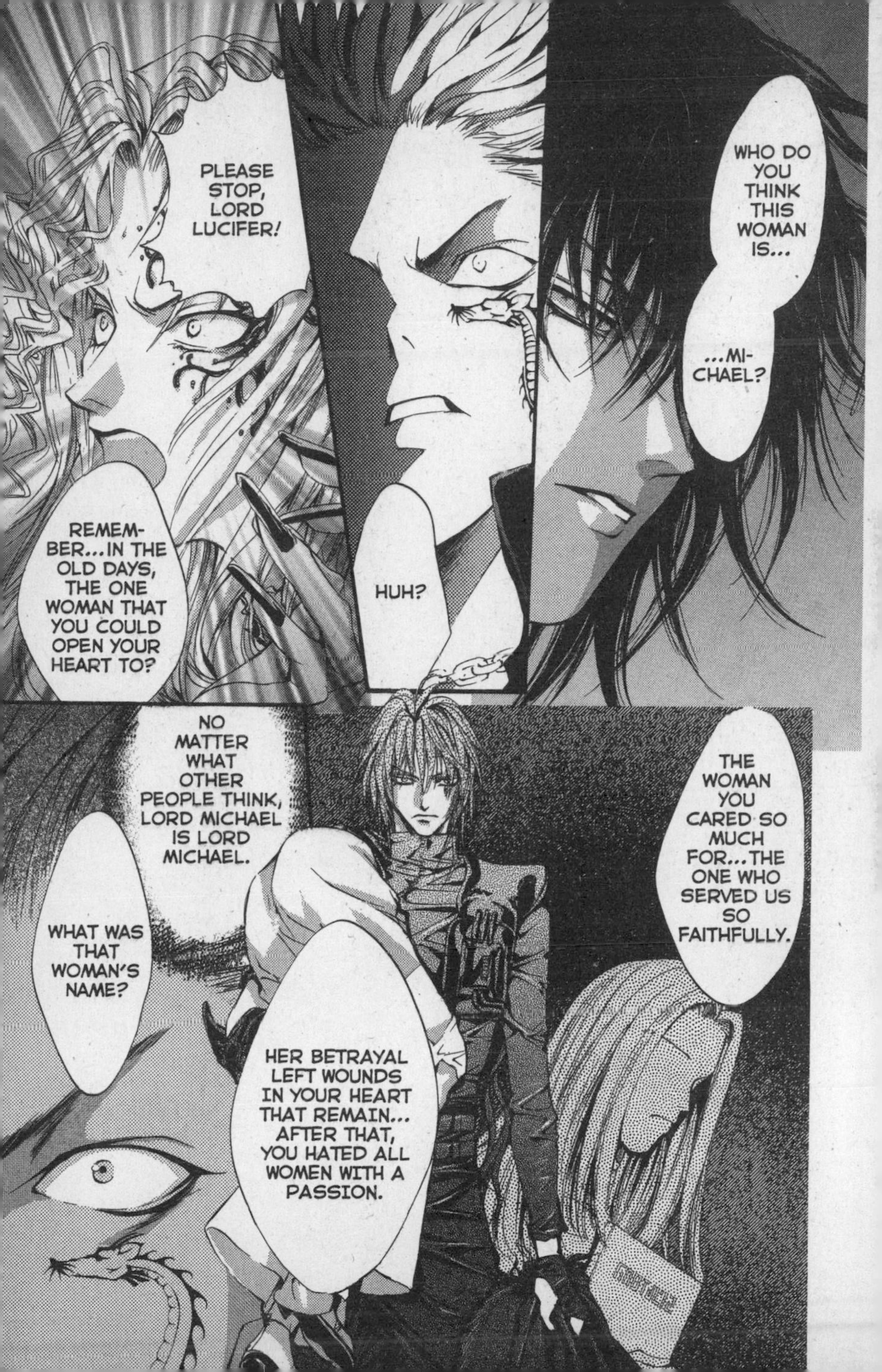
WHO DO YOU THINK THIS WOMAN IS...
...MI-CHAEL?
HUH?
PLEASE STOP, LORD LUCIFER!
REMEMBER... IN THE OLD DAYS, THE ONE WOMAN THAT YOU COULD OPEN YOUR HEART TO?
THE WOMAN YOU CARED SO MUCH FOR... THE ONE WHO SERVED US SO FAITHFULLY.
HER BETRAYAL LEFT WOUNDS IN YOUR HEART THAT REMAIN... AFTER THAT, YOU HATED ALL WOMEN WITH A PASSION.
WHAT WAS THAT WOMAN'S NAME?
NO MATTER WHAT OTHER PEOPLE THINK, LORD MICHAEL IS LORD MICHAEL.

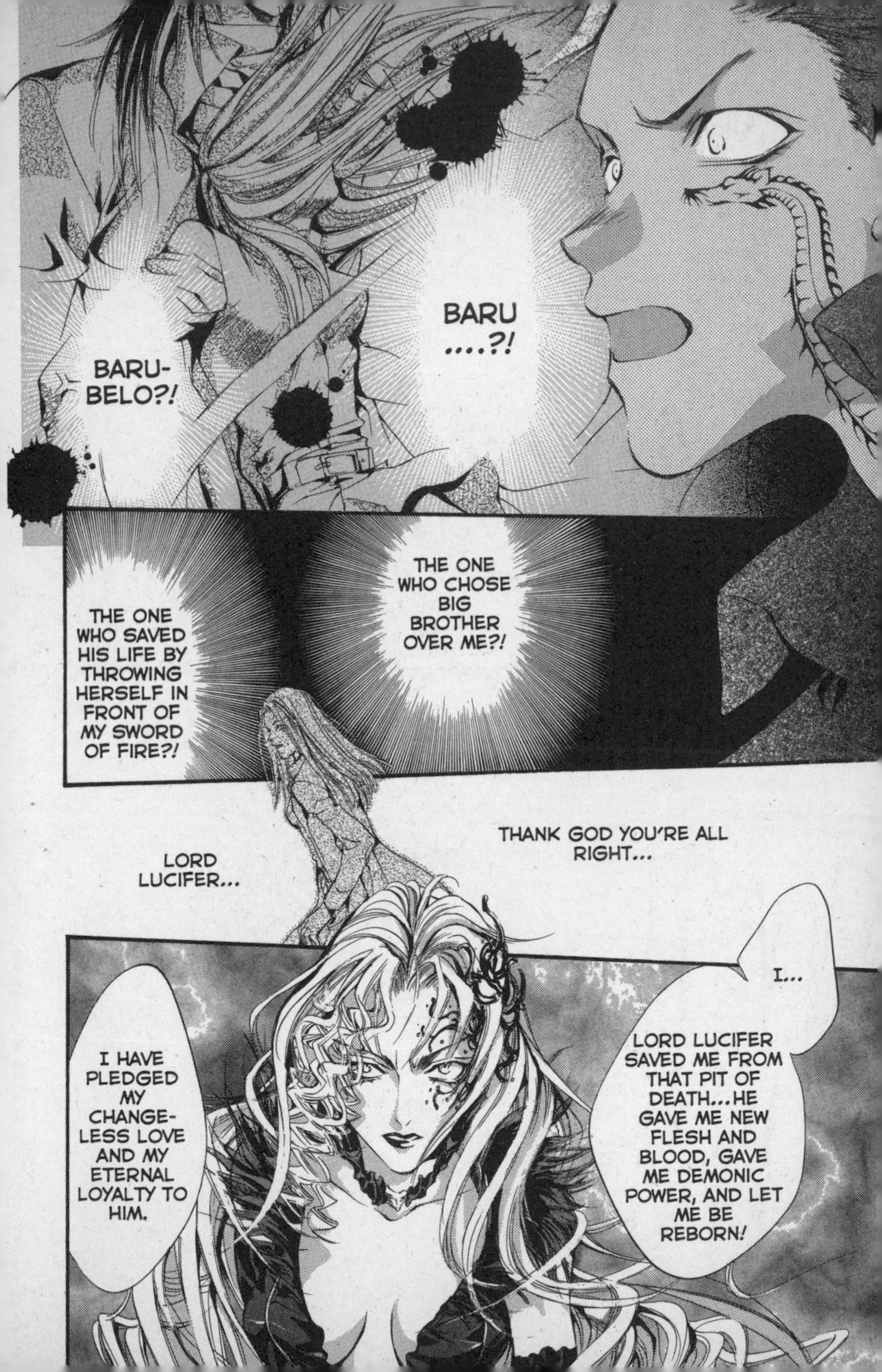
BARU ....?!
BARU-BELO?!
THE ONE WHO CHOSE BIG BROTHER OVER ME?!
THE ONE WHO SAVED HIS LIFE BY THROWING HERSELF IN FRONT OF MY SWORD OF FIRE?!
THANK GOD YOU'RE ALL RIGHT...
LORD LUCIFER...
I...
LORD LUCIFER SAVED ME FROM THAT PIT OF DEATH...HE GAVE ME NEW FLESH AND BLOOD, GAVE ME DEMONIC POWER, AND LET ME BE REBORN!
I HAVE PLEDGED MY CHANGELESS LOVE AND MY ETERNAL LOYALTY TO HIM.

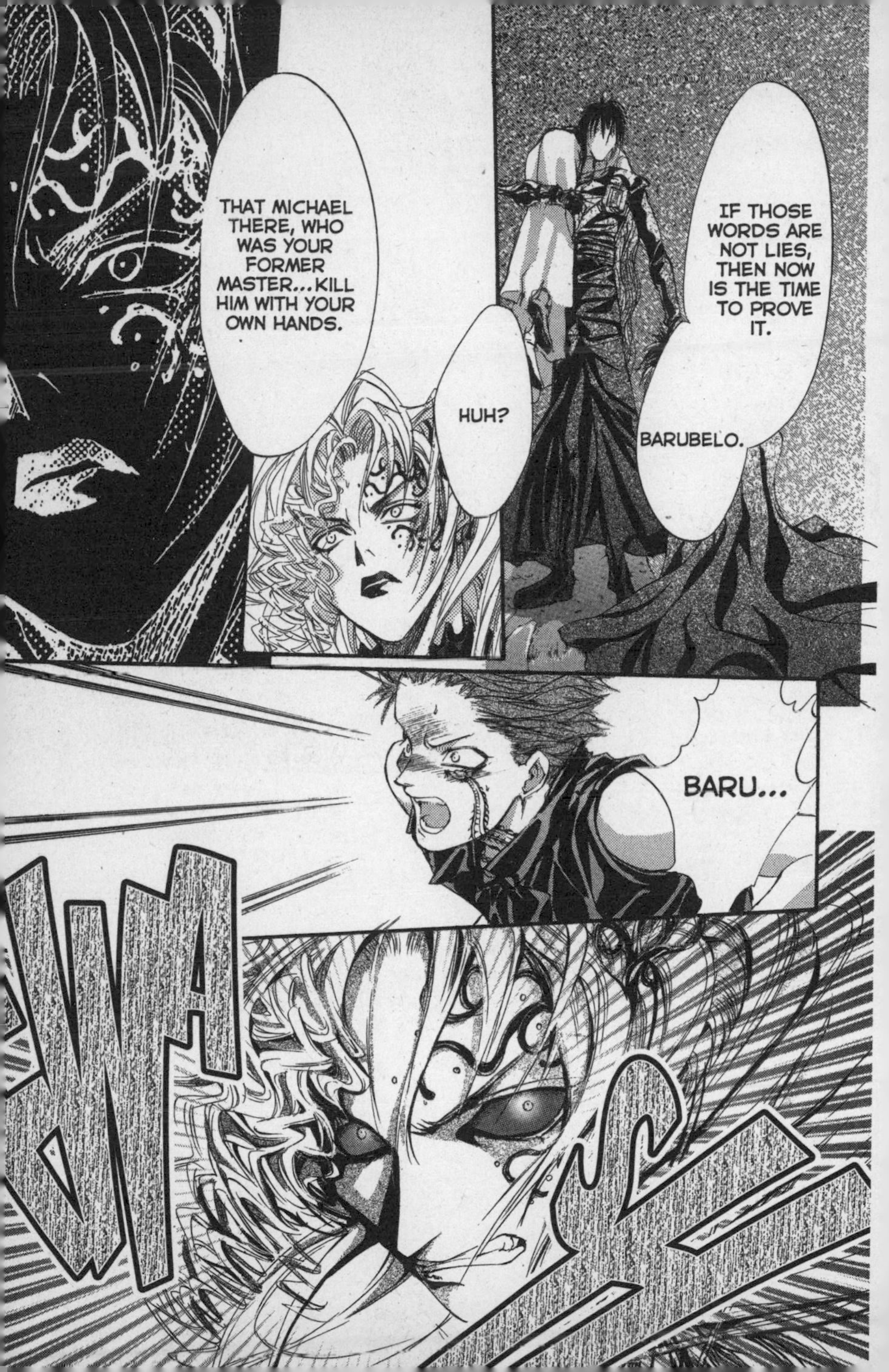
IF THOSE WORDS ARE NOT LIES, THEN NOW IS THE TIME TO PROVE IT.
BARUBELO.
HUH?
THAT MICHAEL THERE, WHO WAS YOUR FORMER MASTER...KILL HIM WITH YOUR OWN HANDS.
BARU...

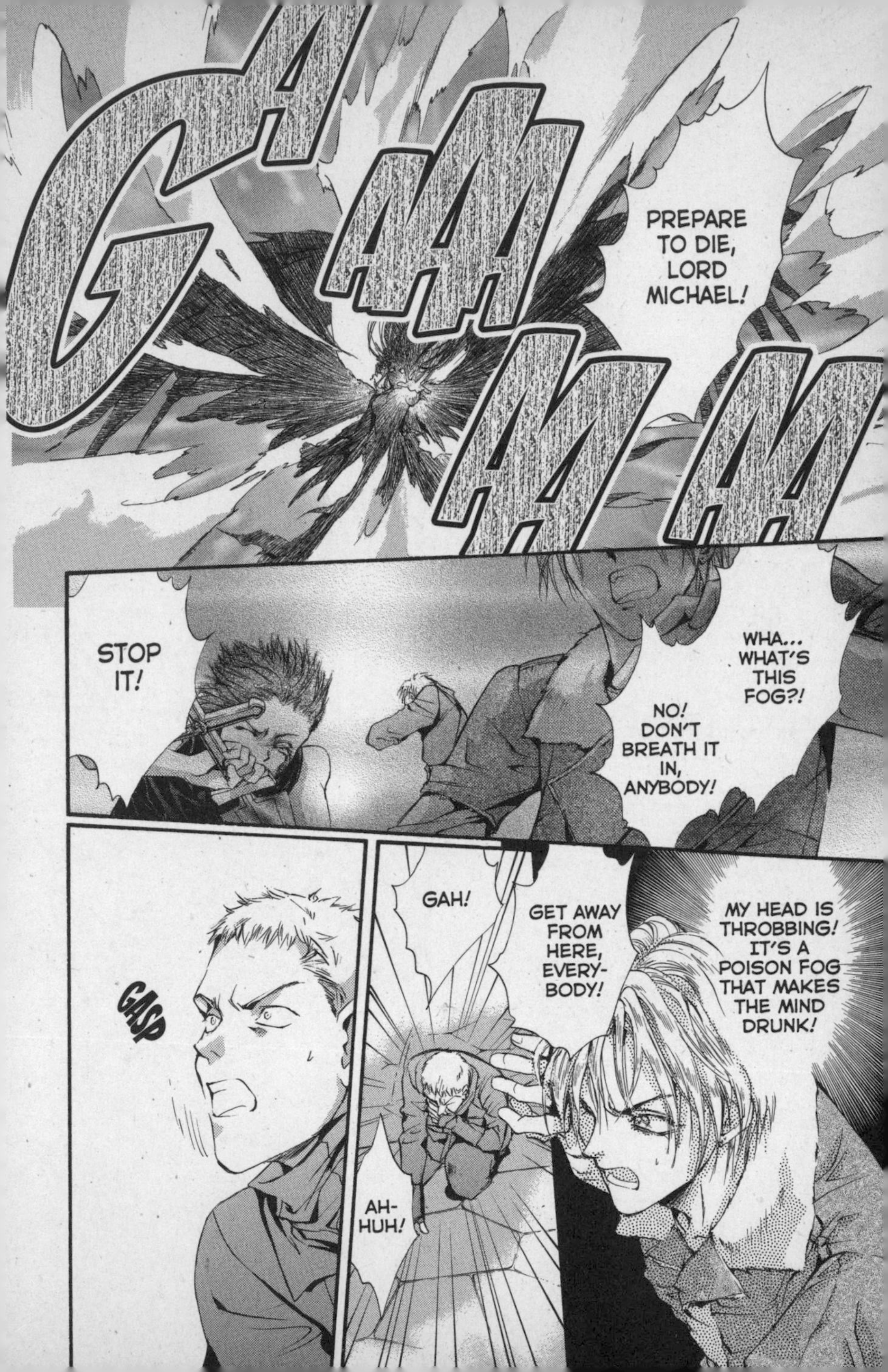
GAMMM
PREPARE TO DIE, LORD MICHAEL!
WHA... WHAT'S THIS FOG?!
NO! DON'T BREATH IT IN, ANYBODY!
STOP IT!
MY HEAD IS THROBBING! IT'S A POISON FOG THAT MAKES THE MIND DRUNK!
GET AWAY FROM HERE, EVERY-BODY!
GAH!
AH-HUH!
GASP

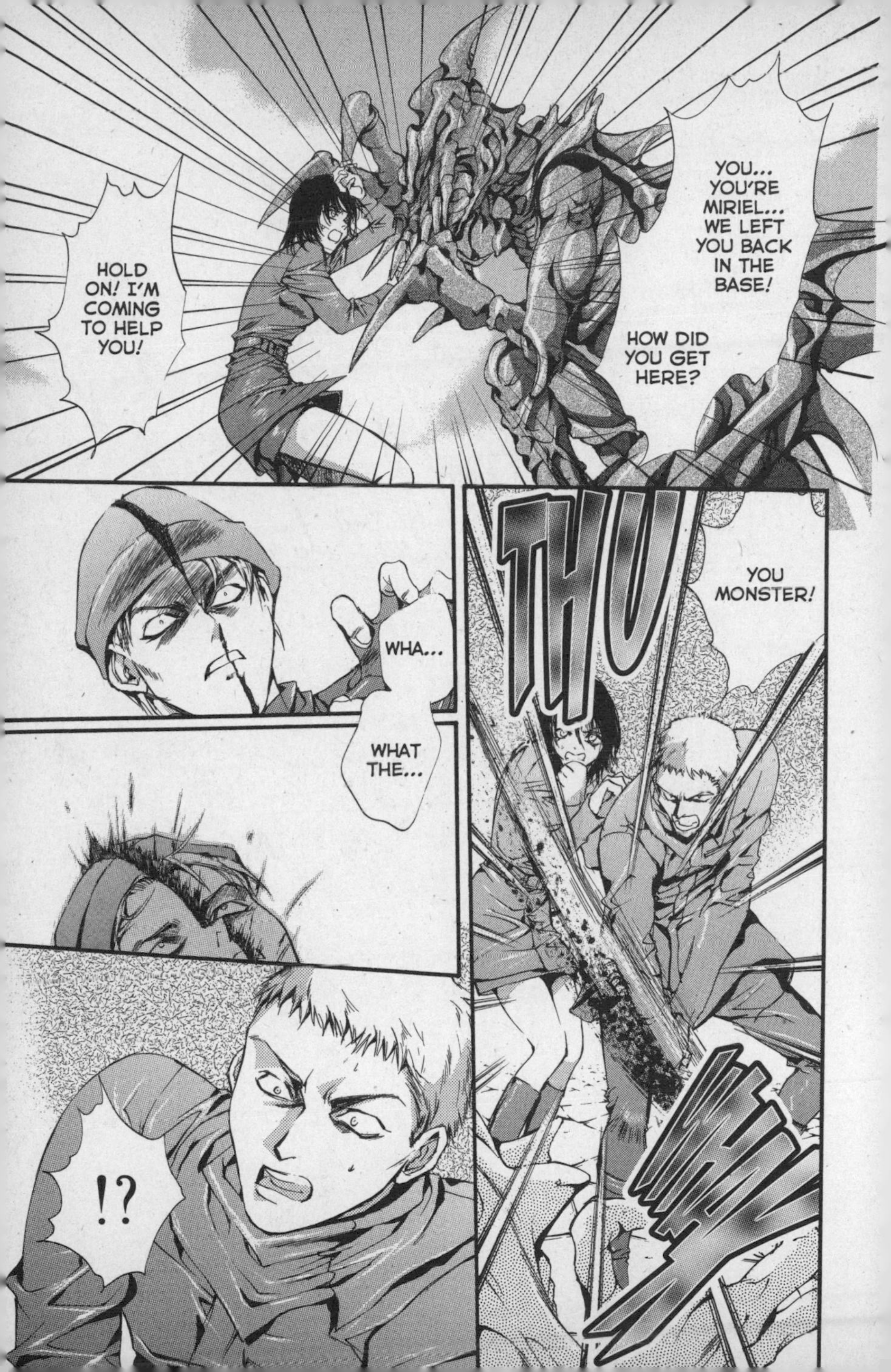
YOU... YOU'RE MIRIEL... WE LEFT YOU BACK IN THE BASE!
HOW DID YOU GET HERE?
HOLD ON! I'M COMING TO HELP YOU!
THU
YOU MONSTER!
WHA...
WHAT THE...
!?

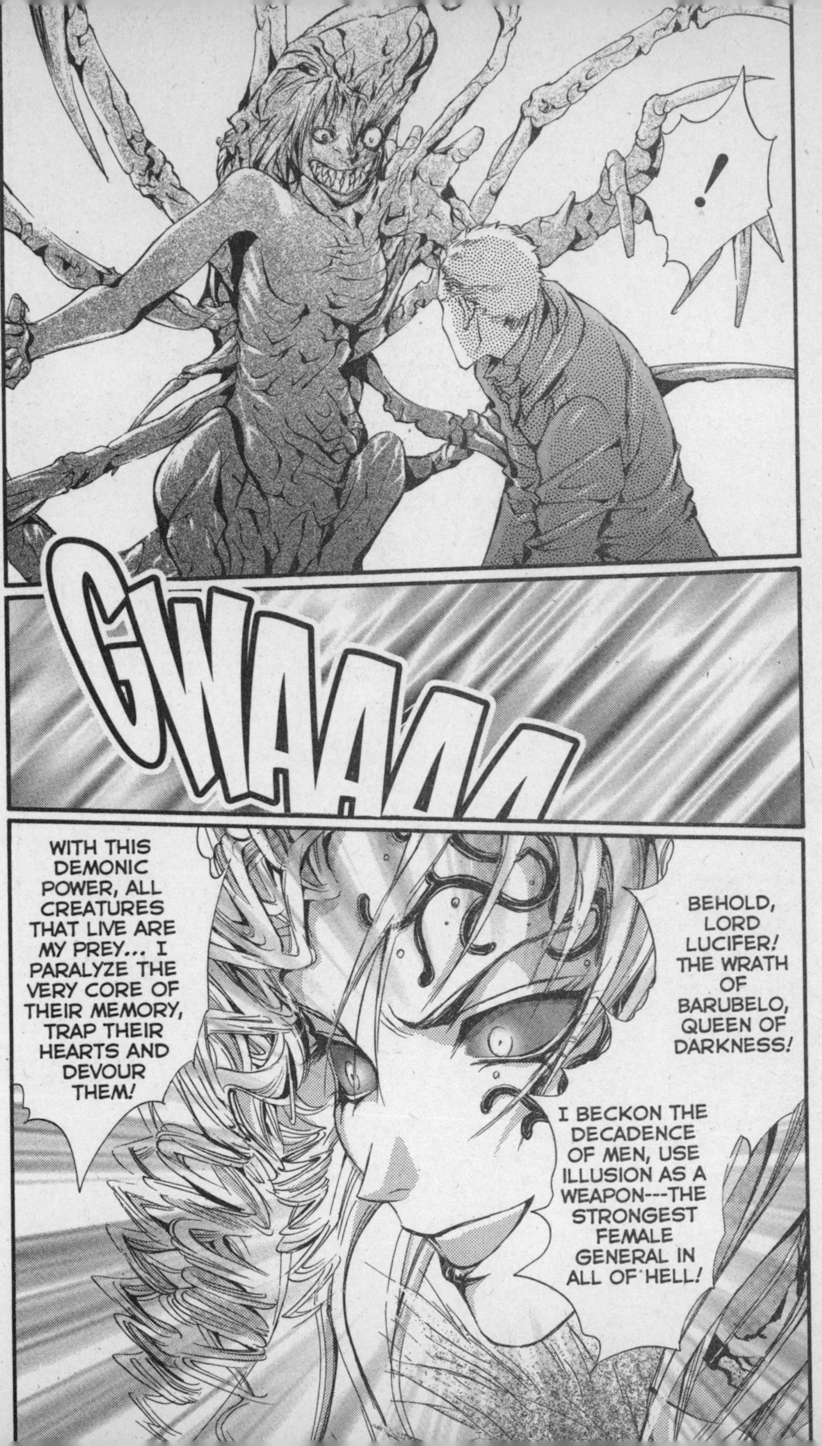
!
GWAAAA
BEHOLD, LORD LUCIFER! THE WRATH OF BARUBELO, QUEEN OF DARKNESS!
I BECKON THE DECADENCE OF MEN, USE ILLUSION AS A WEAPON---THE STRONGEST FEMALE GENERAL IN ALL OF HELL!
WITH THIS DEMONIC POWER, ALL CREATURES THAT LIVE ARE MY PREY... I PARALYZE THE VERY CORE OF THEIR MEMORY, TRAP THEIR HEARTS AND DEVOUR THEM!

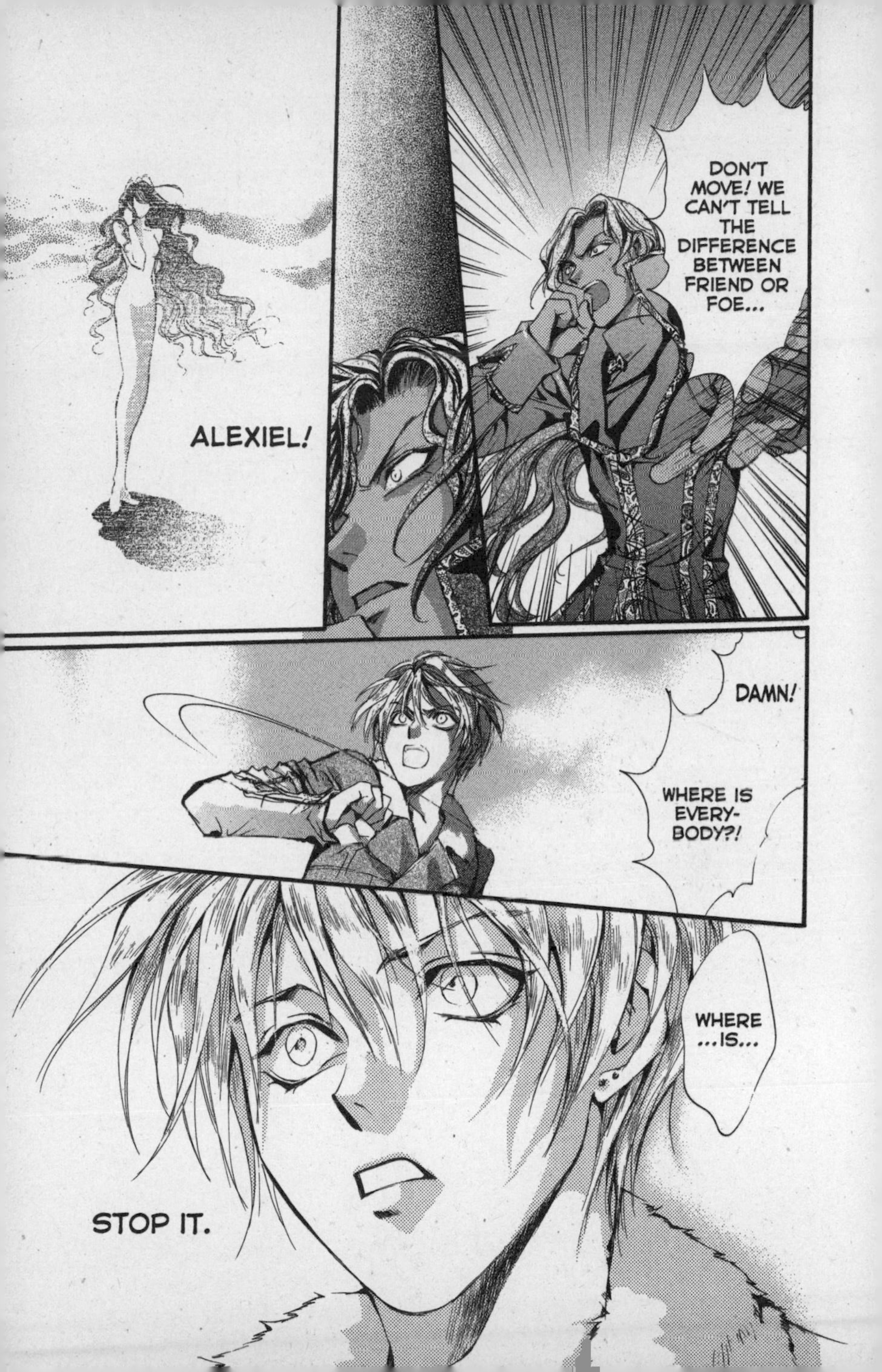
DON'T MOVE! WE CAN'T TELL THE DIFFERENCE BETWEEN FRIEND OR FOE...
ALEXIEL!
DAMN!
WHERE IS EVERY-BODY?!
WHERE ...IS...
STOP IT.

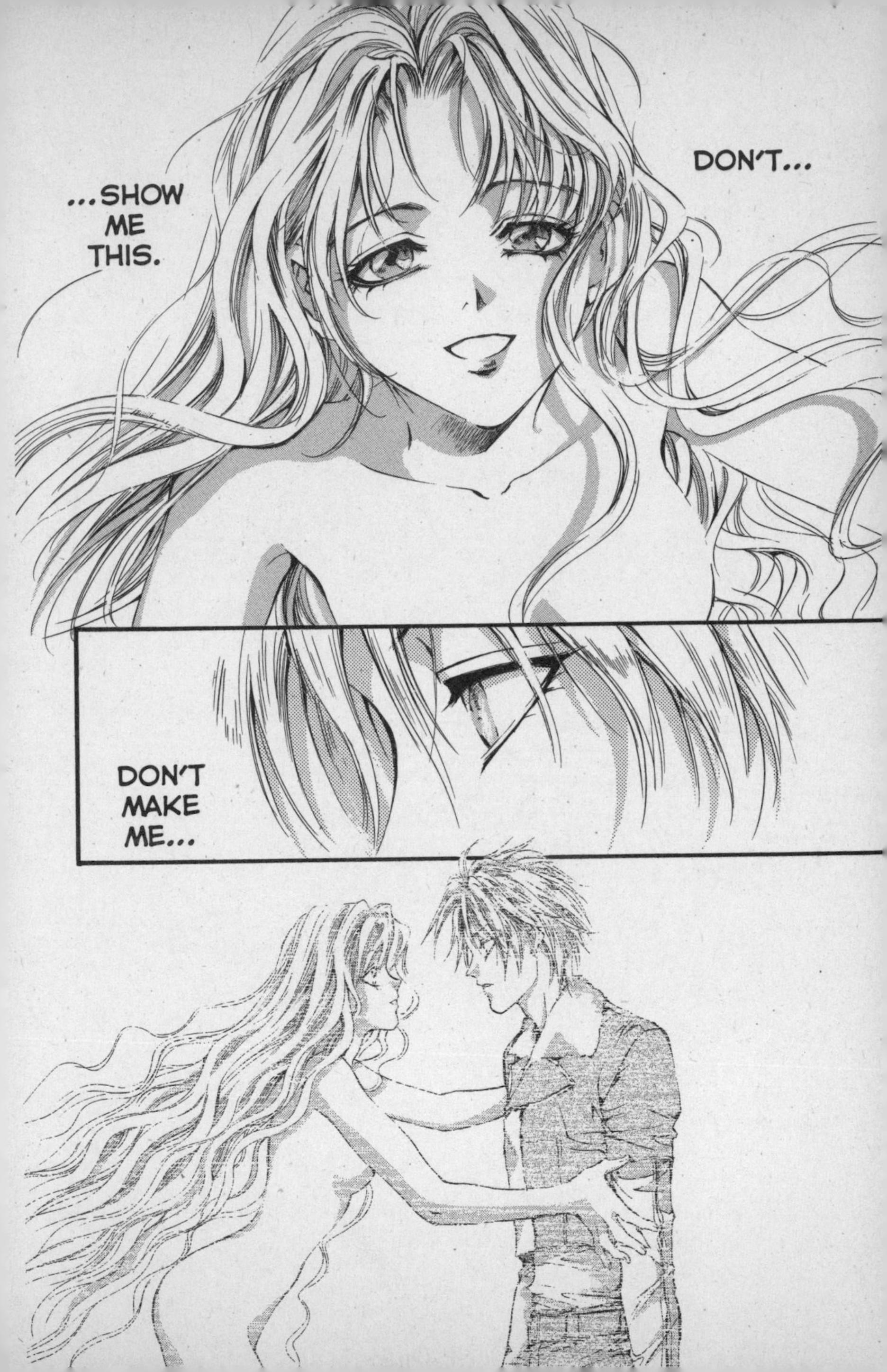
DON'T...
...SHOW ME THIS.
DON'T MAKE ME...

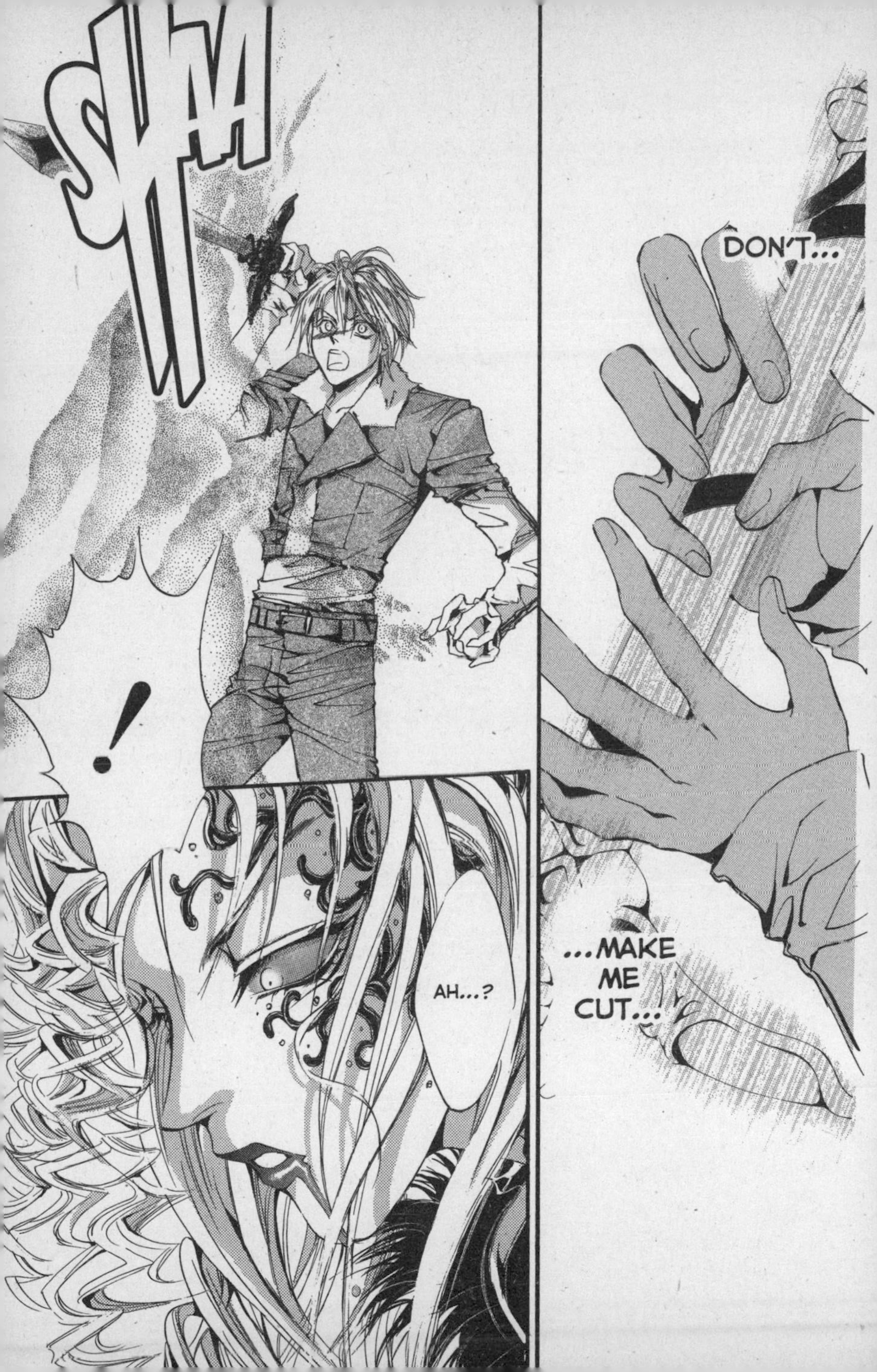
DON'T...
...MAKE ME CUT...
SHAA
!
AH...?

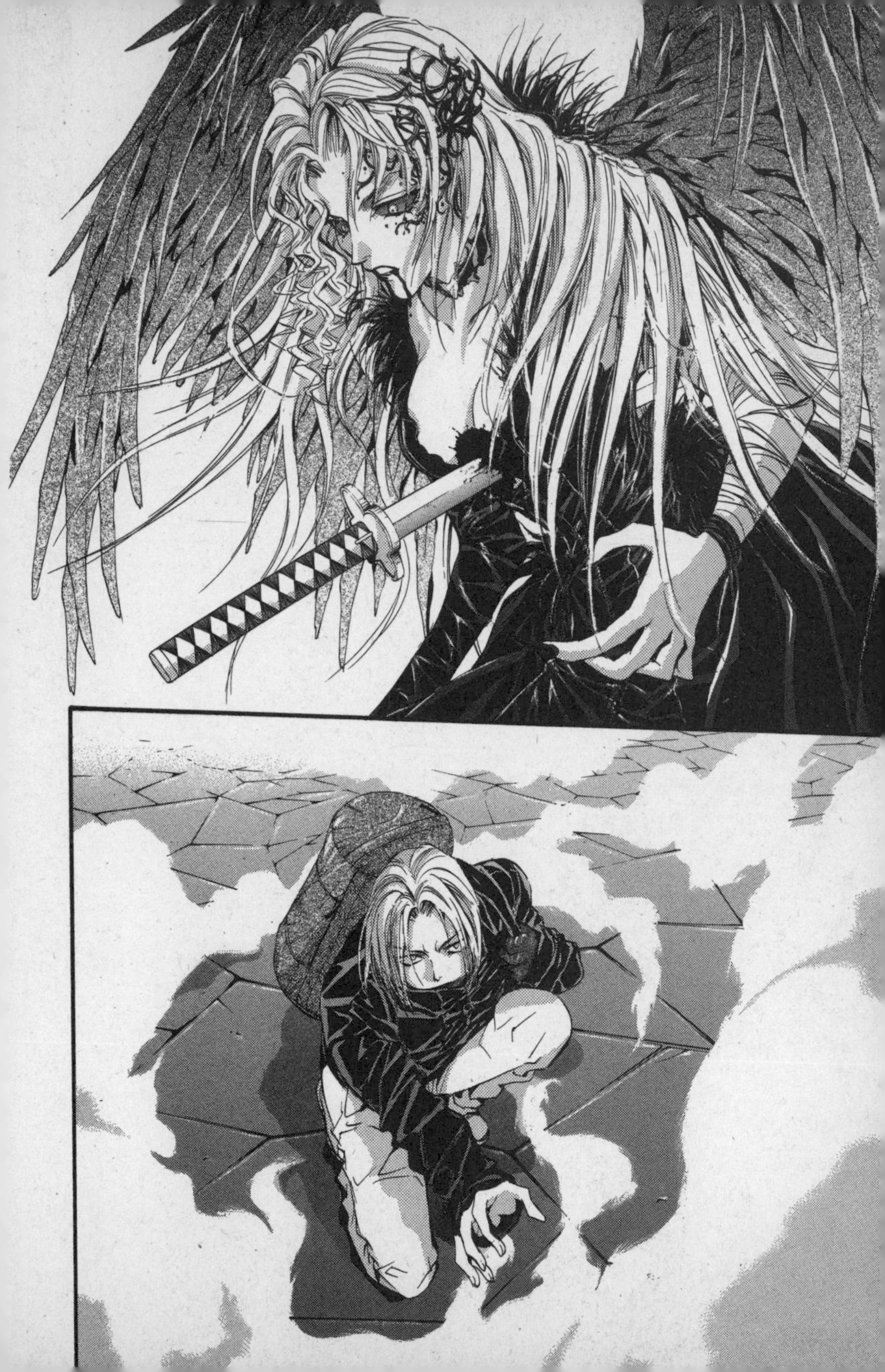

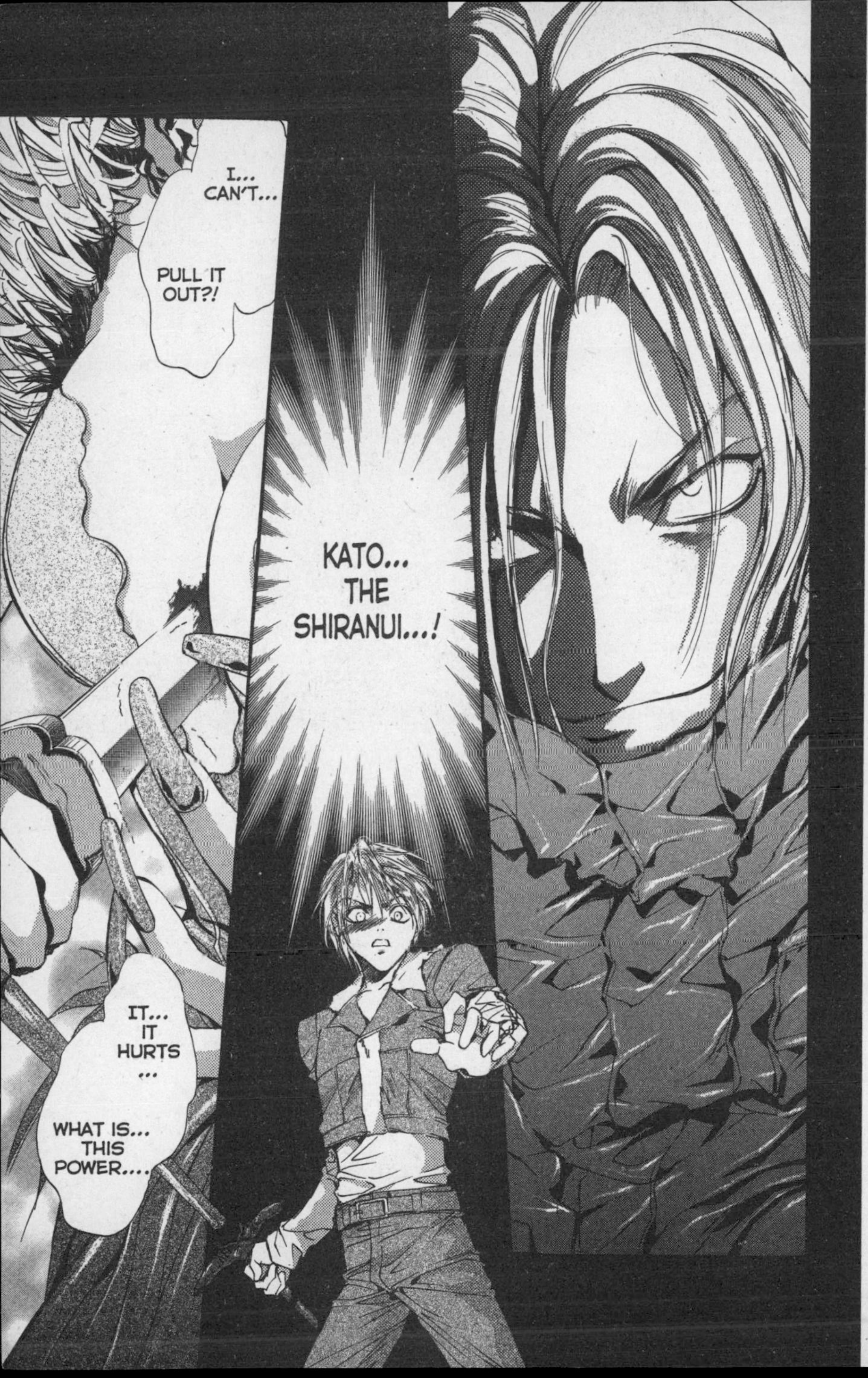
KATO... THE SHIRANUI...!
I... CAN'T...
PULL IT OUT?!
IT... IT HURTS...
WHAT IS... THIS POWER....

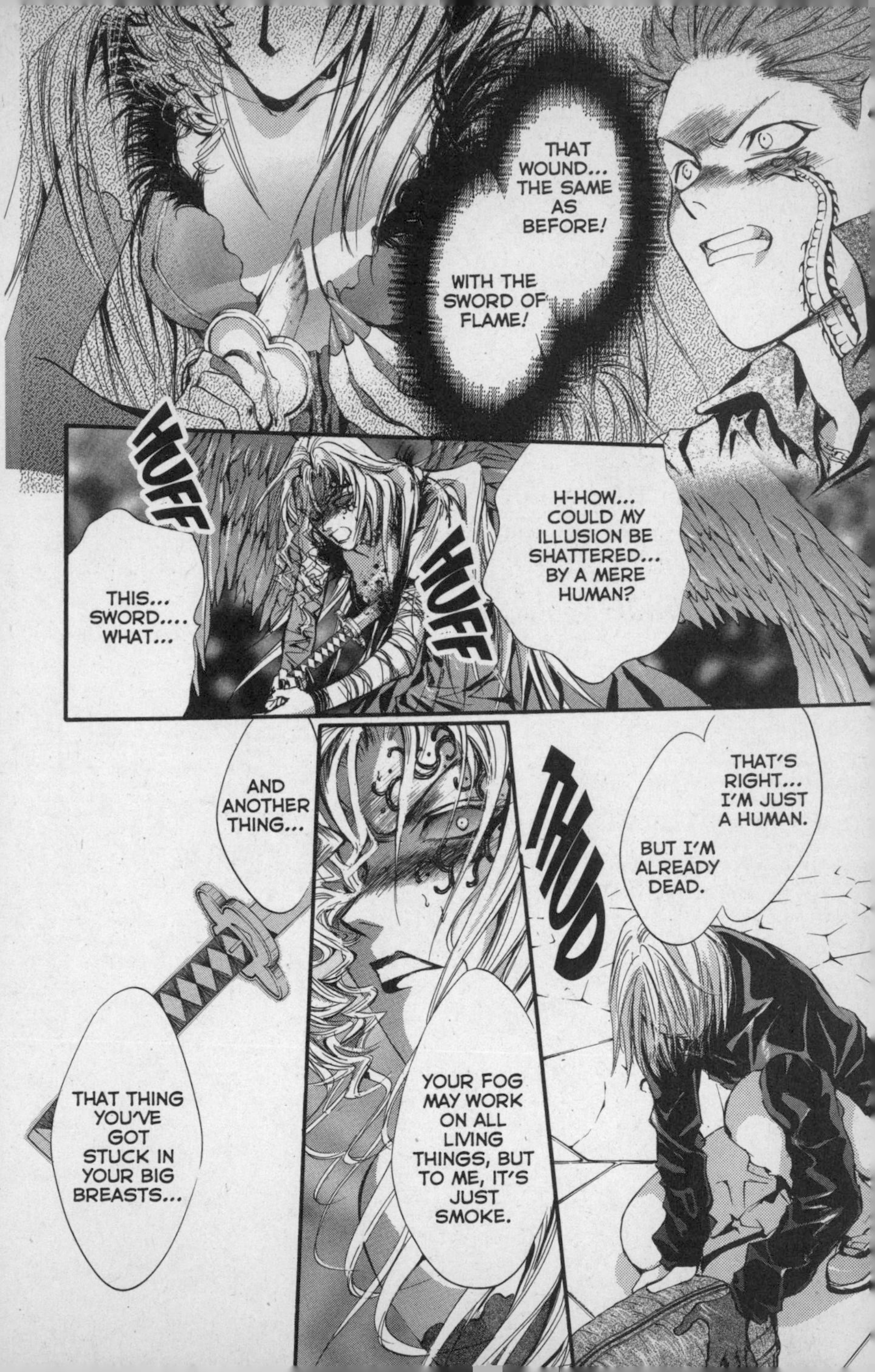
THAT WOUND... THE SAME AS BEFORE!
WITH THE SWORD OF FLAME!
H-HOW... COULD MY ILLUSION BE SHATTERED... BY A MERE HUMAN?
HUFF
HUFF
THIS... SWORD.... WHAT...
THAT'S RIGHT... I'M JUST A HUMAN.
BUT I'M ALREADY DEAD.
THUD
YOUR FOG MAY WORK ON ALL LIVING THINGS, BUT TO ME, IT'S JUST SMOKE.
AND ANOTHER THING...
THAT THING YOU'VE GOT STUCK IN YOUR BIG BREASTS...

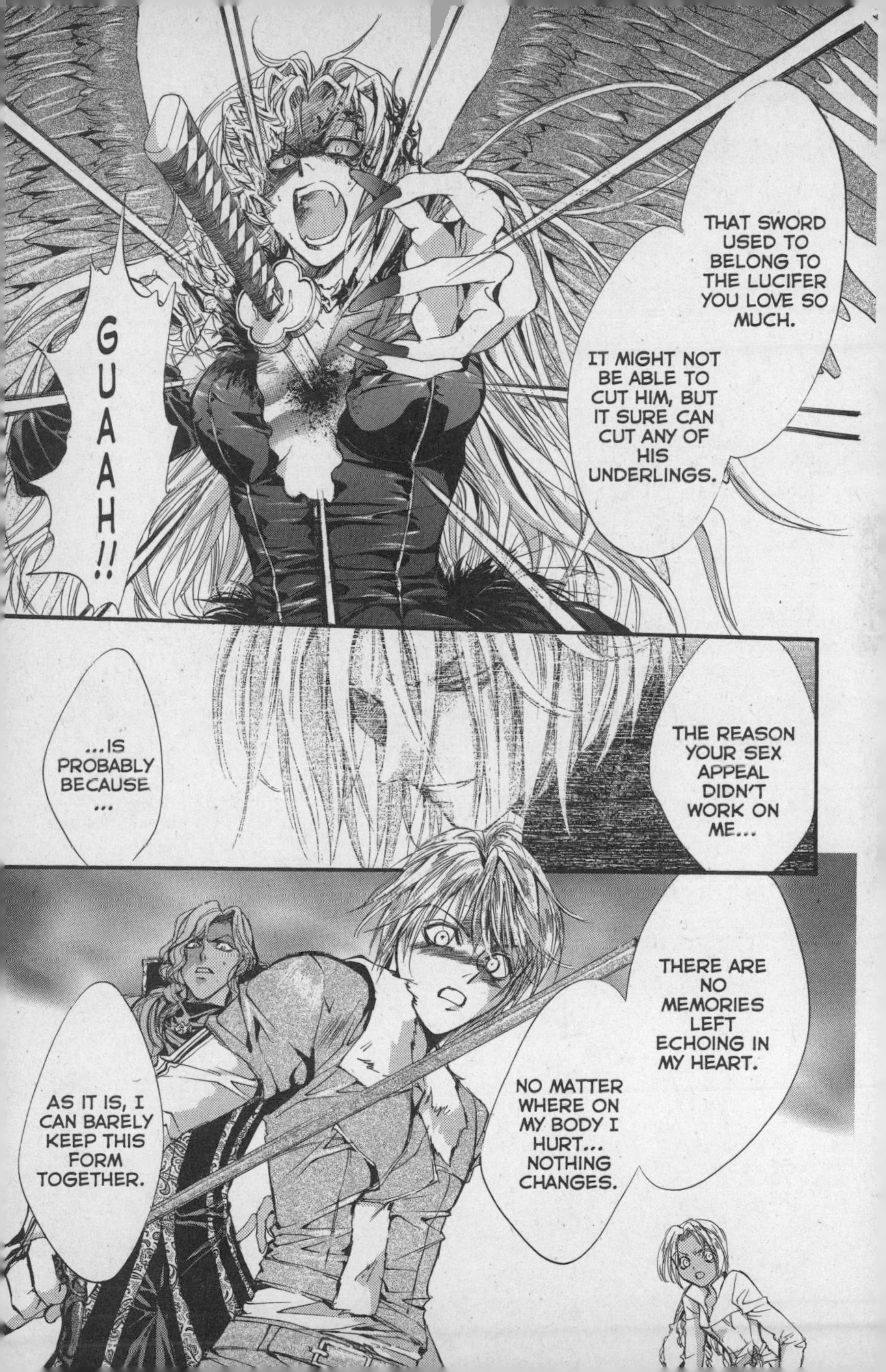
THAT SWORD USED TO BELONG TO THE LUCIFER YOU LOVE SO MUCH.
IT MIGHT NOT BE ABLE TO CUT HIM, BUT IT SURE CAN CUT ANY OF HIS UNDERLINGS.
GUAAH!!
THE REASON YOUR SEX APPEAL DIDN'T WORK ON ME...
...IS PROBABLY BECAUSE ...
THERE ARE NO MEMORIES LEFT ECHOING IN MY HEART.
NO MATTER WHERE ON MY BODY I HURT... NOTHING CHANGES.
AS IT IS, I CAN BARELY KEEP THIS FORM TOGETHER.

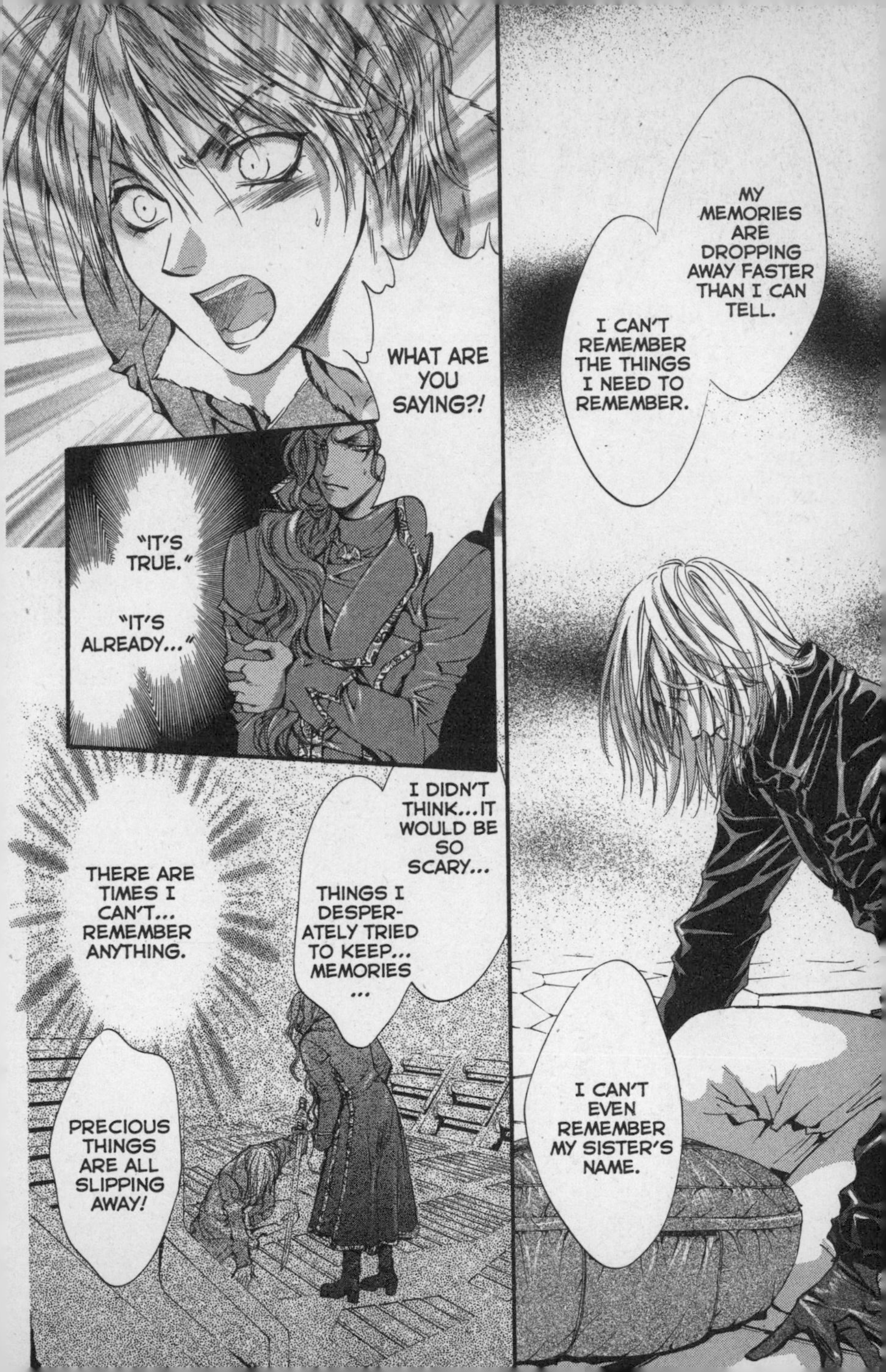
MY MEMORIES ARE DROPPING AWAY FASTER THAN I CAN TELL.
I CAN'T REMEMBER THE THINGS I NEED TO REMEMBER.
I CAN'T EVEN REMEMBER MY SISTER'S NAME.
WHAT ARE YOU SAYING?!
"IT'S TRUE."
"IT'S ALREADY..."
I DIDN'T THINK...IT WOULD BE SO SCARY...
THINGS I DESPER-ATELY TRIED TO KEEP... MEMORIES ...
THERE ARE TIMES I CAN'T... REMEMBER ANYTHING.
PRECIOUS THINGS ARE ALL SLIPPING AWAY!

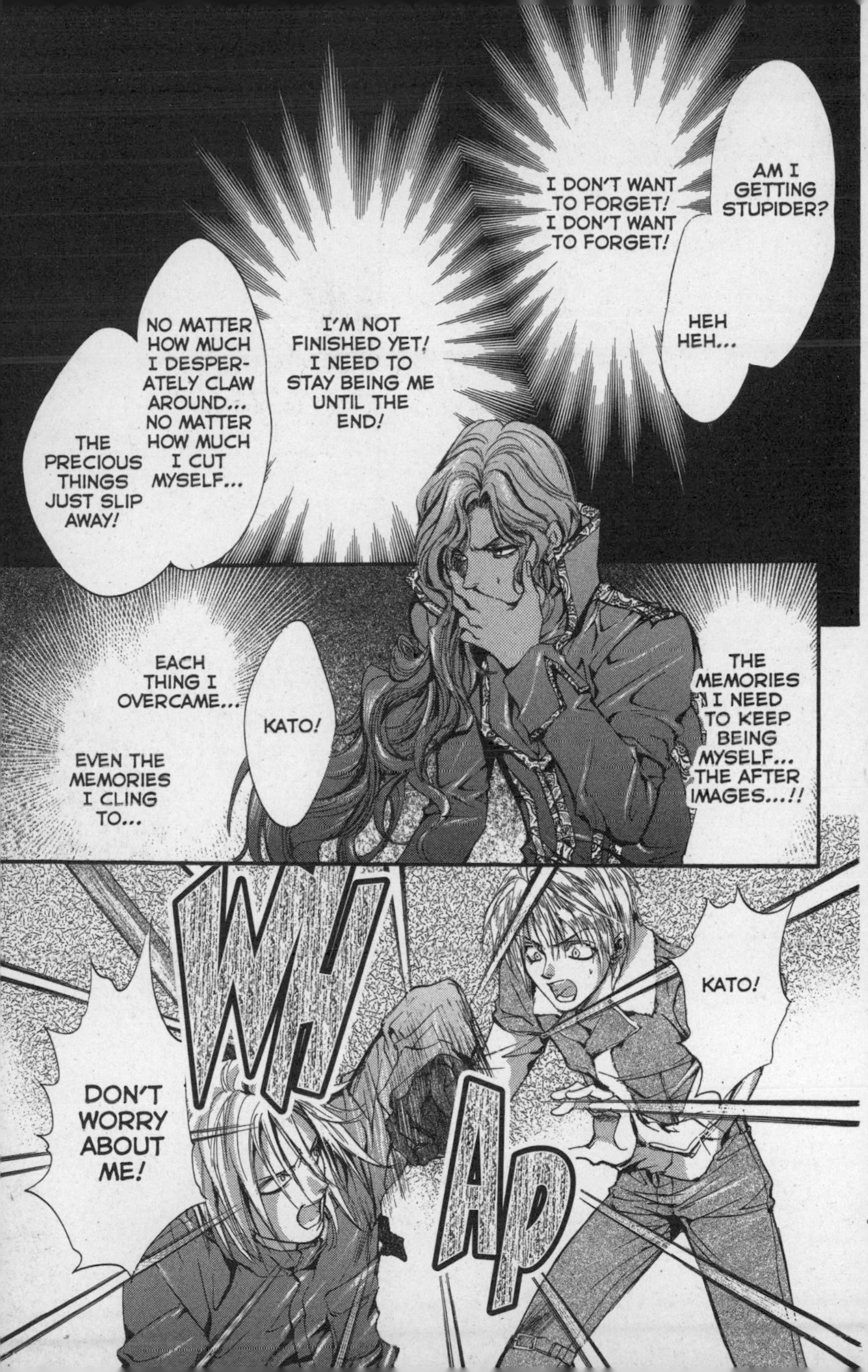
AM I GETTING STUPIDER?
HEH HEH...
I DON'T WANT TO FORGET! I DON'T WANT TO FORGET!
I'M NOT FINISHED YET! I NEED TO STAY BEING ME UNTIL THE END!
NO MATTER HOW MUCH I DESPER-ATELY CLAW AROUND... NO MATTER HOW MUCH I CUT MYSELF...
THE PRECIOUS THINGS JUST SLIP AWAY!
THE MEMORIES I NEED TO KEEP BEING MYSELF... THE AFTER IMAGES...!!
KATO!
EACH THING I OVERCAME...
EVEN THE MEMORIES I CLING TO...
KATO!
WHAP
DON'T WORRY ABOUT ME!

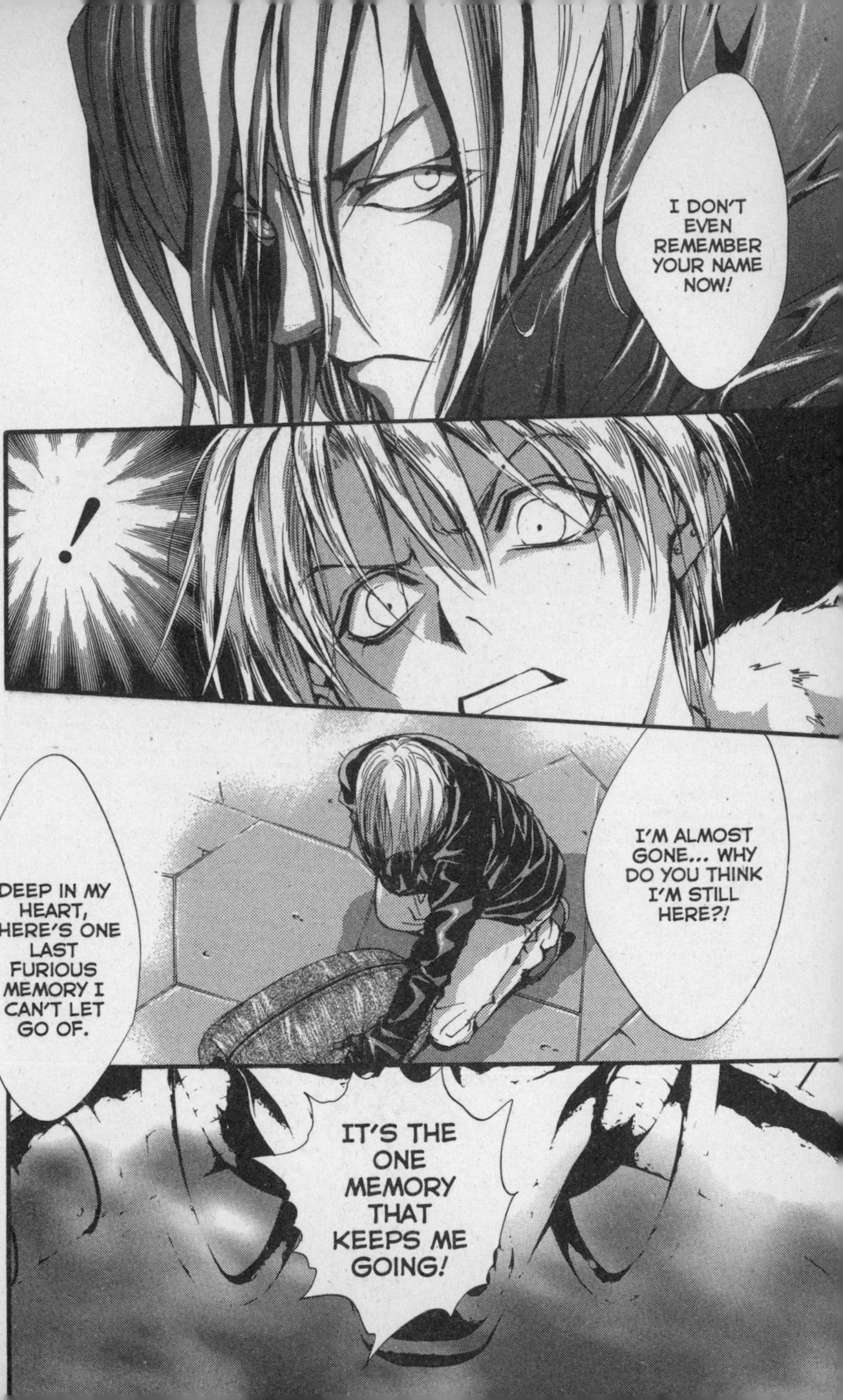
I DON'T EVEN REMEMBER YOUR NAME NOW!
!
I'M ALMOST GONE... WHY DO YOU THINK I'M STILL HERE?!
DEEP IN MY HEART, THERE'S ONE LAST FURIOUS MEMORY I CAN'T LET GO OF.
IT'S THE ONE MEMORY THAT KEEPS ME GOING!

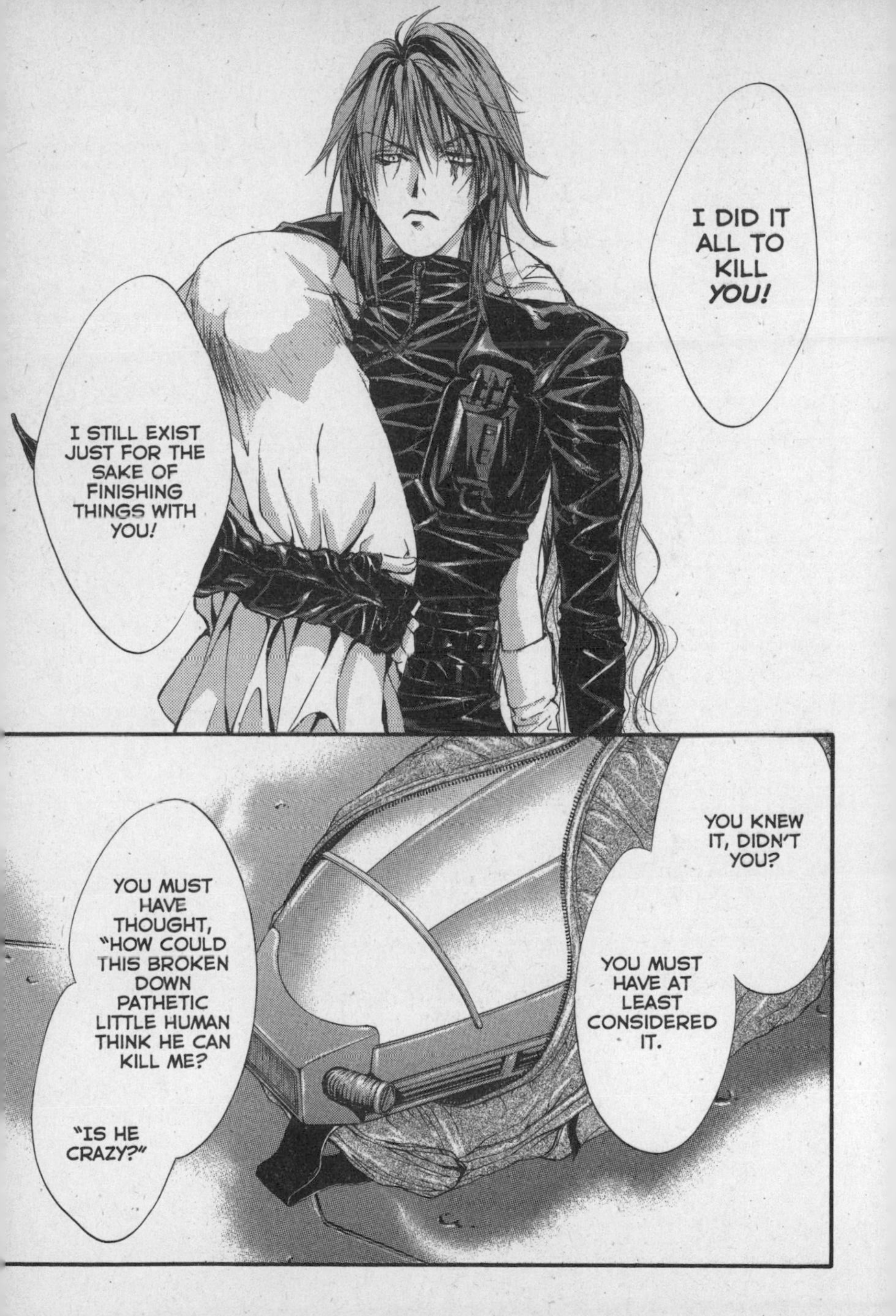
I DID IT ALL TO KILL *YOU!*
I STILL EXIST JUST FOR THE SAKE OF FINISHING THINGS WITH YOU!
YOU KNEW IT, DIDN'T YOU?
YOU MUST HAVE AT LEAST CONSIDERED IT.
YOU MUST HAVE THOUGHT, "HOW COULD THIS BROKEN DOWN PATHETIC LITTLE HUMAN THINK HE CAN KILL ME?
"IS HE CRAZY?"

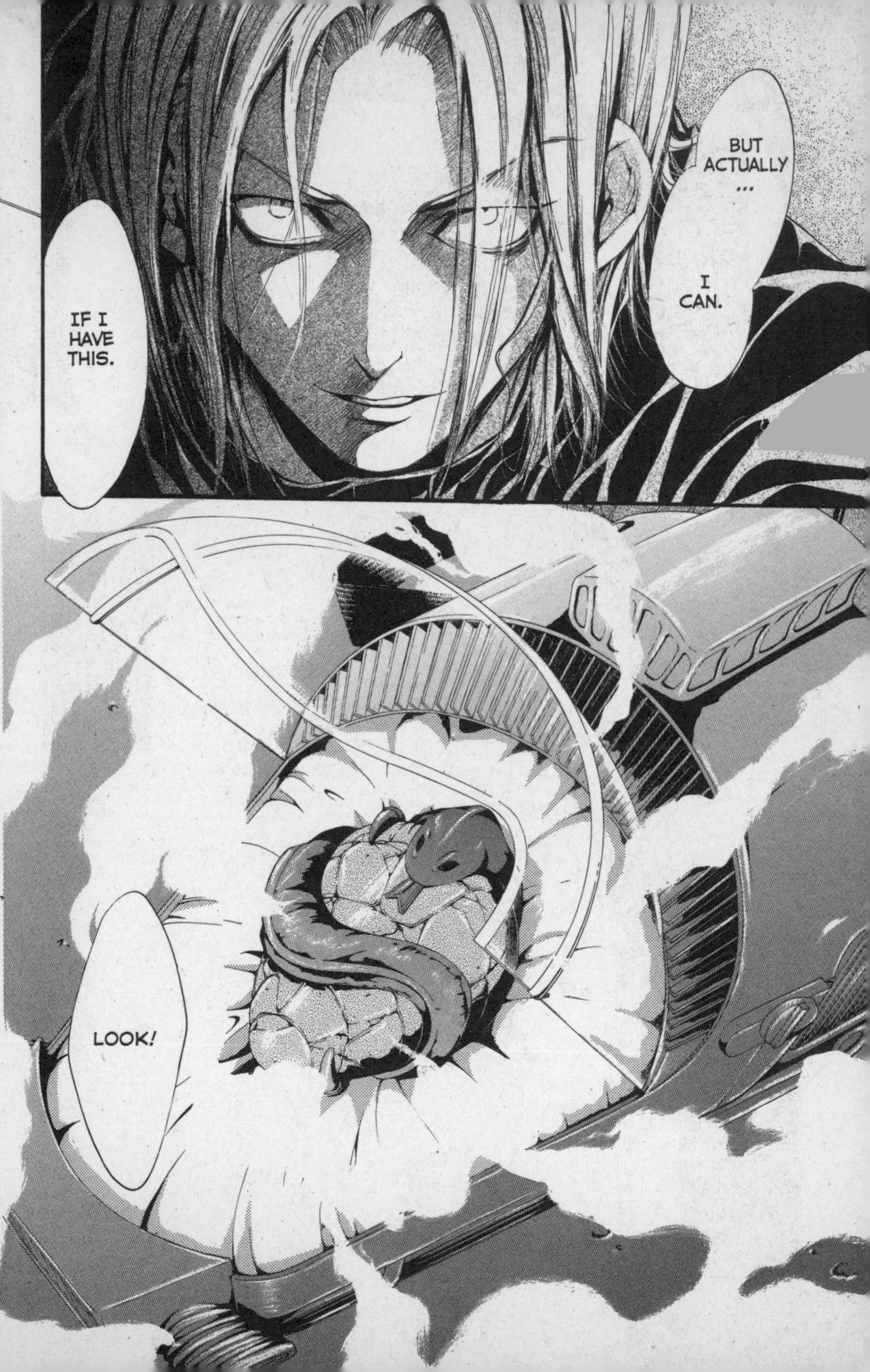
BUT ACTUALLY ...
I CAN.
IF I HAVE THIS.
LOOK!

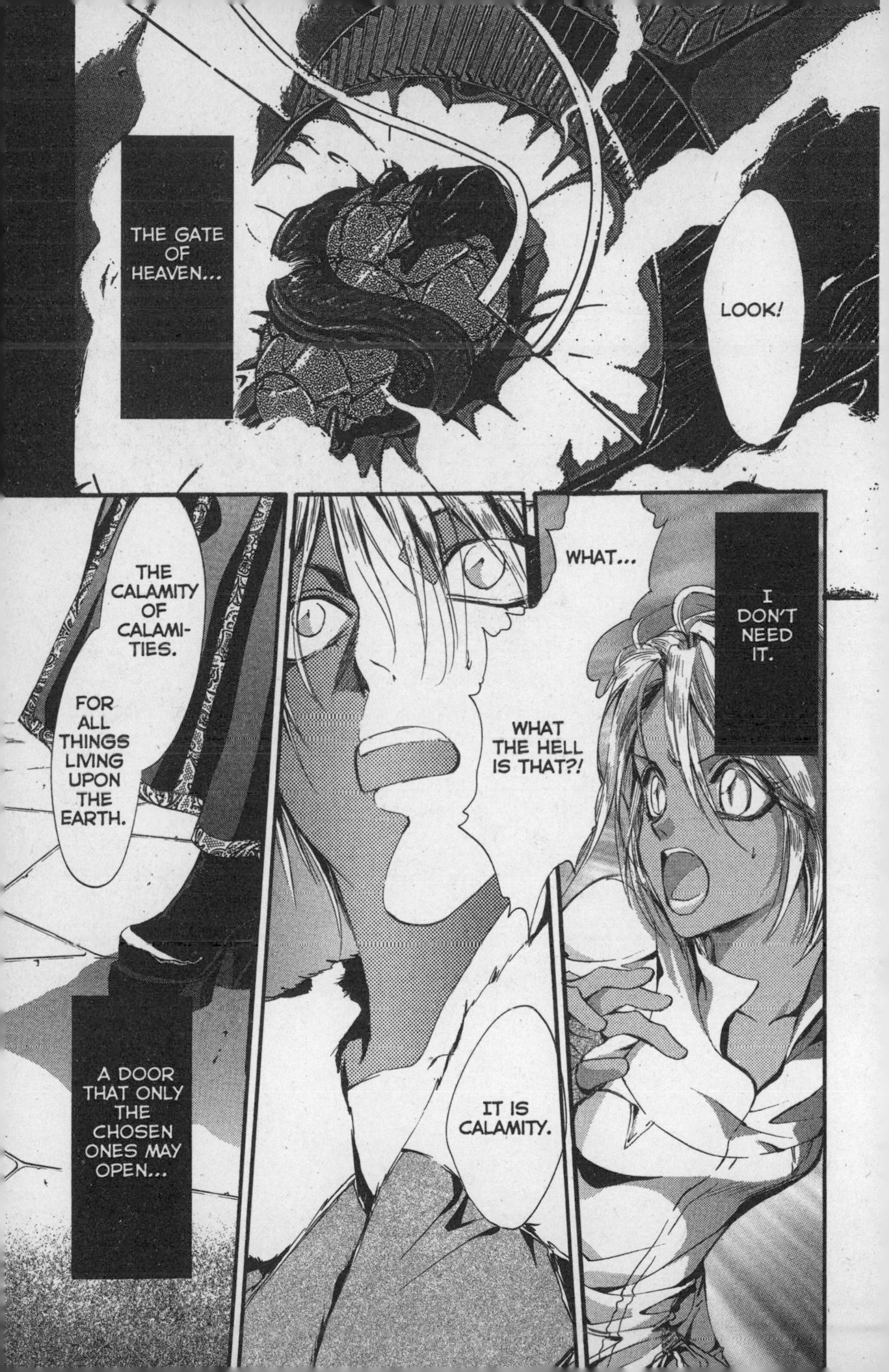

LOOK!
THE GATE OF HEAVEN...
I DON'T NEED IT.
WHAT...
WHAT THE HELL IS THAT?!
IT IS CALAMITY.
THE CALAMITY OF CALAMITIES.
FOR ALL THINGS LIVING UPON THE EARTH.
A DOOR THAT ONLY THE CHOSEN ONES MAY OPEN...

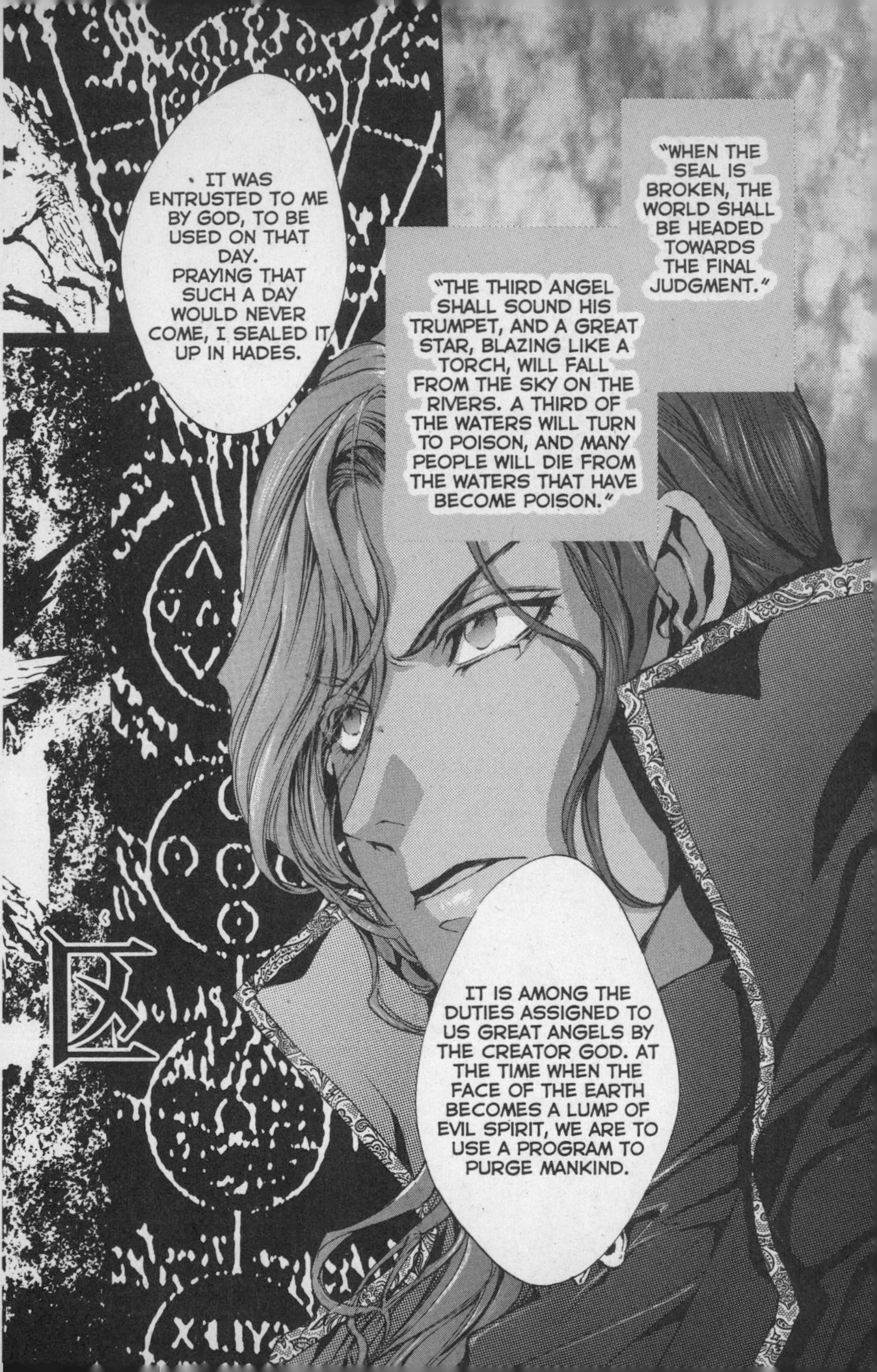
"WHEN THE SEAL IS BROKEN, THE WORLD SHALL BE HEADED TOWARDS THE FINAL JUDGMENT."
"THE THIRD ANGEL SHALL SOUND HIS TRUMPET, AND A GREAT STAR, BLAZING LIKE A TORCH, WILL FALL FROM THE SKY ON THE RIVERS. A THIRD OF THE WATERS WILL TURN TO POISON, AND MANY PEOPLE WILL DIE FROM THE WATERS THAT HAVE BECOME POISON."
IT WAS ENTRUSTED TO ME BY GOD, TO BE USED ON THAT DAY. PRAYING THAT SUCH A DAY WOULD NEVER COME, I SEALED IT UP IN HADES.
IT IS AMONG THE DUTIES ASSIGNED TO US GREAT ANGELS BY THE CREATOR GOD. AT THE TIME WHEN THE FACE OF THE EARTH BECOMES A LUMP OF EVIL SPIRIT, WE ARE TO USE A PROGRAM TO PURGE MANKIND.

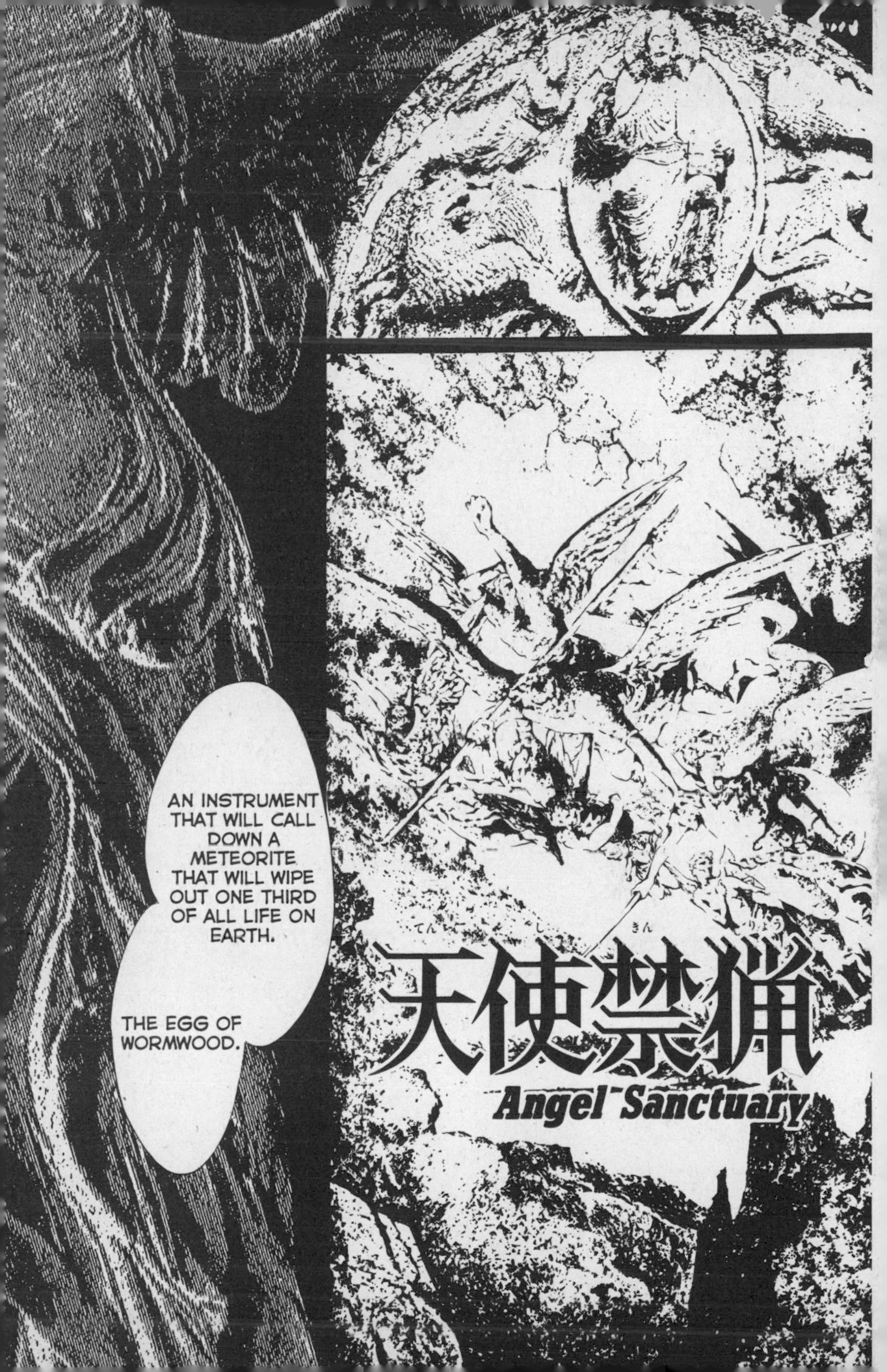

てん し きん りょう
天使禁猟
Angel Sanctuary
AN INSTRUMENT THAT WILL CALL DOWN A METEORITE THAT WILL WIPE OUT ONE THIRD OF ALL LIFE ON EARTH.
THE EGG OF WORMWOOD.

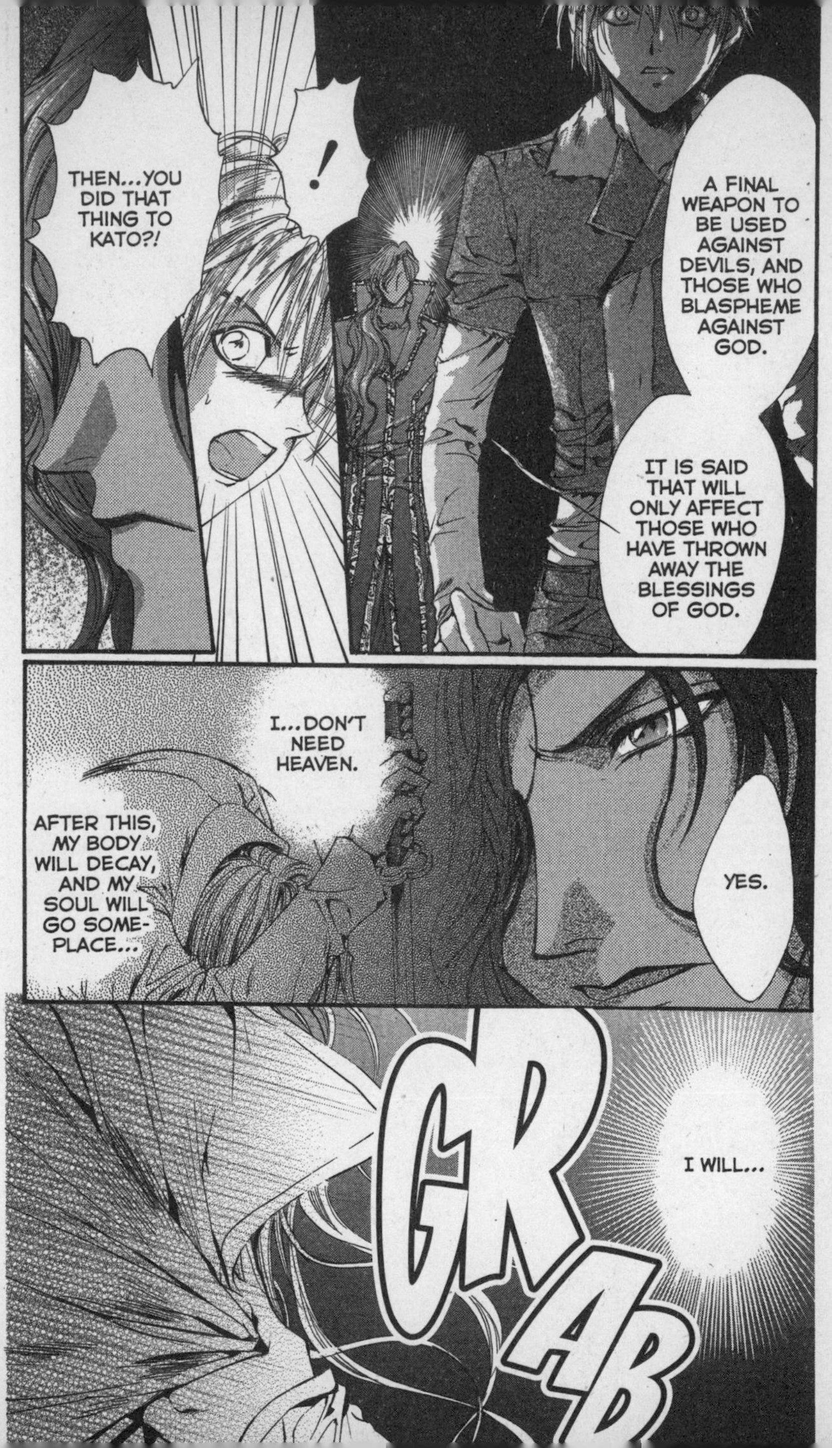
A FINAL WEAPON TO BE USED AGAINST DEVILS, AND THOSE WHO BLASPHEME AGAINST GOD.
IT IS SAID THAT WILL ONLY AFFECT THOSE WHO HAVE THROWN AWAY THE BLESSINGS OF GOD.
!
THEN...YOU DID THAT THING TO KATO?!
YES.
I...DON'T NEED HEAVEN.
AFTER THIS, MY BODY WILL DECAY, AND MY SOUL WILL GO SOME-PLACE...
I WILL...
GRAB

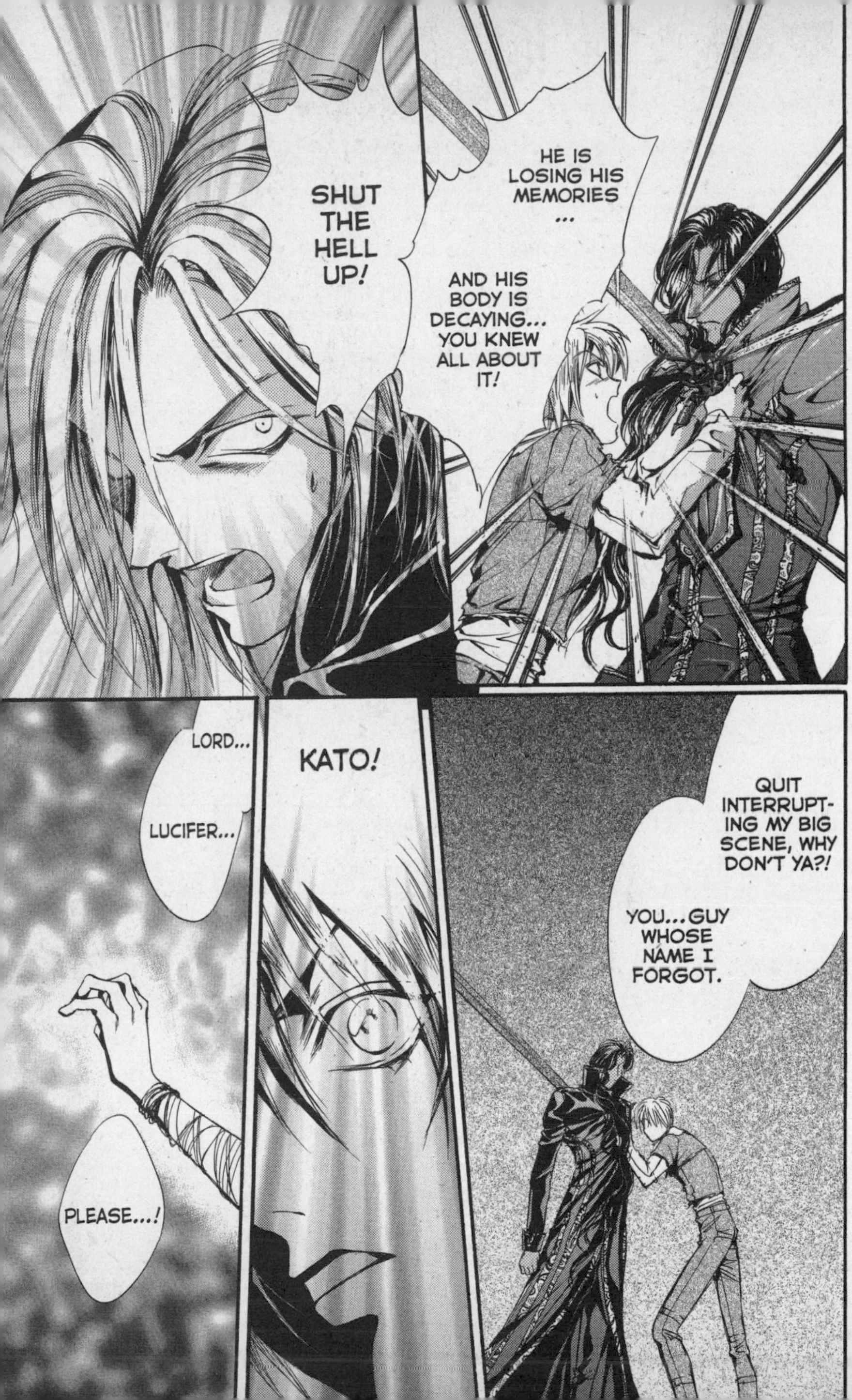
HE IS LOSING HIS MEMORIES...
AND HIS BODY IS DECAYING... YOU KNEW ALL ABOUT IT!
SHUT THE HELL UP!
QUIT INTERRUPTING MY BIG SCENE, WHY DON'T YA?!
YOU...GUY WHOSE NAME I FORGOT.
KATO!
LORD...
LUCIFER...
PLEASE...!

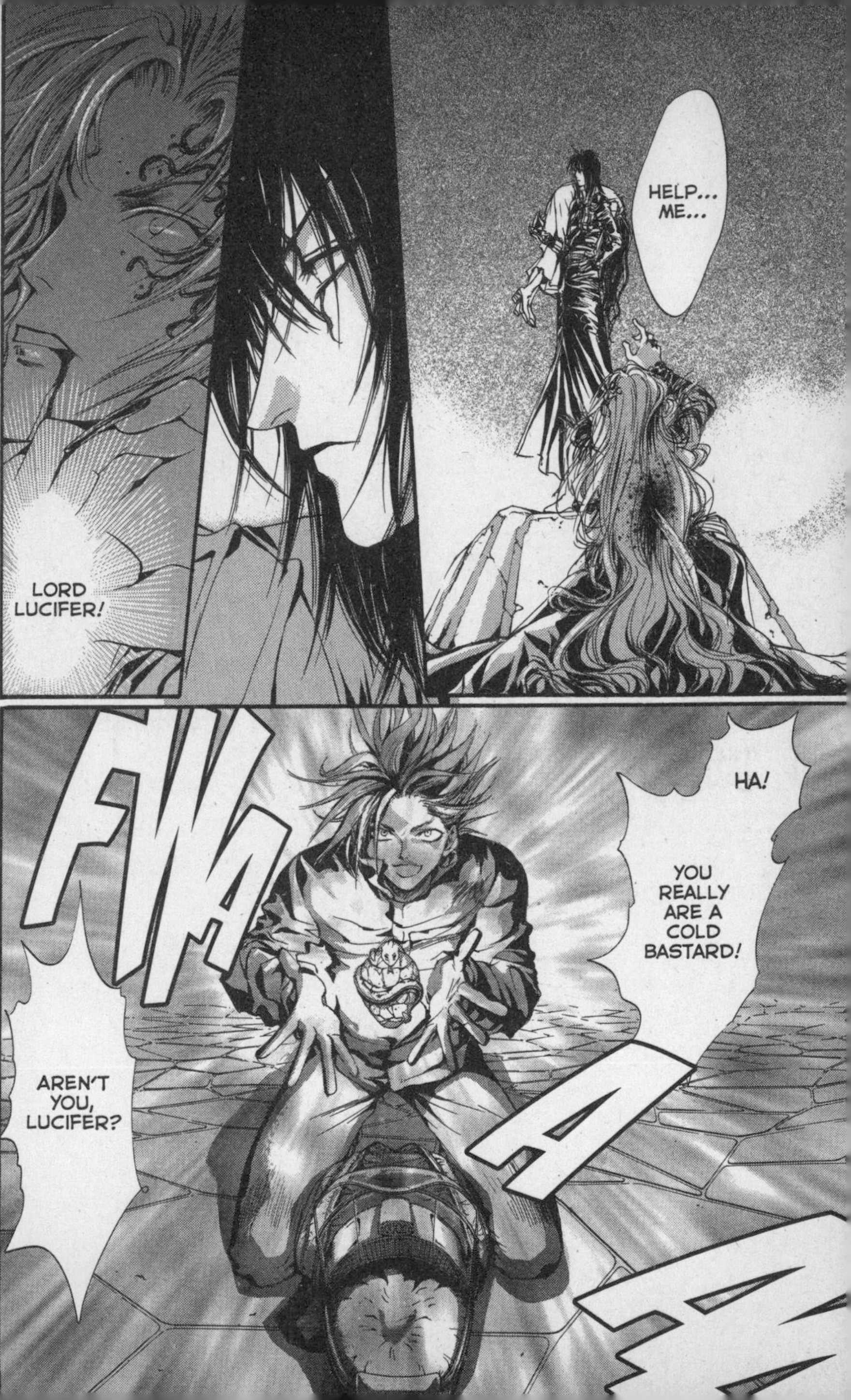
HELP... ME...
LORD LUCIFER!
HA!
YOU REALLY ARE A COLD BASTARD!
FWA
AREN'T YOU, LUCIFER?
A

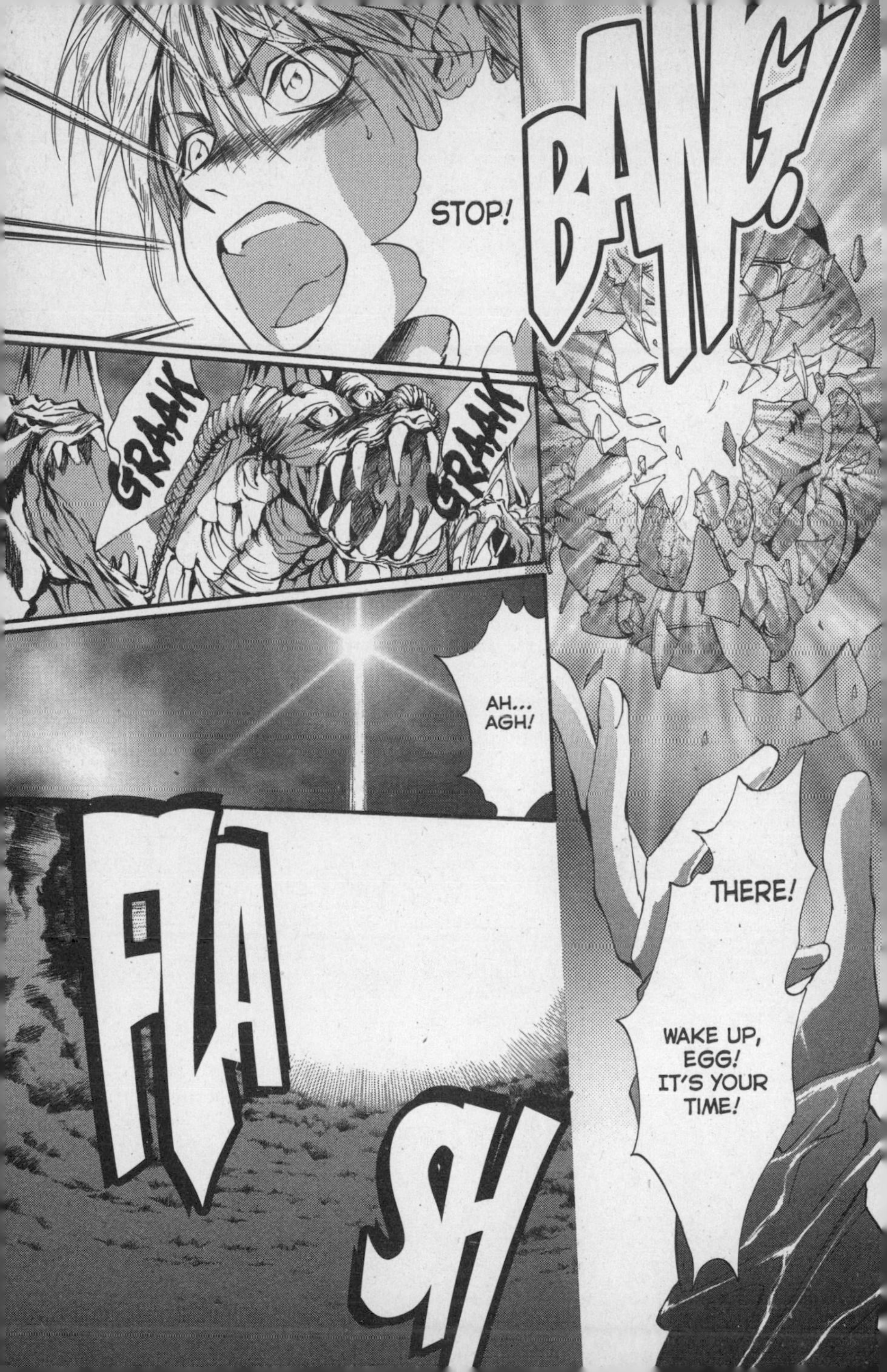
BANG!
THERE!
WAKE UP, EGG! IT'S YOUR TIME!
STOP!
GRAAK
GRAAK
AH... AGH!
FLASH

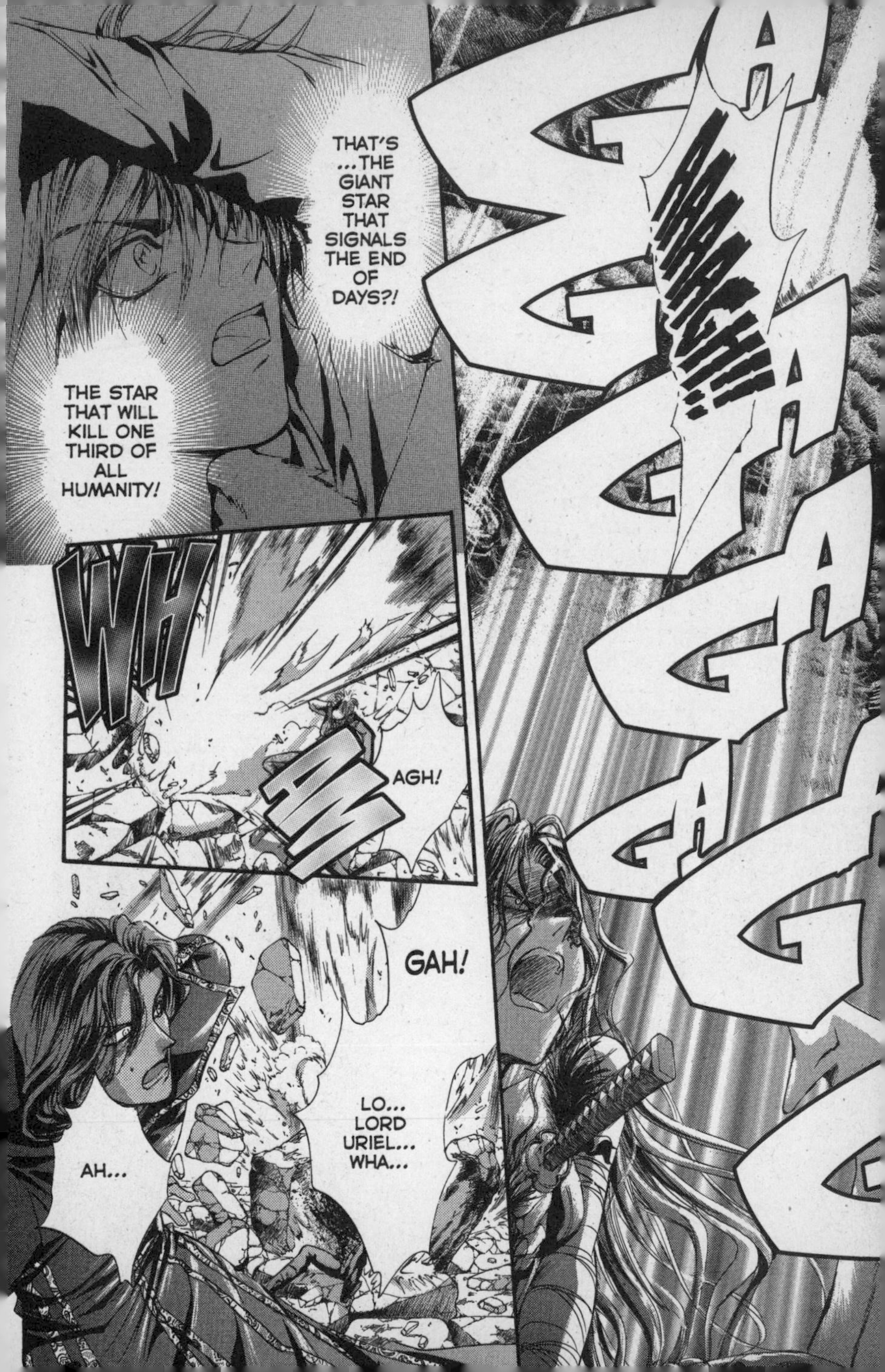
AAAAGH!!!
THAT'S ...THE GIANT STAR THAT SIGNALS THE END OF DAYS?!
THE STAR THAT WILL KILL ONE THIRD OF ALL HUMANITY!
WHAM
AGH!
GAH!
LO... LORD URIEL... WHA...
AH...

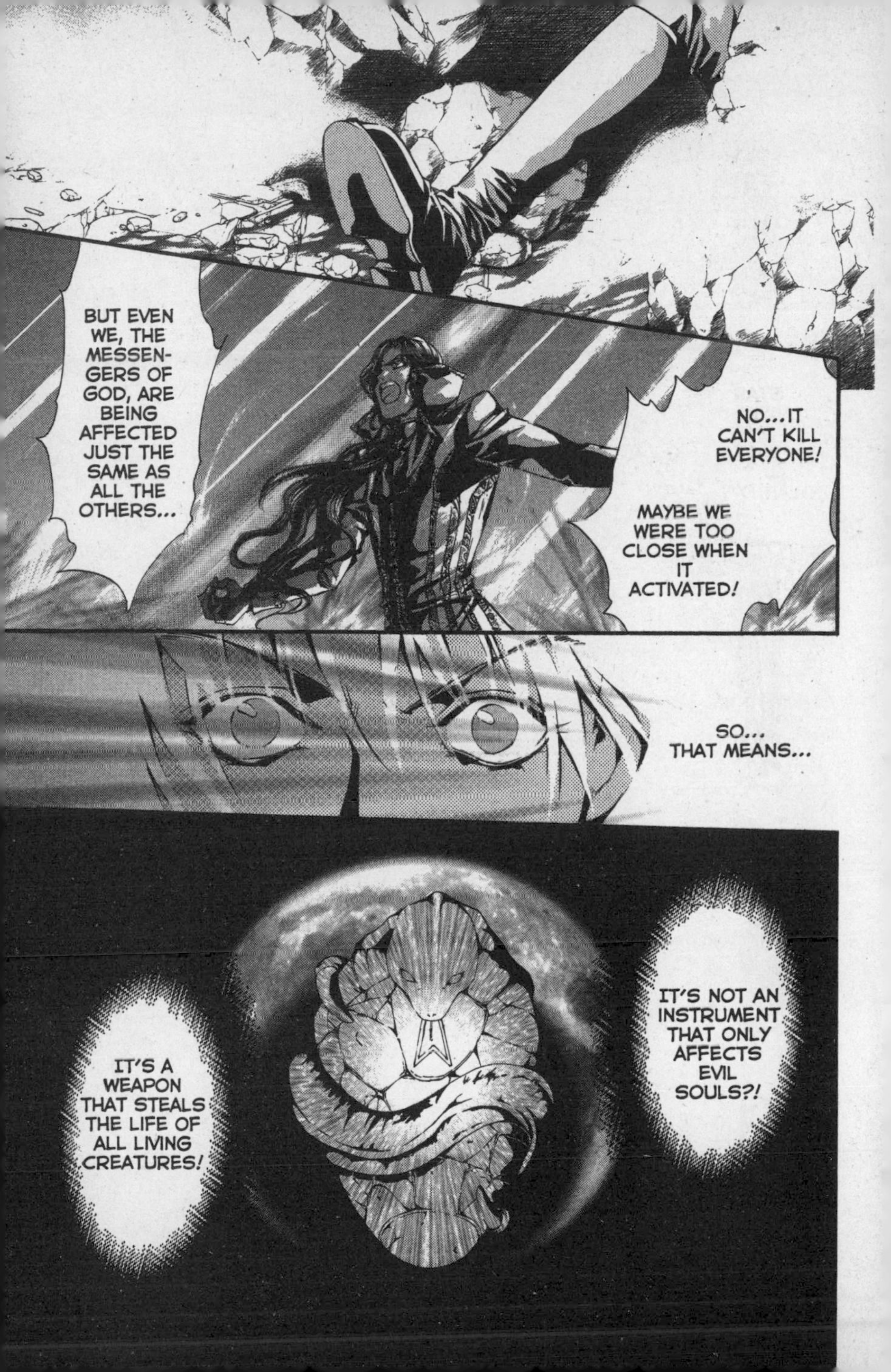
NO...IT CAN'T KILL EVERYONE!
MAYBE WE WERE TOO CLOSE WHEN IT ACTIVATED!
BUT EVEN WE, THE MESSENGERS OF GOD, ARE BEING AFFECTED JUST THE SAME AS ALL THE OTHERS...
SO... THAT MEANS...
IT'S NOT AN INSTRUMENT THAT ONLY AFFECTS EVIL SOULS?!
IT'S A WEAPON THAT STEALS THE LIFE OF ALL LIVING CREATURES!

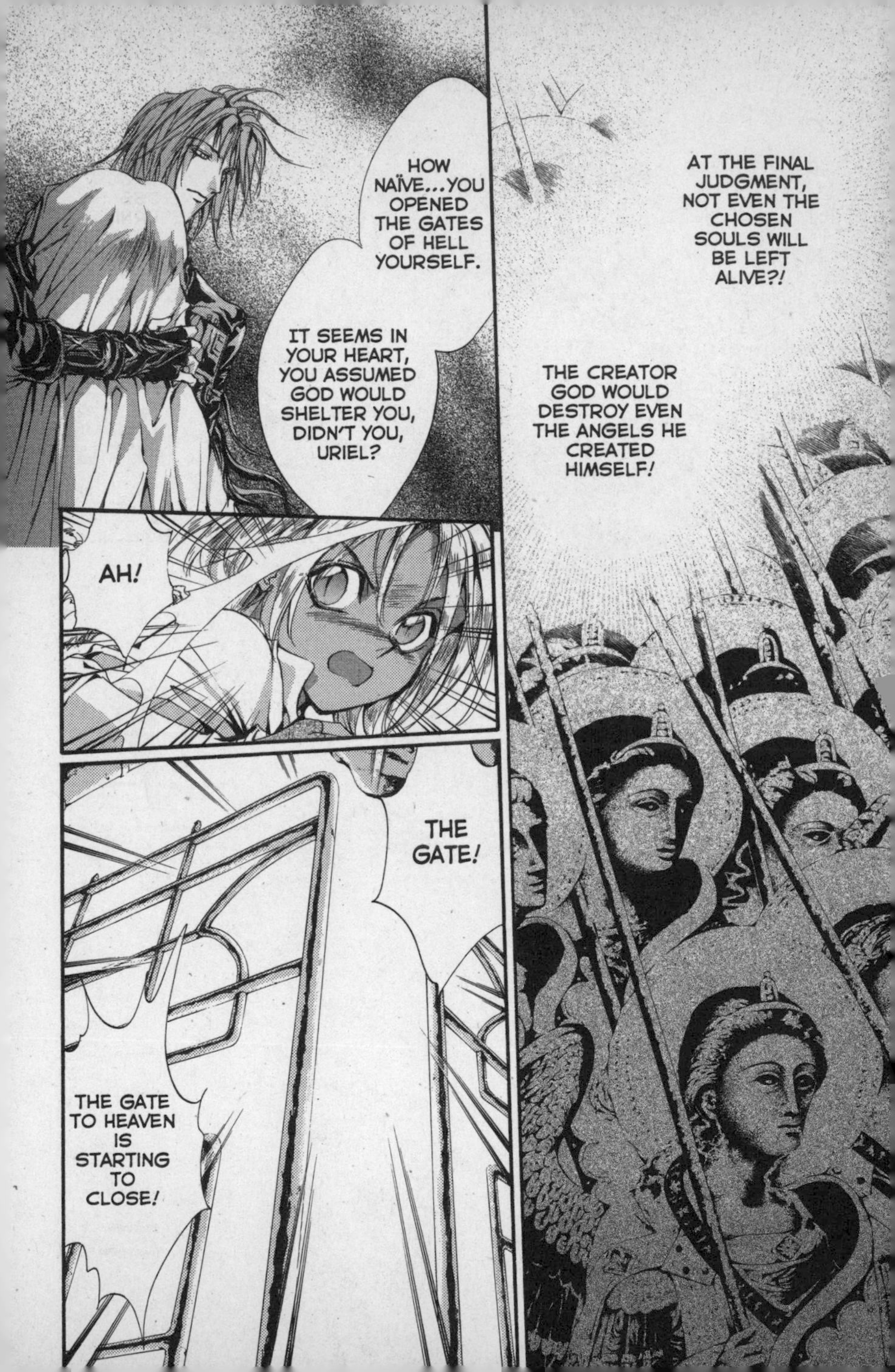
AT THE FINAL JUDGMENT, NOT EVEN THE CHOSEN SOULS WILL BE LEFT ALIVE?!
THE CREATOR GOD WOULD DESTROY EVEN THE ANGELS HE CREATED HIMSELF!
HOW NAÏVE...YOU OPENED THE GATES OF HELL YOURSELF.
IT SEEMS IN YOUR HEART, YOU ASSUMED GOD WOULD SHELTER YOU, DIDN'T YOU, URIEL?
AH!
THE GATE!
THE GATE TO HEAVEN IS STARTING TO CLOSE!

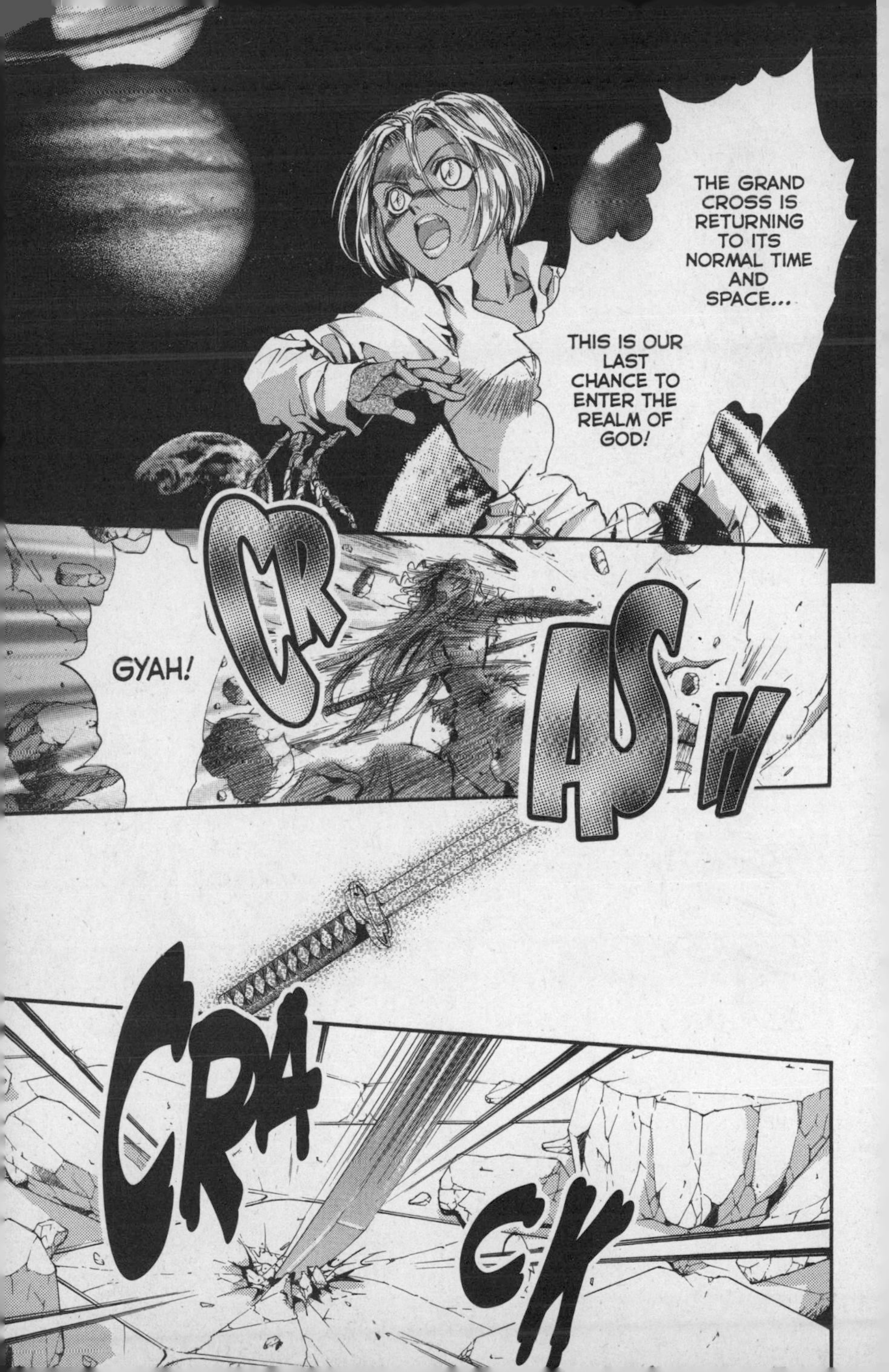

THE GRAND CROSS IS RETURNING TO ITS NORMAL TIME AND SPACE...
THIS IS OUR LAST CHANCE TO ENTER THE REALM OF GOD!
CRASH
GYAH!
CRACK

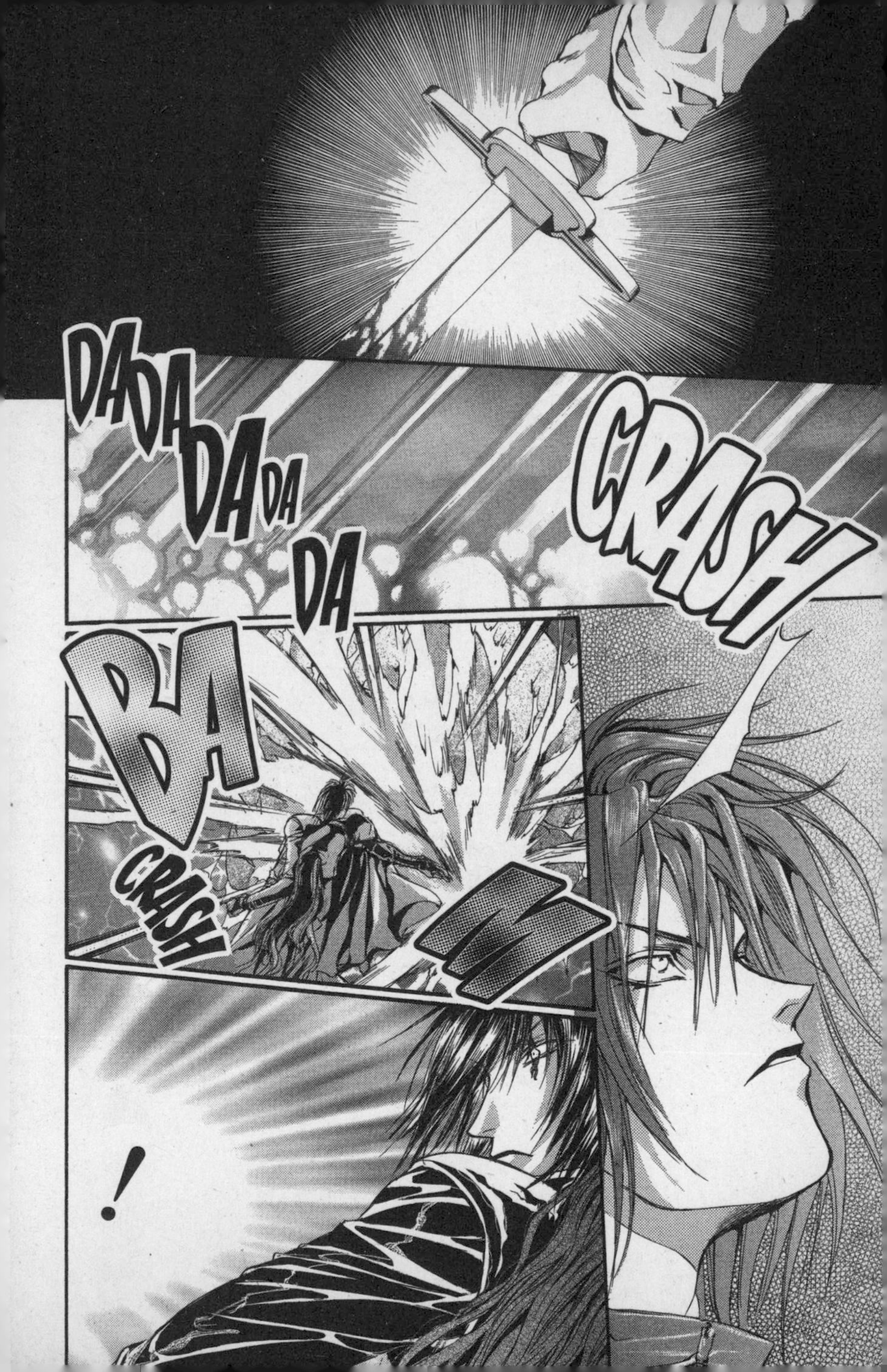
CRASH
DADADA
DA
DA
DA
BA
CRASH
!

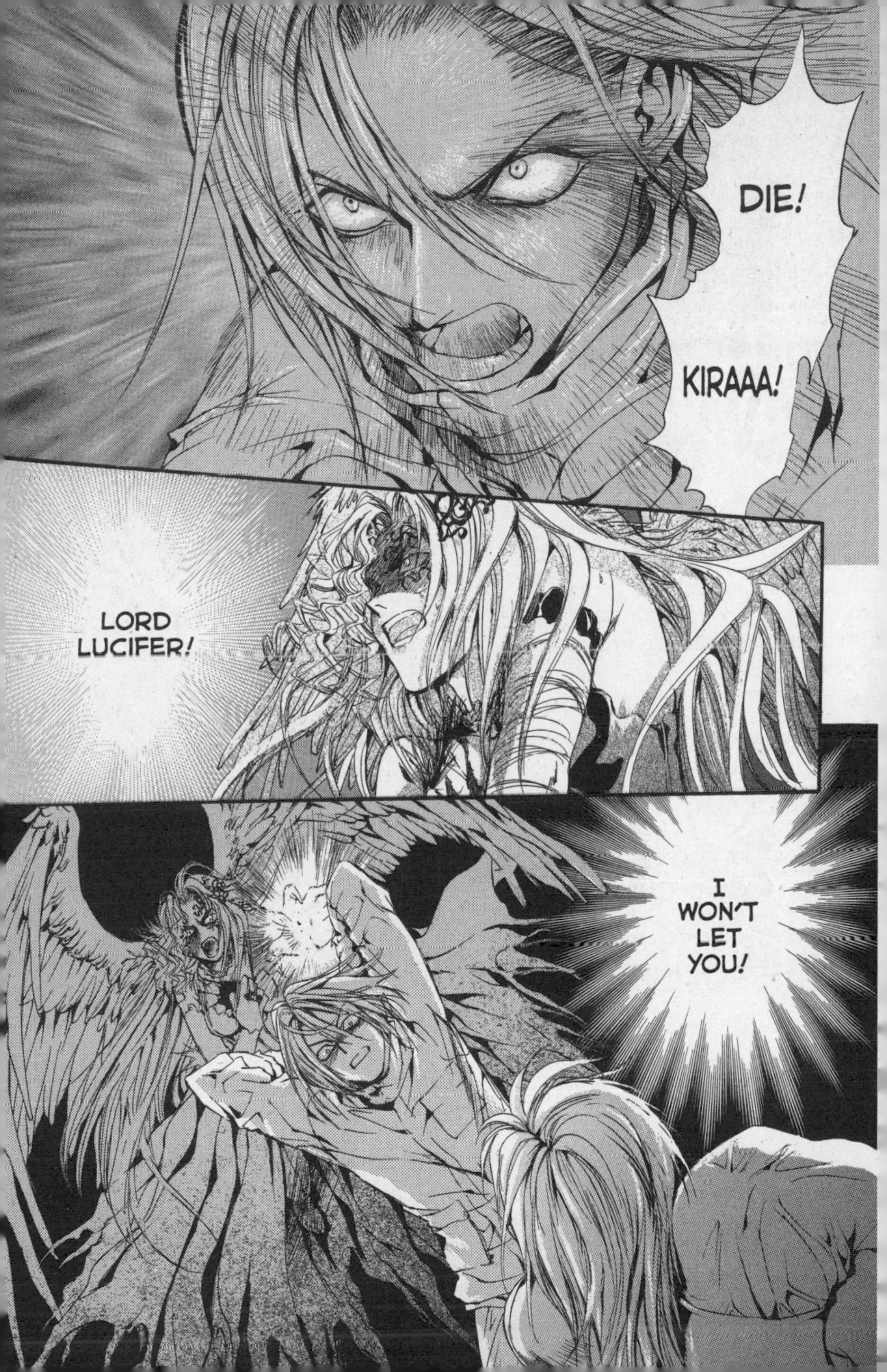
DIE!
KIRAAA!
LORD LUCIFER!
I WON'T LET YOU!

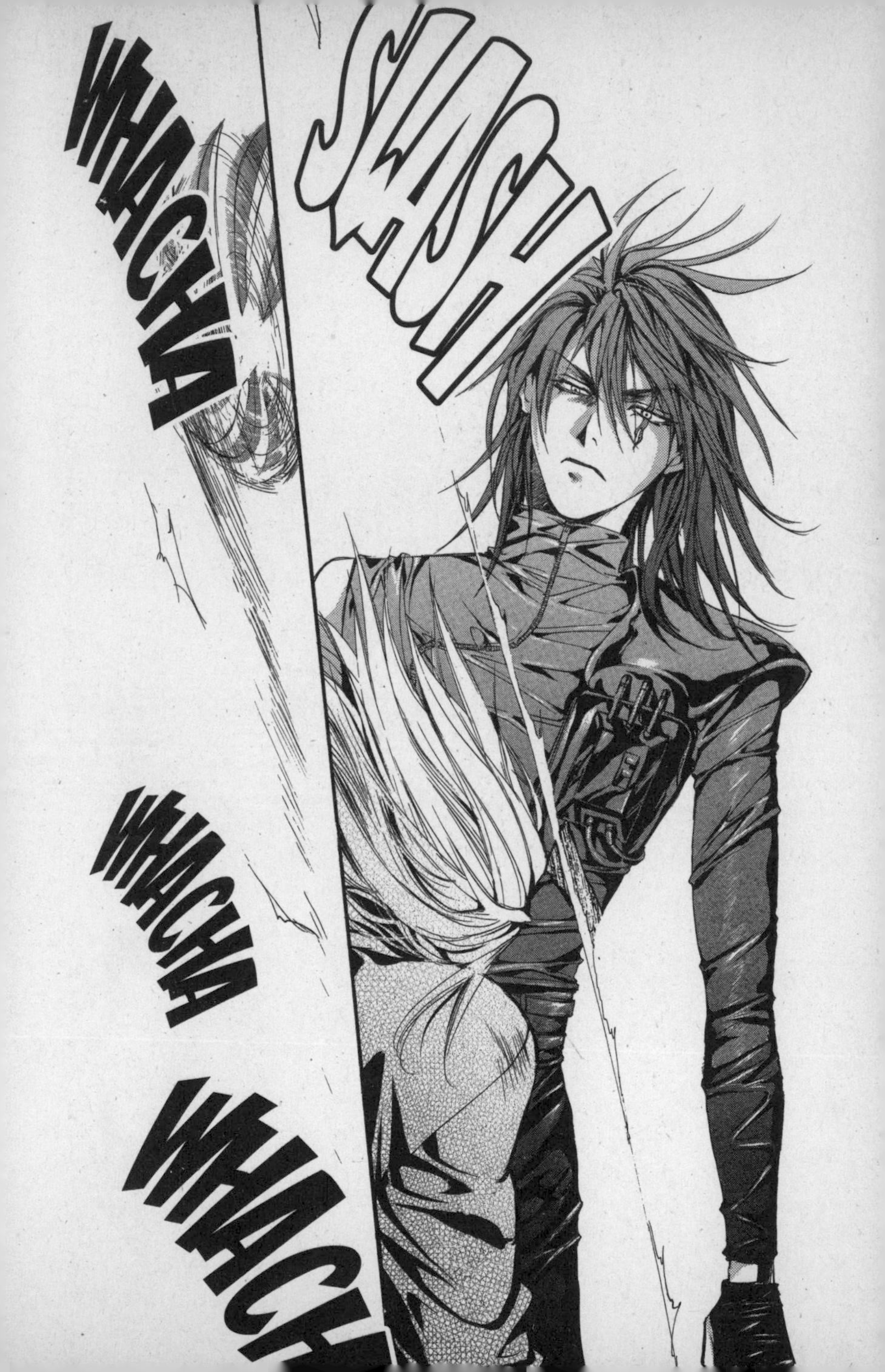
SLASH
WHACHA
WHACHA
WHACH

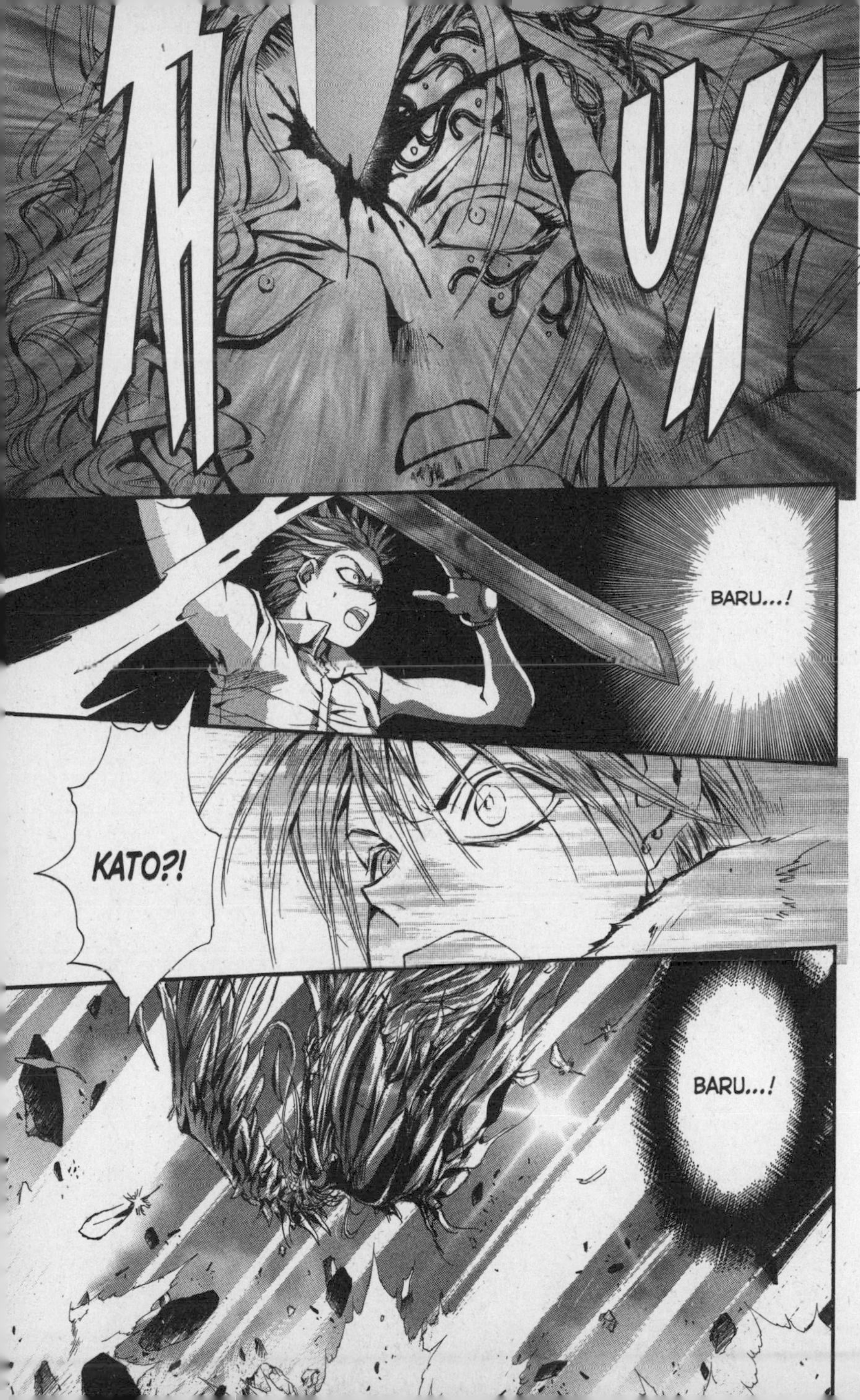
BARU...!
KATO?!
BARU...!

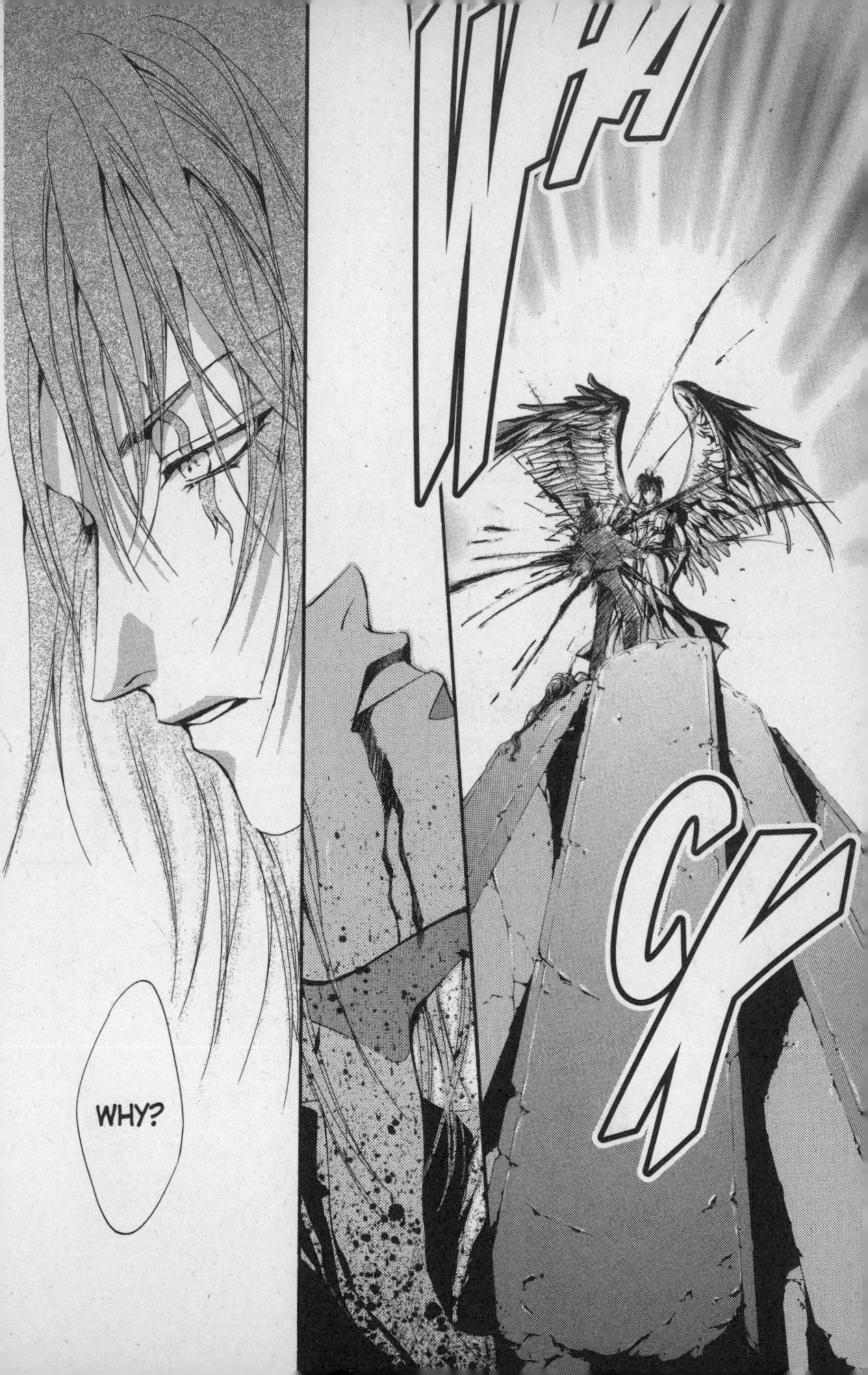
GK
WHY?

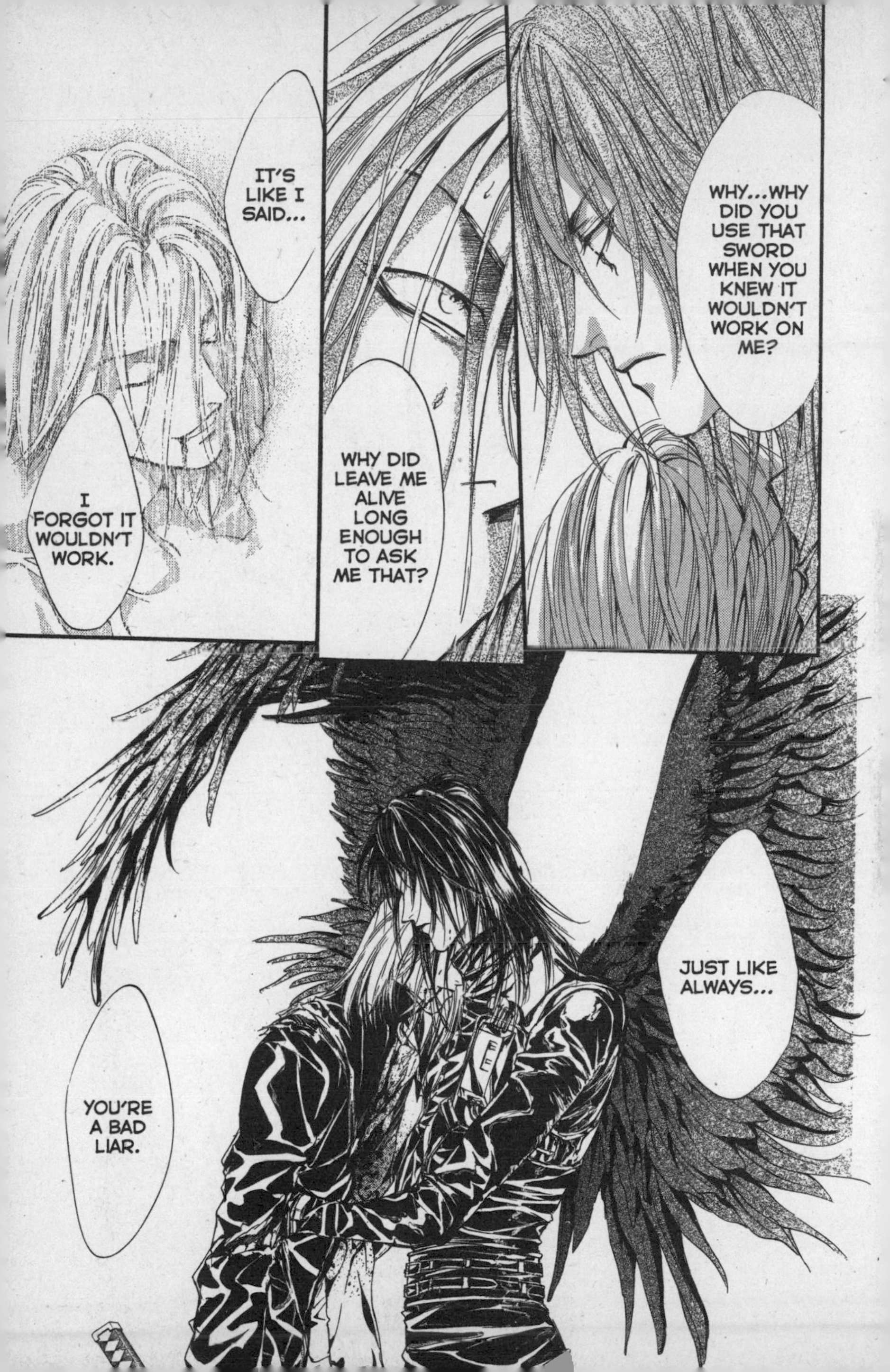
WHY...WHY DID YOU USE THAT SWORD WHEN YOU KNEW IT WOULDN'T WORK ON ME?
WHY DID LEAVE ME ALIVE LONG ENOUGH TO ASK ME THAT?
IT'S LIKE I SAID...
I FORGOT IT WOULDN'T WORK.
JUST LIKE ALWAYS...
YOU'RE A BAD LIAR.

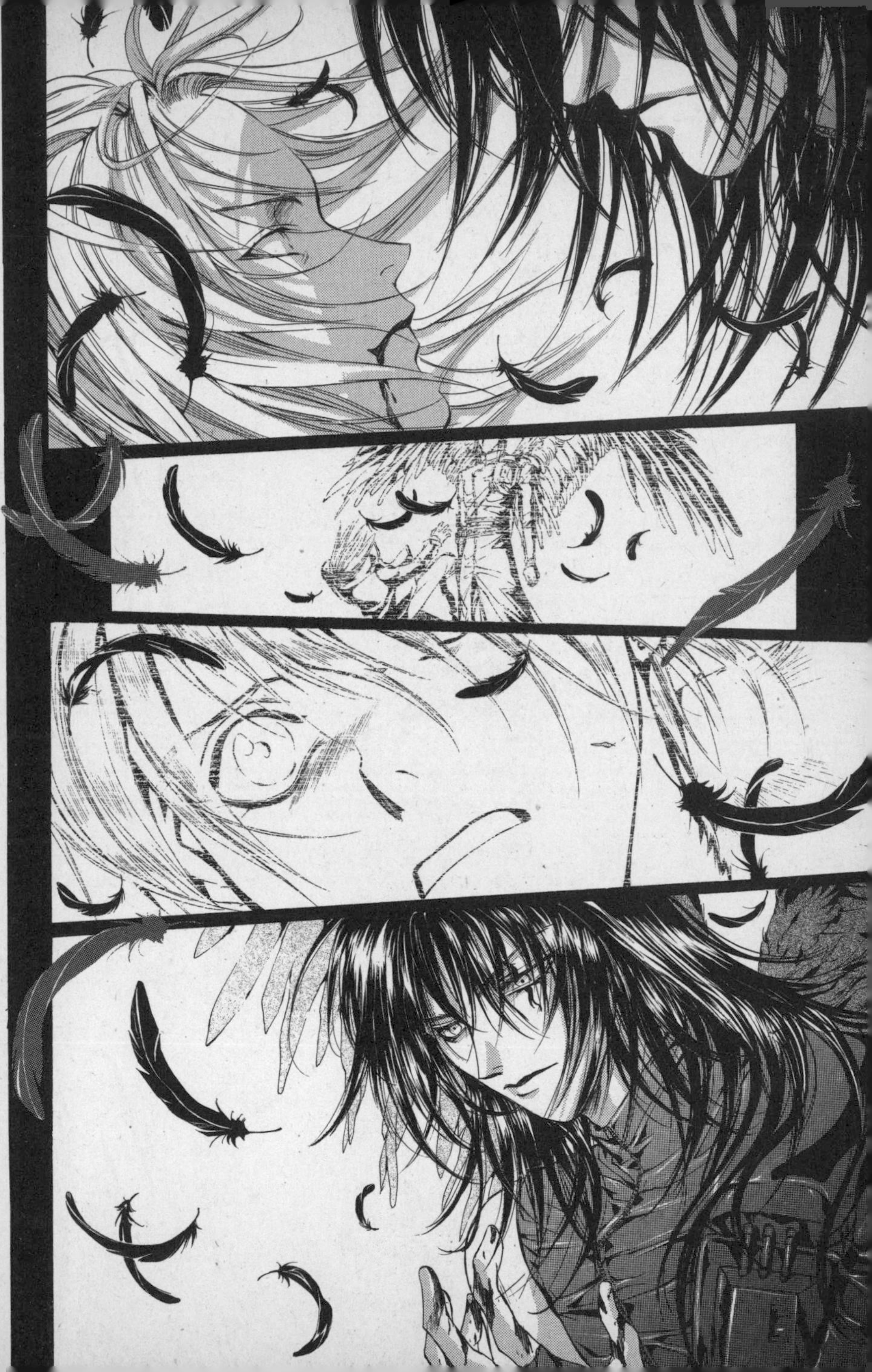

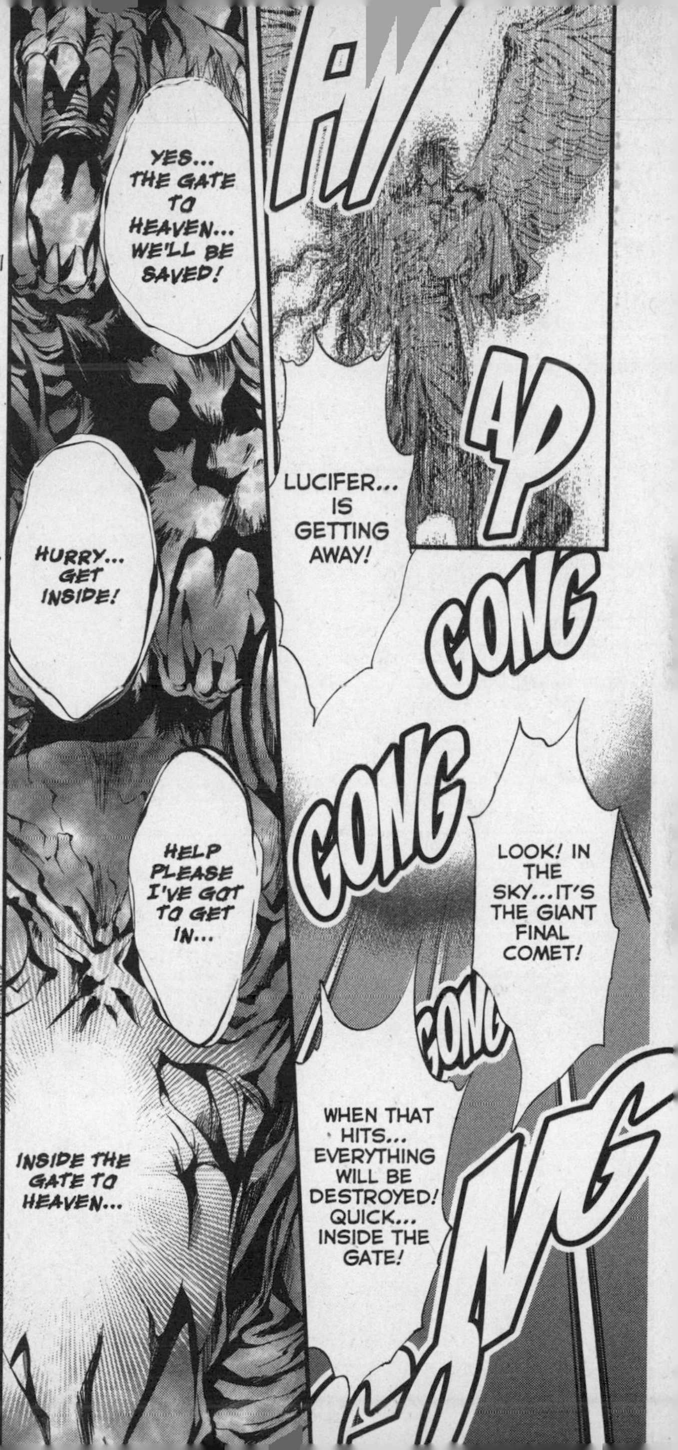
AP
LUCIFER... IS GETTING AWAY!
GONG
GONG
LOOK! IN THE SKY...IT'S THE GIANT FINAL COMET!
GONG
WHEN THAT HITS... EVERYTHING WILL BE DESTROYED! QUICK... INSIDE THE GATE!
YES... THE GATE TO HEAVEN... WE'LL BE SAVED!
HURRY... GET INSIDE!
HELP PLEASE I'VE GOT TO GET IN...
INSIDE THE GATE TO HEAVEN...

I'm wondering if I didn't go a little too far with Barubelo. I should have made her more of an evil woman. I assume everyone figured out that Barubelo is Baru. Thanks for remembering her. In this volume there is a mistake...I wrote "Bel" when it's supposed to be "Baru." It was really hard to draw Barubelo's design and movement. Lucifer's, too. And all the demons were pretty tough.
Oh, hey...the Angel Sanct OVA went on sale! I get really happy every time I see the ad for it on TV. It looks really good! The movement of Rosiel's hair is incredible. Please go out and buy it.

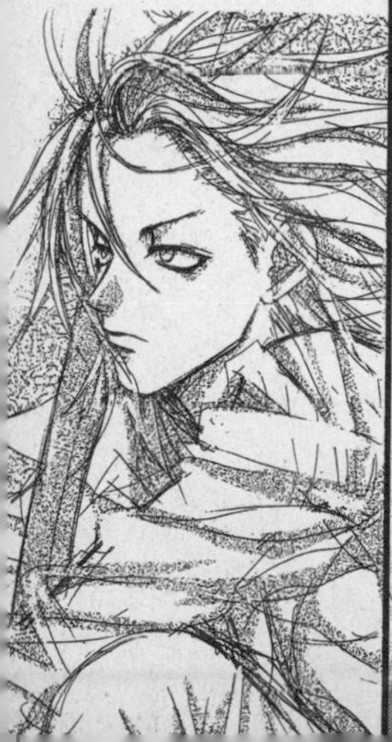

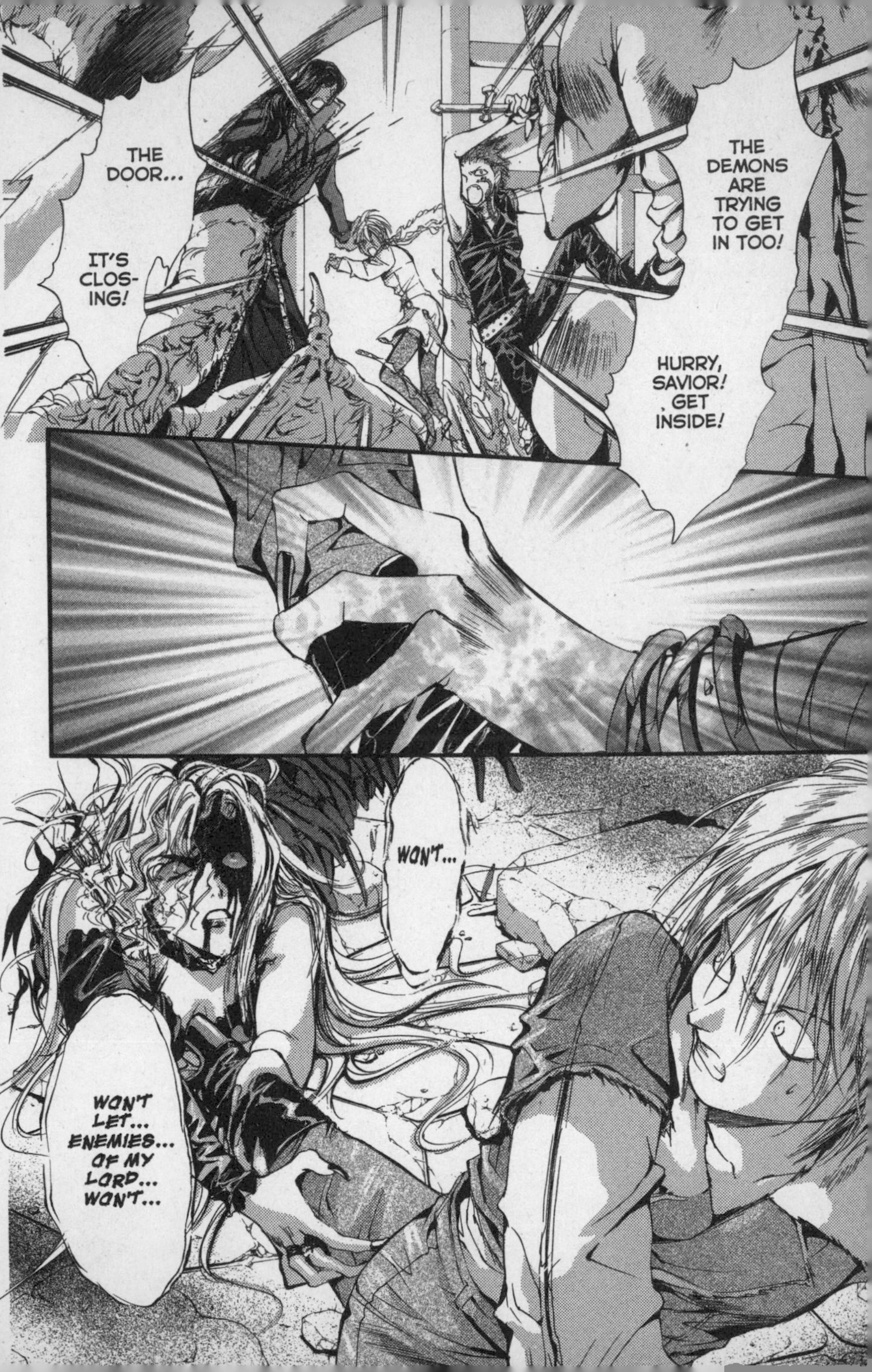
THE DEMONS ARE TRYING TO GET IN TOO!
THE DOOR...
IT'S CLOSING!
HURRY, SAVIOR! GET INSIDE!
WON'T...
WON'T LET... ENEMIES... OF MY LORD... WON'T...

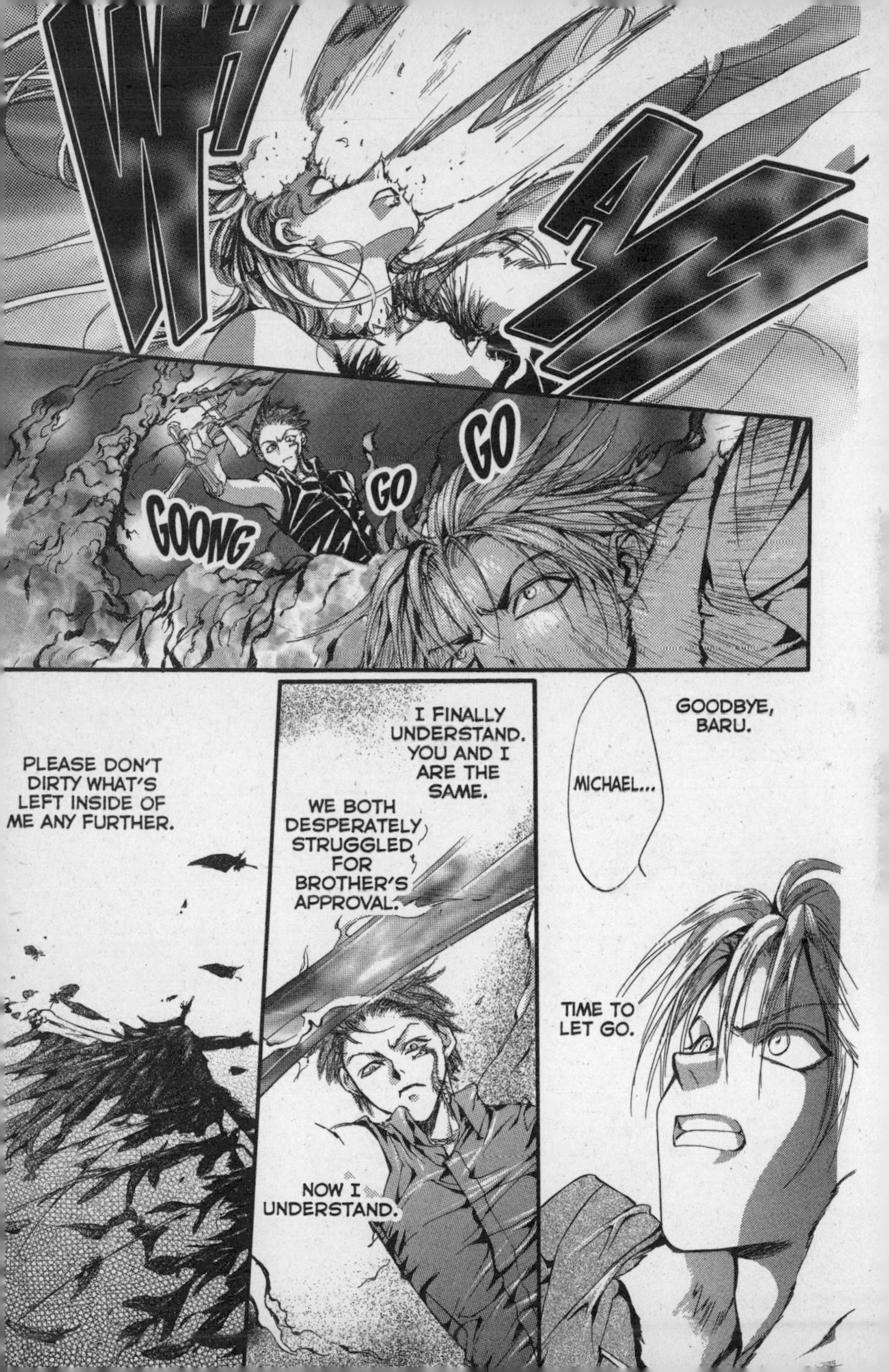
GO
GO
GOONG
GOODBYE, BARU.
MICHAEL...
TIME TO LET GO.
I FINALLY UNDERSTAND. YOU AND I ARE THE SAME.
WE BOTH DESPERATELY STRUGGLED FOR BROTHER'S APPROVAL.
NOW I UNDERSTAND.
PLEASE DON'T DIRTY WHAT'S LEFT INSIDE OF ME ANY FURTHER.

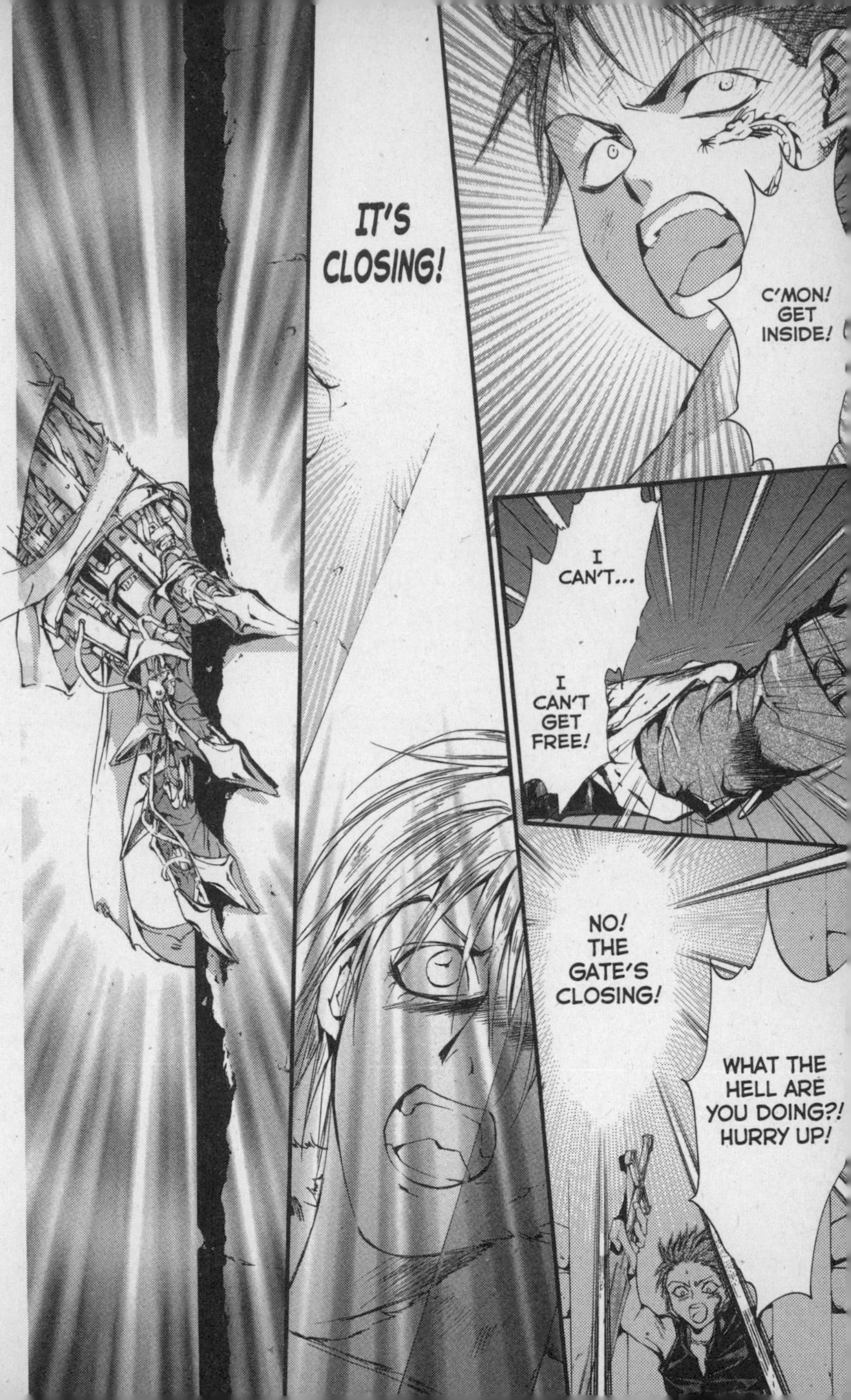
C'MON! GET INSIDE!
I CAN'T...
I CAN'T GET FREE!
NO! THE GATE'S CLOSING!
WHAT THE HELL ARE YOU DOING?! HURRY UP!
IT'S CLOSING!

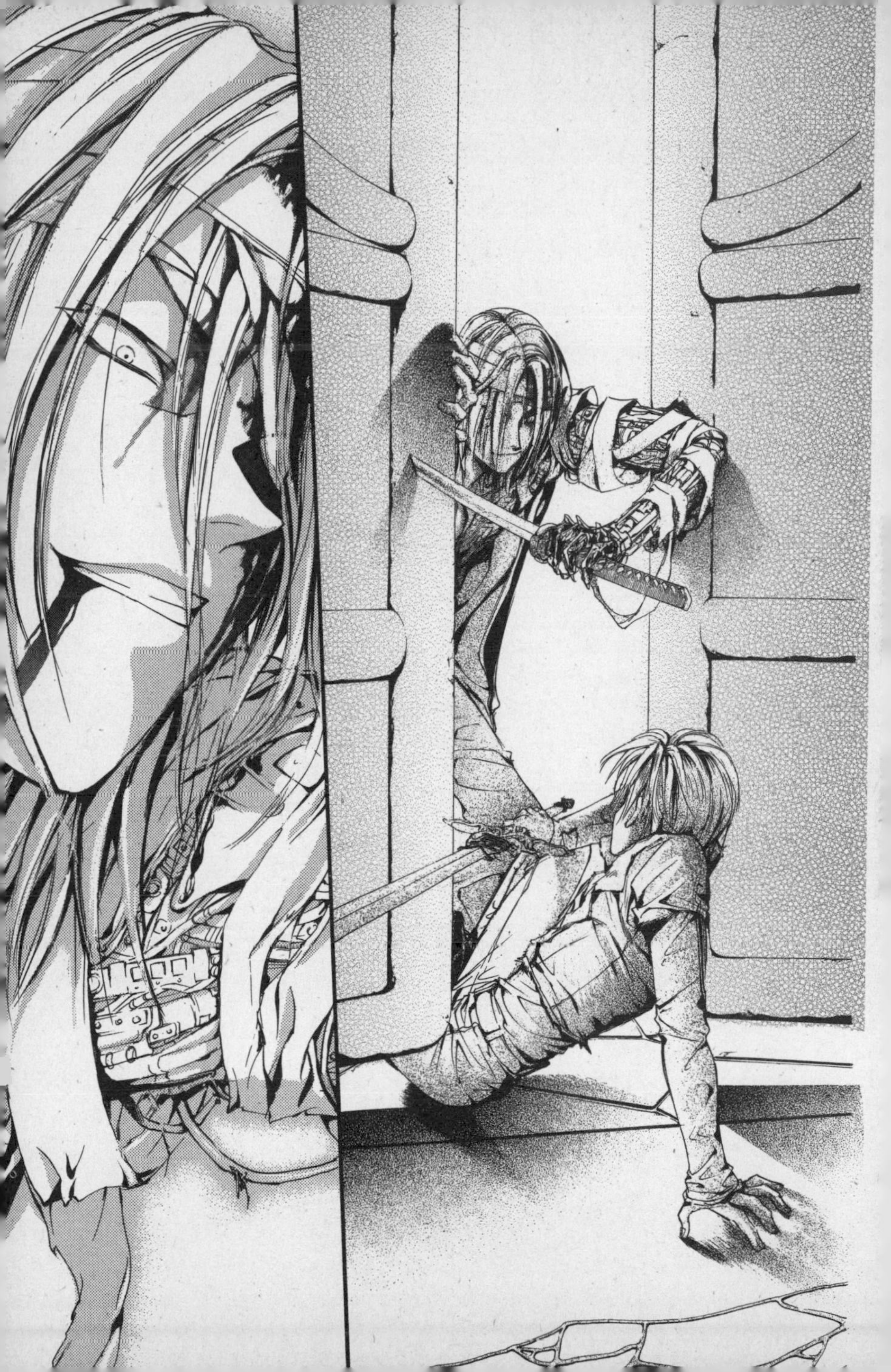

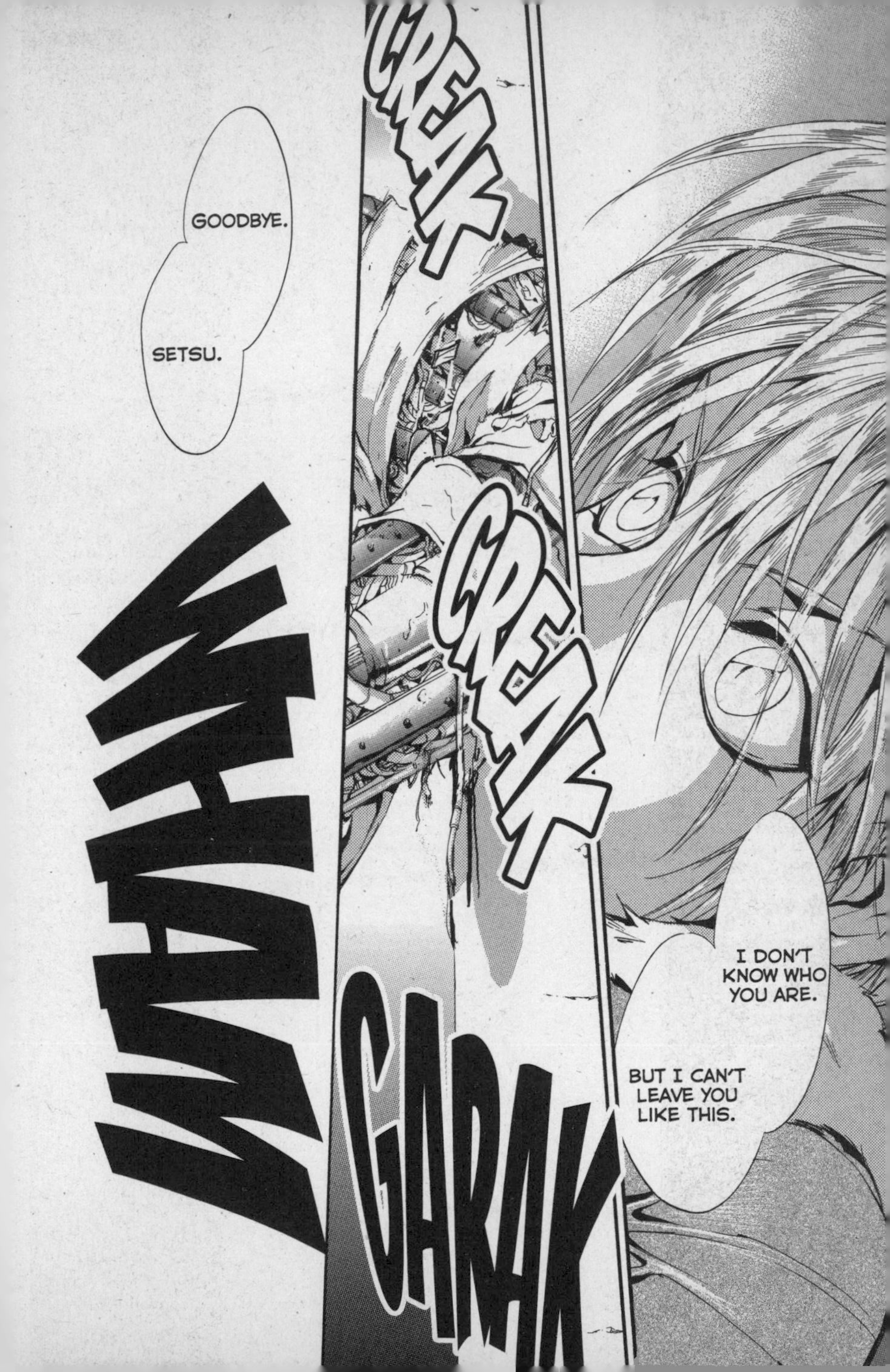
I DON'T KNOW WHO YOU ARE.
BUT I CAN'T LEAVE YOU LIKE THIS.
CREAK
CREAK
GARAK
GOODBYE.
SETSU.

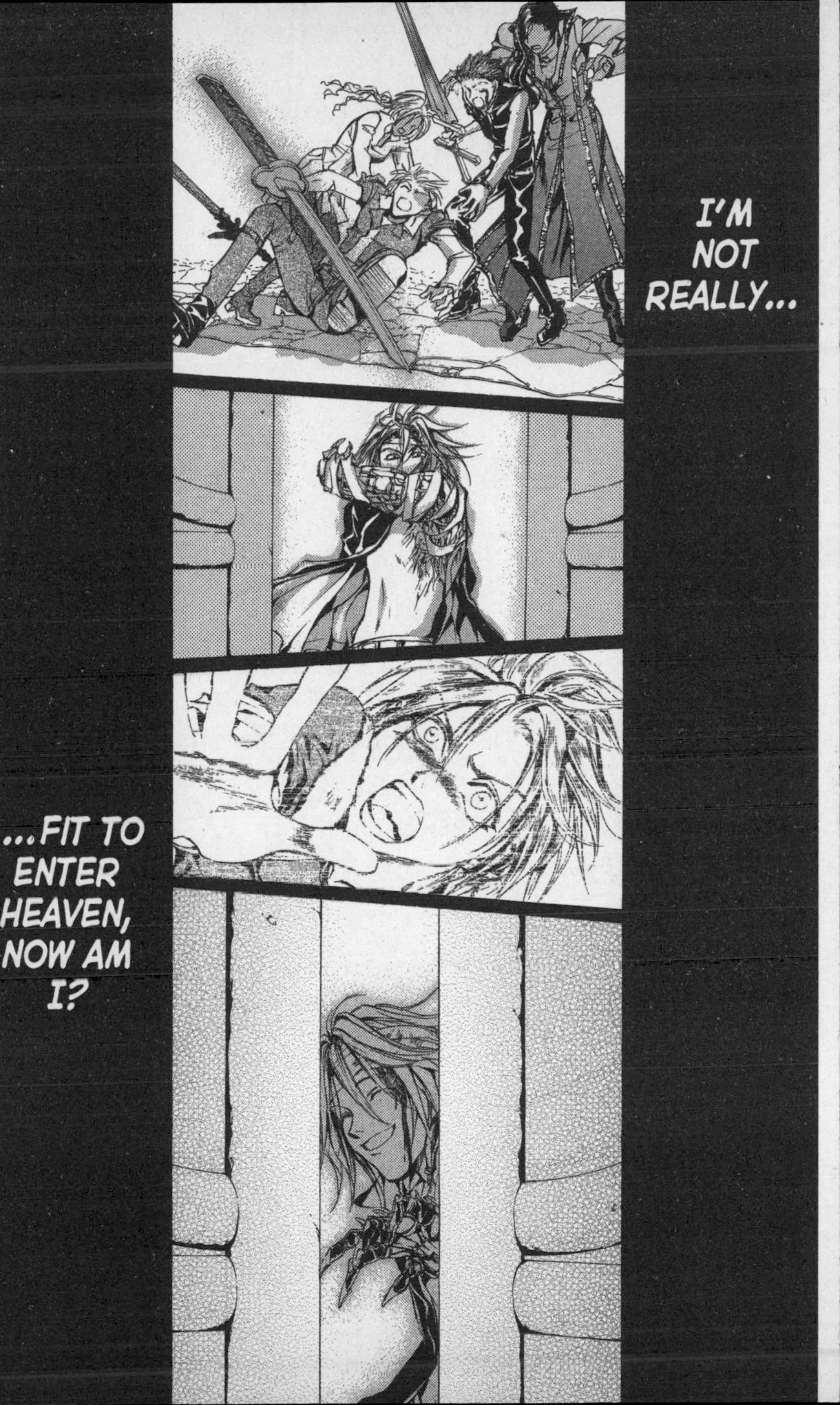
I'M NOT REALLY...
...FIT TO ENTER HEAVEN, NOW AM I?

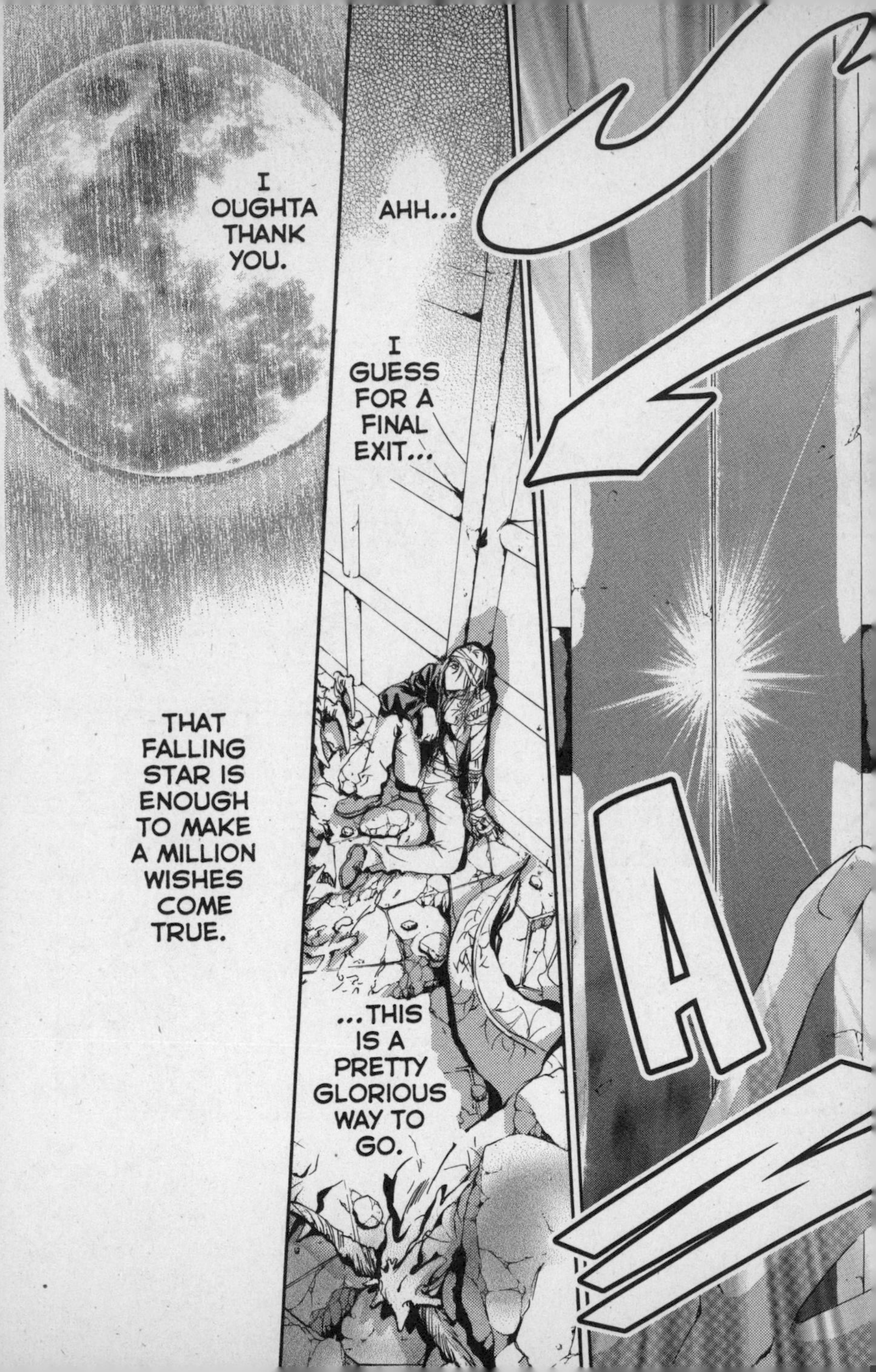
AHH...
I GUESS FOR A FINAL EXIT...
...THIS IS A PRETTY GLORIOUS WAY TO GO.
I OUGHTA THANK YOU.
THAT FALLING STAR IS ENOUGH TO MAKE A MILLION WISHES COME TRUE.

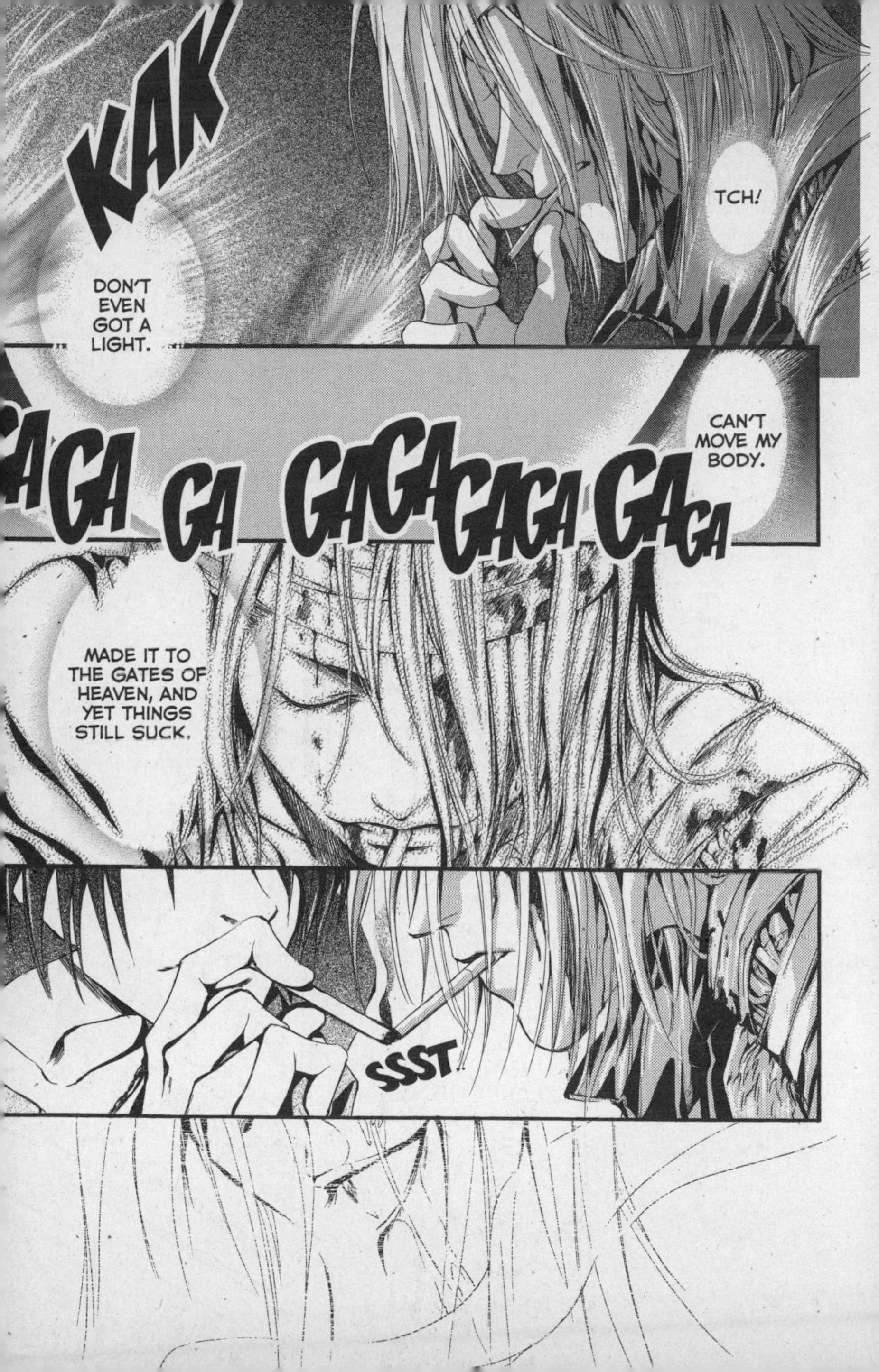
TCH!
KAK
DON'T EVEN GOT A LIGHT.
CAN'T MOVE MY BODY.
GAGA GA GAGAGAGA GAGA
MADE IT TO THE GATES OF HEAVEN, AND YET THINGS STILL SUCK.
SSST.

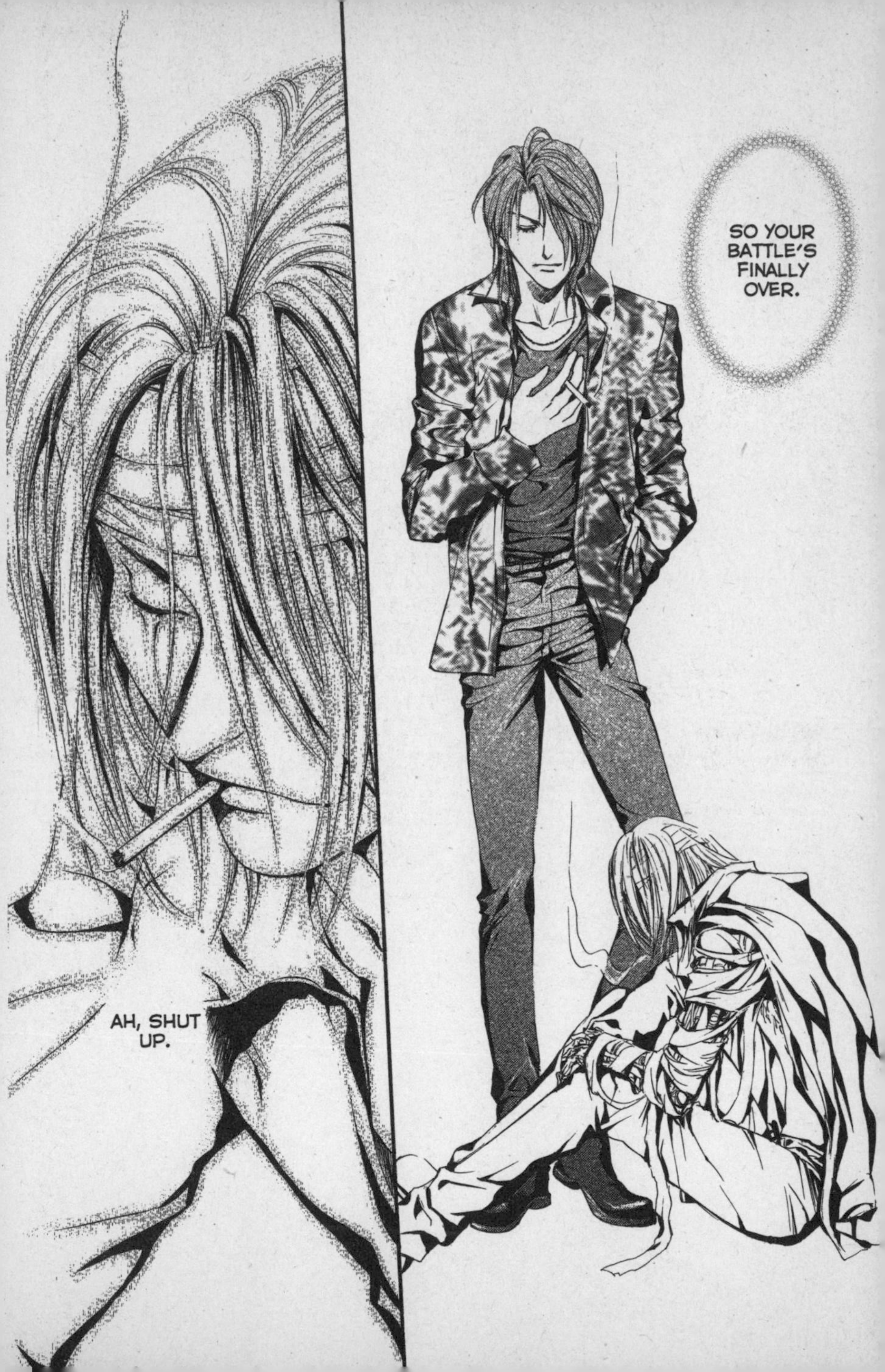
SO YOUR BATTLE'S FINALLY OVER.
AH, SHUT UP.

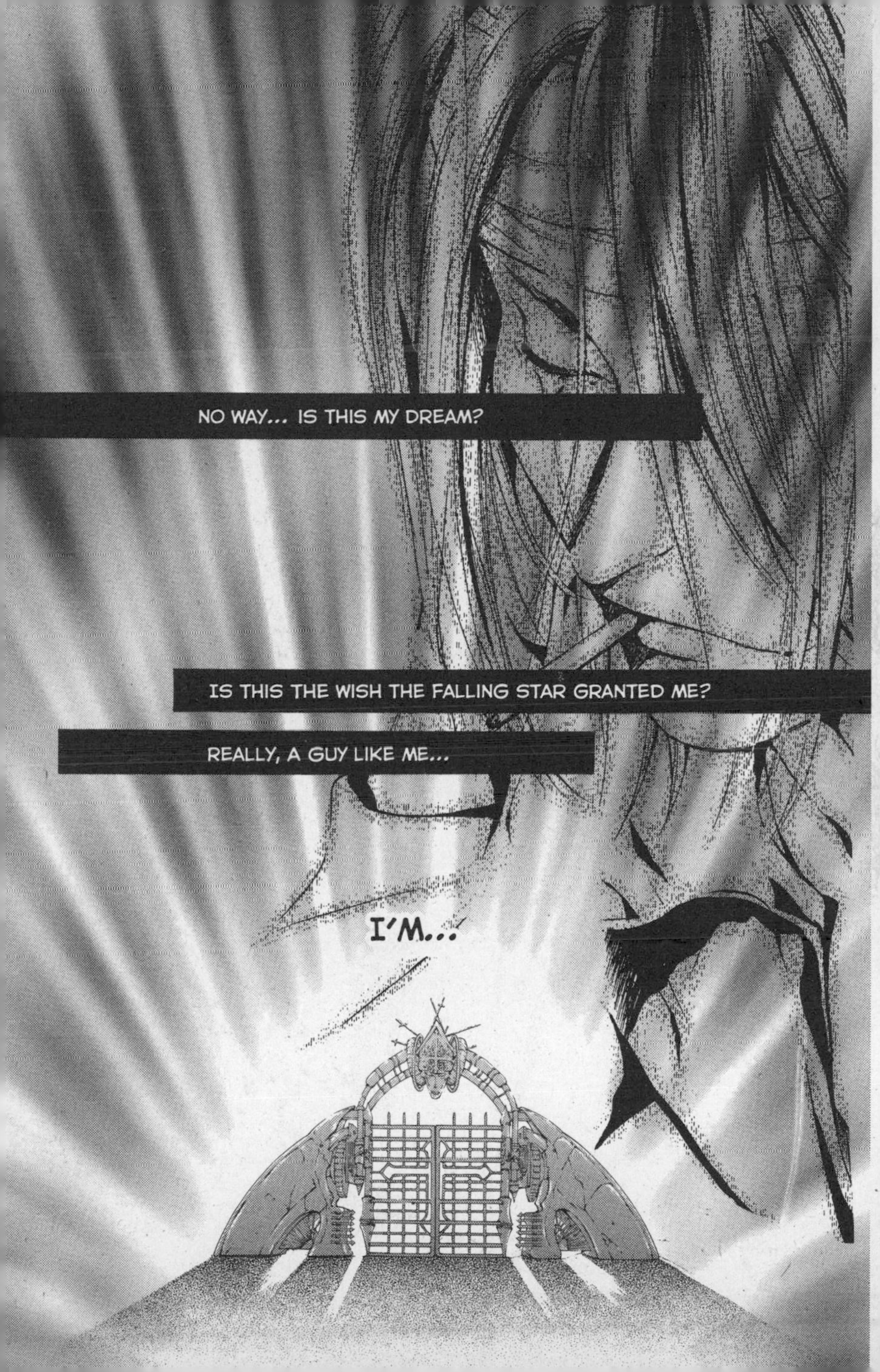
NO WAY... IS THIS MY DREAM?
IS THIS THE WISH THE FALLING STAR GRANTED ME?
REALLY, A GUY LIKE ME...
I'M...

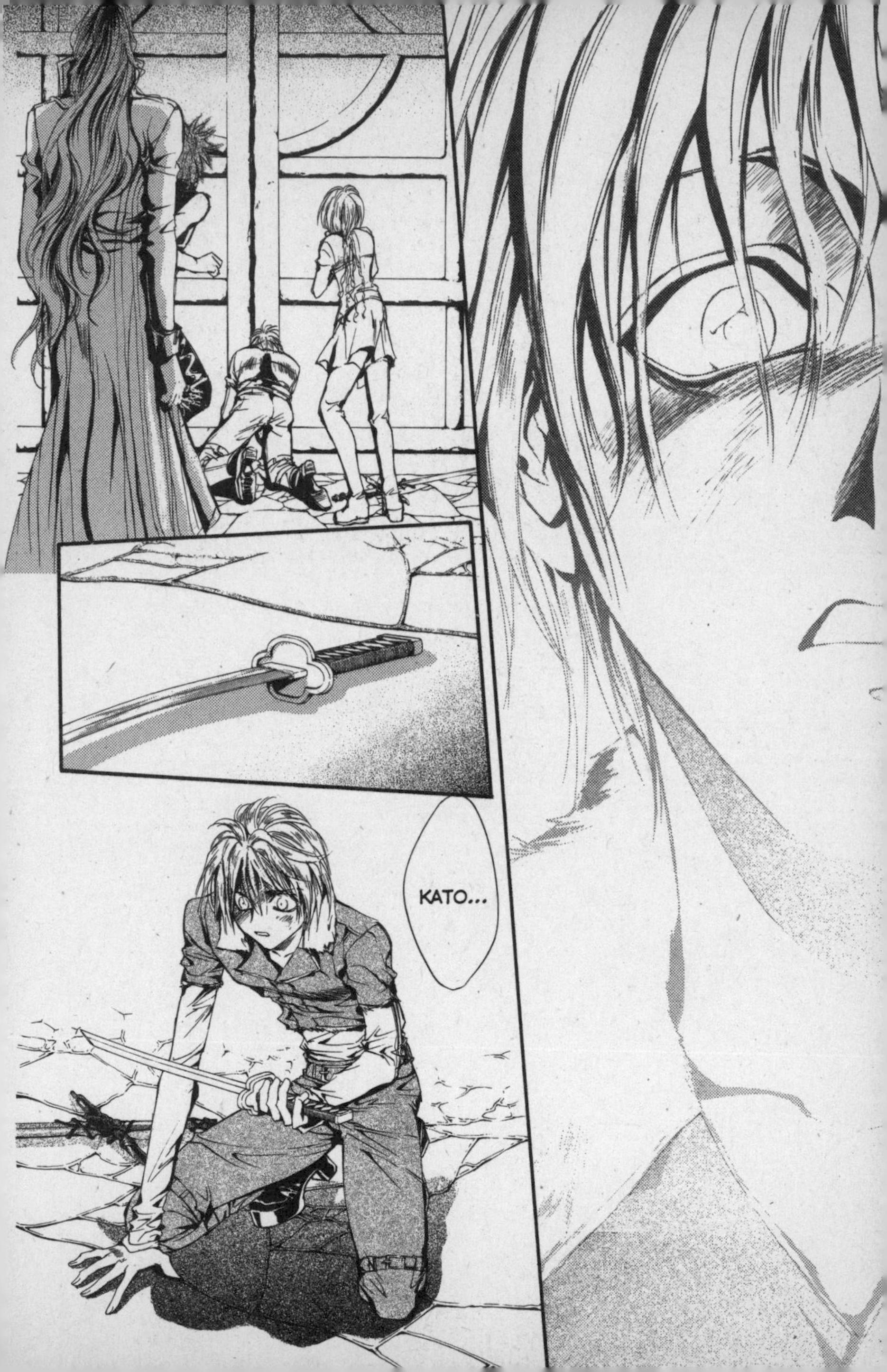
KATO...

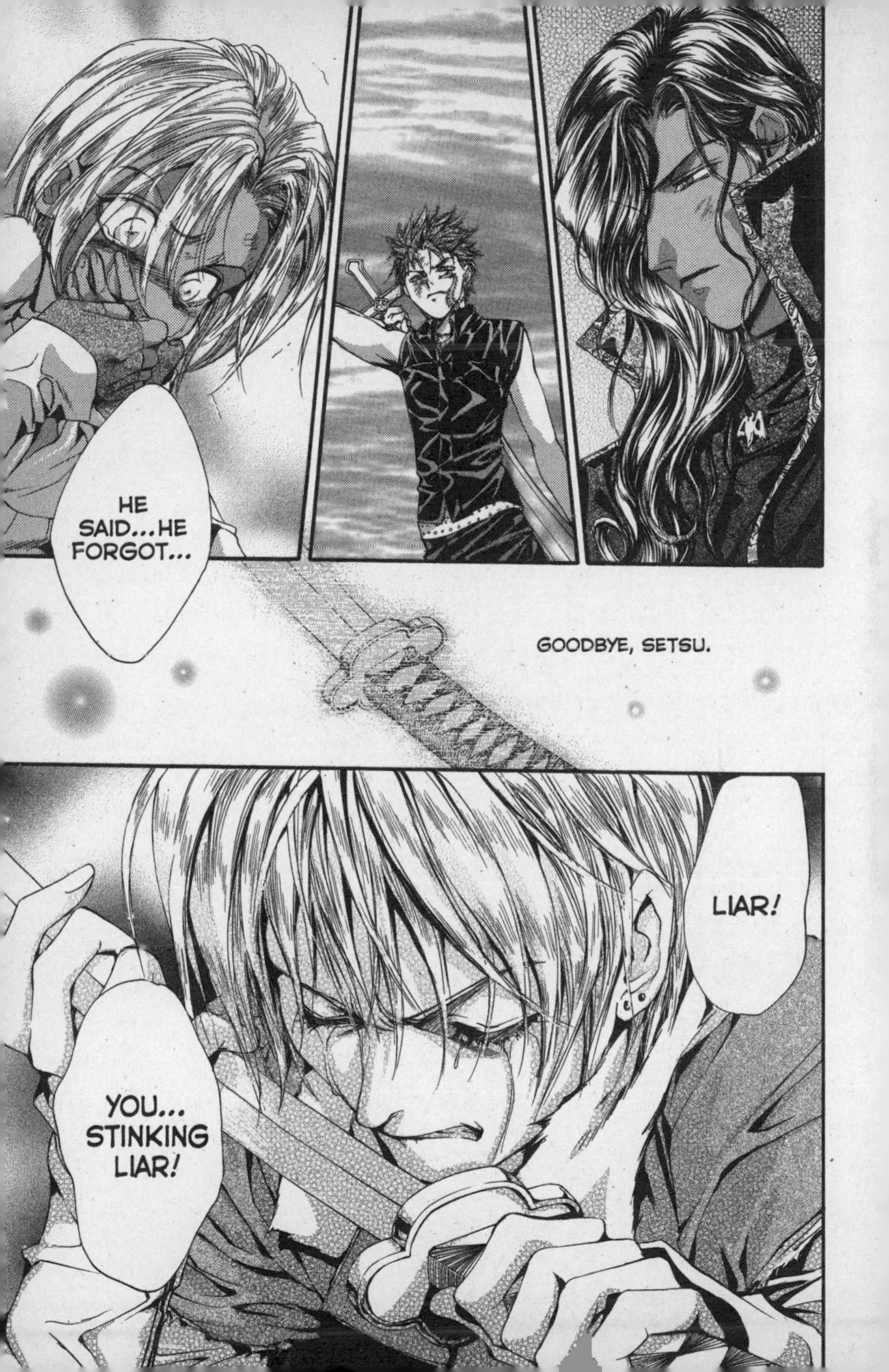
HE SAID...HE FORGOT...
GOODBYE, SETSU.
LIAR!
YOU... STINKING LIAR!

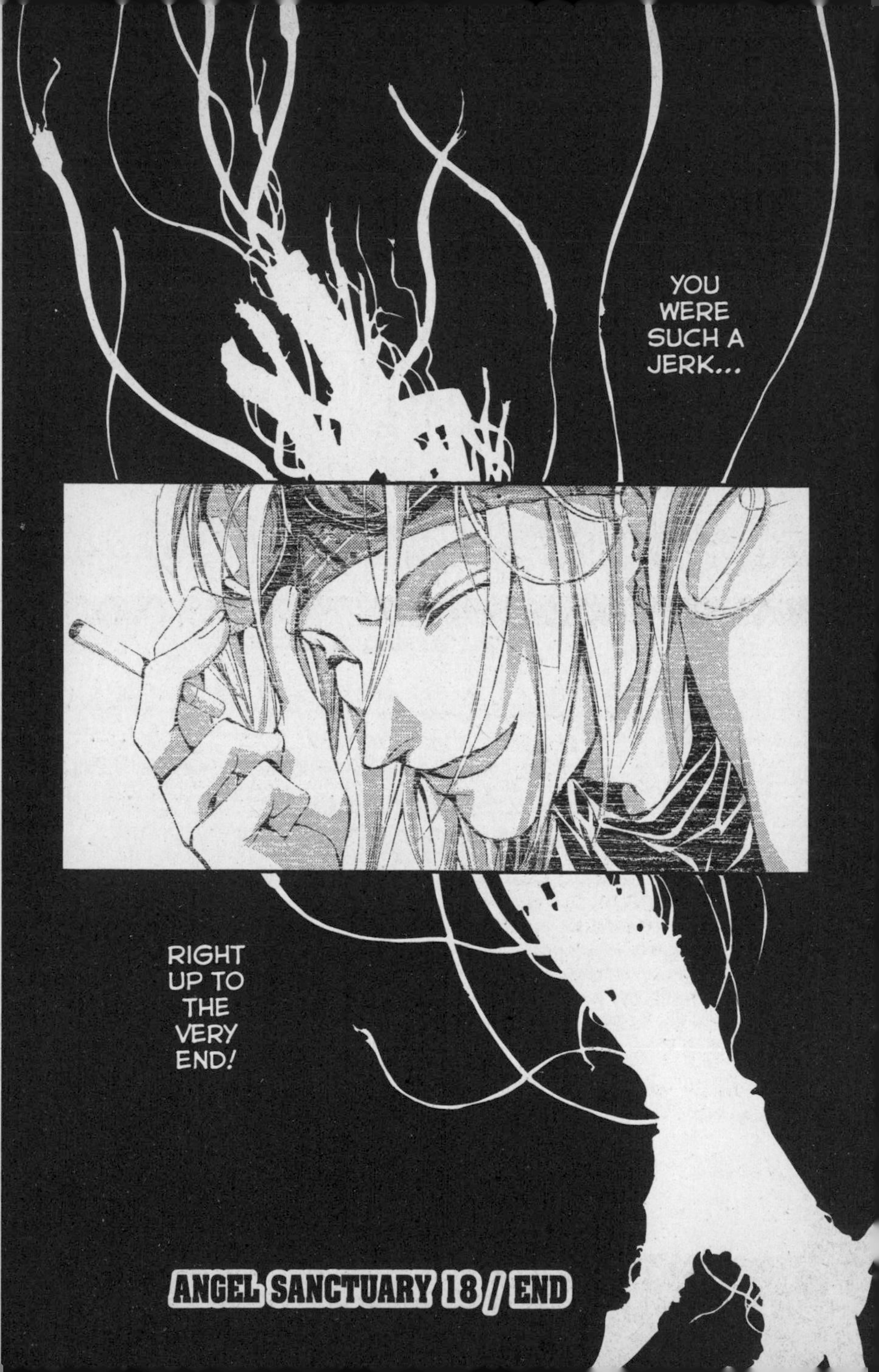
YOU WERE SUCH A JERK...
RIGHT UP TO THE VERY END!
ANGEL SANCTUARY 18 / END

Raphy Katan Rosiel Uriel Arachne Asmo Hatter

Sevy Capitol Mika Raciel Rosiel Kira Kato Riru Sara Setsuna Kurai Boys Noiz L. Astoroth

↑ ALL 20 MEMBERS OF THE CAST. really packed in.

What do you think? We put out vol. 18 right after vol. 17, and it felt like we really pushed it. The sketch above is the original for the spread I talked about in the last volume, with all the characters lined up. All the good guys and the bad guys are packed in there, so there were too many people for me to give proper attention to. I had to drop some of them. The pose Arachne used was intended for Asmodeus. There are so many people, and I would have hated to try coloring them all! The splash page is long enough, so I wanted to try this.

But even the initial sketch was tough! Anyway...this is the last time Kato makes an appearance. So volume 18 is his book. It came a little quicker than I originally planned, but the closer I got to the end, I knew each page was getting harder to draw, so I wanted to do each one perfectly. I didn't want to let go of him. He was a strange character that gradually got more and more popular, and I really enjoyed drawing him. There were a lot of readers who identified with his life that seemed to go nowhere. He was popular to the end, and a lot of people actually cried to see him go. I'm grateful to hear that. At the end, all he could see was the light of the falling star and Kira, who he should have hated. It was like he was finally free from the curses that had plagued him. That was the vision he saw. Just like Lailah and Metatron, the last person who came to him was the one he loved. So his story had some confusing and troubling parts to it.

Now that this volume is done, "Angel Sanctuary" is heading into the final countdown! Even I know this is the moment of truth, so I'm hanging in there. I look forward to hearing everyone's comments!

I've been to see Micchi, TM Revolution, Rapitts and Gackt in concert. They were all great!

Alexiel
NEXT ACCESS
Angel

···TO BE CONTINUED

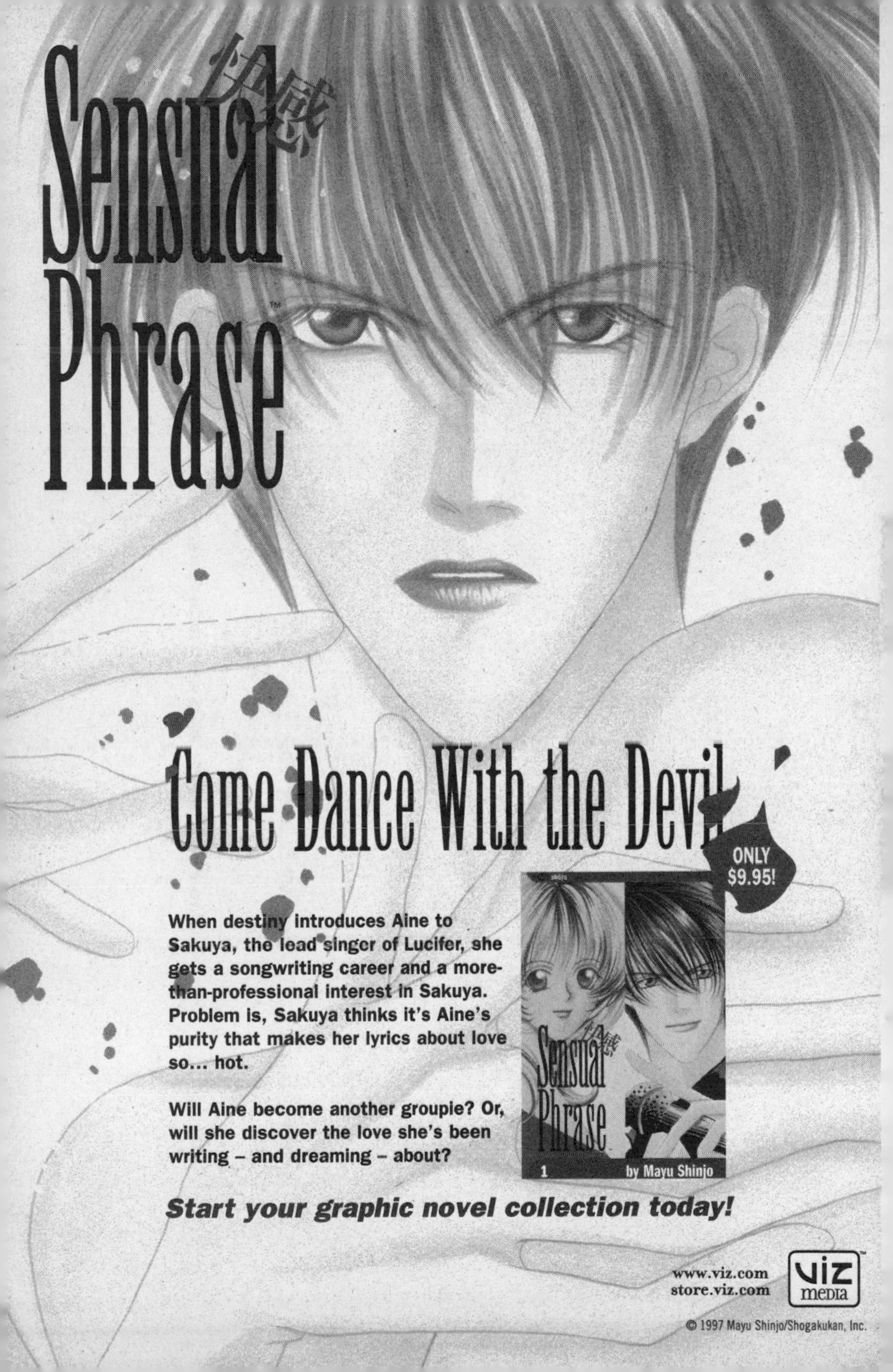
Sensual Phrase™
快感
Come Dance With the Devil
ONLY $9.95!
When destiny introduces Aine to Sakuya, the lead singer of Lucifer, she gets a songwriting career and a more-than-professional interest in Sakuya. Problem is, Sakuya thinks it's Aine's purity that makes her lyrics about love so... hot.
Will Aine become another groupie? Or, will she discover the love she's been writing – and dreaming – about?
Sensual Phrase
1
by Mayu Shinjo
Start your graphic novel collection today!
www.viz.com
store.viz.com
VIZ MEDIA
© 1997 Mayu Shinjo/Shogakukan, Inc.

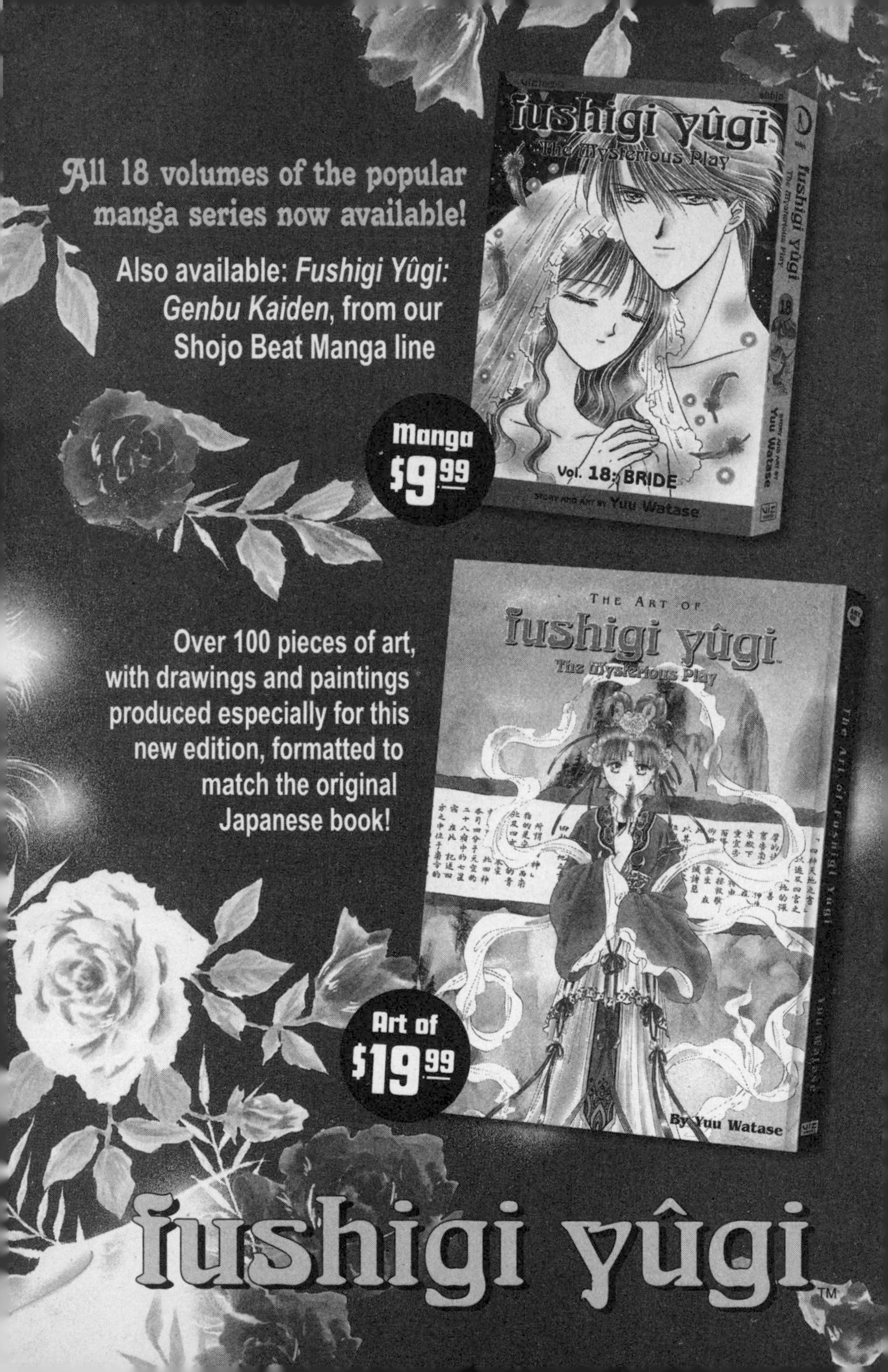
All 18 volumes of the popular manga series now available!
Also available: Fushigi Yûgi: Genbu Kaiden, from our Shojo Beat Manga line
fushigi yûgi
The Mysterious Play
Vol. 18: BRIDE
STORY AND ART BY Yuu Watase
Manga $9.99
Over 100 pieces of art, with drawings and paintings produced especially for this new edition, formatted to match the original Japanese book!
THE ART OF
fushigi yûgi
The Mysterious Play
By Yuu Watase
Art of $19.99
fushigi yûgi™

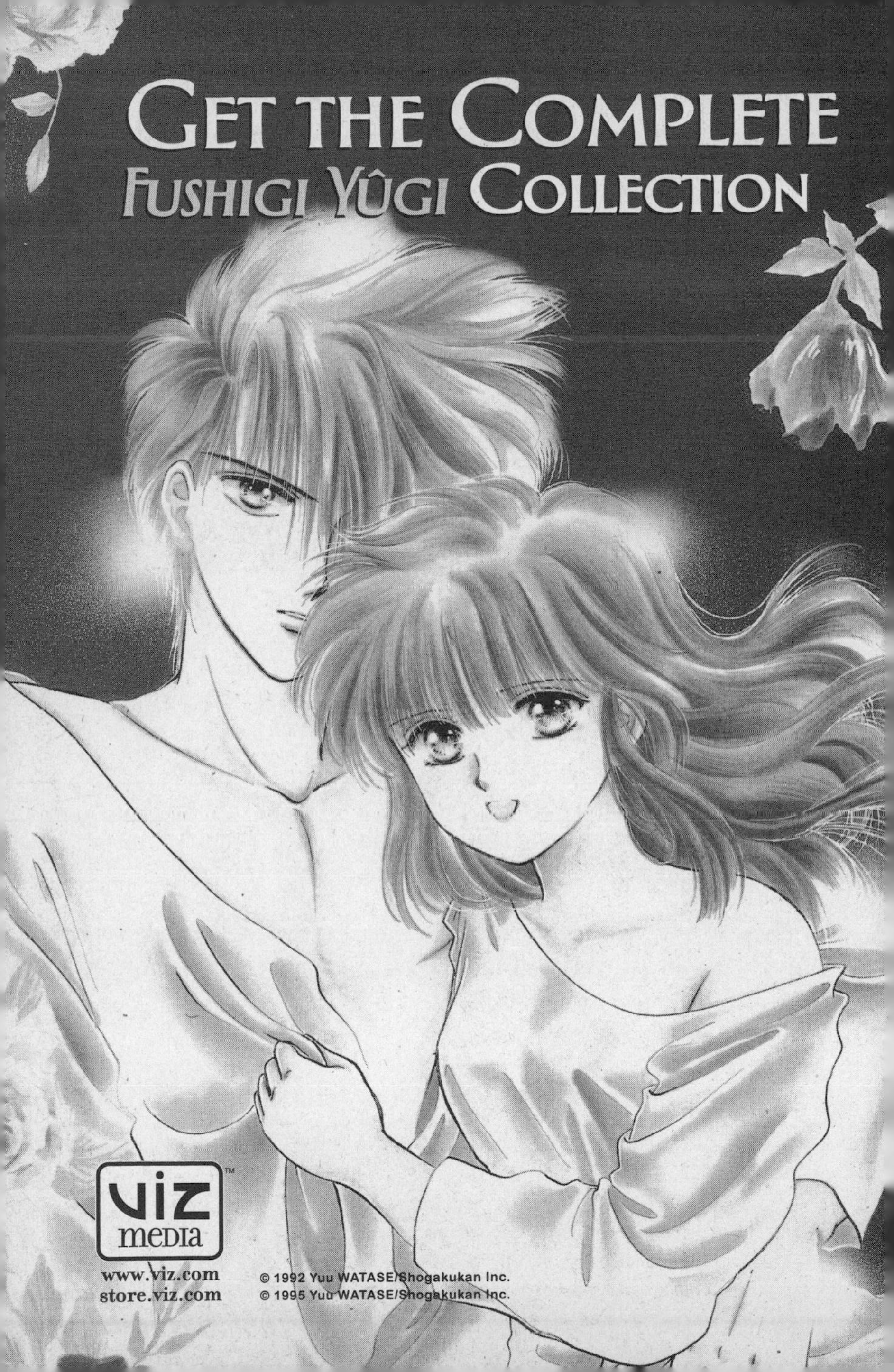
GET THE COMPLETE
FUSHIGI YÛGI COLLECTION
VIZ media
www.viz.com
store.viz.com
© 1992 Yuu WATASE/Shogakukan Inc.
© 1995 Yuu WATASE/Shogakukan Inc.